EDMUND BURKE AND IRELAND

This pioneering study of Edmund Burke's engagement with Irish politics and culture argues that Burke's influential early writings on aesthetics are intimately connected to his lifelong political concerns. The concept of the sublime, which lay at the heart of his aesthetics, addressed itself primarily to the experience of terror, and it is this spectre that haunts Burke's political imagination throughout his career. Luke Gibbons argues that this anxious aesthetics found expression in his preoccupation with political terror, whether in colonial Ireland and India, or revolutionary America and France. Burke's preoccupation with violence, sympathy, and pain allowed him to explore the dark side of the Enlightenment, but from a position no less committed to the plight of the oppressed, and to political emancipation. This major reassessment of a key political and cultural figure will appeal to Irish studies and postcolonial specialists, political theorists and students of Romanticism.

Luke Gibbons is the Keough Family Professor of Irish Studies at the University of Notre Dame, Indiana. He has written extensively on Irish literature, history, the visual arts, film, and popular culture. He is the author of *Transformations in Irish Culture* (1996), *The Quiet Man* (2002), and co-author of *Cinema and Ireland* (1988).

EDMUND BURKE AND IRELAND

Aesthetics, politics, and the colonial sublime

LUKE GIBBONS

PUBLISHED BY THE PRESS SYNDICATE OF THE UNIVERSITY OF CAMBRIDGE
The Pitt Building, Trumpington Street, Cambridge, United Kingdom

CAMBRIDGE UNIVERSITY PRESS
The Edinburgh Building, Cambridge, CB2 2RU, UK
40 West 20th Street, New York, NY 10011–4211, USA
477 Williamstown Road, Port Melbourne, VIC 3207, Australia
Ruiz de Alarcón 13, 28014 Madrid, Spain
Dock House, The Waterfront, Cape Town 8001, South Africa

http://www.cambridge.org

© Luke Gibbons 2003

This book is in copyright. Subject to statutory exception
and to the provisions of relevant collective licensing agreements,
no reproduction of any part may take place without
the written permission of Cambridge University Press.

First published 2003

Printed in the United Kingdom at the University Press, Cambridge

Typeface Adobe Garamond 11/12.5 pt.   *System* LATEX 2$_\varepsilon$ [TB]

A catalogue record for this book is available from the British Library

ISBN 0 521 81060 4 hardback

For Dolores

To use his own words... Burke's Sublime and Beautiful had more charms for him, than all the speculations of Mr. Paine on the Rights of Man.

Thomas Russell, as reported in R. R. Madden,
The United Irishmen: Their Lives and Times, 3rd series, ii (1846)

Edmund Burke has Gog's [John Keogh's] boys now on a visit to Beaconsfield, and writes him a letter in their praise... Flattering Gog to carry his point. Is that *sublime* or *beautiful*?

Theobald Wolfe Tone, *Journal*, 5 September 1791

[On] Ireland, America, and India, he [Burke] was at every point on the side of the future.

Harold Laski, *Political Thought in England from Locke to Bentham* (1950)

Contents

List of illustrations　　　　　　　　　　　　　　　　*page* ix
Preface　　　　　　　　　　　　　　　　　　　　　　　xi

　　Introduction: Edmund Burke, Ireland, and the colonial
　　sublime　　　　　　　　　　　　　　　　　　　　　　1

PART I　THE POLITICS OF PAIN

1　'This king of terrors': Edmund Burke and the aesthetics of
　　executions　　　　　　　　　　　　　　　　　　　　21

2　'*Philoctetes*' and colonial Ireland: the wounded body as national
　　narrative　　　　　　　　　　　　　　　　　　　　　39

PART II　SYMPATHY AND THE SUBLIME

3　The sympathetic sublime: Edmund Burke, Adam Smith,
　　and the politics of pain　　　　　　　　　　　　　　83

4　Did Edmund Burke cause the Great Famine? Commerce,
　　culture, and colonialism　　　　　　　　　　　　　121

PART III　COLONIALISM AND THE ENLIGHTENMENT

5　'Tranquillity tinged with terror': the sublime and agrarian
　　insurgency　　　　　　　　　　　　　　　　　　　147

6　Burke and colonialism: the Enlightenment and cultural
　　diversity　　　　　　　　　　　　　　　　　　　　166

PART IV PROGRESS AND PRIMITIVISM

7 'Subtilized into savages': Burke, progress, and primitivism   183

8 'The return of the native': the United Irishmen, culture, and colonialism   208

Conclusion: towards a post-colonial Enlightenment   230

Notes   239
Index   288

Illustrations

1. James Barry, 'Philoctetes on the Island of Lemnos' (1770). Reproduced by permission of the Pinacoteca Nazionale di Bologna — *page* 42
2. James Barry, Study for "Philoctetes on the Island of Lemnos" (1770). Reproduced by permission of the Tate Gallery, London — 45
3. James Barry, 'Self-Portrait' (1803). Reproduced by permission of the National Gallery of Ireland — 47
4. Caravaggio, 'The Supper at Emmaus'. Reproduced by permission of the National Gallery, London — 48
5. James Barry, 'The Fall of Satan' (1777) © Hunterian Art Gallery, University of Glasgow — 49
6. James Barry, 'The Baptism of the King of Cashel by St Patrick' (1801) (sketch: original painting executed in 1763). Reproduced by permission of the National Gallery, Ireland — 70
7. James Barry, 'Philoctetes' (*c.* 1790s). Reproduced by permission of the Tate Gallery, London — 76
8. John Vanderlyn, 'Murder of Jane McCrea' (1804). Reproduced by permission of the Wadsworth Atheneum, Hartford. Purchased by the Wadsworth Atheneum — 187
9. 'The Affecting History of the Dreadful Distresses of Frederic Manheim's Family' (1800). Private collection — 192
10. 'A Narrative of the Captivity, Sufferings and Removes of Mrs. Mary Rowlandson' (1773). Private collection — 198
11. Paul Revere, 'Bloody Massacre Perpetrated in King-Street, Boston' (1770). Private collection — 199
12. 'Review of the Lion of Old England' (1794). Reproduced by permission of the National Library, Ireland — 224

Preface

This basic argument of this book is that Edmund Burke's aesthetics take up where his politics ostensibly leave off, allowing him to negotiate some of the 'deepest obligations written on the heart' (to use his own formulation) that could not always be reconciled with his official public persona as a British statesman. The concept of the sublime, which lay at the heart of his aesthetics, addressed itself primarily to the experience of fear and terror, and it is this spectre that haunted Burke's political imagination throughout his career. This found expression primarily in his preoccupation with political terror, whether in colonial Ireland and India, or revolutionary America and France. The complexity of Burke's theories of violence, sympathy, and pain, as outlined in his *A Philosophical Enquiry in the Origin of our Ideas of the Sublime and Beautiful* (1757), provided him with a set of diagnostic tools to probe the dark side of the Enlightenment, particularly as it was used to justify colonial expansion, religious bigotry, or political repression. This is not to turn Burke – one of the emblematic figures of conservative thought – into a revolutionary where none was intended (though Mary Wollstonecraft did remark that had he lived in France, he would most likely have been a Jacobin). It is rather to argue that he was a man deeply divided against himself, a very fusion of the opposites yoked together in his concept of the sublime.

Several critics have drawn attention to the manner in which Burke's obsession with the depredations of Warren Hastings in India, and the reign of terror during the French Revolution, are prefigured in his aesthetic writings, but are unable to account for his early preoccupation with fear and violence. It is my contention that these can be traced in part to the formative Irish milieu of his aesthetic writings – a set of experiences that prefigured his later abiding concerns with the violence of colonialism and modernity. Conversely, those who, like Conor Cruise O'Brien, sounded the colonial notes in Burke's 'Great Melody', have failed to address the relation between this discordant strain in his politics, and his troubled aesthetic writings. This applies with less force to a more recent attempt to retrieve Burke's political reputation from a post-colonial perspective, Uday Singh Mehta's *Liberalism and Empire*, which, unlike O'Brien, follows the logic of Burke's rage against empire to a critique of Britishness itself, and the complicity of liberalism with the despotism of colonialism. The present study can be seen as complementing Mehta's focus on India by integrating Burke's aesthetics and his Irish background more fully into these searching critiques of colonialism.

In recent decades, and from diverse points of view, scholars, most notably Seamus Deane, W. J. McCormack, and Terry Eagleton, have sought to address the Irish dimension in Burke's work, drawing on both his politics and his aesthetics to explore the Gothic recesses of eighteenth-century Irish culture. It is in this spirit that I trace in Burke's theory of the sublime a fraught theoretical engagement with the political turbulence of his own upbringing, and the unresolved anxieties of a Catholic background, raised in the shadow of the Penal Laws. Burke's immediate family had direct links with some of the most traumatic state executions in early and mid-eighteenth-century Ireland, and with the outbreak of the first major wave of agrarian terror in the Whiteboy campaign of the 1760s, the aesthetics of the sublime acquired an intense personal urgency in Burke's life. Members of Burke's maternal family were directly implicated in the Whiteboy movement, and his last sustained visit to Ireland may have been to organize covertly the defence of Whiteboy suspects. But the concern with the body in pain – a central theme of the *Enquiry* – extends beyond these individual cases, for the trope of the injured body recurs as a national allegory of the plight of colonial Ireland in the eighteenth century. In terms of the new, neo-stoical concepts of civil society that evolved in the eighteenth century, the body in pain, and its attendant 'right to complain', proved an embarrassment to the Enlightenment, and came to be identified with the losers of history, and the ominous category of 'doomed' peoples. I argue that what is often construed as a counter-Enlightenment current in the writings of Swift and Burke derives from their determination to reinstate the wounds of history into the public sphere, and, by extension, 'obsolete' or 'traditional' societies into the course of history. For the Enlightenment (particularly its Scottish variant, as exemplified by Adam Smith), the injured body was incapable of looking beyond itself, and hence of attaining the universal or cosmopolitan stance required to operate in the civic sphere. By contrast, Burke's aesthetics outline an alternative, radical form of sensibility – the 'sympathetic sublime' – in which the acknowledgement of oppression need not lead to self-absorption, but may actually enhance the capacity to identify with the plight of others.

For this reason, not the least of the ironies of Burke's colonial sublime is that, in an Irish context, its cultural logic led ultimately to the political project of the United Irishmen, the radical movement which sought to bring the revolutionary energies of America and France to bear on the political upheavals in Ireland in the 1790s. Transplanted from the venerable oak of the ancient constitution in Britain onto the tree of liberty in late eighteenth-century Ireland, Burke's concept of tradition – in this case, the subaltern culture of his Gaelic, Catholic background – bore fruit in a grafting of a radical strain of Romanticism onto Enlightenment thought. As such, the politics of the sublime affords the possibility of a more grounded, ethnographic Enlightenment, sensitive to cultural differences, inherited loyalties, and the contingencies of time and place. Though easily construed as a counter-Enlightenment, it offers the possibility of a alternative vision of social change which questions the logic that modernity only extends to the victors, leaving the powerless casualties of history in its wake.

In many ways, the debts incurred in writing this book seem to emanate, like Burkean antiquity, from a time out of mind. I wish to thank my commissioning editor, Ray Ryan, and the fine production team at Cambridge, Rachel deWachter, Sheila Kane, Neil de Cort and Paul Watt, for steering the book through the various stages of its publication. I also wish to express my gratitude to the Keough Institute for Irish Studies at the University of Notre Dame for financial assistance during this process. I owe a debt to Peter Mew, formerly of the Philosophy Department, Trinity College, Dublin, for enabling me to study aesthetics in the first place, and members of the English Department at Trinity College, and my former colleagues at Dublin City University, for providing an intellectual environment which facilitated interdisciplinary research. I am very grateful to Tom Bartlett, Claire Connolly, Pia Conti, Fintan Cullen, Chris Fox, Michael Griffin, Siobhán Kilfeather, Greg Kucich, Joep Leerssen, W. J. McCormack, Breandán MacSuibhne, Willa Murphy, Eamonn O'Ciardha, Kevin O'Neill, William Pressly, Ann Rigney, Jim Smyth, Fiona Stafford, Nathan Wallace, John P. Waters, and Kevin Whelan for much needed guidance, encouragement and critical debate during my long hibernation in the eighteenth century. Mary Burgess Smyth, Joe Cleary, Farrel Corcoran, Paul Christensen, Ann Bernard Kearney, Rachael Dowling, Tom Duddy, Terry Eagleton, Marjorie Howes, Richard Kearney, Declan Kiberd, David Lloyd, Catherine Morris, Emer Nolan, Niamh O'Sullivan, Clair Wills, and Robert Young have ensured that the friendship of Burke's 'little platoon' can still be a reality at the dawn of a new century. Kevin Whelan cast his meticulous eye over the entire manuscript, bringing his own knowledge of the textual underground of eighteenth-century Ireland to bear on it. More than any other scholar, Seamus Deane has helped critics to read the colonial dark of Burke and eighteenth-century Ireland, and this study would not have been possible without his sustained critical and intellectual support over many years. If I single out Tadhg Foley for special mention, it is because he often converted what seemed like the mountain gloom of eighteenth-century aesthetics into mountain glory – even if I have seldom been able to attain his scholarly heights. Such progress as I have made is due to my family, and, above all, to Dolores, Laura, and Barry, who constantly lifted my spirits when this book threatened to become Gibbons's decline and fall.

Introduction: Edmund Burke, Ireland, and the colonial sublime

> As to your general Politicks in Ireland, they are so sublimely profound, there is such a grandeur of meanness in them, that they pass my expression and indeed my comprehension. Passiveness and servility seem to be natural companions just as Violence and Tyranny.
> Edmund Burke to Charles O'Hara, 7 January, 1776

Writing about the resurgence of the aesthetic concept of the sublime as a key term in contemporary cultural debates, Jean-François Lyotard remarks that it is uniquely capable of 'bearing pictorial or otherwise expressive witness to the inexpressible', to the contradictory feelings of 'pleasure and pain, joy and anxiety, exaltation and depression' that have characterized modernity in the aftermath of the Holocaust and the nuclear age. Though first promulgated in the eighteenth century, the sublime, according to Lyotard, 'is the only mode of artistic sensibility to characterize the modern'. Having disappeared from the lexicon of art for over a century, Lyotard contends that it resurfaced as a mode of figuration in the avant-garde work of the American abstract artist Barnett Newman in the late 1940s.[1] Since its re-emergence, the sublime, as a liminal form of experience which gestures towards the 'inexpressible' and the 'unrepresentable', has been variously invoked by critics and cultural historians as the most appropriate category (or anti-category) for mapping the terrors of the twentieth century, and its grim historical antecedents – the Holocaust (Lyotard),[2] 'the slave sublime' and the millions who died in the middle passage between Africa and America (Paul Gilroy), the depredations of British colonialism in India (Sara Suleri), the reign of terror in the French Revolution (Ronald Paulson), the limits of human endurance in polar exploration (Francis Spufford), intimations of nuclear catastrophe in our own time (Frances Ferguson; Rob Wilson), or more generally, the anguish of the body in pain (David Morris; Steven Bruhm).[3] 'It remains to the art historian', Lyotard adds, 'to explain how the word sublime reappeared in the language of a Jewish painter from New York during the forties', noting, in a revealing aside, that Newman had 'read

Edmund Burke's *Inquiry [into... the Sublime and Beautiful]* and criticized what he saw as Burke's over "surrealist" description of the sublime work'.[4]

If it is incumbent on art history to explain the re-emergence of the sublime in the shadow of the Holocaust in the post-World War Two period, the task facing Irish cultural history is to explain how this mythos of terror was formulated in the first place in the colonial context of eighteenth-century Ireland, in the aesthetic writings of the young Edmund Burke (1730–97).[5] Burke's *A Philosophical Enquiry into the Origin of our Ideas of the Sublime and Beautiful* was published in 1757, when he was twenty-seven years old, but was begun at least ten years earlier, during his period as a student at Trinity College, Dublin.[6] What was unusual, and indeed unsettling, about the shift in cultural sensibility effected by the *Enquiry* was its identification of 'terror', and the figure of the body in pain, as the basis of the most intense forms of aesthetic experience. According to Burke, in a formulation that launched a thousand Gothic quests:

Whatever is fitted in any sort to excite the ideas of pain, and danger, that is to say, whatever is in any sort terrible, or is conversant about terrible objects, or operates in a manner analogous to terror, is a source of the *sublime*; that is, it is productive of the strongest emotion which the mind is capable of feeling... When danger or pain press too nearly, they are incapable of giving any delight, and are simply terrible; but at certain distances, and with certain modifications, they may be, and they are delightful, as we everyday experience. (*Enquiry*, 39–40)[7]

It is this aesthetics of shock, dependent on the proximity of danger or pain but giving rise nonetheless to ambivalent, agreeable sensations, which Burke links to the emotional rapture of the sublime. The provenance of some of the central ideas in the *Enquiry* can be traced to Burke's adolescence in Dublin, as is evident in a remarkable letter written to Richard Shackleton on 25 January 1745, describing a storm in which the River Liffey burst its banks alongside his family home on Arran Quay. Burke, then fifteen years of age, reassures his friend that he will endeavour to reply to his previous letter:

tho' every thing around me conspires to excite in me a Contrary disposition, the melancholy gloom of the Day, the whistling winds, and the hoarse rumblings of the Swoln Liffy, with the flood which even where I write lays close siege to our whole Street... yet the joy of conversing with my friend, can dispel the cloudiness of the Day[,] Lull the winds and stop the rapid passage of the flood...

The young Burke was, perhaps, expecting a lot of the power of friendship and conversation to calm the storm, but, as we shall see, his later attempts to infuse abstract social relations, particularly in the face of adversity, with the emotional charge of friendship and 'sympathy' owes much to his formative experiences in Ireland. In the next part of his letter to Shackleton, Burke gives an on-the-spot report of how the river is about to engulf their house, while he continues writing in the best sensational tradition of the epistolary novel: 'now the water comes up to the first floor of the House threatning us every minute with rising a great deal higher the Consequence of which would infallibly be the fall of the house and to add to our misfortune the inhabitants of the other Quay secur'd by their situation deride the poor prisoners...I can't Stir without apparent Danger to my life.'

Far from being despondent, however, the prospects of doom and self-destruction force him in on himself, rousing his innermost resources in what may be seen as a rehearsal for arguments later outlined in the *Enquiry*:

It gives me pleasure to see nature in those great tho' terrible Scenes, it fills the mind with grand ideas, and turns the Soul in upon herself. This together with the sedentary Life I lead forc'd some reflections on me which would not otherwise have occurrd. I consider'd how little man is yet in [h]is own mind how great! he is Lord and Master of all things yet Scarce can command any[;] he is given a freedom of his will, but wherefore? was it but to torment and perplex him the more? How little avails this freedom if the objects he is to act upon be not as much disposd to obey as he to Command...If but one element happens to encroach a Little on the other what confusion may it not Create in his affairs, what Havock, what destruction!

It is possible to see in this a foreshadowing of Burke's attentiveness throughout his writings to the contingencies of time and place, to the capacity of local circumstances or unforeseen events to topple grand schemes to improve the human condition. Just as nature in its 'great tho' terrible scenes' may transfer some of its strength and grandeur to the beholder, so also in society, those seeking to wield unrestrained power may often unwittingly defeat their imperious designs by empowering their victims, pushing them to equally unrestrained acts of resistance:

what well Laid and what better executed S[c]heme...is there but what a Small Change of nature is sufficient to defeat and entirely abolish...The Servant Destined to his use confines, menaces, and frequently destroys this mighty this feeble Lord![8]

The servant, in other words, may well strike back. In what follows, I will argue that much of Burke's abiding concerns with colonial oppression, whether in Ireland, America, or India, are bound up with his acute awareness of the capacity of the servant to rise up against intolerable abuses of state power: 'When you drive him hard, the boar will surely turn upon the hunters.'[9] This is one of the primary sources of the 'fear' and 'terror' that lies at the heart of the colonial sublime.

One particular manifestation of state power recurs in Burke's writings: the ultimate deterrent of the death penalty, and the horrific spectacle of public executions. Though the aim was undoubtedly to cow and to intimidate, the severity of the punishment was such that, in keeping with the operation of the sublime, the sympathy of the crowd often passed to the hapless victim, thus undermining state power at the very moment of its triumph. Sympathy, in fact, plays a key role in Burke's conception of the sublime, extending its remit from self-preservation in the face of danger to include wider social sentiments and the well-being of others. In a crucial departure from dominant Enlightenment thinking, Burke stresses the capacity of the endangered or injured body to think of others, as if to emphasize that the individual, even in pain or under duress, is still a social being. It is significant that in the midst of a tumultuous storm, when his own life is threatened, the young Burke casts his eyes across the river where evidently some citizens, assured of their own safety, were enjoying the spectacle of seeing others suffer: 'and to add to our misfortune the inhabitants of the other Quay secur'd by their situation deride the other prisoners'. Scenes such as these in which spectators, secure from danger, are indifferent to the misfortune of fellow human beings, troubled Burke greatly, and his theory of the sublime can be seen as an attempt to prevent the aesthetic from becoming, in effect, an anaesthetic. Underlying this was a determination to remove the voyeuristic detachment from these spectacles of suffering, emphasizing the true horror that underpinned the colonial sublime.

It is for this reason that Burke sought to displace the primacy of *vision*, the sovereignty of sight, from its central position in theories of aesthetic experience. Whereas the new aesthetic theories promulgated by his French contemporaries such as Diderot and Rousseau looked to clarity and transparency as the ruling principles of art, Burke instead argued that darkness, obscurity and indistinctness are responsible for the most powerful aesthetic emotions. 'A clear idea', he noted in a masterly understatement, 'is therefore another name for a little idea' (*Enquiry*, 63). Having assailed the visual basis of the metaphor of 'enlightenment' (but not necessarily, as we shall see, the idea of the Enlightenment itself), Burke proposed that words were superior to images in negotiating the terrors of the sublime. It is difficult not to see in this a presentiment of the 'Irish Gothic' and many of the darker impulses that have animated Irish culture during the past two centuries – the preference for obscurity over clarity, the expressive force of the word over the mimetic powers of the image, the fascination with beauty and terror, and, above all, the volatile intersection between aesthetics and politics.

This is not to construe Burke as laying the foundational fictions for those creative energies, whether in literature or art, that sought to come to terms with the more violent and turbulent manifestations of Irish culture. Burke abhorred, as we shall see, the very idea of 'foundations',[10] and his writings might better be considered as 'exemplary' texts, in the special sense that he attached to the concept. An exemplary text or event, to adapt Seamus Deane's formulation, is both a culminating moment in a process or series of events already under way, but is also a disruptive, originating moment in the subversion of that process, an omen of things to come.[11] 'A well-timed stroke of sublimity', wrote Burke's classical precursor, Longinus, 'scatters everything before it like a thunderbolt', and it is in this sense that the exemplary events that come under the aegis of the sublime represent an irruption into the continuum of history.[12] In Burke's own eschatology, as I outline in Chapters 1 and 5, the events in Munster surrounding the Whiteboy disturbances in the 1760s, leading to what he referred to as the 'judicial murder' of his kinsman Fr Nicholas Sheehy in 1766, were early warning flashes of the storm that was to unleash its full fury against the Catholic population in the 1790s. But they were not just portents of the future: as he argued in an historical manoeuvre that was to receive its most forceful exposition in his *Reflections on the Revolution in France* (1790), modern terror was also the culmination of a process that could be traced to the proselytizing zeal of Cromwell, and particularly to the devastating impact of the Cromwellian plantations in Ireland.

Burke's often-mentioned 'clairvoyance' may derive from his exceptional capacity to identify certain moments or events, often far from auspicious at the outset, as fulcrums in time that tilt the balance of history for decades, or even centuries, to come.[13] In several chapters below, I examine how pivotal events such as the execution of Fr Nicholas Sheehy (Chapter 1), the march to Versailles on 5/6 October 1789 (Chapter 7), or seemingly more random events such as the murder of Jane McCrea during the American Revolution (Chapter 7), the violation of young women in India (Chapter 3), or the brutal punishment meted out to a virtually unknown Catholic soldier, Private James Hyland, in the British army in Tipperary in 1795 (Chapter 3), function for Burke as 'disasters in the moral' sphere, the social equivalents, as he put it, of a 'miracle in the physical order of things'.[14] 'By miracle', David Bromwich observes, 'Burke evidently means the visible token of disaster, an event that gives a sublime shock.'[15] Such prodigies in the human world need not always occur on a grand scale but can often turn on the kind of details that escape the epic sweep of historical vision:

> The death of a man at a critical juncture, his disgust, his retreat, his disgrace, have brought innumerable calamities on a whole nation. A common soldier, a child, a girl at the door of an inn, have changed the face of fortune and almost of nature.[16]

The sublime, Burke noted in the *Enquiry*, is mainly concerned with greatness and magnitude, but vertiginous details, and 'littleness' of the kind 'in tracing which the imagination is lost as well as the sense' (*Enquiry*, 72), can also induce profound disorientation, and thereby constitute a source of fear and terror.

An exemplary event for Burke has much in common with the later romantic cult of 'the fragment', a piece of history that is disconnected enough from its putative whole to have a discrete existence by itself, but yet which still points to something beyond it, however indeterminate. Such events possess the narrative potential and semantic range of dramatic representations, except they do not take place at one remove from reality. They exemplify what might be termed an 'aesthetics of the actual', and it is by means of this dramaturgy of the real that Burke's aesthetics often picks up where his politics leaves off, gesturing towards recalcitrant or clandestine areas of experience that elude the scripts of official political discourse. Displaying the opacity of symptoms rather than the lucidity of signs, exemplary events cannot be read at face value and function instead, in Burke's own terminology, as 'convulsions' or 'paroxysms' in the body politic. It is as if the more disturbing the event, the greater the resistance to realism or graphic clarity. In keeping with his critique of vision, Burke writes that 'when painters have attempted to give us clear representations of...terrible ideas, they have I think almost always failed; insomuch that I have been at a loss, in all the pictures I have seen of hell, whether the painter did not intend something ludicrous'. By contrast:

> there are many things of a very affecting nature, which can seldom occur in the reality, but the words which represent them often do; and thus they have an opportunity of making a deep impression and taking root in the mind, whilst the idea of the reality was transient; and to some perhaps never really occurred in any shape, to whom it is notwithstanding very affecting, as war, death, famine, &c. (*Enquiry*, 173–4)

The mention of 'famine' is salutary here as an event which not only points to the future course of Irish history, but which may also have a provenance in Burke's own troubled past. In her recent analysis of Burke's aesthetics from a post-colonial perspective, Sara Suleri discerns in the category of the sublime a proleptic foray into politics, a preliminary assaying of the 'deranged plot of colonialism' that was to dominate so much of Burke's subsequent political career:

While Burke's treatise on the sublime predates his active involvement in the politics of the colonization of India, it constitutes a figurative repository that would prove invaluable to the indefatigable eloquence of his parliamentary years. The *Enquiry*... provides in itself an incipient map of his political consciousness: as a study of the psychic proximity of aesthetic discourse with the concomitant intimacy of cultural terror.[17]

In a similar vein, Ronald Paulson points to the manner in which Burke's response to the French Revolution is framed in terms of the tensions between terror and beauty worked out in the *Enquiry* in the 1750s:

I think we can begin to see where Burke's imagery of the revolution in fact came from and what it meant to him. It was the terrible of his sublime... Burke's solution to the confrontation with this unthinkable phenomenon, the French Revolution (one already adopted to some degree in his attacks on Hastings's Indian depredations), was to fit it into the framework of aesthetic categories he had worked out for himself thirty years before. He is not unaware of that other category, the beautiful, associated by him... with the mother, the queen, the chivalry that surrounds her.[18]

Suleri and Paulson are correct to note the intricate relations between Burke's aesthetics and politics, but they are faced with the difficulty of explaining how his youthful theory of the sublime anticipates his involvement in public life. It is true that the *Enquiry* was published several decades before his obsessive concerns with India and France, but it was not conceived in a political vacuum, for it does not predate his intimacy with the 'cultural terror' of the Ireland of his upbringing. As Michel Fuchs point out, the ineluctable political nature of Burke's concept of the sublime is clear from the very outset: 'examining closely the examples he gives of "noxious things" that legitimately produce terror, we are struck by the fact that social institutions account for a large number of them: capital punishment, despotic heads of state, Kings, military chiefs, heads of families... and, of course, God'.[19] It is important for Burke's argument that the capacity to induce awe and terror is not necessarily diminished by the legitimacy of these institutions, but when they are illegitimate, and rule by fear alone, the sublime is present in all its terrifying force. In this respect, as Fuchs avers, Burke did not have to venture far to experience its effects at first hand, with the additional threats of war, famine and collective violence:

There is nothing surprising about the sublime being the fundamental category of *A Philosophical Enquiry* since it is also the fundamental characteristic of daily life in Ireland... Wherever one casts one's eyes, one saw only dangers and threats; even the powerful, who were everything in Ireland, would be as nothing without the constant support of London and its constant threats against the colony's majority.[20]

Burke's anxious aesthetics, with its intimations of ruin and catastrophe, prefigured not only the Great Famine of 1845–51, as I shall argue in Chapter 4, but may have resulted from his own experience of famine as a young boy raised in the Cork countryside in 1740–1, where the combined failure of both the potato and cereal crop due to a devastating 'arctic' winter led to the death of one-third of the population of the county. As a 'symptomatology' of social life, Burke's aesthetics provided him with a set of diagnostic skills which enabled him to probe the 'cultural terror' beneath surface appearances, alerting him in particular to the deceptive calm of social contentment or tranquillity in colonial societies. This, to use one of his favourite metaphors, was often little more than a thin crust of top-soil, belying the volcanic turbulence underneath. 'In our Indian government', he wrote, in words that applied equally to Ireland, 'whatever grievance is borne is denied to exist; and all mute despair, and sullen patience, is construed into content and satisfaction.'[21]

Burke's reading of eighteenth-century Ireland, therefore, would be at variance with recent attempts in Irish historiography to construe the surface contentment over much of the century as evidence of a deeper social consensus consistent with an *ancien* rather than a colonial regime. According to S. J. Connolly:

Despite the recent history of conquest and warfare and the political and religious tensions that resulted, this was not a society held down by force. Instead, government depended on the continued willingness of the many, most of the time, to accept the domination of a few

– even if this, he adds in a crucial aside, was only 'because they lacked the ability to establish, or possibly even to imagine, an alternative'.[22] This attempt to make Ireland post-colonial before its time by erasing all traces of colonialism in the first place, overlooks the fact, as Thomas Bartlett has pointed out, that the dominant Protestant interest was alienated from the hostile majority Catholic population in a way that had few parallels in Europe. As Bartlett puts it: 'Surely this image of a ruling elite entirely cut off from those whom it rules by bonds of affection (Burke's view) but yet surrounded by a watchful and unreconciled majority, is a main feature of a "colonial base"?'[23] This would certainly accord with Burke's view of an unbridgeable chasm between, on the one hand, 'the colonial garrison' or 'the English colonies in Ireland', as he described them, and, on the other, 'a conquered people, whom the victors delighted to trample upon, and were not at all afraid to provoke'.[24] For Burke, the rot in Ireland was not confined to the top but had infected the entire social and political system. In a letter to Dr John Curry of the Catholic Committee, he wrote that his attachment to Ireland was motivated by

> an utter abhorrence to all kinds of public injustice and oppression, the worst species of which are those which being converted into maxims of state, and blending themselves with law and jurisprudence corrupt the very fountains of all equity, and subvert all the purposes of Government. From these principles I have ever had a particular detestation to the penal system in Ireland.[25]

Such an elementary breakdown in the political order – 'the practice of making the extreme medicine of the constitution its daily bread' (*Reflections*, 154) – vitiates the right to rule, and his warning about India was to prove prophetic in Ireland with the founding of the radical United Irishmen in the 1790s: 'I must beg to observe, that, if we are not able to contrive some method of governing India *well*, which will not of necessity become the means of governing Great Britain ill, a ground is laid for their eternal separation.'[26]

Connolly concedes that where law and order were concerned, 'two notorious cases, those of Sir James Cotter in 1720 and Fr Nicholas Sheehy in 1766' may seem to contest the picture of a consensual social order, but he seeks to accommodate them within his harmonious vision of a cohesive, non-colonial dispensation. In the case of Sheehy's execution, he contends that it was at most a local disturbance, with no wider cultural or political implications:

> The real question is whether this one case of assassination by legal process can be taken as reflecting on the system as a whole... The judicial murder of Sheehy was... the high point of a particularly vicious local conflict, its very notoriety, both at the time and later, marking it out as an exceptional event.[27]

It is striking that the two examples of 'exceptional events' which Connolly adduces may have had a direct bearing on the fraught circumstances of Burke's upbringing in eighteenth-century Ireland, for in both cases he had familial connections with these victims of official terror.[28] The case of Sheehy impinged on him personally, and it was only 'exceptional' for Burke in that the violation of the due process placed it entirely outside the legal system, thus calling its very legitimacy into question. If such 'exceptions' stood in isolation from the colonial regime, it was because they were forced underground into a submerged cultural space where they acquired a new cultural valency, reconstituting themselves, in Burke's own words, by virtue of 'an interior history of Ireland – the genuine voice of its records and monuments – which speaks a very different language' from the triumphalist histories of conquest and confiscation in Temple and Clarendon.[29] What was 'exceptional' at an official level thus became 'exemplary' in relation to a competing subaltern culture, opening up precisely the alternative moral economy of Gaelic, Catholic Ireland which Connolly claims to have been non-existent, or at least ineffectual. This may indeed have been politically dormant – or biding its time – in the early decades of the century,[30] but in terms of Burke's theory of the sublime, this surface consensus is little more than 'a sort of tranquillity tinged with terror' (*Enquiry*, 136), a convulsion waiting to happen. Considered from this perspective, the shock of state violence unleashed in Munster in the 1760s, and on a general scale in the 1790s, could only serve to arouse a subjugated culture 'from the quiet sleep of death', releasing 'the ghosts from the ruins of castles and churches' that haunted the land.[31] This was the basis of the Gothic register in which Burke expresses his fears about the excessive violence of colonial regimes, whether in Ireland or in India: because the injuries of the past are scarcely healed, it needed little to reopen the deep wounds that festered beneath the illusory outward composure of the body politic.

This theme of a festering wound, of the body in pain, is a recurrent motif in eighteenth-century Irish culture. In its most dramatic form, as I discuss in Chapter 2, it is embodied in the abject figure of Philoctetes, the wounded outcast of Sophocles's tragedy who, abandoned on an island, comes to represent the plight of an abandoned people. Philoctetes resurfaced in the English literary canon in the pioneering translation by Swift's friend, Dr Thomas Sheridan, in 1725, but received his most powerful visual expression in a painting by James Barry, executed in 1771, and in subsequent prints issued by Barry to coincide with successive phases in the campaign for Catholic emancipation. As a national allegory, the drama of Philoctetes is uniquely well placed to expose the underside of the Enlightenment that haunted Burke, its indifference towards the casualties of progress or the victims of history. As I argue below, leading figures in the Scottish Enlightenment such as David Hume and Adam Smith linked expressions of 'sympathy' to a desire to emulate others' wealth and good fortune, thus providing a spur for one's own self-advancement, but were reluctant to extend compassion, not to mention justice, to those who lost out on modernization, or who were consigned to the fate of 'doomed' cultures. By contrast, Burke was troubled by the other side of modernity, the victims of progress and utility:

> Men are rarely without some sympathy in the sufferings of others; but in the immense and diversified mass of human misery, which may be pitied, but cannot be relieved, mankind must make a choice. Our sympathy is always more forcibly attracted towards the misfortunes of certain persons, and in certain descriptions: and this sympathetic attraction discovers, beyond a possibility of mistake, our mental affinities, and elective affections.[32]

Many of Burke's (and, it might be added, Swift's) ostensible 'counter-Enlightenment' stances come from this concern with the body in pain, and a refusal to countenance advances in civility and modernity that disavowed the cost of progress. Projected onto a social level, this sympathy for the injured body extended to cultures on the receiving end of colonialism, amounting at times to an almost Nietzschean acknowledgement of the violence sedimented in universalist schemes of human emancipation and improvement. But, like Swift, Burke is not just concerned to acknowledge pain: equally crucial, as I argue in Chapter 3, is the assertion of the right to complain, to protest not only against injustice but against the new neo-stoical conception of the citizen, exemplified by Adam Smith's *The Theory of Moral Sentiments* (1759), which sought to purge the body and its discontents from the public sphere. For Burke, injustice acquires an extra cruel dimension when the cries of the sufferer are taken themselves as measures of disloyalty, hence warranting further oppression. As he wrote of the indifference of the Protestant Ascendancy to the plight of the Catholic population in Ireland at the beginning of the decade that was to culminate in the carnage of the 1798 rebellion:

> They were quite certain, that no complaints of the natives would be heard on this side of the water [i.e. in England], with any other sentiments than those of contempt and indignation. Their cries served only to augment their torture. ('Langrishe', iii, 321)

In arguing thus, Burke's critique of the Enlightenment may be taken to exemplify what Albert O. Hirschman, in his typology of reactions to the Enlightenment, has designated 'the perversity thesis', according to which grand schemes to advance the cause of progress and liberty often relapse into the very barbarism they set out to eliminate.[33] Certainly, this was the thinking that informed Burke's notorious comparison of the Jacobins in France to 'American savages' (*Reflections*, 159), and, in Chapter 7, I argue that so far from being a trait shared only by the Jacobins, this abiding fear on Burke's part of a reversion from civility into savagery can be traced closer to home in the conduct of the British government during the American Revolution, and particularly to the practice of employing and manipulating Iroquois Indians as agents of terror. Colonial regimes not only brought out the savage in others, they brought it out in themselves. If there is any train of thought linking Burke's indictments of colonial rule in Ireland, India or America, it is the fatal logic whereby colonial regimes end up perpetuating the worst traits of the societies they endeavour to civilize: 'the medicine of state corrupted into its poison' (*Reflections*, 126). Nor were ideological rigidity and doctrinaire ideas of progress confined to the Jacobins. In Chapter 4, I argue that Burke's own writings were subjected to the 'perversity thesis' in that his authority was invoked by ideologues in the British Treasury to justify the iron laws of economic rationality that presided over the catastrophe of the Great Irish Famine.[34] This rested on a fundamental misunderstanding of Burke's conception of the radical differences between the forms of crisis manifested in the Irish and the British economies, and, at a more philosophical level, of his determination to bring the obligations of the heart, based on the medieval right of necessity and the most basic forms of mutual concern, to bear on the 'metaphysical' abstractions of political economy.

It remains to seen, however, whether Burke's preoccupation with the injured body, and, by extension, with the victims of progress in its revolutionary or colonial guise, is a rejection of the Enlightenment or, as I suggest, an extension of it into what was then the unfamiliar terrain of cultural or 'group rights', and a more culturally nuanced approach to universal norms of justice and equality. Burke is often understood as espousing a defence of tradition and 'cultural particularism' against abstract ideas of human rights and the ordinances of universal reason. His grounding of morality in 'sympathy', of the kind that lends itself to personal or communal ties, is consistent with this sense of local allegiance, and is given eloquent expression in one of the most famous passages in the *Reflections*:

To be attached to the subdivision, to love the little platoon we belong to in society, is the first principle (the germ as it were) of public affections. It is the first link in the series by which we proceed towards a love to our country and to mankind. (*Reflections*, 135)

But, as is clear from this formulation, it by no means follows that our allegiances are *restricted* to local horizons – the suggestion, rather, is that more extensive or wide-ranging forms of solidarity or 'fraternity' cannot dispense with these primary affections: 'The love to the whole is not extinguished by this subordinate partiality' (*Reflections*, 315). One of the implications of Burke's linking of sympathy with the discontinuities and 'defamiliarizing' tactics of the sublime, which I examine in Chapter 3, is precisely to extend its remit across cultural boundaries, to embrace the shock of the strange with the emotional involvement we bring from our own culture. Hence, in his protracted campaign to bring Warren Hastings before the bar of public opinion, Burke uses all his rhetorical powers to speak as if from personal experience of a remote country, India, that he had never visited. In this juxtaposition of proximity and distance, familiarity and estrangement, it is possible to discern a version of the 'sympathetic sublime' that possesses the global reach of universalist theories of human rights, but without the calculus of abstraction, or the insensitivity to time and place, that characterized progress and universal reason in much mainstream Enlightenment thought.

It is worth surmising whether this is what the United Irishman Thomas Russell, a returned soldier from India, had in mind when he remarked on one occasion that he preferred Burke's *Enquiry into the Sublime and Beautiful* to the political ideas of Thomas Paine.[35] Not least of the ironies of the radical sensibility generated by the 'sympathetic sublime' is that in Ireland it lent itself to the revolutionary programmes of the United Irishmen rather than to incremental reforms of the kind advocated by Burke. It was in the writings and political activities of the United Irishmen in the 1790s that the political ramifications of the colonial sublime assumed insurgent material form, giving the universalism and civic humanism of republican ideology a local habitation through an engagement with agrarian movements (through alliances with the Defenders, the Catholic peasant underground organization), popular ballads, native music, the Irish language (Russell published the first Gaelic magazine, *Bolg an tSolair*, in 1795) – in short, the first revolutionary stirrings of an emergent cultural nationalism, energized by a radical Enlightenment project.

Part of Burke's theoretical aversion to republicanism was due to its metaphysical speculations on foundations, its fixation on abstract ideals of 'natural rights' and 'natural liberty', and their related primitivist recastings of pre-modern societies as mythic 'states of nature'. So far from celebrating cultural diversity, primitivism negated what Seamus Deane has referred to as the 'specific density' of native cultures, construing 'tradition' and actual lived history as a fall from the purity of the original founding principles. Under the aegis of the Scottish Enlightenment, Gaelic culture itself was removed, in the guise of Celticism, to the Ossianic fiction of a remote past conjured up in the imagination of James Macpherson. By contrast, the United Irishmen's active engagement with Gaelic and vernacular culture, and the politics of the recent past in Ireland, can be seen as an attempt to appropriate Burkean notions of tradition and local allegiances for an advanced revolutionary project. Tradition in England may have acted as a stabilizing principle, as exemplified by the mythic continuity which Burke attached to the 'ancient constitution', but in Ireland, as he was all too aware, tradition was a disruptive force, drawing attention to successive phases of confiscation and bloodshed perpetrated by colonial conquest. This is the Gothic bequest which we have noted above in relation to Burke, the indelible stain on the family escutcheon that resurfaced as a motif in the distinctively Irish literary genre of 'the national tale of terror'.[36] As Burke wrote in the 1790s of Protestant celebrations of Cromwell and King William: 'One would not think that decorum, to say nothing of policy, would permit them to call up, by magic charms, the grounds, reasons, and principles of those terrible confiscatory and exterminatory periods' ('Richard Burke', vi, 77) when they established their rule. Tradition in this context was little more than revisiting the scene of a crime, the return of the repressed in the public sphere. As Iain McCalman has written of the ambivalence of this aspect of Burke's politics in the 1790s:

Throughout the 1790s Burke thus found himself advancing ideas and political programmes for Ireland which contradicted his counter-revolutionary crusade in England... [For Burke] Irish Jacobinism, as distinct from its wanton English strain, stemmed from terrible hunger, distress, and injustice. If such sympathy did not push Burke into becoming a republican revolutionary like Irish Whig counterparts Arthur O'Connor and Wolfe Tone, he verged on complicity.[37]

It was precisely this grounding of abstract republican ideals in the grievances of the dispossessed that provided the impetus for the mass mobilization of the United Irishman, and for their nascent vernacular vision of universal liberty.[38] As the storm clouds gathered over Ireland in the 1790s, and sectarian strife broke out on a scale unimaginable in the 1760s, even Burke appeared to be infected by revolutionary contagion, and the need to infuse the restless energy of the sublime into the propagation of the Catholic cause is a recurrent note in his writings of this period. Though he stopped short initially from advocating violent resistance, even this had changed by 1795, with the rise of the mass agrarian movement known as the Defenders. In a letter to Dr Hussey, the first President of Maynooth, Burke attributes the horrors of Orange pogroms against Catholics in Armagh to the misguided caution of the Catholic clergy:

I am not at all surprised at it; and consider it as one of the natural consequences of a measure better intended than considerd – that of the Catholick Clergys persuading the Laity to give up their Arms. Dreadful it is; but it is now plain enough, that Catholick *Defenderism* is the only restraint upon Protestant Ascendency.[39]

To the extent that his aesthetic concerns are engaged with his politics, Burke's writings reveal a character divided against itself, as if his early theories were following their logical, or rather pathological, course through his troubled personality. Burke is often presented as a relic of a feudal age, a Don Quixote tilting at windmills of his own making, but in many ways he was an intellectual before his time, if not also, as Mary Wollstonecraft suggested, a revolutionary out of place.[40] This raises the crucial question of whether bringing Burke's aesthetics to bear on his politics is to read him against the grain, conveniently overlooking those aspects of his political philosophy defending the monarchy, state religion, aristocracy, inequality, and so on, that have identified him as one of the patron saints of conservatism. These are undoubtedly the familiar signposts on the Burkean landscape, pointing to the main thoroughfares in his thought, and in terms of his own aesthetic categories, these images of stability and accumulated order find expression in the domain of 'the beautiful' – or its later, more irregular counterpart, 'the picturesque'. My concern in this study, however, is less with this recognizable terrain than with those unapproved roads that have received less inspection, or which seem to be at odds with his more public (and not so public) pronouncements. Some of these positions certainly seem difficult to reconcile with the main currents of his political thought, but, as I shall argue, they are less inexplicable when considered in the light of his aesthetic theories. To be sure, this will result in a partial and selective reading, but in another sense it is more comprehensive in that it attempts to integrate his powerful aesthetic writings into his wider moral and political vision.

The irony of placing a simplistic emphasis on Burke's conservatism while ignoring the unresolved counter-currents in his thought is that while the defense of aristocracy and hierarchy seems antiquated by contemporary standards, his aesthetic theories, and particularly his disturbing concept of the sublime, have received a whole new lease of life in contemporary critical debates. The shelf life of many of his key political ideas may thus have passed, but reformulated in terms of his aesthetics, it may be that some of his more critical stances on the Enlightenment, colonialism and indigenous cultures have had to await the end of the twentieth century for their moment to come. As Raymond Williams has written, in a characteristically astute analysis:

> The confutation of Burke on the French Revolution is now a one-finger exercise in politics and history... This sort of thing is indeed so easy that we may be in danger of missing a more general point, which has less to do with his condemnations than with his attachments, and less with his position than with his manner of thinking... Burke's writing is an articulated experience, and as such has a validity which can survive even the demolition of its general conclusions.[41]

Williams continues: 'It is not that the eloquence survives where the cause has failed', but if by eloquence is meant Burke's profound and unsettling aesthetic sensibility, both at the level of theory and practice, then there is indeed a sense in which his 'eloquence' picks up where his cause has failed. Aesthetics for Burke is not just a matter (as Williams put it elsewhere) of 'grace after meals', but permeates his presentation of self from his earliest days, calling, in the process, for a radical revision of one-dimensional views of his work and thought. Burke's overt political loyalties and allegiances, in keeping with his writings, were very much a product of their time, but critics of his crusade against the French Revolution often fail to point out that proponents of modernity such as Adam Smith, and many other leading lights of the Scottish and English Enlightenments, did not rush to embrace republican principles either. Indeed, by the mid 1790s, some of the most influential strands in British radicalism had begun to distance themelves from Jacobinism, seeking to annex Burke's rhetoric of the British constitution for their own purposes in the refurbished myth of the 'freeborn Englishman' and ancient liberties, thereby muting their critique of the monarchy and the British constitution.[42]

In the final analysis, the question whether Burke's ideas can be disentangled from the constricting political horizons of his own era is no different from whether Greek (and hence European) concepts of democracy can be disassociated from the institutions of slavery which facilitated them; or, closer to our own time, whether Jefferson's republican vision of life, liberty and the pursuit of happiness is irrevocably bound up with slavery and the racial segregation which disfigured American democracy in its formative phase. In such circumstances, it is not necessarily the 'universality' of theory, its transcendence of time and place, that speaks to the present moment, but rather its malleability and openness to history, its capacity to change with the times. This is pre-eminently the tenor of Burke's philosophy, its lack of theoretical closure being due in part to the fact that it carried within itself many unresolved and dissonant narratives which threatened at times, like the power of the sublime, to topple his own paeans to the 'great oak' of the British constitution. For Burke, there is not simply one past, but as David Bromwich emphasizes, using Burke's own terminology, 'a choice of inheritance' (*Reflections*, 120), a range of alternative pasts that point towards different possibilities in the present and the future. To the extent that history can be lost, it is also 'something we have to strive to retain', and in this, Burke's extraordinary eloquence often comes across as an echo-chamber, carrying the voices of the endangered and the oppressed that would otherwise have been consigned to oblivion.[43] This clamour of voices in Burke's language has to do with his impassioned and often reckless concern to address the fate of the 'others' of empire, the excluded majorities, whether in Ireland, India or America, whose cultures were violated in the name of progress and civilization. In retrieving these lost narratives in Burke's work, we are perhaps, as Foucault argues, utilizing rather than simply commenting on a writer's life, and what he says about Nietzsche could equally apply to Burke: 'The only valid tribute to thought such as Nietzsche's is precisely to use it, to deform it, to make it groan and protest.'[44] It is as if, subject to the attrition of history, these ideas themselves are akin to the voices of the vanquished, crying out to be heard across the centuries.

Living in an era that proclaims the end of history, and that has witnessed the ambivalent legacies of modernity and globalization, it is worth recalling Burke's salutary warnings against the kind of strident optimism in Enlightenment thinking that coexisted with nonchalant hostility towards its excluded 'others'. One of the consequences of the dissociation between art and morality in Enlightenment thought was that the 'aesthetic', and culture in general, was requisitioned to act as a consolation for politics, granting minorities or marginalized groups an exotic or imaginative after-life – 'romantic Ireland', the 'noble savage', the 'last of the race' – to compensate for their exclusion from citizenship in the public sphere. By closing the gap between culture and politics, Burke cuts off this escape route, seeing in the imagination haunted by terror an unrequited rage for justice. The concept of the sublime offers no comforting illusions, but serves to remind us that there is indeed a price for progress, and that only those societies offer hope for the future who settle their debt to the past.

PART I

The politics of pain

I

'This king of terrors': Edmund Burke and the aesthetics of executions

> I see that you have but one way of relieving the poor in Ireland. They call for bread, and you give them 'not a Stone', but the Gallows.
> Edmund Burke to John Ridge, 1763

> There are very few pains, however exquisite, which are not preferred to death; nay, what generally makes pain itself, if I may say so, more painful, is, that it is considered an emissary of this king of terrors.
> Edmund Burke, *Enquiry into the Sublime and Beautiful* (1757)

In one of the many mischievous asides in what may justly be seen as the anarchist's cookbook of nineteenth-century Ireland, Thomas Moore's *Memoirs of Captain Rock*, the notorious Captain informs us that the date of his birth, 15 March 1766, was a portent of the misfortunes which were to befall his native land. In the midst of the first major outbreak of agrarian insurgency in Ireland, the Whiteboy agitation that racked Munster in the early 1760s:

I came into the world – on the very day (as my mother has often mentioned to me, making the sign of the cross on her breast at the same time,) when Father Sheehy, the good parish priest of Clogheen, was hanged at Clonmell, on the testimony of a perjured witness, for the crime of which he was as innocent as the babe unborn. This execution of Father Sheehy was one of those *coups d'état* of the Irish authorities, which they used to perform at stated intervals, and which saved them the trouble of further atrocities for some time to come.[1]

The gibbet on which Fr Nicholas Sheehy was hung, drawn and quartered threw a shadow over the Irish political landscape which extended well into the next century. 'The account of the persecution and judicial murder of Father Nicholas Sheehy, of Clogheen', wrote R. R. Madden, 'is an epitome in itself of the history of Ireland at that period, of its persecuted people, of the character of their oppressors.'[2] Innumerable ballads and elegies mourned his death, and within ten years the *Freeman's Journal* reported that the 'deluded people were made to think him a saint, and to carry away a great deal of the earth that covered his body, as a sacred relic'.³ His fate was recounted in one of the earliest nationalist historical novels of the nineteenth century, and came to exemplify, in the popular imagination, the persecution of Catholics under the Penal Laws in the eighteenth century.⁴

Fr Nicholas Sheehy was arrested three times on suspicion of being a Whiteboy organizer in the Tipperary/Limerick region before his eventual indictment for the murder of an informer, one John Bridge, in 1766.⁵ The Whiteboy movement, the first of many agrarian secret societies to stalk the Irish countryside until the end of the nineteenth century, emerged in 1761 in an area of North Munster embracing the counties Tipperary, Limerick, and Cork. The Whiteboys derived their name from the practice of disguising themselves in white sheets or female clothing, and their immediate grievances were economic, in particular the bitterly resented payment of tithes to the established Protestant Church, and the sudden upsurge in land enclosures brought on by the pressures of the Seven Years War. In the eyes of the authorities, however, this agrarian unrest was merely a pretext for reactivating residual Jacobite sympathies among the disaffected Catholic population labouring under the oppressive Penal Laws introduced after the Williamite settlement, and as such was a symptom of a deeper crisis involving a threat of 'popish insurrection' and a treasonable alliance with France.

For one official in Dublin Castle, Edmund Burke, the terror of the 1760s represented an acutely personal crisis that went to the heart of his deepest familial and political allegiances. In the earliest account of agrarian disorders in Munster dating from October 1761, an alarmist letter from William Fant to the Lord Lieutenant of Ireland reported sightings of the Pretender dressed as a woman at meetings organized by Burke's maternal relatives and childhood friends, the Nagles and Hennessys, who lived in the Blackwater valley in north County Cork.⁶ These personal links implicating Burke with the Whiteboys extended to Fr Nicholas Sheehy himself, who was related to Burke through marriage.⁷ The alarm registered in Burke's private writings during this period betrays an emotional intensity bordering on frenzy. As he wrote from England to his friend, Charles O'Hara, an MP in the Irish Parliament:

We are all in a Blaze here with your plots, assassinations, massacres, Rebellions, moonlight armies, French Officers and French money. Are you not ashamed? You who told me if they could get no discovery from Sheehy, they would cool and leave off their detestable plot mongering. You think well of Ireland; but I think rightly of it; and know that their unmeaning Senseless malice is insatiable; *cedamus patria*! I am told, that these miserable wretches whom they have hanged, died with one voice declaring their innocence: but truly for my part, I want no man dying, or risen from the dead, to tell me that lies are lies, and nonsense is nonsense... I assure you I look upon these things with horror, and cannot talk of such proceedings as the effects of an innocent credulity.

Throughout the decade of the 1760s, he confides to O'Hara that he cannot even bear to contemplate what is going on, or raise it to the level of consciousness: 'My Sollicitude for Ireland is growing rather less anxious than it was', he writes, 'I endeavour to remove it from my mind as much as I can', and again: 'I hate to think of Ireland, though my thoughts involuntarily take that turn, and whenever they do meet only with objects of grief or indignation.'[8] This politics of 'periphrasis', as he was later to call it,[9] is akin to that precipitated by the experience of the sublime, as enunciated in Burke's earlier treatise on aesthetics, the *Enquiry*:

The passion caused by the great and sublime... is that state of the soul, in which all its motions are suspended, with some degrees of horror... Hence arises the great power of the sublime, that far from being produced by them, it anticipates our reasonings, and hurries us on by an irresistible force. (*Enquiry*, 57)

As an aesthetic of extreme situations, Burke's theory of the sublime may be seen not only as a philosophical enquiry but also as a fraught, highly mediated response to the turbulent colonial landscape of eighteenth-century Ireland. The sublime strains at the inexpressible, at what lies beyond representation in both its aesthetic and political senses, and is thus significant, as Sara Suleri argues in relation to Burke's writings on India, 'less for its contribution to modern theories of imperialism than for its passionate recognition of the dubieties inherent in any narrative of colonial possession'.[10] It is in this sense that it weighed heavily on Burke's divided emotional loyalties in Ireland, caught between his official political persona in the early 1760s as private secretary to William Gerard Hamilton, Chief Secretary to the Lord Lieutenant at Dublin Castle, and the divergent 'obligations written on the heart' by his upbringing in the Gaelic, Catholic milieu of his maternal family, the Nagles, in north County Cork.[11]

Burke's *Enquiry*, a landmark in the history of aesthetics, was published in 1757, and as such predates the outbreak of Whiteboy agitation in the 1760s. But the political anxieties precipitated by the underlying causes of unrest in Munster had already impinged on Burke's formative years, as is clear from his direct family connection with another example of state terror, the execution of the leading Jacobite sympathizer, James Cotter, in 1720. Cotter's execution, according to L. M. Cullen, 'was easily the most traumatic political event of the first half of the century in Ireland, having no parallel in the rest of Ireland and providing in recollection on both sides the spark which set alight the sectarian tensions in Munster in the early 1760s'. Like Sheehy's death, it released a flood of popular emotion, giving rise to no less than twenty *caoins* (keens) or laments in Gaelic poetry alone.[12] Burke's family was deeply entangled in this event, for his father, Richard Burke, would appear to have acted as Cotter's attorney during the ill-fated trial. It may be that his father's subsequent conforming to Protestantism was even prompted by the 'witch hunts' which followed the trial, and anti-Catholic plots against the Nagle and Hennessy families over their alleged Jacobite connections surfaced again in 1731–2 and 1733.[13] Some commentators have cast doubt on the connections between Burke's father and Cotter but there is another important connection, showing that relations with the Cotter circle persisted until 1757, the year of publication of the *Enquiry*. On 30 May 1757, the *Corke Journal* related that two notes for substantial sums of money payable to the recently deceased Joseph Nagle were not endorsed before his death, and readers of the paper are asked to deliver the notes to either the original vendors, to David Nagle, nephew and administrator of the estate, 'or to Richard Burke, Attorney, at his house in Lower Ormonde Quay, Dublin'.[14] Joseph Nagle, a Counsellor-at-Law, was one of the most resolute defenders of the Catholic interest under the Penal Laws, and for that reason, according to his niece, Nano Nagle, was 'the most disliked by the Protestants of any Catholic in the Kingdom'.[15] His brother, Garret Nagle, and James Cotter were married to two sisters, and Joseph and Garret were named in informers' reports in the 1730s as being the main agents for the Jacobite cause in Munster. Both were acquitted following an investigation by the Parliament in Dublin, but throughout this period Joseph was fighting another extended battle to hold on, as a Catholic, to his estates.[16] That Burke's family was drawn into the legal affairs of perhaps the most marked proponent of the Catholic cause in Munster shows that the extended fallout from the Cotter affair, and its seditious taint of Jacobitism, was still making its presence felt in the formative period in which he wrote the *Enquiry*.[17]

SHOWS OF FORCE: THEATRICALITY AND TERROR

Set against this troubled background, the frequent examples of state executions adduced in the *Enquiry* to demonstrate the terrors of the sublime, acquire a morbid personal dimension in Burke's life. To support his general argument that ideas of pain and terror are of a greater intensity than any satiation induced by pleasure, Burke cites the example of the hideous torture inflicted on the attempted French regicide, Robert Damiens, during his execution in 1757: 'I am in great doubt, whether any man could be found who would earn a life of the most perfect satisfaction, at the price of ending it in the torments, which justice inflicted in a few hours on the late unfortunate regicide in France' (*Enquiry*, 39). There are indications that the *Enquiry* was initially conceived in 1747 in the tense political atmosphere following a threatened Jacobite uprising in Ireland, and it may be, as James Boulton suggests, that the extraordinary public interest in the execution of the Scottish Jacobite leader, Lord Lovat, for high treason in London in April 1747 provided the impetus for the remarkable passage in which Burke argues that dramatic reenactments of suffering on the stage pale in comparison to displays of real pain:[18]

Chuse a day on which to represent the most sublime and affecting tragedy we have; appoint the most favourite actors; spare no cost upon the scenes and decorations; unite the greatest efforts of poetry, painting and music; and when you have collected your audience, just at the moment when their minds are erect with expectation, let it be reported that a state criminal of high rank is on the point of being executed in the adjoining square; in a moment the emptiness of the theatre would demonstrate the comparative weakness of the imitative arts, and proclaim the triumph of the real sympathy. (*Enquiry*, 47)

The reservations expressed in Burke's aesthetic theory about fictional displays of pain are not directed at their dramatic nature, but at their exploitation as a form of public spectacle: 'it is a show and a spectacle, not a play, that is exhibited', as Burke wrote later of the deterioration of drama on the London stage ('Third Letter', v, 337).[19] Lurid displays of violence facilitated a kind of aesthetic detachment which Burke found deeply objectionable, as is clear from his later response to what he perceived as the gross humiliations inflicted on Louis XVI by the stage managers of the French Revolution:

Some tears might be drawn from me, if such a spectacle were exhibited on the stage. I should be truly ashamed of finding in myself that superficial, theatric sense of painted distress, whilst I could exult over it in real life. With such a perverted mind, I could never venture to shew my face at a tragedy. (*Reflections*, 175)

It is sentiments such as these which prompt Frans De Bruyn's perceptive comment that 'Burke unfolds a curiously literal-minded theory of tragedy in his *Reflections*, one that virtually ignores the distinction between tragic events in real life and dramatic tragedy as an *imitation* of reality. This denial of aesthetic distance is already apparent in his earliest consideration of the effects of tragic representation on a theatre audience.'[20] Thus, as a young student at Trinity College, Dublin, Burke expresses his distaste for scenes of grotesque violence in drama:

> we should long ago have seen farcical Scenes excluded from Tragedy... for as Miracles are unnecessary to convince thinking Men; so are Prodigies to please Men of Taste. I scarce remember a taking Tragedy of the *English*, in which there is not some Body butchered on the Stage; but what is the greatest Hindrance to the laying aside this barbarous Practice, is the Passion the People have for the Actor's Dying; but this Practice of fighting and killing is so far from having the desired Effect, in raising Terror that it carries something ridiculous with it.

Burke proceeds to argue that a minimalist staging of a 'Couple of Men clattering Foils' will give a far greater idea of combat than graphic attempts at realism. To determine the limits of dramatic representation in this way, however, is not to eschew all forms of artistic mediation, and remove violence entirely from public view: 'if judiciously manag'd', he writes, 'the Narrative' will convey what spectacle cannot do, and 'will not only raise a greater Idea than Representation possibly can, but perhaps than such a real Combat would'. What is required is not a captive but a sympathetic, 'thinking Audience', who would complete mentally what is not depicted on stage: 'the ill-natur'd don't care to see a generous Distress, but dancing Buffooneries and *Harlequin* eases them of these, as well as all other Thoughts'.[21] Burke's worst fears concerning the ostentatious use of spectacle to pander to indolent imaginations were realized over forty years later in the street theatre and processions of the French Revolution. 'A cheap, bloodless reformation, a guiltless liberty, appear flat and vapid' to the intoxicated taste of those who have taken to the streets:

> There must be a great change of scene; there must be a magnificent stage effect; there must be a grand spectacle to rouze the imagination, grown torpid with the lazy enjoyment of sixty years security, and the still unanimating repose of public prosperity. (*Reflections*, 156)

Burke's thinking here is evolving towards the idea of theatre as orchestrating *exemplary* actions or events, scenes which do not seek to include everything but by a 'judicious' dramatic economy, summon up the whole in the minds of the audience. This argument is developed in the section on language in the *Enquiry* where he takes issue with simplistic, mimetic theories of language, according to which the meaning of words is bound up with graphic representations, or the mental images that accompany them. He asks us to reflect on a statement such as, 'I shall go to Italy next summer.' This is easily understood; yet, in order to grasp its meaning, there is no need to engage in Tristram Shandy-type exercises painstakingly outlining the minutiae of the journey:

> no body has by this painted in his imagination the exact figure of the speaker passing by land or by water, or both; sometimes on horseback, sometimes in a carriage; with all the particulars of the journey. Still less has he any idea of Italy, the country to which I proposed to go; or of the greenness of the fields, the ripening of the fruits, and the warmth of the air, with the change to this from a different season, which are the ideas for which the word *summer* is substituted. (*Enquiry*, 170)

– and so on. This anti-pictorial principle applies with greater force to general terms such as 'wise, valiant, generous, good and great' which have clear reference or 'application' to real objects in the world: 'these words, by having no application, ought to be un-operative; but when words commonly sacred to great occasions are used, we are affected by them even without the occasions' (*Enquiry*, 166). In these cases, meanings are carried over from their original contexts through habit and custom, the usages which we share as members of an interpretative community. Words depend for their effect not on 'representation' or their mimetic power, but on their evocative capacity generated through social usage: the aim is 'to affect rather by sympathy than by imitation' (*Enquiry*, 172). Affective response is achieved at the expense of graphic clarity, particularly in the case of those words which have the greatest emotional impact on our lives:

> There are many things of a very affecting nature, which can seldom occur in the reality, but the words which represent them often do; and thus they have an opportunity of making a deep impression and taking root in the mind, whilst the idea of the reality was transient; and to some perhaps never really occurred in any shape, to whom it is notwithstanding very affecting, as war, death, famine, &c. (*Enquiry*, 173–4)

From this it is clear that the staging of tragic events, or scenes of suffering, achieve their desired effects not through graphic clarity or excessive details, but through the flow of sympathy which emanates from the moral imagination. In this way they act in an exemplary manner, attaching awe and reverence to abstract principles such as justice, authority, and providence which are inculcated through our participation in a common, albeit hierarchical, culture. Exemplary events possess a symbolic power over and above their own particularity in that they do not simply illustrate the basic tenets of a system, but define and instil them in the minds of beholders. As an example, Burke cited the importance of the Sacheverell trial in

1709–10 in forming the self-images of the Whigs in a period of instability and uncertainty:

> It was carried on for the express purpose of stating the true grounds and principles of the Revolution; what the Commons emphatically called their *foundation*. It was carried on...in order, by a juridical sentence of the highest authority, to confirm and fix Whig principles...and to fix them in the extent and with the limitations with which it was meant they should be understood by posterity.[22]

There is little doubt that Burke also saw the impeachment of Warren Hastings in this light, a sustained dramatic performance designed to influence policy, changing the perceptions of what was permissible in colonial rule and in furthering the interests of empire.

The difficulty for Burke, however, with these kinds of exemplary events or actions is that as test cases, in which the stability of the system itself is at stake, their performative force requires a deep insight in the circumstances of their staging. and a careful calibration of their theatrical effects. Otherwise, they run the risk of unleashing forces which, as Burke was all too aware from outbreaks of popular tumult and the fury of crowds, threaten to expose the fragility and even the legitimacy of the entire social order. Thus the ultimate expression of the politics of the sublime, the staging of public executions, can instil awe and reverence among the populace for the 'dread majesty' (*Enquiry*, 67) of the sovereign, but if these displays of terror are mismanaged through excess and blood-lust on the part of the law itself, they may succeed only in inciting the very rage and popular savagery they were meant to subdue.[23] Explaining the fear and trembling induced by the very idea of the Almighty, Burke writes that

> whilst we contemplate so vast an object, under the arm, as it were, of almighty power, and invested upon every side with omnipresence, we shrink into the minuteness of our own nature, and are, in a manner, annihilated before him. And though a consideration of his other attributes may relieve in some measure our apprehensions; yet no conviction of the justice with which it is exercised, nor the mercy with which it is tempered, can wholly remove the terror that naturally arises from a force which nothing can withstand. If we rejoice, we rejoice with trembling...
> (*Enquiry*, 68)

But this does not exhaust the entire operation of the sublime, for there is also a counter-movement which mitigates our fear of annihilation, and enhances our own self-image and self-esteem. This occurs when we are enabled, through imaginative identification, to partake of some of the power possessed by the awesome object or occasion with which we are confronted. By means of an expansion of our mental faculties, filling in the picture, as it were, through our own endeavour, we appropriate to ourselves some of the power of the object that threatens to overwhelm our senses. For this to transpire, however, it is vital that the full force or terror of the object in question be withheld from view through a 'judicious obscurity' (*Enquiry*, 59), so that we have to rise to the occasion ourselves to meet the challenge to our well-being. Hence Burke endorses the kind of striving associated with emulation or ambition which:

> produces a sort of swelling and triumph that is extremely grateful to the human mind; and the swelling is never more perceived, nor operates with more force, than when without danger we are conversant with terrible objects, the mind always claiming to itself some part of the dignity and importance of the things which it contemplates. (*Enquiry*, 50–1)

Crucially, for this restorative process to take effect, the danger has to be at one remove to facilitate the internalization of an external power. It is when these conditions are not in place that the whole theatrical display of authority comes unstuck, and society is exposed to the unmitigated savagery of the 'simply terrible' (*Enquiry*, 40).[24] For Burke, this breakdown of aesthetic authority was nowhere more evident than in the 'farces' enacted by the revolutionary Assembly in France:

> They act like the comedians of a fair before a riotous audience; they act amidst the tumultuous cries of a mixed mob of ferocious men, and of women lost to shame, who, according to their insolent fancies, direct, control, applaud, explode them; and sometimes mix and take their seats amongst them; domineering over them with a strange mixture of servile petulance and proud presumptuous authority. As they have inverted order in all things, the gallery is in the place of the house. (*Reflections*, 161)

THE MASQUE OF DEATH AND THE MORAL ECONOMY

This is the spectre that continually haunts Burke throughout his career, and which accounts for his determination to dissociate the restorative powers of the Glorious Revolution of 1688 from the destructive energies unleashed by the French Revolution. Burke was at pains to point out that the Glorious Revolution was directed not at the monarchy as such, but against what were considered the serious abuses and irregularities which threatened to destroy the institution under the corrupt reign of James II. So far from being an uncritical apologist for the existing order, Burke was willing to accept that, as he put it, 'an irregular, convulsive movement may be necessary to throw off an irregular, convulsive disease' (*Reflections*, 109). However, as is clear from the metaphor of 'disease', revolution in these circumstances is seen as *restorative*, a means of returning the corrupted body politic to its former healthy state:

> The [Glorious] Revolution was made to preserve our *antient* indisputable laws and liberties, and that *antient* constitution of government which is our only security for law and liberty... We wished at the period of the Revolution, and do now wish, to derive all we possess as *an inheritance from our forefathers*... All the reformations we have hitherto made have proceeded upon the principle of reference to antiquity. (*Reflections*, 117)

Burke's measured response to the Revolution of 1688 helps us to understand the role of violence in maintaining the legitimacy of the state. In terms of the aesthetic categories outlined in the *Enquiry*, the violence of 'the sublime' is required to restore order and instil awe and respect, but to maintain social harmony and tranquillity it is necessary to utilize the ameliorating influence of 'the beautiful'. This elicits affection and loyalty, tempering the show of force that constitutes the sublime by the silent operation of custom and tradition, the 'soft collar of social esteem... which made power gentle, and obedience liberal' (*Reflections*, 170–1). This latter component is essential to convert state violence into non-coercive forms of social regulation and control. As a number of historians have recently argued, while exercises of power under aristocratic hegemony in the eighteenth century such as charity and patronage were clearly paternalist and discretionary, an element of volition also entered into the harsh world of law and order, with considerable latitude being exercised in the actual enforcement of the draconian laws on the statute books. Thus, while the number of capital crimes grew from about 50 in 1688 to over 200 by the early nineteenth century, in actuality the rate of hangings decreased steadily throughout this period.[25] Executions came to depend increasingly on their *symbolic* power rather than their frequency, on the grounds that exemplary shows of strength were more effective in cowing the population than overexposure to horror and cruelty. That the primary purpose of executions was public display, rather than the infliction of pain on the victim, is clear from the practice of hanging suicides and mutilating dead bodies, leaving them rotting on gibbets or, in the case of state criminals, their heads impaled on spikes.

In keeping with the argument outlined in the *Enquiry*, Burke's profound uneasiness about such theatres of pain turned precisely on their exemplary status, their capacity either to induce allegiance through awe and fear, or, when badly stage-managed, to provoke hostility and resentment of the kind that alienated the population entirely from the judicial system. In his courageous attack on the punishment of two homosexuals in the pillory in 1788, which led to the death of one of the unfortunate victims, Burke argued that it is the duty of lawmakers 'to proportion that punishment so that it should not exceed the extent of the crime, and to provide that it should be of that kind, which was calculated to operate as an example and prevent crimes, than to oppress and torment the convicted criminal'.[26] Just as his objections to graphic excess in his theory of meaning turned on its replacement by sympathy and the solidarity of an interpretative community, so also the efficacy of violence, like the revolution of 1688, depended not on the macabre powers of spectacle, but on the possession of a deeper, common culture, 'the secret, unseen, but irrefragible bond of habitual intercourse' that holds society together, even in the face of profound social and political antagonisms. The aesthetic impact of executions, with their calculated theatrical effects, reinforces communal norms, if only because they utilize a shared repertoire of cultural codes to stage the masque of death.[27] But in the absence of such complex cultural codes, the horrors of the sublime have no restorative or invigorating effects on the populace, and state violence degenerates into unmitigated terror. In the case of the persecution of the two homosexuals, Burke argues that if 'justice, rigid, was solely attended to, and all sight of mercy lost, and forgone', this was tantamount to violating the coronation oath of the King, and to 'commit[ing] perjury, because his Majesty, when he was crowned, and invested with executive government, has solemnly sworn to temper justice with mercy'.[28] The very recourse to excessive terror indicates that the underlying connective tissue of society has broken down, thus calling the legitimacy of the system itself into question. Burke had little difficulty in following through this logic in relation to the French Revolution, but that it might also apply in the case of colonial rule in Ireland and India was a prospect too disturbing to contemplate.

To contrast the grim manifestations of state violence in radically different social settings, we have only to turn to the reactions of the authorities to the most serious outbreaks of disorder in late eighteenth-century Ireland and Britain. Notwithstanding the imputations of savagery and barbarity to the various secret societies that stalked the countryside, very few fatalities occurred during the first major eruption of Whiteboy agitation in the 1760s. Yet a greater number of Whiteboys were hanged in this period than were executed after the Gordon riots in London, which accounted for as many as 700 deaths.[29] Within a few months of the original outbreak in 1761–2, some 237 Whiteboy suspects were in jail, leading L. M. Cullen to observe:

The scale and unprecedented character of these arrests has not been given sufficient attention. To put them in context, they were probably far more numerous than the arrests in any Irish county in the troubled months of early 1798, with the possible exception of Carlow.[30]

As we shall see below, Burke was deeply concerned at the savage reprisals meted out to the Whiteboys,[31] and there are many echoes of this traumatic period in his passionate pleas for a measured and temperate approach to the punishment of the Gordon rioters almost twenty years later. Burke had a personal grievance against the rioters, in that their anger was directed at the meagre concessions granted to Catholics in the Relief Act of 1778, legislation introduced by Sir George Savile, but orchestrated at one remove by Burke himself.[32] The house of the Chief Justice, Lord Mansfield, was burned by the rioters, and Burke's own life was in danger as the crowd resurrected old canards that he was a secret papist, and a Jesuit in disguise. Instead of taking refuge, however, Burke sought to meet the threat head on and insisted on mingling with the crowds, having to draw his sword on one occasion to defend himself. In a letter written to Richard Shackleton, he recounts: 'During that Week of Havock and Destruction... I spent part of the next day in the street amidst this wild assembly into whose hands I deliverd myself informing them who I was... My friends had come to persuade me to go out of Town, representing (from their kindness to me) the danger to be much greater than it was.'[33]

Though the animus of the mob was directed at the cause to which Burke had the most enduring personal commitment throughout his life, that of Catholic reform, the sentencing of sixty-two rioters to death in the immediate aftermath of the riots touched a raw nerve that recalls his response to the Whiteboy agitation: 'I really feel uneasy on this business', he wrote to Sir Grey Cooper, 'and should consider it as a sort of personal favour, if you could do something to limit the severity and extent of the law on this point.' He expanded on the reasons for his anxiety:

The executions... will be undoubtedly too many to serve any good purpose. Great slaughter attended the suppression of the tumults; and this ought to be taken into discount from the execution of the law. For God's sake entreat of Lord North to take a view of the sum total of the deaths, before any are ordered for execution; for, by not doing something of this kind, people are decoyed in detail into severities they never would have dreamed of, if they had the whole in their view at once. The scene [of the recent executions] in Surrey would have affected the hardest heart that ever was in an human breast. Justice and mercy have not such opposite interests as people are apt to imagine.[34]

Burke had no qualms about inflicting the severest punishment on the leaders of the riots, who were clearly identifiable and who consciously espoused bigoted principles, but that was not the course taken by the law. It concentrated instead on those who were caught up in the disturbances, very many of whom were 'a poor thoughtless set of creatures, very little aware of the nature of their offence...I have all the reason in the world to believe that they did not know their offence was capital' ('Reflections on Executions', v, 519). In language drawn from the *Enquiry*, Burke argues that these people were swept away in the frenzy of the protests and 'by the contagion of a sort of fashion, were carried to these excesses' ('Reflections on Executions', v, 520). Burke was adamant that individuals should not be singled out as scapegoats for offences that owe their existence to the excesses of popular protests. This applied with even more force when those who are earliest convicted appear to get the harshest treatment, a misguided policy which makes it seem as if the law operates 'by chance or under the influence of passion', lacking 'any steady principle of equity' ('Reflections on Executions', v, 516). In these circumstances, executions fail completely to act as object lessons for wrongdoers, since, due to the arbitrariness of sentencing policy, the victims 'are always looked upon rather as unlucky than criminal' ('Reflections on Executions', v, 520). Whereas Henry Fielding had argued that the need to set an example may require the punishment to be far in excess of the crime – hanging someone for the theft of a few shillings – Burke saw such clear injustices as calling the law itself into question: 'A severe and cruel penalty for a crime of a light nature is as bad and iniquitous as the crime which it pretends to punish' ('Impeachment', vii, 114).[35] Failing to act in an exemplary fashion, arbitrary shows of terror undermine the very basis of law. On these grounds, the reign of terror perpetrated in Munster in the 1760s and repeated, to Burke's great alarm, in the savage reprisals directed at Catholics in the 1790s, amounted not simply to an abuse of power, but to an indictment of the entire social system.

One of Burke's most original contributions to the discourse of power and domination is his insistence that even in its most awesome displays of terror, the state still requires an underlying cultural frame to render its dramaturgy of violence intelligible. As many recent reappraisals of the history of penology have emphasized, the emergence of the modern penal system was due to the passing of the old moral economy, and its associated forms of paternalism and public culture. These turned on a mutual recognition of hierarchical values held by plebs and patricians alike, and it was in this communal space that public executions made the maximum impact. According to Michel Foucault, this system began to break up with the fragmentation of modern society which converted the crowd into the more unmanageable mob that threatened to overrun and take control of these spectacles of pain. The result was that punishment began to dispense with theatricality to the point where it virtually disappeared from public view, depending instead on the 'audience' to conjure up the horror in the mind's eye.[36]

For Burke, however, this privatization of disciplinary regimes does not dispense with theatricality, in the sense of performative public culture, but rather presupposes it. As we have seen, it is precisely this internalization of terror that accounts for the empowering effects of the sublime. On this reasoning, even the 'individualistic' instinct of self-preservation which forms the basis of the sublime, and upon which the death penalty operates as the ultimate deterrent, requires a prior process of socialization. This can be seen from the dynamics of mass or collective action, a phenomenon which held a fatal fascination for Burke from his earliest years. The recklessness of individuals engaged in collective violence shows that, contrary to the Hobbesian view, self-preservation is not a basic, 'pre-social' determinant of behaviour, but needs to be acquired and socially cultivated like other human passions. If governments or indeed other exemplars of public order do not show respect for human life, then it is unlikely that individuals will respect it either:

Men, who see their lives respected and thought of value by others, come to respect that gift of God themselves. To have compassion for oneself, or to care, more or less, for one's own life, is a lesson to be learned just as any other; and I believe it will be found, that conspiracies have been most common and most desperate where their punishment has been most extensive and most severe. ('Reflections on Executions', v, 517)

Or as he expresses it in the *Reflections*, with a characteristic historical dimension: 'Respecting your forefathers, you would have been taught to respect yourselves' (*Reflections*, 123).

THE REVENGE OF THE REPRESSED

In this statement, we can trace an abiding set of concerns on Burke's part that links his aesthetics of the sublime with his earliest experiences as a student in Dublin, and particularly his response to the Jacobite fear which gripped Ireland in 1745–6. Writing to Richard Shackleton in April 1746, the young Burke remarks that 'This pretender who gave us so much disturbance for some time past is at length with his adherents entirely defeated and himself as some say taken prisoner', before going on to express his own concern at the fate of the rebels:

[T]is strange to see how the minds of people are in a few days changed, the very men who but awhile ago while they were alarmd by his progress so heartily cursed and hated those unfortunate creatures are now all pity and wish it could be terminated without bloodshed. I am sure I share in the general compassion, tis indeed melancholy to consider the state of those unhappy gentlemen who engag'd in this affair (as for the rest they lose but their lives) who have thrown away their lives and fortunes and destroy'd their families for ever in what I beleive they thought a just Cause.[37]

This disregard for self-preservation can be attributed to the debilitating rather than the empowering effects of the sublime. Instead of internalizing or privatizing the power with which we are confronted, the individual looks to solidarity or 'imitation' (*Enquiry*, 49–50) of others for the strength that is missing within: loud sounds or tumultuous noise are particularly disposed towards producing this form of sympathetic 'contagion', as Burke proceeds to note in the *Enquiry*:

Excessive loudness alone is sufficient to overpower the soul, to suspend its action, and to fill it with terror. The noise of vast cataracts, raging storms, thunder, or artillery, awakes a great and aweful sensation in the mind, though we can observe no nicety or artifice in those sorts of music. The shouting of multitudes has a similar effect; and by the sole strength of the sound, so amazes and confounds the imagination, that in this staggering, and hurry of the mind, the best established tempers can scarcely forbear being borne down, and joining in the common cry, and common resolution of the crowd. (*Enquiry*, 82)

On the terms of the *Enquiry*, such reckless abandon is produced when 'danger or pain press too nearly... and are simply terrible' (*Enquiry*, 40). This is the inevitable outcome when zealotry and randomness intervene in the judicial process, spreading the nets of punishment and reprisals so wide as to pose a threat to virtually an entire community. In this case, the aesthetic distance from danger required to cultivate awe and reverence is removed, and terror incites counter-terror from the crowd, with all its destructive impulses. That Burke may have been prompted by an actual example of the fury of the crowd in such circumstances during his writing of the *Enquiry* is suggested by a passage in a letter from Dublin to Shackleton, in which he notes ruefully: 'There was a young fellow hanged here yesterday for robbing his master of a few guineas. A few days later another was pardoned for the murder of five men. Was not that justice?' Certainly the mob had no doubts where justice lay, for the hanging excited public outrage, ending in a riot.[38]

For Burke, a policy of vengeful state executions is counter-productive in that it evokes sympathy for the victims and directs the odium of the public towards government rather than those who break the law. He seemed acutely aware of how 'tenderness' towards the criminal is elicited from the public, and, with an eye for the kind of harrowing details that evoke sympathy, goes so far as to recommend particular caution when dealing with the body after execution: 'great care should be taken, that their bodies may not be delivered to their friends, or to others, who may make them objects of compassion, or even veneration' ('Reflections on Executions', v, 516–17). In this ghoulish aside, it is possible to detect once more the restless ghost of Nicholas Sheehy. 'It is not easily conceived', Burke wrote in one of his youthful notebooks,

> what use funeral ceremonies are to mankind. Triffling as they may seem, they nourish humanity, they soften in some measure the rigour of Death, and they inspire humble, sober and becoming thoughts. They throw a decent Veil over the weak and dishonourable circumstances of our Nature. What shall we say to that philosophy that would strip it naked.[39]

It is difficult to avoid the conclusion, given Burke's direct connection to both the Cotter and Sheehy cases noted above, that he was drawing here on his insights into an alternative moral economy to that of the official colonial regime in Ireland, that exemplified by the potentially subversive practices of 'keening' and wakes in Gaelic culture. 'Keens', wrote Thomas Crofton Croker, 'are also a medium through which the disaffected circulate their mischievous principles', and both physical and symbolic control of the corpse became a political struggle, as if the dead lived beyond the grave in the popular imagination: 'When the awful sentence of death has been pronounced by the judge on an Irish culprit, it is not unusual for him to petition that his body may be given to his friends after execution, and, if this is granted, he meets his fate with fortitude and resignation.'[40] By the end of the eighteenth century in Ireland, two powerful political dirges – Eibhlín Ní Chonaill's 'Caoineadh Airt Ui Laoghaire' and William Drennan's very different martial anthem 'The Wake of William Orr' – had helped to usher in a new dramaturgy of death in which mourning, speeches from the dock, and stage-managed funerals became themselves extraordinary weapons of resistance.

Hence the fears expressed by Burke regarding the capacity of the crowd during an execution – and, by extension, the general populace affected by it – to seize the mobilizing power of rituals for their own ends, when the authorities had failed abjectly through their own excesses to exploit them. As an example of an inhuman 'philosophy that would strip [death] naked', he had only to recall what he described as the 'horrors of the Munster circuit' in the 1760s. Nicholas Sheehy's head was impaled on a spike over the jail in Clonmel for twenty years, when it was finally recovered by his sister, Catherine, who was married, as we have seen, to Richard Burke, Edmund's first cousin. This awareness of the symbolic power of death indicates that it may have been the same sister who, during Sheehy's 'melancholy [funeral] procession smeared the door-posts of [his parish priest], Dr Egan's house, with the blood still reeking from his body', on account of the priest's refusal to defend him in court. Soon afterwards, the head of another cousin, Edmund Sheehy, was snatched after his execution by a young woman who escaped through the crowd with it in her apron, followed by the executioner.[41] A similar macabre act of defiance followed in Co. Kilkenny when the chests of six Whiteboys were ritually scored in public before their heads were cut off, as a reprisal for a dramatic rescue of prisoners. In a demented state, the wife of one of the victims, Mrs John Brennan, carried the severed head of her husband through the streets of Kilkenny, lamenting his death and attempting to raise money for his funeral.[42] Edmund Burke's prediction that unrestrained terror on the part of the state would incense rather than intimidate the populace was borne out four years later in a grim postscript to Nicholas Sheehy's death, reporting an incident that took place in Co. Offaly, almost 40 miles from the scene of his execution:

On Thursday the 6th a man was executed at Philipstown for murder; during the execution, the mob (which was very great) were remarkably quiet, but as soon as it was over, they stoned the hangman to death, and the body lay for two or three days under the gallows. The unfortunate creature was the person who hung Sheehy the priest, which is supposed to be the reason for the outrage.[43]

In this theatre of cruelty, the curtain may fall but the action is far from over if the audience's rage for justice remains unrequited. Death, in Irish culture, was certainly not the end of the drama, and it may be this which inspired the story that towards the end of his life Burke expressed fears that the fate of the undead might befall his own body. According to one report, he issued instructions for his own burial, stipulating that his body be transferred from its wooden coffin to a leaden casket and buried in an unknown spot, lest the French revolutionaries, if they triumphed in England, dig it up and defile his memory.[44] The story may be anecdotal; but the anxiety underlying it is not.[45] In his first 'Letter on a Regicide

Peace', Burke reserved his most scathing invective for the disrepect which the Jacobins showed for the dead, a practice, he believed, which reduced them to the level of little more than cannibals:

> To all this let us join the practice of cannibalism... By cannibalism I mean their devouring, as a nutriment of their ferocity, some part of the bodies of those they have murdered... By cannibalism I mean also to signify all their nameless, unmanly, and abominable insults on the bodies of those they slaughter. ('First Letter', v, 212)[46]

It is not just his own inner demons but the culture of his upbringing that is speaking through him here. The belief that the dead cannot rest in peace until the ghosts of past injustices have been allayed may have been partly what Burke had in mind when he characterized the sublime as 'a sort of tranquility shadowed with horror': 'When we have suffered from any violent emotion, the mind naturally continues in something like the same condition, after the cause which produced it has ceased to operate. The tossing of the sea remains after the storm' (*Enquiry*, 34, 35). Surface calm belies the torrents within, whether at the level of the individual or society, and it is to one such illusory façade, the stoical composure of the self in the throes of acute pain, that we shall now turn.

2

'Philoctetes' *and colonial Ireland:*
the wounded body as national narrative

> It will gradually become apparent that at particular moments when there is within a society a crisis of belief — that is, when some central idea or ideology or cultural construct has ceased to elicit a population's belief either because it is manifestly fictitious or because it has for some reason been divested of ordinary forms of substantiation — the material factualness of the human body will be borrowed to lend that cultural construct the aura of 'realness' and 'certainty'.
>
> Elaine Scarry, *The Body in Pain*

> The wound is ever bleeding
>
> Paschal Grousset, *Ireland's Disease* (1879)

'It has been said', wrote Thomas Moore, under the alias of the insurgent chief, Captain Rock, 'that "you may trace Ireland through the Statute-book of England, as a wounded man in a crowd is tracked by his blood".'[1] The image of Ireland as a wounded body, publicly dismembered and desecrated in the staged spectacle of the execution of Fr Nicholas Sheehy as we have seen in Chapter 1, pervades the literature and art of eighteenth-century Ireland. In terms of the 'manly' ideals of virtue, and the affirmative principles of self-command and civic spirit promoted by the Enlightenment, the body wracked by pain cut a pitiful figure. Lacking dignity and even agency, it had more to do with the losers of history, and with those left behind by progress, than with narratives of emancipation and self-determination. In due course, such unbecoming displays of human frailty became the subject of romantic pathos, and were relegated at best to narratives of nostalgia and regret, or, at worst, to a sullen melancholia, a condition to which 'the Celts' were considered unduly susceptible. But that is not how Moore's Captain Rock sees it, and he is not slow to point out that suffering inflicted by injustice may give rise to profound social convulsions as well as to more docile forms of acceptance and resignation:

To reproach a country thus trained, with its riotous and sanguinary habits – to expect moderation from a people kept constantly on the rack of oppression, is like Mercury, in Aeschylus, cooly lecturing Prometheus, on the exceeding want of good temper and tractableness he exhibits – while the only grievance, forsooth, he has to complain of, is being riveted by his legs and arms to a rock, and having a wedge of eternal adamant driven into his breast.[2]

The image of a suffering body abandoned on a rock calls to mind not only the defiant heroism of Prometheus but the more problematic, abject figure of Philoctetes, the wounded Greek warrior in Sophocles's tragedy who refused to hide his offensive, suppurating wound.[3] The fate of Philoctetes featured prominently in late eighteenth- and early nineteenth-century debates on sentimentalism and tragedy, in paintings by François Boucher, William Blake, Jean-Germain Drouais, Pierre-Paul Prud'hon, and in literary works or translations by Herder, Wordsworth, André Gide and, closer to our own time, Derek Walcott and Seamus Heaney.[4] Lessing's major treatise on aesthetics, the *Laocoön* (1766), turns on a contrast between the torment of Laocoon (as represented in the famous classical statue) and the suffering of Philoctetes, and critics as diverse as Adam Smith, Herder, and Hegel also invoked Sophocles's tragedy in discussing the proprieties of representing pain.[5] But it was to eighteenth-century Ireland that the plight of Philoctetes spoke most eloquently. Sophocles's play was introduced into the modern English literary canon through a translation by Dr Thomas Sheridan, Swift's closest Irish friend and fellow political propagandist. This reappropriation of the injured, malodorous body of Philoctetes for a radical political project culminated at the end of the eighteenth century in the extraordinary painting and series of engravings issued by the Irish painter and republican sympathizer, James Barry, to chart successive phases in the Irish struggle for Catholic emancipation. One of the powerful legacies bequeathed by Philoctetes in Sophocles's play was the depiction of the suffering body as a site of solidarity with others, rather than a narcissistic obsession with one's own wounds. In the work of Barry, this involved retrieving the injured body from romantic isolation and abjection, and reintegrating it into the emancipatory narratives of the Enlightenment. It is to this complex set of codings between the aesthetics of the sublime and the figure of the body in pain that this chapter will be mainly addressed.

'ON ANOTHER MAN'S WOUND': THE THEATRICALITY OF THE IMAGE

In Greek mythology, the story of Philoctetes recounts how a great warrior, armed with the magic bow of Hercules, comes to grief having been bitten on the foot by a serpent and abandoned by his comrades, at the behest of Odysseus, on the deserted isle of Lemnos.[6] There he languished with his festering wound for ten years until the Greeks finally realize, as an oracle had foretold, that Troy cannot be captured without the wounded warrior and his magic bow. Sophocles's play deals with the return of Odysseus and Neoptolemus, the son of Achilles, to the island in an attempt to inveigle Philoctetes to rejoin the Greek camp. The scheming Odysseus persuades Neoptolemus to relieve the beleaguered hero of his bow by deceit and leave him at the mercy of the elements, but such are the tears and lamentations of the outcast when his wound begins to suppurate once more that Neoptolemus changes heart and finally goes to his aid. He tries to convince the warrior to accompany them to Troy, as the fate of Greek civilization depends on it. Having been twice bitten, as it were, Philoctetes is unyielding, and prefers to nurse his grievance. The impasse is resolved when Hercules, in the form of a *deus ex machina*, intervenes in the action to assure Philoctetes that his ailment will be cured if he identifies with a public cause greater than his own grievances, and goes to Troy. Each party, he advises, requires the mutual recognition of the other to achieve their desired results:

> Son of Achilles... remember this,
> Without his aid thou canst not conquer Troy,
> Nor Philoctetes without thee succeed.[7]

When the Irish artist James Barry presented his canvas 'Philoctetes on the Island of Lemnos' (Fig. 1) to the Accademia Clementina at Bologna in 1770, it was among the first paintings of the forlorn Greek archer to be executed since antiquity.[8] What is remarkable about Barry's work is his determination to undo the isolation of pain which, as Elaine Scarry has argued, is the most unbearable aspect of all physical suffering.[9] One of the paradoxes of pain is that by its very insistence on the privacy of intense bodily experience, it registers a profound need for social contact, for the presence of another: 'It brings with it', writes Scarry, 'all the solitude of absolute privacy with none of its safety, all the self-exposure of the utterly public with none of its possibility for camaraderie or shared experience.' As an example of the isolation of pain, Scarry cites the paintings of Francis Bacon in which a solitary figure 'is made emphatically alone by his position on a dais, by an arbitrary box placed over him... yet while he is intensely separate from the viewer (a separation Bacon wanted to heighten further by having the canvasses covered with glass) he is simultaneously mercilessly exposed to us'. In these harrowing images, it is difficult to know whether it is the physical suffering or the experience of abandonment which comes across as the greatest source of terror. This provides the pretext for Scarry's

Fig. 1 James Barry, 'Philoctetes on the Island of Lemnos' (1770)

comments on the desolate setting in which Sophocles places the wounded figure of Philoctetes :

> The background against which we watch and hear the agonized writhing of the wounded hero, writhing which so repelled his shipmates that they abandoned him here – is a small island of jagged rocks at once utterly cut off from homeland and humanity and utterly open to the elements.[10]

As if he had foreseen the helpless fate of Francis Bacon's victims, Barry sets out to remove the invisible cage surrounding the body in pain, exposing it not to the gaze of a detached spectator but to the ministrations of a sympathetic, participant observer. In so doing, Barry was insistent on an irreducible social dimension in the aesthetics of pain, thus setting his face firmly against a dominant trend in eighteenth-century and early nineteenth-century art which, in the contemporary terminology of Michael Fried, eschewed a social 'theatrical' mode of address for a more interiorized aesthetic experience of 'absorption'.[11] By 'absorption', Fried means a mode of representation first systematically theorized by Diderot which sought to repudiate the presence of the spectator in front of the canvas – a strategy, ironically, which was adopted in order 'to persuade its audience of the truthfulness of its representations'. The reason for this, in Fried's concise summary, is that:

> nothing was more abortive of that act of persuasion than when a painter's dramatis personae seemed by virtue of the character of their actions and expressions to evince even a partial consciousness of being beheld... the immediate task of the painter was therefore to extinguish or forestall that consciousness by entirely engrossing or, as I chiefly say, *absorbing* his dramatis personae in their actions and states of mind. A personage so absorbed appeared unconscious or oblivious of everything but the object of his or her absorption, as if to all intents and purposes there were nothing and no one else in the world... Diderot's conception of painting... insisted as never before on an absolute discontinuity between actors and beholders, representation and audience.[12]

From this it is clear that the absorptive vision not only obviates the presence of the beholder, but also removes art from its location in the exhibition arena and, by extension, public space in general. In effect, what we are witnessing here is the emergence of the aesthetic as a disinterested system of value, cut off from its moorings in the external world and secured against the incursions of 'extra-aesthetic contingency'.[13] In Diderot's art criticism, as Fried sees it, a series of compositional norms are prescribed which emphasise the autonomy and 'inner control' of the work:

Hence the importance in Diderot's writings of a dynamic ideal of compositional unity according to which the various elements in a painting were to be combined to form a perspicuously closed and self-sufficient structure which would so to speak seal off the world of the representation from that of the viewer... 'The canvas encloses all the space and there is no one beyond it,' Diderot wrote in his *Pensées détachées sur la peinture*.[14]

The kinds of contemplative states which lend themselves to the absorptive vision – reading, sewing, blowing a soap bubble, building a card castle, to cite some of Fried's examples – may indeed be such that the subjects of the painting are perfectly happy to be left alone, concentrating intently on the activity at hand.[15] But what of a situation in which being left alone is a source of fear and dread, and where the solicitations of another may not be regarded as an interruption but may be yearned for as a matter of survival? In describing how isolation is intrinsic to the helplessness which torturers hope to induce in their victims, Elaine Scarry observes:

In this closed world where conversation is displaced by interrogation, where human speech is broken off in confession and disintegrates into human cries... in this world of broken and severed voices, it is not surprising that the most powerful and healing moment is often that in which a human voice, though still severed, floating free, somehow reaches the person whose sole reality had become his own unthinkable isolation, his deep corporeal engulfment... [The] voices... that return to the prisoner his most elemental political ground as well as his psychic content and density are finally almost physiological in their power of alteration.[16]

In this connection, it is striking that when Philoctetes in Sophocles's play first encounters Neoptolemus and the chorus, his most immediate wish is for them to speak so that he can hear their once familiar accents:

> Speak!... Let me hear the sound
> Of your long wished-for voices. Do not look
> With horror on me, but in kind compassion
> Pity a wretch deserted and forlorn
> In this sad place. Oh! if ye come as friends,
> Speak then, and answer – hold some converse with me,
> For this at least from man to man is due.
>
> (*Philoctetes*, 104)

Hence it may be the case, as Fried contends, that under the internal composure of absorption, the subjects of a painting are so engrossed in their actions as to be oblivious of everything 'beyond the work', but this is hardly sufficient to describe the plight of Philoctetes or, for that matter, anyone else in a state of extreme duress. In Sophocles's drama, the warrior's tears and cries of woe finally impress themselves upon Neoptolemus, and he

Fig. 2 James Barry, Study for 'Philoctetes on the Island of Lemnos' (1770)

responds with 'kind compassion' rather than with the detached gaze of someone cut off from the action. But as Barry chooses to include only one figure – that of the abandoned hero – in the pictorial field, where is the missing participant, the other 'long-wished for voice'?

In Barry's painting, and indeed in many of his other works, this role falls on the viewer, standing in the public space in which the picture is exhibited. The beholder is addressed not as a disembodied spectator, whose physical presence does not matter, but as a public citizen, immersed in the everyday business of the world. That Barry was fully aware of the extent to which the injured body is explicitly on display is clear from the inscription he attached to the preliminary drawing (Fig. 2) for the 'Philoctetes', which purports to explain the awkward posture of the ulcerous foot: 'There will appear more Agony & ye disordered leg will be more distinctly mark'd by having it stretched out in air and without any support from ye rock he sits on' (Pressly, *James Barry*, 25). The body is on show as if attempting, however pathetically, to attract notice, to catch the attention of a sympathetic beholder – a posture which led Richard Payne Knight to remonstrate that the ulcerated foot in Barry's picture, 'though less faithfully represented than such things are in the paintings of Hemskirk and Jan Steen, is more disgusting, as being upon a larger scale'.[17] In the painting, this theatrical presentation of the body is augmented by the peculiar flatness of the landscape in the background, the embankment, as William Pressly writes, amounting to little 'more than a stage curtain ending in a sharp thin edge'. The pronounced lack of pictorial depth directs the attention of the viewer almost entirely to the immediate foreground, thus accentuating the distinctive spatial logic which, in Robert R. Wark's estimation, represents Barry's most original contribution to eighteenth-century art.

According to Wark, the most radical aspect of this compositional strategy of Barry's lay in his stark compression of pictorial space, which all but removes any semblance of aesthetic distance between the spectator and the pictorial field. The scale of objects derives not from the laws of perspective, or even from their internal relationship to each other (as recommended by Diderot), but from their relationship to the *viewer outside* the frame: in several paintings, objects which overlap others and thus are clearly in front are nevertheless 'given the same actual size so that the spectator automatically assumes them all equidistant'.[18] In what could function as a description of the *Philoctetes*, Wark writes of Barry's 'Birth of Venus' (1772):

In all... these pictures the objects represented are close to the picture plane, that is the artist does not suggest that there is much space between us and the figures. In the 'Birth of Venus', though a whole ocean is indicated in the background, Barry has brought the figures to within what appears to be no more than a foot or so of the front spatial boundary of the picture... [As a result] the ocean is devoid of life, and appears (at least towards the right hand side of the scene) as hardly more than a backdrop. (Wark, 'James Barry', 93–4)

This anomalous spatial logic is also evident in one of Barry's most vivid realizations, his powerful late 'Self Portrait' (Fig. 3). In the latter, as Wark points out, the statuary in the background appears, by virtue of its size and surface treatment, to be so close to the picture plane as to leave virtually no room for Barry's own body in front:

there is practically no space suggested between the head and the picture plane. Foreshortened elements such as the right shoulder or the picture Barry is holding, go flat; hence the space we mentally provide for the head is hardly behind the picture plane at all. (Wark, 'James Barry', 127)

The imaginative effect of this dramatic foregrounding is that Barry's physical presence is pushed out of the visual field into an area normally considered out of bounds for pictorial representation, the public exhibition space occupied by the spectator.

Fig. 3 James Barry, 'Self-Portrait' (1803)

In the course of developing his argument that the renunciation of theatricality was instrumental in the rise of the autonomy of art, Fried has occasion to contrast the absorptive vision of painters such as Courbet with the theatrical use of pictorial space in the work of Caravaggio. In Courbet's early paintings, the location of the spectator in front of the painting is eliminated not so much through exclusion (as in eighteenth-century art)

Fig. 4 Caravaggio, 'The Supper at Emmaus'

but by the seemingly opposite process of *inclusion*, spiriting the beholder into the interior space of the canvas. The body of the beholder is, as it were, dematerialized, in keeping with the disinterestedness of the absorptive, aesthetic attitude. By way of contrast with this practice, Fried cites the physical emplacement of the spectator in some of Caravaggio's major works. Citing Rudolf Wittkower's well-known discussion of the 'Supper at Emmaus' (Fig. 4), Fried notes how Caravaggio increases the emotional and dramatic impact of the scene by foreshortening Christ's right arm and the outflung arm of a disciple to such an extent that 'they seem to break through the picture plane and reach into the space in which we stand'. This effect is reinforced by the precarious position of the fruit basket balancing on the edge of the table, 'which may at any moment land at our feet'. By opening up the scene in this way, Caravaggio's aim was 'to increase the *participation* of the worshipper in the mystery rendered in the picture', a project which, as Fried points out, is diametrically opposed to Courbet's attempt to dispense altogether with the external onlooker.[19] In both painters the boundaries of the picture surface are breached, but whereas Courbet is attempting to draw the beholder into the work, Caravaggio is striving to bring the work to the beholder, opening it up to the exigencies of the world outside the picture.

Fig. 5 James Barry, 'The Fall of Satan' (1777)

Barry's practice is in keeping with this latter direct mode of address, and is seen at its most pronounced in the claustrophobic images based on Milton, 'Satan and his Legions Hurling Defiance toward the Vault of Heaven' and the earlier 'The Fall of Satan' (Fig. 5). In these prints, and in the imposing 'Tartarus' section of his vast canvas 'Elysium and Tartarus and the State of Final Retribution' (1778–84), the flailing limbs of the rebel angels seem to tumble forward into a dark, vertiginous chasm which is not even reassuringly cut off from the spectator by the bottom edge of the frame: 'the dramatic intensity with which the edge of it is brought forward', writes Wark, 'seems almost to put us inside it, while the tight mass of bodies falling in front is not conducive to a spacious or calm effect' (Wark, 'James Barry', 111). Wark goes on to suggest that in this radical transformation of visual space, with its consequent unsettling of the beholder, Barry's practice may indeed have been indebted to Caravaggio, while setting him apart from the neo-classical protocols observed by his contemporaries (with, perhaps, the notable exception of William Blake or, as Thomas Crow suggests, Drouais in France):

> the spatial qualities of Barry's work cannot be...easily accounted for. There is little in earlier English art which he might have known that would have offered suggestions, and not much in his own day. To be sure, many of his contemporaries frequently brought their figures close to the picture plane – Reynolds, Romney, West and Flaxman to mention a few – but they were hardly working in this way early enough to have great influence on Barry, and certainly not in the seemingly 'compressed' type of space we have found him using.... Indeed I think one must go back to mid sixteenth and early seventeenth century Italian painting before anything really comparable is seen. Caravaggio and the early Roman Baroque painters frequently suggested the sort of active, compressed space we have seen in some of Barry's work...[20] (Wark, 'James Barry', 135)

THE CRYING GAME: SPACE, TIME, AND TEARS

If we return to the 'Philoctetes' in the light of this discussion, it is clear that Barry is not just presenting but *confronting* the viewer with the attrition of pain on the human body. Background and pictorial depth are all but dispensed with, and the physical mass of the wounded figure is exaggerated, in order to thrust the scene into the forefront of the viewer's line of vision. This abolition of distance is further intensified by the fact that Barry, in a striking breach of neo-classical decorum, shows the mighty warrior shedding tears, thus exposing the frailty of a powerful male body on the verge of breakdown.[21] One of the central tenets of neo-classicism was the concept of *propriety*, the belief that virtue was best served by self-possession and by placing an embargo on excessive shows of feeling, even in the face of the most extreme suffering. Hence the praise which critics such as Lessing and Winckelmann lavished on the moral grandeur and marmoreal calm of the famous statue of the 'Laocoon', which appeared to vindicate this conquest of pain. As Winckelmann described it in a famous passage:

> As the depths of the sea always remain calm, however much the surface may be raging, so the expression in the figures of the Greeks, under every form of passion, shows a great and self-collected soul. This spirit is portrayed in the countenance of Laokoon, and not in the countenance alone, under the most violent suffering... This pain expresses itself, however, without any violence, both in the features and in the whole posture. He raises no terrible shriek, such as Virgil makes his Laokoon utter, for the opening of the mouth does not admit it; it is rather an anxious and suppressed sigh... Laokoon suffers, but he suffers as the Philoktetes of Sophokles; his misery pierces us to the very soul, but inspires us with a wish that we could endure misery like that great man.[22]

It was this passage which drew forth from Lessing his extended reflections on the 'Laokoon', and his attempts to clearly demarcate the limits of representation in the visual arts. Lessing agreed with Winckelmann's account of the statue, but objected to the comparison with Sophocles's drama, and to the wider argument that both of these works owed their moral grandeur to an ennobling suppression of feelings in Greek society. For one thing, Philoctetes in Sophocles's drama does not evince anything like a calm countenance, and the fact that he was elevated to the status of a tragic hero notwithstanding his howls and screams showed that, unlike their more barbaric Spartan neighbours, the refined Greeks did *not* seek to curtail expressions of bodily pain. As is clear from their epic poetry, even many of Homer's heroes nodded in this respect. The reason the *statue* of Laokoon displayed such composure in the throes of suffering has more to do with the specific demands of visual representation – 'the peculiar conditions of... art, and its necessary limits and wants' (*Laokoon*, 22) – than with the general codes of behaviour prevailing in Greek culture.

Due to their essentially *spatial* character and their devotion to physical beauty, restraints are called for in the visual arts which are not necessary in the *temporally* unfolding forms of literature and drama. According to Lessing, a dramatist can permit a stricken protagonist to indulge in weeping and wailing because elsewhere in the play, indeed for the most part of the action, it can be shown that he adopts a manly bearing more in keeping with a hero:

> Were it really unbecoming in a man to shriek under the violence of bodily pain, what prejudice could this slight and transitory impropriety excite in us against one in whose favour we are already prepossessed by his other virtues? Virgil's Laokoon shrieks, but this shrieking Laokoon is the same man whom we already know and love as a farsighted patriot and affectionate father. We attribute his cries not to his character, but solely to his intolerable suffering. (*Laokoon*, 23)

Momentary lapses into what might be considered effeminate behaviour, in other words, are permissible in a sequential narrative because of its capacity to present other more uplifting traits of character which efface this ignoble trail of tears. But this is not possible in the spatial medium of painting, which is restricted to capturing *a single* moment in a life history, and *one* perspective on an action or event. For this reason, it is vital that the painter does not import into a pictorial representation the temporal structure of drama, or the multifaceted aspects of a personality or event that lend themselves to narrative exposition. Contrasting the imperturbability of the statue of Laokoon, then, with the fitful drama of Philoctetes, Lessing laid the basis for a dissociation between literature ('poetry') and the visual arts ('painting'), that has presided over the subsequent development of both artistic practice and criticism down to the modern period:

Poetry and painting, both are imitative arts... However they make use of entirely different means for their imitations; and from the difference of these means all the specific rules for each art are to be derived. *Painting* uses figures and colours in *space. Poetry* articulates tones in *time*. The signs of the former are *natural*. Those of the latter are *arbitrary*.[23]

Barry's abiding preoccupation with the theatricality of the image, and his determination to evoke the sufferings of Philoctetes in pictorial form against the influential arguments of German aesthetics, may be seen as a pre-emptive strike, emanating from Irish culture, against this fateful divergence between word and image, time and space, and narrative and spectacle in the arts. In his efforts to absolve Philoctetes of the imputation of 'effeminacy', Lessing has recourse to a series of general observations on the essential humanity which underscored the Greek concept of the hero. The warrior's complaints, he writes, may betray his humanity, but his 'actions are those of a hero': 'The two combined constitute the human hero, who is neither effeminate nor hard, but now the one, now the other, as now nature, now principle and duty, require' (*Laokoon*, 31). It is clear from this that Lessing has a sequential process in mind, in which alternating states of heroic fortitude and susceptibility to feeling succeed one another. The crucial point, however, is that they not be present at the one time, for this would deeply compromise the manly demeanour of a hero and, by implication, the civic credentials of virtue. Because the visual arts are restricted to capturing one point in time, Lessing therefore recommends that the artist stops short of depicting the moment when pain actually becomes manifest. This instils a sense of expectancy into the work, presenting the spectator with intimations of mortality rather than with its stark delineation. It is on these grounds that the *Laokoon* receives his unstinted praise for it does not seize upon the instant when the noble hero breaks down under duress, but shows him still capable of mobilizing all his resources to maintain his dignity and self-control. The more debasing effects of suffering repel rather than attract the viewer, according to Lessing, and are best left to the imagination.

From this perspective, Barry's painting of Philoctetes represents an affront to the austerity of the image, as if insisting that painting can still assume the burden of narrative, albeit at the point of breakdown. The banished hero is unapologetically portrayed in all his vulnerabilty, at precisely the stage where he succumbs to weeping, and the heroic and the human are not presented alternately, but are run together in one strained composition. Unlike Lessing, who is concerned to mitigate the humiliation of yielding to the torments of the body, Barry has no misgivings about exposing the unacceptable face of pain. In a characteristic observation made in Italy at the time he painted the 'Philoctetes', he expressed his aversion to those viewers in polite society who

affect such nice feelings and so much sensibility, as not to be able to bear the sight of pictures where the action turns upon any circumstance of distress; [or who] have such extreme good nature as to turn off with disgust from the whole class of affecting subjects which agitate and call forth our feeling for the distresses of our species, and which the wisest nations have ever regarded as the noblest, most useful, and most interesting subjects, both for painting and for poetry... I am ashamed to be obliged to combat such silly affectations, they are beneath men who have either head or heart; they are unworthy of women, who have either education or simplicity of manners; they would disgrace even waiting-maids and sentimental milleners.[24]

What is noticeable in this observation of Barry's is his determination to prove, contrary to Lessing, that painting *is* a suitable vehicle for the expression of pain, and his equally emphatic insistence that the need to look suffering in the eye cuts across both gender and class boundaries. It is the wound in the body, this visible breach in the boundary between self and other, which brings out the latent theatricality in painting, and opens up both the self-contained individual and the autonomous work of art to narratives beyond what Fried terms their own 'internal dynamic necessity'. For Lessing, it is not isolation as such but its accompaniment by pain which transforms Philoctetes's predicament into one requiring intervention by others. To be alone, he argues, in conditions where we retain our 'health, strength, and industry', is not a form of deprivation, and 'has certainly no great claim upon our sympathy', as the example of Robinson Crusoe illustrates. In this case, the individual 'can gradually learn to dispense with all *external aid*' (*Laokoon*, 27, my italics), and isolation is turned into the more creative category of solitude. But in the event of pain and injury, he admits, 'when the solitary one possesses no control over his own body', there is an importuning for aid, a direct address to the other. In effect, pain forces our feelings out into the open, breaking down our illusions of privacy and self-reliance. For this reason, Lessing has little difficulty in recommending the emotional excess of suffering as a fit subject for the performance-based medium of drama, in which the interplay of different actors is negotiated through a sequential narrative: 'All stoicism is undramatical', he writes, 'and our sympathy is always proportioned to the suffering expressed by the object which interests us' (*Laokoon*, 11). But it is precisely the same logic which dictates that stoicism preside over the expression of pain in the visual arts, where the image is impervious to both the theatrical awareness of 'the other', and the passage of time. The key contribution which the visual arts make to the civilizing process is partly to be accounted for by the transfer of the internal composure of the work to the comportment of the 'disembodied' spectator, cultivating a form of equipoise and self-possession very similar to the inner control of Fried's mode of absorption.

Barry, however, was not at all convinced that such refinement and equanimity was adequate as a response to distress and suffering in either drama or painting. He equated this regulation of 'the outward man by a torpid, inanimate composure' with the 'indifference' of Puritanism, in which 'the tongue spoke almost without moving the lips, and the circumstances of a murder were related with as little emotion as an ordinary mercantile transaction' ('Inquiry', ii, 292). It is by rejecting such 'inanimate composure', and resorting to tears and cries of woe as forms of communicative action, that Philoctetes signals his refusal to accept his fate, to 'comply then and be happy' (*Philoctetes*, 129), as the chorus fatalistically advises him. The contrast between the theatrical excess of Barry's work and an aesthetics of containment can perhaps best be seen by comparing the 'Philoctetes' with a painting discussed by Fried, Greuze's portrait of a 'Young Girl with a Dead Canary', which was executed five years earlier. Both paintings depict disconsolate individuals shedding tears, and both even feature a dead bird, lying on its back in the foreground. But there the resemblance ends. For Fried, Greuze's painting shows an individual totally engrossed with herself, making 'perspicuous the depth and intensity of the young girl's absorption in her grief' (Fried, *Absorption and Theatricality*, 59). The extent to which the spectator is unacknowledged and placed outside the frame is clear from Diderot's contemporary response where he tries to imagine a spectator vainly attempting to console the girl, reading between the lines her loss of innocence:

> my child, your sadness is very profound, very considered! What is the meaning of this abstracted, melancholy air? What! For a bird! You are not crying. You are grieved, and thought accompanies your grief. There, there, my child, open up your heart to me. Tell me the truth. Is the death of this bird really what makes you withdraw so firmly and sadly within yourself?... You lower your eyes; you do not answer me.[25]

The contrast with Philoctetes could not be greater. The tears of the stricken warrior are not withdrawal symptoms but distress signals, expressing a desire to escape from, rather than retreat into, the seclusion of the self. It is in this sense that we may speak of the 'theatricality' of tears, even if they are spontaneous and entirely sincere. As Jay Caplan points out in relation to the emergence of the cult of sentimentalism in eighteenth-century drama, crying was considered a form of contagion: to be moved to tears was bound up with the capacity *to move others*, whether they be characters in the action, the readers or spectators of the work, or indeed the authors of the texts themselves:

> Somatic and semantic, biological and dialogical, the tear at once expresses our universally sensitive nature and addresses itself to our fellows... the pleasure of 'being moved and shedding tears' is always implicitly shared, just as a tear appeals to interlocutors past, present, and future.[26]

Hence the tears which Philoctetes sheds are not a form of self-indulgence but an expression of the inadequacy of unshared emotion, and are directed at an absent audience – even if they go, as in Sophocles's drama, 'Unheeded, save when babbling echo mourns / In bitterest notes responsive to his woe' (*Philoctetes*, 103). For Barry, the beholder of the painting, absent and yet present, constitutes this audience, offering the isolated body crying out in pain a release from entrapment by its own echo, and from the agony of self-absorption.

THE 'INTELLIGENT EYE': ART AND ALLEGORY

James Barry's rejection of the neo-classical aesthetics of absorption, and its relegation of the body in pain to the private domain of sensibility rather than the public sphere of justice, was central to his overall project of restructuring Enlightenment notions of sympathy by means of the transformative vision of art. Raising physical pain to the level of tragedy, and extending the remit of *virtú* to include hitherto 'effeminate' forms of behaviour such as crying, can be seen as part of an overall attempt to inscribe the body itself, with all its discontents, onto public life. Barry's lack of embarrassment over the materiality of the flesh was articulated at a visual level by his willingness to entertain a level of opacity within the image that was deemed inimical to the absorptive ideals of illusion and transparency. For Diderot, it was vital that a painting be immediately intelligible and strive towards pure opticality: 'I turn my back on the painter who offers me an emblem, a logogriph to decipher', he wrote, 'If the scene is one, clear, simple and unified, I will grasp its ensemble at a glance.'[27] Barry was no less intent on making a decisive impact on the spectator, but from a diametrically opposite point of view: considerable background knowledge and a civic humanist education (albeit radically redefined within Barry's sense of the term) were the prerequisites for a true comprehension of great art. For this reason, Barry proposed, it is impossible 'that an illiterate man could make anything of true art', since art requires 'the acquisition of that comprehensive thought, that necessary knowledge of all the parts of history, and the characters who act in it; that power of inventing and adding to it, and that judgement of making the old and new matter consistent and of one embodied substance' ('Inquiry', ii, 252).

In arguing thus, Barry is making a case for *allegory*, for freighting the image with the kind of verbal infrastructure or symbolic meaning that requires active involvement on the part of the beholder. It was the overt acknowledgement of this 'extra-aesthetic' dimension beyond the frame, with its consequent denial of the disembodied, voyeuristic spectator, which led to the demise of allegory with the rise of new 'aesthetic' conceptions of art in the late eighteenth century. As Maureen Quilligan writes:

The reader's involvement in allegory is perhaps more arduous than in any other genre... If he is something of a voyeur in relationship to orthodox narrative organized along the lines of verisimilitude, then he is the central character in an allegory. The narrative may be said to 'read' him. Nor does his centrality derive from a position of passivity, simply receiving doctrine; the process is more one of collusion. The reader's participation in the fiction must be active... What distinguishes allegory from other sophisticated forms of self-reflexive fiction therefore, is the part the reader must play in order for the fiction to be perfected – and *perfected primarily in realms outside the fiction*. (My italics)[28]

Allegory, in other words, is the narrative equivalent in history painting of the theatricality of the image, in that it presupposes the presence of an active, interpretative spectator who 'completes' the meaning of the work. It is not difficult to see, therefore, why Barry should insist on the importance of what he referred to as the 'intelligent eye',[29] for it was clearly bound up with his desire to elevate the 'mechanical' art of painting to the intellectual level of literature, and the discursive powers of language in general. The fact that Philoctetes's claims on our sympathy are not compromised by allowing his body to register his torments is consistent with this attempt to endow sensual expression, whether through the flesh or the 'embodied substance' of painting, with the dignity and resolve of *virtu*. Yet there were also dangers involved in making too much of the erudition required for a proper response to art. For one thing, it tended to fly in the face of Barry's democratic conception of painting, of its public responsibility to cultivate *virtu*, as he put it, not only in the charmed circles of St James but also among the less fortunate denizens of Wapping ('Inquiry', ii, 220). Secondly, there was the possibility that in placing too much emphasis on content and meaning, the idea could overwhelm the image, relegating art to the mere illustrative and servile function he was determined to avoid.

For this reason, the question of allegory moved to centre-stage in Barry's theatre of the image. Referring to the 'most unfavourable kind' of allegory in the hieroglyphs of ancient Egyptian art, 'where nothing was shewn for itself but as the symbol and type of some other thing' ('Lectures', i, 356), Barry objected that the material encasement of these images contributes as little to their meaning as the shape and colour of letters to the meaning of a word. This attenuation of the sign also informed the rigid and static referents attached to allegorical figures in Cesare Ripa's enormously influential *Iconologia* (1593), which Barry, with characteristic understatement, dismissed as merely 'the offal of the imagination' ('Lectures', i, 468). Having drawn attention to the pitfalls presented by allegory, however, Barry turned his attention to those occasions 'where the allegoric composition may (when in the hands of a wise, ingenious and feeling artist) be adopted' ('Lectures', i, 469–70). There may be difficulties, for example, in doing justice to an important historical event, for even though it may appeal to our emotions 'it would not fill the mind, and come home to all the occasions of general application like the allegoric composition' ('Lectures', i, 469). Hence his willingness to accept 'mixed forms' which combined the literal and the figural, and in which the wider significance of a historical personage or state of affairs is brought out at an allegorical level. These compositions are only successful, however, when the painter attends to the 'embodied substance' of the figures, in the sense of visual details and material forms, and not just to the general ideas – when, that is:

the subject or action is substantially and fully explained by the figures themselves: as it would have been in any particular historical or invented fact. The insignia of the figures can add nothing to the explication and interest of the action; though they raise the personages, from being mere historic individuals, into the abstract, and more sublime characters of Time, Eternity, Rage, and Envy. ('Lectures', i, 470)

As against the neo-classical orthodoxy, enshrined in Sir Joshua Reynolds's *Discourses on Art*, which held that the physicality of the body must be suppressed in an allegorical figure to make way for higher-level meanings, Barry insisted that the corporeality of the body enhanced the operation of all but the most stilted forms of allegory.[30] It is this which leads John Barrell to observe in relation to Barry's last major painting, 'The Birth of Pandora', that the capacity of the central figure of Pandora to act as a personification of civic unity is not jeopardized by her obvious sexuality and erotic allure. Though the spectator, who is addressed as a male,

is intended to find in Pandora a purely formal and ideal representation of civic unity...he may instead find an object of desire, and the provocative pose she has adopted, passive, ornamented and displayed, does nothing to discourage this. Indeed, it seems that to find the one he must find the other: Pandora must appear as an object of desire, to encourage him to desire what, as symbol, she represents.[31]

By recreating the body politic ('civic unity') in the image of actual, eroticized bodies (as against the conventional female forms usually associated with male inspired ideals of *virtu*), allegorical painting for Barry could achieve at the level of figuration what had not yet been realized in the politics of civic humanism. It is as if allegory itself incorporated the juxtaposition of male and female, reason and sentiment, abstract meaning and sensual expression, without which the public sphere could not be considered truly egalitarian – as well as undoing these binaries in the process. In this respect, Barry was prepared to temper his criticism of the 'monstrous' forms which, in his opinion, defaced ancient Egyptian art to make allowance for one enigmatic figure which cast its spell over him – that of the sphinx. In praising the placing of a sphinx on the helmet of the sculpture of Minerva made by Phidias for the Parthenon (Minerva's indeterminate sexuality already posing something of an enigma), he wrote:

This ingenious symbol comprehends more than a mere union of even the bodily force of Ajax and the intellectual provident skill of Ulysses; for the head and breasts show it to be feminine, and consequently endowed with all the interesting advantages derived from the superior sensibilities and affectionate tenderness of the heart, which so happily and necessarily accompany the female or maternal character through all animal nature, and which, by the capacious reason of humanity, becomes sublimated into a Cordelia, an Aristopateira, the heroic daughter of my Diagoras; or into a character which appears even superior to either of them, namely, the Irish princess, whose interesting story is related by Dr Thorkelin from an old unsuspicious Danish record.[32]

The prospect which the sphinx presents of a powerful male (possessing 'bodily force' and 'intellectual provident skill') who nevertheless displays female attributes, is reminiscent of the charges of 'effeminacy' which were levelled at Philoctetes' emotional excess, and which, until the onset of the age of sensibility, had all but eliminated him from the pantheon of tragic heroes. As Barrell suggests, it may even be the case that Pandora was envisaged by Barry as a complementary figure to Philoctetes, for she assumes virtually the same bodily posture, extending to the raised and bound left foot.[33] The fact that the train of associations in Barry's reflections on allegory culminates in an example drawn from Irish mythology raises the possibility that the figure of the stricken Philoctetes himself may constitute a national allegory, an embodiment of the pitiful state of the Catholic population in Barry's own native Ireland. Like the Greek warrior, 'the Irish Princess' who is the subject of the Icelandic scholar Thorkelin's obscure Irish saga was also forced into exile, and was reduced to the menial status of a slave in another country.[34] As we shall see, it was this aspect of Philoctetes, the reduction of a highly civilized warrior to an ignoble condition of slavery and 'savagery', which first brought him to the attention of writers and artists intent on exposing the injustices of colonial rule in eighteenth-century Ireland.

SOLIDARITY AND THE INJURED BODY

Here and there... one comes upon an isolated play, an exceptional film, an extraordinary novel that is not just incidentally but centrally and uninterruptedly about the nature of bodily pain. In Sophocles's *Philoctetes*, the fate of an entire civilization is suspended in order to allow the ambassadors of that civilization to stop and take account of the nature of the human body, the wound in that body, the pain in that wound. (Scarry, *Body in Pain*)

The paradox in James Barry's *Philoctetes* whereby the stark isolation of the wounded warrior addresses an absent spectator is brilliantly captured in Herder's *Essay on the Origin of Language* (1771), in which he testifies to the social address of language, even in an apparently pre-linguistic, sub-human state:

A suffering animal, no less than the hero Philoctetus, will whine, will moan when pain befalls it, even though it be abandoned on a desert island, without sight or trace or hope of a fellow creature... It is as though it could sigh out part of its pain and at least draw in from the empty air space new strength of endurance as it fills the unhearing winds with its moans.[35]

As Simon Richter argues, this seems to point to a non-social, physiological explanation for the origin of language, one, moreover, that lends itself to primal, expressivist interpretations of the healing power of language. On this reading, it is not communication with another that effects the talking cure, but the sheer ability to voice one's suffering, as if the expiration of air itself acts as a poultice drawing out the pain: 'Philoctetes feels pain; with his scream, he almost feels some relief.' But in fact this physiological grounding of pain is not the full picture where Herder, or for that matter Barry, is concerned. The most important aspect of this seemingly primal or instinctual response is that, rather than being 'autistically grounded in the body of each individual',[36] it is already directed towards others, even in their absence. As Herder himself puts it:

So little did nature create us a severed block of rock, as egotistic monads... even the chords whose sound and strain do not arise from choice and slow deliberation, whose very nature the probing of reason has not as yet been able to fathom, even they – though there is no awareness of sympathy from outside – are aligned in their entire performance for a going outward towards other creatures. The plucked chord performs its natural duty: it sounds! It calls for an echo from one that feels alike, even if none is there, even if it does not hope or expect that such another might answer. (Herder, 'Essay', 87)

In arguing that nature itself is socially directed, Herder seems to be striving for a form of expression that possesses the physical force of a biological reflex, but is nonetheless the product of language and culture. Crucially, the somatic component is not seen as a foundation, a pre-social or pre-linguistic substratum, but as an element diffused throughout an entire system: 'vestiges of [the] sounds of nature', he explains in an apt analogy, 'are not the roots as such: they are the sap that enlivens the roots of language' (Herder, 'Essay', 91). It is for this reason, as Richter perceptively remarks, that Herder's 'Philoctetes is more like us than he is like Rousseau's pre-linguistic primitive.'[37] It is not, therefore, the physical expression as such that conveys meaning, but its insertion in a complex network of human ties and associations. A tear by itself 'is just a cold drop of water', just as 'a weary breath – half a sigh – which dies so movingly on pain distorted lips' is but 'an empty draft of air': 'Severed from everything else, torn away, deprived of their life, they are, to be sure, no more than ciphers, and the voice of nature turns into an arbitrary penciled symbol' (Herder, 'Essay', 90). To explain how they are subsequently endowed with emotive meaning, Herder has recourse to the formative influence of childhood experiences on our acquisition of language:

> The words, the tone, the turn of this gruesome ballad or the like touched our souls when we heard it for the first time in our childhood with I know not what host of connotations of shudder, awe, fear, fright, joy. Speak the word, and like a throng of ghosts those connotations arise of a sudden in their dark majesty from the grave of the soul: they obscure inside the word the pure limpid concept that could be grasped only in their absence. (Herder, 'Essay', 98)

This, as we shall see in Chapter 3, is derived from Edmund Burke's *Enquiry into the Sublime and Beautiful*: what is important for Herder's purposes is that it allows him to attach the somatic force of expressive language to its material properties of sound, tone, and rhythm.

Though they might appear to be involuntary, instinctual reactions, cries of pain such as Philoctetes emits on his deserted island are social from the outset, craving by their very public nature for the presence of another human being. As if with Barry's later prints of Philoctetes in mind, Herder writes of 'this weak, this sentient being':

> However lonesome and alone it may seem to be, however exposed to every hostile storm of the universe, yet it is not alone: It stands allied to all nature! Strung with delicate chords; but nature hid sounds in those chords which, when called forth and encouraged, can arouse other beings of equally delicate build, can communicate, as though along an invisible chain, to a distant heart a spark that makes it feel for this unseen being. These sighs, these sounds are language. (Herder, 'Essay', 88)

Reduced, then, to the most primordial human condition, the body in pain, as exemplified by Philoctetes, is still capable of transcending its own self-absorption, and thinking of others, through the secret chords of sympathy threaded like filigree through our most elemental responses to pain. It is true that, at first, this takes the form of a desire to be delivered from one's agony, as when Philoctetes, on first encountering the young visitor to his island, Neoptolemus, implores him not to look

> With horror on me, but in kind compassion
> Pity a wretch deserted and forlorn
> In this sad place.   (*Philoctetes*, 104)

and proceeds to acquaint him with the story of his betrayal by Ulysses and his fellow Greeks who left him in pain and bereft of any consolation:

>   – no kind companion left
> To minister or needful food or balm
> To my sad wounds. On every side I looked,
> And saw nothing but woe; of that indeed
> Measure too full. For day succeeded day,
> And still no comfort came; myself alone
> Could to myself the means of life afford,
> In this poor grotto.   (*Philoctetes*, 105)

But in a striking act of imaginative empathy on hearing of Neoptolemus's (alleged) suffering at the hand of the scheming Ulysses, and of the death of his father, Achilles, Philoctetes attends to his young visitor's plight while still nursing his own grievances:

> PHIL.   Permit me, son,
>   To mourn his fate, ere I attend to thine. [*He weeps*]
> NEO.   Alas! thou needst not weep for others' woes,
>   Thou hast enough already of thy own.
>   (*Philoctetes*, 107)

This concern for others, even in the midst of his own agony, is again apparent when, in the expectation of returning to Greece, he asks Neoptolemus, on account of his howls and the stench of his wound, to place him out of harm's way on the ship to cause least offence to the passengers. As Charles Segal observes: 'For all his external savagery, the outcast has both a capacity for deeper communication and ultimately a truer power to persuade than the artful persuader, Odysseus [Ulysses]':

Reaching out of his loneliness and abandonment, he [Philoctetes] invokes those basic ties of civilized humanity from which he is cut off. He calls Neoptolemus *teknon*, 'child', and entreats him 'by your father, by your mother, by whatever in your house (*oikos*) is dear to you' (*prosphiles*). For all the rudeness of his house that is no house, this castaway can convey the affection or *philia* that a house should contain.[38]

    It is this capacity for solidarity in pain where, instead of turning in on himself, Philoctetes in the throes of agony still finds the capacity to sympathize with others, which finally wins Neoptolemus over, and persuades him to reject the manipulative intrigues of Ulysses. At stake here is a predicament that went to the heart of Enlightenment theories of progress. Ulysses uses reason and guile to advance what is perceived as the common good – in this case, victory at Troy – but is willing to employ any stratagem, no matter how unscrupulous, to attain this objective. In his use of instrumental reason, he attaches priority exclusively to the 'technology' of progress, Philoctetes' magic bow, without sparing any thought for its owner, and the price he must pay for being deprived of his means of subsistence.[39] By virtue of his 'savage' hunting state and habitation in the wilderness, Philoctetes in his eighteenth-century incarnation may thus be seen as an embodiment of the profound injustices visited upon the losers of history, and, in particular, those 'primitive' societies consigned to the ominous category of 'doomed peoples' before the march of progress. Who, wrote Herder somewhat optimistically, could remain indifferent in the face of such suffering: 'what fibres of steel, what power to plug all inlets of sensibility are needed for a man to be deaf and hard against this?'(Herder, 'Essay', 96). But Ulysses embodies precisely such a form of civility with iron in its soul. For him, Philoctetes is an eminently dispensable means to a highly desirable end. In this, as Adorno and Horkheimer argued, the cunning of Ulysses represents that 'dialectic of the Enlightenment' whereby the forces of reason and secularism repeated, albeit in a modern, progressive guise, the cult of sacrifice to the gods which it prided itself on overcoming. Progress, like the deities of old, exacts a heavy cost in human lives, as it dooms its casualties to extinction – 'the deceit of a priestly rationalization of death by means of an apotheosis of the predestined victim'.[40]

Whereas for Ulysses, the bow – and by extension, instrumental reason – can be separated from its owner, for Neoptolemus, by contrast, the turning point occurs when he realizes that, for justice to be done, Philoctetes must accompany his bow, and the injured body be reintegrated into the course of history. Neoptolemus's task, after his cruel deception of Philoctetes has been discovered, is to deliver him from his self-absorption by winning his trust again, cultivating his ability to look through others' eyes. This forgetting of his wounds on Philoctetes's part is not entirely an act of healing, for there is no reassurance of a happy ending:

> PHIL.   My sufferings past I could forget; but oh!
> I dread the woes to come; for well I know
> When once the mind's corrupted it brings forth
> Unnumbered crimes, and ills to ills succeed.
> *(Philoctetes*, 135)

The unabated nature of suffering, however, does not prevent him from the ultimate gesture of solidarity with others, the identification with the great public cause of the conquest of Troy with which the play ends. It is true that for this to take effect, the introduction of Hercules, in the form of a *deus ex machina*, is required, but as Alasdair MacIntyre points out, the recourse to this device indicates not so much 'an arbitrary disentangling by the intrusion of the supernatural, but the discovery of a standard for action which merely human resources have been unable to supply'.[41] Certainly, there is no possibility of an impartial standard of justice by means of which the clash in values between Ulysses and Neoptolemus can be settled; indeed, it is precisely this detachment of justice from its connection to actual human suffering that is implied by Ulysses' recourse to instrumental reason. Yet the intervention of Hercules is not entirely a bolt from the blue, for it has, in fact, a history. Hercules is Philoctetes's oldest friend, and the donor of his magic bow in the first place, which was given as a gift when Philoctetes had come to the aid of the dying Hercules by lighting the funeral pyre that delivered him from his agony.[42] Hercules's 'reappearance' at the end, then, may be seen as an acknowledgement of the capacity of the injured body to re-enter history, acting not simply as an avatar of revenge but as the bearer of justice. By the same token, the reactivation of Philoctetes's capacity for trust and friendship in the light of Hercules's intervention derives not so much from a renunciation of his past suffering, and a recourse to atemporal standards of justice, but from his ability to connect with an alternative version of the past which points to the future, transforming his own profound grievances into a renewed pursuit of a reformulated common good.[43]

'ROARING ON THE RACK': SWIFT, SHERIDAN, AND THE INJURED BODY

According to Adorno and Horkeimer, the justification of sacrifice in the interests of progress can be traced to the cannibalistic 'idea of the collective body, the tribe, into which the blood of its slaughtered member would flow back as energy'. In the modern world, they contend, practices such as mass emigration 'by which in times of hunger an entire age group of youths is ritually required to emigrate, bear unmistakable traces of such barbaric and transfigured rationality'.[44] For a powerful eighteenth-century precursor of this critique of the dark side of the Enlightenment, we have only to turn to the savage irony of Jonathan Swift's *A Modest Proposal* (1729), in which cannibalism, the eating of young children, is justified in the name of social engineering and economic rationality. As Carole Fabricant points out, underlying this dystopian vision is Swift's persistent refusal to write the suffering body out of history, particularly as it impressed itself upon him in the dismal spectacle of the Irish poor, and the political and economic 'tyranny' which gave rise to their wretched condition:

His writings show us why a studied avoidance of this suffering, or an evocation of its existence by coldly detached, 'scientific' analysts devoid of a morally or ideologically engaged standpoint, not only fails to convey a truthful picture but, even worse, functions to perpetuate the very mentality responsible for the suffering in the first place.[45]

The belief that one should not hide oppression, and that the right to protest over one's suffering is the most basic of all civil liberties, was a distinctive component of the 'patriotic' ideology in Ireland from its first enunciation in William Molyneux's *The Case of Ireland Stated* (1698): '*We Are in a Miserable Condition indeed*', wrote Molyneux, '*if we may not be allow'd to* Complain, *when we think we are Hurt.*'[46] These sentiments received their most trenchant formulation in Swift's *Drapier's Letters*, where it is stated, with Molyneux explicitly in mind, that the erosion of freedom in Ireland under colonial rule is such that:

> those who have used *Power* to cramp *Liberty* have gone so far as to Resent even the *Liberty of Complaining*, altho' a Man upon the Rack was never known to be refused the Liberty of *Roaring* as loud as thought fit.[47]

With his characteristic barbed irony, Swift proceeded to point out that opposing certain kinds of enslavement through abstract appeals to virtue and natural rights is as useful, to adapt his own comparison, as a beautiful prospect to a man in a dungeon:

> As to myself, it hath been my Misfortune to begin and pursue it [i.e. resistance to oppression] upon a wrong Foundation. For having detected... Frauds and Falsehoods... I foolishly *disdained* to have Recourse to *Whining, Lamenting* and *Crying for Mercy*, but rather chose to appeal to *Law* and Liberty and the *Common Rights of Mankind*, without considering what *Climate* I was in. (*Drapier's Letters*, v, 116–17)

If a nation is humiliated to such an extent that it has to struggle for even the right to ventilate its own sufferings, then this is not an index of its own abasement but rather of the intensity of oppression:

> The Provocation must needs have been Great, which would stir up an obscure indolent Drapier to become an *Author*... It is a known story of the Dumb Boy, whose Tongue forced a passage for Speech by the Horrour of seeing a Dagger at his Father's Throat. This may lessen the Wonder that a Tradesman hid in Privacy and Silence should *cry out* when the Life and Being of his Political *Mother* are attempted before his face, and by so infamous a Hand. (*Drapier's Letters*, v, 110–11)

Swift's assertion of the right to 'roar on the rack' was contained in his notorious fourth Drapier's Letter, 'To the Whole People of Ireland', which was published in October 1724, to coincide with the arrival of the new Lord Lieutenant, Lord Carteret, in Ireland.[48] Carteret regarded those passages in the letter demanding legislative independence as treasonable, and it was immediately prosecuted for sedition. The printer, John Harding, already a seasoned veteran of state prosecutions, was imprisoned, and a reward of £300 offered for the identity of the author, whose name was, in fact, an open secret all over Dublin. While Carteret and the Privy Council waited for an informer to claim the £300 reward, a verse of scripture appeared 'fix'd up in publick Places about the city': 'And the people said unto Saul, Shall Jonathan die, who hath wrought this great salvation in Israel? God forbid.' In case the message was lost, a contemporary newspaper which carried the report of the political graffiti tendentiously explained the allegorical resonances to the public: 'The Conceit lies in this, that the suspected Author of the said Pamphlet is called *Jonathan*; we are told also, that his Sir-Name begins with an *S*.'[49]

It was against this background of the deployment of allegory to circulate open secrets in public space that Dr Thomas Sheridan, Swift's close friend, fellow wit and publicist, chose to introduce the pain-racked, malodorous figure of Philoctetes into the modern English canon. A preface to one of Sheridan's publications claimed that 'a double Meaning is of double use',[50] and when his pioneering translation, published in 1725, was dedicated to Lady Carteret, wife of the Lord Lieutenant, her husband, Lord Carteret, himself a distinguished classical scholar, cannot have been slow to read between the lines of the text. In the year of its publication, 1725, Sheridan found himself in trouble with the Lord Lieutenant when, having procured an appointment as a clergyman in Co. Cork on Carteret's recommendation, he rather unwisely delivered a sermon on the text, 'Sufficient unto the day is the evil thereof', on 1 August, the anniversary of the Hanoverian Succession.[51] If, as Charles Segal suggests, Philoctetes's debility in Sophocles's drama 'signifies the waning vitality of a wounded world order where the legitimate king, or in this case the legitimate bearer of the heroic and moral values of kingship, is injured, enfeebled, and exiled',[52] then Sheridan's long-standing Jacobite associations may have added an additional seditious dimension to his translation of the play. When the cunning Ulysses manoeuvres the magic bow from Philoctetes's hand, the deceived warrior protests in Sheridan's translation:

> That I, who did the Son of Jove succeed,
> In Right of thee, must never more enjoy thee –
> But by a cursed Usurpation seiz'd,
> By one who had no Right to thy Succession.[53]

which leads the chorus to exclaim, as if the author of the translation is covering his tracks in case he attracts the same attention as his friend Swift:

> Whate'er this Person has express'd
> You shoul'd interpret it the best,
> Nor wrest his Meaning to invidious Sense,
> The publick Orders he obey'd
> Justly in ev'rything he said,
> And well contriv'd it for his Friends Defence.
> (Sheridan, *Philoctetes*, 41)

The analogies between Philoctetes's island and the indifferent response in London to the economic plight of Ireland as described by Swift are evident in the wounded warrior's complaint that:

> My woful Case was neither heard at Home,
> Nor ev'n among the *Greeks* – but those who cast
> Me out smile at my Wrongs, and keep them secret.
> ... No sailor steers
> With willing Sails to these inhuman Shores;
> No trade; no harbours; here no Mortal dwells
> With hospitable Care to tend a Stranger.
> (Sheridan, *Philoctetes*, 10–11)

This is consistent with the image of a kingdom reduced to slavery – a common charge in Protestant patriot discourse – with which Philoctetes confronts the deceitful Ulysses, accusing him of showing contempt for liberty:

> PHIL. Alas, my father has begot a slave!
>   To gen'rous Freedom I'm a perfect Stranger.
> UL. Not so. But equal to those mighty Princes
>   With whom you're destin'd to demolish *Troy*.
> PHIL. Who I! all Racks I rather wou'd endure;
>   I'd rather live for ever here alone.[54]
> (Sheridan, *Philoctetes*, 37)

In *The Intelligencer*, which he co-wrote with Swift, Sheridan devoted two issues to a defence of the Drapier, and hence it is not surprising that the distinctive trope of the rack should recur throughout *Philoctetes*, as when the chorus bemoan the warrior's tragic fate:

> But never did I hear or see
> A man so rack'd before,
> As Philoctetes seems to me,
> What suff'rings can be more?

> He never did an Act was wrong
> But justice still maintain'd:
> I wonder much that he so long,
> Such Torments has sustain'd.[55]
>   (Sheridan, *Philoctetes*, 25)

Critics have frequently drawn attention to the contradictions inherent in Swift's (and William Molyneux's) claim to speak for the whole people of Ireland, while being part of an Anglo-Irish Protestant elite that introduced the Penal Laws, a form of civil apartheid, against Catholics.[56] Swift's abiding preoccupation with poverty, however, and the spectre of famine and cannibalism which haunts his works, evince a scarcely concealed concern for the plight of the common people, and, as Joseph McMinn argues, it was through Thomas Sheridan, more than any other acquaintance, that he came into contact with the destitution of Gaelic Ireland.[57] Sheridan expressed his own 'sincere compassion' for the appalling poverty he witnessed in the Irish countryside, and in his picture of the abandoned Philoctetes, relying on rags, herbs, and the blood of animals to survive, it is possible to discern echoes of his own description of the Irish poor in the *Intelligencer*, 'who are sunk to the lowest Degree of Misery and Poverty, whose Houses are Dunghills, whose Victuals are the Blood of their Cattle, or the Herbs in the Field; and whose Cloathing to the Dishonour of God and Man is Nakedness'.[58] Part of the political acumen of Sophocles's play lies in its determination to show that 'savagery', the existence of human beings in a primitive 'state of nature', is not always superseded by progress, but may in fact be produced by it. This lies at the heart of Swift's animus against improving schemes and abstract conceptions of progress which were conveniently inured to the cries of their victims. As we shall see, it was this rejection of emotional restraint, and an insistence on the right of injured parties to inveigh against injustice, which was central to the reworking of Enlightenment responses to the wounded body in eighteenth-century Ireland.

ALLEGORY AS SEMANTIC WOUND

The more eloquent passages in the work are the wounds...conflict has left in the theory. (Theodor Adorno, 'The Curious Realist: On Siegfried Kracauer')

For Swift and Sheridan, notwithstanding the taints of Jacobitism and their evident concern for the Irish poor, protests against English 'tyranny' were couched mainly (but not exclusively) in Patriot terms, from the point of view of the ruling Protestant interest in Ireland. By the late eighteenth century, however, with the rise of the Catholic Committee and, in England, the influence of Edmund Burke on colonial policy in Ireland, demands for liberty and freedom became more inclusive, directly embracing the Catholic cause as well as more traditional patriot concerns. For Burke, the general condition of Ireland under the Penal Laws was no better than slavery, and the degradation of the Irish such as to be analogous to the condition of a diseased limb on the British body politic: 'I never can forget that I am an Irishman. I flatter myself perhaps; but I think, I would shed my blood rather than see the Limb I belong to oppressed and defrauded of its due nourishment.'[59] Or, in what Conor Cruise O'Brien describes as 'the closest glimpse we get of the festering wound of Philoctetes' in relation to Burke,[60] the Catholic population under the Penal Laws are again described by him as being better off dead than in the position of 'a feverish being', kept 'above ground an animated mass of putrefaction, corrupted himself, and corrupting all around him'.[61]

That a diseased limb, and more particularly the wounded foot, was emblematic of the afflictions of Ireland is clear from James Barry's pioneering history painting, 'The Baptism of the King of Cashel by St Patrick' (1762/3: Fig. 6), the exhibition of which in 1763 brought the young painter from Cork to the attention of Edmund Burke, who subsequently befriended him, extending to him patronage and financial support.[62] This is probably the earliest publicly exhibited painting with a recognizably cultural nationalist theme in the history of Irish art, if not in the history of art itself, and its evocation of Ireland's heroic past achieved quasi-official status by virtue of its being hung in the Irish House of Commons until the building was seriously damaged by fire in 1791. The picture portrays an incident related in Geoffrey Keating's *History of Ireland* (c. 1633) in which St Patrick accidentally stuck his crozier through the foot of Aongus, the King of Munster, while baptising him at Cashel.[63] Though the immolation of the King causes consternation among his followers, Aongus bears his pain with fortitude on the assumption that the act was part of the ceremony. There seems little doubt, as William Pressly suggests, that the noble bearing of the King throughout his agonizing ordeal was meant to show the virtuous state of ancient Ireland to its colonial detractors, in keeping with the efforts of contemporary propagandists, such as the native Catholic historian Charles O'Conor, to vindicate Irish claims to be descended from a civilization as advanced as that of ancient Greece (the Doric column, in the immediate background of Barry's picture, echoes visually the native dolmen on the distant landscape).[64] Aongus shares with Philoctetes the

Fig. 6 James Barry, 'The Baptism of the King of Cashel by St Patrick' (1801) (sketch: original painting executed in 1763)

fact that his experience of pain does not prevent him identifying with a higher ideal, but it is striking that the ideal in question involves a form of cultural conversion, stepping outside (albeit with an injured foot) the boundaries of his own culture to embrace a new, Christian dispensation.[65] Instead of forcing the mind inward, in a mode of self-absorption, pain turns it outward towards Enlightenment ideals of cross-cultural sympathy and solidarity, reinforced by the mapping of ancient Ireland onto the universal ethos of classical antiquity.[66] That Philoctetes in Barry's later painting does not show quite the same reserve under pain as Aongus, testifies not so much to his weakness as to the extremes of his oppression as an emblem of eighteenth-century Ireland, and the abject state into which a once great civilization has fallen under the yoke of the Penal Laws.

In his indictment of the Penal Laws, Edmund Burke directed his most scathing invective at the manner in which they interfered with tenure and inheritance. By leaving it open for a usurping son to disinherit his father by the mere expedient of a conversion to Protestantism, the legal system had undermined the deep affective ties between patriarchy and property:

> By this law the tenure and value of a Roman Catholic in his real property is not only rendered extremely limited, and altogether precarious; but the paternal power is in all such families so enervated, that it may well be considered as entirely taken away; even the principle upon which it is founded seems to be directly reversed... The paternal power thus being wholly abrogated, it is evident that by the last regulation the power of a husband over his wife is also considerably impaired; because if it be in her power, whenever she pleases, to subtract the children from his protection and obedience, she herself by that hold inevitably acquires a power and superiority over her husband. ('Popery Laws', vi, 8, 10–11)

The logic of colonial rule, in other words, is that it reduces men to the condition of women, a transgression of gender relations which, in Burke's eyes, can only lead to profound social instability, if not to revolution itself. Yet in terms of the renewed interest in sentimentalism which was informing contemporary aesthetic debates, and to which Burke himself made such a major contribution, it is not clear if this erosion of male authority was entirely to be regretted, particularly in so far as it questioned 'manly' ideas of fortitude and self-restraint, the duty to keep one's counsel and evince a stoic-like bearing in circumstances of great distress. As Burke himself confessed to Thomas Burgh in 1780, when it came to the question of Ireland even he was not able to feign a calm countenance:

> I am not, however, stoic enough to be able to affirm with truth, or hypocrite enough affectedly to pretend, that I am wholly unmoved at the difficulty which you, and others of my friends in Ireland, have found in vindicating my conduct towards my native country. It undoubtedly hurts me in some degree; but the wound is not very deep.[67]

It would seem, indeed, that the constant dilemma which faced that section of the Catholic intelligentsia with Whig sympathies in eighteenth-century Ireland was whether to gain the confidence and respect of their masters by maintaining their equanimity, or else to end the charade of silence and resignation by speaking out against their oppression and working actively to abolish the Penal Laws. The problem with the latter course of action was that it might open a Pandora's box and release pent-up forces that simply could not be contained. As Charles O'Conor, the most articulate champion of the Catholic cause in Ireland, put it with evident caution in 1777 on the eve on the first tentative reforms in the Penal code: 'One argument for our silence in the present conjuncture does not escape me, and it is the best that can be produced. It is that our writing on the subject of our grievances may betray us into indiscretion.'[68] This was an abiding fear of many of the more timorous members of the Catholic Committee which reformers such as O'Conor had to overcome in the late eighteenth century. In the words of O'Conor's grandson, the nineteenth-century historian Matthew O'Conor, the main difficulty facing the leading activists on the Catholic Committee in their opposition to the Penal Laws was that they

> had to contend with the influence of the gentry and clergy, and the unconquerable timidity of a prostrate people. Long habits of slavery had frozen the political courage of the gentry; apprehensive of fresh stories of persecution they deprecated all efforts for redress however temperate and loyal. The watchful jealousy of their oppressors they feared, would be roused by activity on their part, and the exertions of their fellow slaves might produce new contexts and convulsions which would endanger the little property they had saved from the shipwreck of the [Williamite] revolution... The morals of the clergy, their fortitude and... principles of pious resignation concurred with the gentry's pusillanimous fears to counteract the efforts of the active.[69]

As Charles O'Conor saw it, keeping up a show of patience and forbearance in the face of sustained injustice was tantamount to collusion with one's own persecution: 'a silence in regard to the calumnies of our enemies', he wrote to his confidant and fellow-activist Dr John Curry in 1758, 'was in some degree criminal and amounted to an acquiesence to the charges made'.[70] Alluding in an allegorical vein to his friend's skill as a physician, O'Conor wrote of the crisis precipitated by opposition to the initial reforms of the Penal Laws in 1778 that it was vital to convey the message that the well-being of the entire nation, both Catholic and Protestant, depended on restoring health to its diseased parts: 'It is felt that the distress of two-thirds of the inhabitants operates to the weakness of all and occasionally, as at present, throws the whole body politic into fainting fits.'[71] When the crisis seemed to be over, and Sir George Savile's Catholic Relief Bill, engineered by Edmund Burke with the assistance of reformers in Ireland, was assured of a safe passage through Parliament, O'Conor attributed its success to Dr Curry's efforts, and to his painstaking dissection of the political anatomy of oppression in Ireland for over four decades:

After a dead trance of more than forty years, you had the courage to break silence in 1747 and expose the wounds given to a nation through the sides of a small and noxious party. Your example roused others here and in England to abandon their despondency.[72]

It is in the light of this depiction of Ireland as a wounded body that we should view Barry's decision in late 1777 to issue an aquatint of 'Philoctetes', dedicated to Sir George Savile. Barry was indebted to Savile on a number of counts, for in his capacity as one of the vice-presidents of the Society for the Encouragement of Arts, Manufactures, and Commerce, he was directly involved in commissioning (or more accurately, in permitting) Barry's monumental series of paintings on 'The Progress of Human Culture' at the Society's Great Room in the Adelphi. Accordingly, Barry proposed to include his portrait, along with that of Lord Chatham, as one of the judges in the third picture in the series in the Great Room, 'Crowning the Victors at Olympia'. This proposal was not followed through, but instead the portrait of Savile was transferred to the fifth picture, 'The Distribution of Premiums in the Society of Arts', where he is included in the company of such luminaries (and friends of Ireland) as Edmund Burke, Arthur Young, and Dr Johnson. When Savile agreed to front the Catholic Relief Bill in 1778, he was assured of even a higher place in Barry's pantheon of heroes. As Thomas Bartlett points out, rumours began to circulate from mid 1777 that some sort of concession to Catholics was likely, as a possible trade-off for recruitment in the war with America. Among those who expressed alarm over the impending legislation was one of the scions of the Protestant interest, Lord Shannon, a Corkman like Barry, who expressed great alarm over unfounded reports that over 10,000 Catholics were to be armed.[73] It was perhaps Shannon's resistance to any amelioration in the condition of Catholics which led Barry to write to him, early in 1778, warning him of the consequences of blocking reforms. The government, Barry wrote to this hardly sympathetic correspondent, had attempted 'by every method that ingenuity can devise to despoil, distress and torment a great majority consisting of more than threefourths of the inhabitants' of Ireland, and, as a result, it was not surprising that 'in proportion as they have feeling and spirit, they must inexpressibly hate and detest you'. He then entreated Lord Shannon, in terms that call to mind the plight of Philoctetes, to bind up the wound of division in the country and to treat Catholics as fellow citizens. Barry was particularly keen to dispel the prejudice that Catholicism was hostile to civic ideals because of its alleged adherence to absolutism, but he can hardly have endeared himself to the noble Lord, a descendant of the 'upstart earl', Roger Boyle, who came to Ireland in the first wave of plantations, by arguing that it was Protestantism, beginning with Henry VIII, which first advocated 'the absurd, slavish and execrable notion of the *divine, indefeasible, uncontroulable* right of *Kings* and *the passive obedience of subjects*' (Pressly, *James Barry*, 84).

Notwithstanding his desire to ennoble Philoctetes, it is clear from these remarks that Barry was not enamoured with 'stoical endurance' of the kind which lent itself to passive obedience, but was more concerned to bestow dignity on a hero who *refused* to conceal pain, and who sought through his tears and protestations to draw attention to his intolerable situation. It was precisely this aspect of Philoctetes, rather than his stoical endurance, which attracted the notice of another Irish commentator, the Limerick-born critic and theorist Daniel Webb who was a friend and supporter of the leading Patriot politician, Henry Flood.[74] In his treatise, *An Inquiry into the Beauties of Painting*, published in 1760, Webb contrasted the passionate concern with justice in ancient Greek art to the 'cold' and quiescent responses to suffering in Christian art, which amounted virtually to a collusion with oppression:

When St Andrew falls down to worship the cross, on which he is soon to be nailed; we may be improved by such an example of piety and zeal; but we cannot feel for one, who is not concerned for himself. We are not so calm in the sacrifice of Iphegenia; beautiful, innocent, and unhappy; we look upon her as the victim of an unjust decree.[75]

For this reason, 'the violent agitations of the soul, affect us most sensibly, by the total disturbance and alteration which they produce in the countenance' (*Beauties of Painting*, 63–4), and this leads Webb to attack the anaemic qualities of Christ's suffering in Raphael's picture of the Transfiguration, which lends itself to mere sentiment, as against the animated distress of his disciples below, which shows true passion (*Beauties of Painting*, 147–8).[76] The 'violent agitations' of the body should be such, he suggests, that 'had the foot only been discovered [of the Laocoon], the swelled veins, the strained sinews, and the irregular motions of the muscles, might have led us into a conception of those tortures, which are so divinely expressed on the face, so wonderfully marked throughout the whole body' (*Beauties of Painting*, 157–8). This might be seen as a prelude to his comments on Philoctetes, and it would appear that Webb's treatise first prompted Barry's interest in Philoctetes, for it included an encomium to Parrhasius's lost painting of the Greek warrior, as described by the poet Glaucus:

> Drawn by Parrhasius, as in person view'd,
> Sad Philoctetes feels his pains renew'd.
> In his parch'd eyes the deep-sunk tears express
> His endless misery, his dire distress.
> We blame thee, painter, tho' thy art commend;
> 'Twas time his sufferings with himself should end.
>
> (*Beauties of Painting*, 162)

'We cannot', adds Webb, 'well conceive an image more tender, or more affecting than this. Let terror be united with pity, the muse of painting has completed her drama' (*Beauties of Painting*, 162).[77]

This drama is expressed with greater intensity in Barry's 1777 print than in the original painting of Philoctetes by bringing the figure to the very edge of the picture surface, and increasing his size so that he appears almost imprisoned within the image. Consistent with this theatrical device, the inner turmoil of the wounded hero is now registered on his windswept body and also, in proto-romantic fashion, on the storm-racked landscape, which has darkened with a sense of foreboding. In the early 1790s, when storm clouds were gathering over the Irish political landscape as the campaign for Catholic emancipation entered a new, turbulent phase, Barry saw fit to issue a further version of the Philoctetes print (Fig. 7), this time straining towards an even greater sublimity, and adding, as Pressly notes, conspicuous phallic imagery in the shape of a tree limb and the arrow penetrating the dove, 'as if these images of potency were needed to counteract the crippling effects of Philoctetes's wound'.[78]

The resonances of these allegorical images was not confined to Catholic circles, but extended to the newly revived Patriot movement, mobilized by the National Volunteers in 1778. In December 1780, Joseph Pollock, a leading member of the Volunteers, based in Newry, wrote to Barry assuring him that his efforts on behalf of his native country were so well received by the burgeoning patriotic movement in Ireland that he had been elected to the Order of St Patrick, a society described by Pressly as a 'prestigious Dublin patriot's club composed of some of the most prominent liberal barristers and members of the Irish parliament'.[79] The club certainly had some distinguished members in the persons of Henry Grattan, Lord Charlemont, John Philpot Curran and Barry Yelverton, but it hardly possessed the official gravitas of the more pomp-laden Order of the Knights of St Patrick, instituted by the Viceroy, Lord Temple, on St Patrick's Day, 1783. The less elevated title of the earlier debating and drinking club which opened its membership to Barry was 'The Monks of the Screw', so named,

Fig. 7 James Barry, 'Philoctetes' (*c.* 1790s)

a contemporary memoir tells us, because 'the furniture and regulations of their festive apartment were completely *monkish*, and they owed both their title and their foundation to an original society, formed near Newmarket by Lord Avonmore [i.e. Barry Yelverton], of which he drew up the rules in a very quaint and comic monkish verse'.[80] Notwithstanding its lack of reverence for monkish habits, Barry, as a Catholic, would not have felt totally out of place in the society for it numbered amongst its members the liberal Catholic priest and fellow Corkman, the Rev. Arthur O' Leary.

O'Leary's anti-sectarian polemics on behalf of Catholic Relief are quoted by Pollock in his virulently anti-English tract, *Letters to the Men of Ireland, by Owen Roe O'Nial*, one of the earliest manifestos of the Volunteer movement, published in 1779. In these letters, Pollock cited the examples of several small countries such as Holland and Switzerland that had thrown off the yoke of foreign oppression, and gloated at the prospect of an impending American victory over the might of the Empire. It was perhaps with this in mind that Pollock, in his communication with Barry the following year, praised the artist's 1776 print, 'The Phoenix, or the Resurrection of Freedom', which depicted the flight of liberty from Britain to its new home in republican America.[81] In his *Letters to the Men of Ireland*, Pollock went on to inveigh against the caricaturing of the Irish on the English stage, arguing that these are not merely representations but that 'its authors are half-disposed to believe it'. The proscenium arch, it would seem, was not sufficient to protect Irish people from the antics of the stage-Irishman. But, he adds regretfully, 'we need not be surprised at the insults received by those whose passiveness seems to court them'. This leads to a call for Irish citizens to have recourse to radical surgery in treating the malaise of colonial rule. Can they, he asks,

> refuse to change her atmosphere for a purer, and cling to disease and to corruption as if *folly* were virtue, *presumption* piety? We shall not, my countryman! Our eyes are opened, our spirit is risen, and our representatives have caught a portion of the flame. They will no longer be satisfied with TEMPORARY EXPEDIENTS. They will strike at the root of the disease, not attempting [just] to skin and film the ulcerous part...[82]

This may have been the view of Ireland's travails which led Pollock, in his letter to Barry, to single out for special praise the 1777 aquatint of 'Philoctetes'. His description, moreover, of the reception of these prints in the highly political atmosphere of the times must have been greatly encouraging to the beleaguered artist, and could only have confirmed his resolute belief in art as an agent of political literacy: 'I have', wrote Pollock, 'several times been highly gratified by shewing the few sketches of yours which I brought over. Even in the frozen North I have found uneducated men who could admire them.'[83] Notwithstanding Barry's emphasis on the need for an educated eye, Irish viewers, it would seem, did not require much erudition to sympathize with the allegory of Philoctetes.

If allegory, as its etymology indicates, originally meant 'other speech', a kind of severed language with a dual mode of address, then there is a sense in which it may be seen as a semantic wound, a gash opening up a radical incompleteness in the surface meaning of an image, a text or, indeed, a divided nation. In eighteenth-century Ireland, allegory may have been not just a rhetorical sleight-of-hand but the condition of a society divided against itself, for to be Irish in a colonial context, whether as native or settler, was to be profoundly aware of another who also laid claim to one's identity. The experience of the Protestant ruling class was that of being, as Sir Samuel Ferguson put it, 'strangers at home', a phrase which, as Siobhan Kilfeather observes, captures 'the paradox of colonial experience': 'The settlers are never completely at ease in their adopted country, never find it possible to make an uncomplicated self-identification as Irish.'[84] This was even more true of the Catholic Irish whom the Penal Laws had estranged, making them, in Edmund Burke's phrase, 'aliens in their native country, and outlaws without charge or process'.[85] To be Irish in these circumstances was to be 'rendered a foreigner in his native land, only because he retained the religion, along with the property, handed down to him from those who had been the old inhabitants of that land before him'.[86] If part of what is meant by the experience of the sublime is to be transported out of oneself, then it was indeed, as Michel Fuchs avers, the condition of everyday life in colonial Ireland.

From the earliest paintings, James Barry's work represents a sustained engagement with these antinomies of Irish experience. 'Barry, in his religion', wrote the sarcastic Richard Payne Knight, 'was a zealous and, in some respects, bigoted Romanist – though his writings breathe nothing but universal toleration.' This was meant as a withering criticism, but it could well be a vindication of Barry's lifelong attempt to reconcile the embattled culture of his native Catholic background with universalist republican principles. Payne Knight proceeds to accuse Barry of falling into that habit which is most inimical to the creativity of artists, 'the continual imitation of themselves': '[He decided] to exhibit himself as a martyr; which he did by affecting extreme poverty and distress, borne with a spirit that preferred every excess of human misery to the humiliation of dependence, or the meanness of solicitation.'[87] Payne Knight's ire, it would seem, is provoked by Barry's determination to confer dignity, rather than servility, on the body in distress. In a similar manner, the wound of Philoctetes leads not to an endless, narcissistic obsession with his own suffering, but to a capacity to identify with others, whether it be Neoptolemus' suffering at the beginning of the play, or the greater good of the Greek polity at the end.[88] As R. C. Jebb writes of the wounded outcast:

The man who retains the most indelible memory of a wrong may be one who still preserves a corresponding depth of sensibility to kindness; the abiding resentment can co-exist with undiminished quickness of gratitude for benefits, and with loyal readiness to believe in promises.[89]

If a subaltern culture is not in a position to emulate the manly self-possession promulgated by hegemonic ideals of *virtú*, then this may not be a weakness but a source of strength. Stoicism on the part of a victim, as we have seen, often amounts to complicity with oppression, an exercise in self-control achieved at the expense of others. As Lessing acutely observed of Philoctetes's refusal to conceal his sufferings: 'if he had been master of his pain, [it] would have confirmed Neoptolemus in his dissimulation', and would never have brought about a change in his condition, or in the moral sensibility of his young aide (*Laokoon*, 32). By addressing the other, Philoctetes paradoxically empowers himself. Nor is it sufficient that in this exchange 'the other' remain aloof, registering the sentimental response of pity but not the urge to do something to alleviate suffering – 'They only pitied me', Philoctetes observes ruefully, but they took no remedial action: 'in vain I prayed / that they would bear me to my native soil / For none would listen' (*Philoctetes*, 106). It is in this sense, as we have seen, that the spectator in front of Barry's painting is expected to stand in for the absent Neoptolemus, who sees the plight of the injured body as belonging not just to the newly emerging private sphere of sentiment and charity, but to the public sphere of justice and social policy. The spectator is not spirited away, as the aesthetics of absorption would have it, but remains a physical presence, an actual citizen located in the public space in front of the canvas. The aesthetic no longer provides an analgesic for art, but exposes the political as well as the existential reality of the body in pain.

PART II

Sympathy and the sublime

3

The sympathetic sublime: Edmund Burke, Adam Smith, and the politics of pain

> Men are not tied to one another by papers and seals. They are led to associate by resemblances, by conformities, by sympathies. It is with nations as with individuals.
>
> Edmund Burke, 'Letters on a Regicide Peace'

> [Burke's] writings on India are the most sophisticated and moving elaboration on the idea of sympathy – the means through which one develops in oneself a feeling for another person or collectivity of persons.
>
> Uday Singh Mehta, *Liberalism and Empire*

In his *The Theory of Moral Sentiments* (1759), Adam Smith notes with a certain mordant wit that intense bodily pain does not lend itself to the ennobling effects of great tragedy, or indeed to any dignified mode of conduct: 'The loss of a leg may generally be regarded as a more real calamity than the loss of a mistress. It would be a ridiculous tragedy, however, of which the catastrophe was to turn up on a loss of that kind.'[1] For this reason, he takes grave exception to those Greek tragedies which attempted to excite compassion through the representation of physical suffering, particularly as exemplified by the emotional excess of the wounded hero, Philoctetes, in Sophocles's drama, who 'cries out and faints from the extremity of his sufferings' (*Moral Sentiments*, 30):

> We are disgusted with that clamourous grief which, without any delicacy, calls upon our compassion with sighs and tears and importune lamentations. But we reverence that reserved, that silent and majestic sorrow, which discovers itself only in the swelling of the eyes, in the quivering of the lips and cheeks, and in the distant, but affecting, coldness of the whole behaviour. (*Moral Sentiments*, 24)

Written in the aftermath of the battle of Culloden, it is tempting to conclude that in the prostrate figure of Philoctetes, Smith sees the image of a culture itself stretched on the political equivalent of the rack. Unlike Swift or, as we shall see, Burke, the logic of such an analogy in the case of Smith is that the old Gaelic order, the shattered culture of the Highlands (and by extension Ireland), should not protest too much, or dwell on its suppurating wounds. Instead, it should cultivate an emotional reserve and a stoic-like bearing in keeping with the requirement of the empire of sentiments, thereby allowing Scotland to avail itself of the considerable commercial and political benefits of an expanding British empire.

One of the ironies of the formation of Britishness in the late eighteenth and early nineteenth centuries was that Irish national narratives were invoked by Scottish writers as models of successful imperial integration. In his well-known preface to the Waverley novels, Walter Scott paid tribute to the novels of Maria Edgeworth for completing what no legislation or coercion could achieve: consolidating the Act of Union at the level of sentiments as well as politics and commerce:

I felt [wrote Scott] that something might be attempted for my own country, of the same kind with that which Miss Edgeworth so fortunately achieved for Ireland – something which might introduce her natives to those of her sister kingdom in a more favourable light than they had been placed hitherto, and tend to procure sympathy for their virtues and indulgence for their foibles.[2]

The key word here is sympathy: the Union, like the Tin Man in the *Wizard of Oz*, only lacked a heart, and it was left to the secret springs of sympathy to work their way through the sister kingdoms to effect a union of hearts as well as minds. This process was greatly facilitated by an elaborate, new philosophical theory of sympathy, elaborated by the Scottish Enlightenment, and receiving its most influential expressions in the moral philosophy of David Hume and Adam Smith. If this laid the intellectual foundations for a Union of affections and what may be called 'the colonial self', philosophical theory and cultural practice in Ireland pulled in a different direction, towards an aesthetics of terror and disintegration as exemplified by Burke's *Enquiry into the Sublime and Beautiful*. As we shall see, the irony of Walter Scott's looking to Ireland was that it pointed to the instability rather than the stability of the Union, fomenting an aesthetics of extreme situations which challenged and disrupted the integrationist narratives of the Scottish Enlightenment. After all, it was Maria Edgeworth herself who conceded that the harsh political realities of Ireland were such in the early nineteenth century as to militate against the very protocols of narrative order: 'The truth is too strong for fiction, and on all sides pulls it asunder.'[3]

PHILOSOPHY AND CULTURAL IDENTITY

> Even reason and prudence themselves depend, if not for their substance, yet certainly for their colour and bent on our native constitution and complexion.
> (*A Note-book of Edmund Burke*)

In the preface to his first published book, *A Vindication of Natural Society* (1756), Edmund Burke raised an issue that was to preoccupy him for much of his life: the possibility that reason operated by a cunning often not of its own making. Burke's suspicion of reason was not that it was abstract but that it was not abstract enough, for even the most advanced intellectual system-building might conceal within itself 'some Under-plot, of more Consequence than the apparent Design'.[4] It is not just, as Hume would have it, that reason is the slave of the passions but that it may be underscored, whether consciously or not, by some hidden or recondite narratives at odds with the imperatives of its apparently rational arguments.[5] As Burke himself put it in the *Enquiry*: 'It is, I own, not uncommon to be wrong in theory and right in practice; and we are happy that it is so. Men often act right from their feelings, who afterwards reason but ill on them from principle' (*Enquiry*, 53). The *Vindication* itself is a case in point, for even though it is Burke's only 'purely theoretical consideration of politics', the author himself admitted that 'it was not his Design to say all that could possibly be said' (*Vindication*, 9).[6] This has to do, of course, with the notorious irony of the text, and the multiple voices which Burke was not averse to using throughout his career, even in his most public pronouncements: 'he who was master of an irony so grave', as William O'Brien described him, 'as sometimes to be taken by more than the simple for sober earnest'.[7]

It is in this sense that theory, even of the most intellectually rigorous kind, may often be ventriloquizing other recalcitrant areas of experience which do not lend themselves to, or cannot be effectively expressed within, the ordinances of pure reason.[8] At one level, the limitations of theory may have to do with the cultural conditions of reason itself, with the fact that, as Marx put it, 'even the most abstract categories, despite their validity – precisely because of their abstractness – for all epochs, are nevertheless, in the specific character of this abstraction... themselves likewise a product of historical relations'. For Marx, theory was the product of the most advanced stages of historical development, providing modern societies with the universal categories to map out the lineaments of the historical epochs that preceded them.[9] Whatever about the association of universal reason with progress, Marx's point that the emergence of theory, even in its most abstract or universal form, is culturally specific, and hence an expression, however oblique, of the society which gave rise to it, is central to the argument of this chapter.

A contemporary version of this cultural grounding of theory may be found in Fredric Jameson's call for a 'social reading' of philosophical projects or schools of thought which would construe them as 'a symbolic index' of the 'different national contexts' in which they arise. Hence, for Jameson, the critiques of totalization and the relentless 'de-centring' strategies of French post-structuralism make sense against a backdrop of the historic weight of the French Left, and the powerful centralizing forces at work in French society. By contrast, such critiques of 'the centre', and espousals of fragmentation and 'molecular' politics, are singularly inappropriate in the United States, where fragmentation is already the social norm, and the Left is destabilized without the disintegrating logic of post-structuralism. Jameson concludes that 'there is therefore a real problem about the importation and translation of theoretical polemics which have a quite different semantic content in the national situation in which they originate'.[10]

It is within this framework of philosophy as national narrative that I propose to look at eighteenth-century Irish and Scottish philosophy, particularly as represented by the aesthetics of Edmund Burke and the ethical theory of Adam Smith and, to a lesser extent, David Hume. Notwithstanding their direct and highly influential engagements with the various philosophical discourses out of which they emerged, their abiding intellectual concerns can also be seen as densely mediated responses to the acute crises of identity precipitated in their respective cultures by the formation of modern Britain. In replacing 'sovereignty' with a concept of identity based on 'exchange' in both his economics and moral philosophy, for example, and in arguing that the advantages to be gained from free trade more than outweighed the loss in political sovereignty, Adam Smith, according to Michael J. Shapiro, was

> fitting a model of home rule to the need for access to markets... [and] was responding in part to the turmoil produced in connection with the Scottish-English Union, which had been effected in 1707 after a tumultuous national debate in Scotland. The debate had been primarily concerned with the degree of compensation to be gained through an increased trading advantage to be had by giving up a large measure of Scottish sovereignty.

The benefits of 'exchange' surfaced in Smith's moral philosophy as the theory of sympathy, according to which the self is constituted through networks of sentiment or 'fellow-feeling'. The individual, therefore, is reconstituted not as 'the sovereign, self-contained owner or author of actions, but, rather, [as] a dynamic, reflexive, immanently social system of symbolic exchanges'.[11] In this respect, it is striking, as Nicholas Xenos has observed, that the primary orientation of sympathy in Scottish culture was not towards pain and suffering but towards pleasure, motivated by a desire to emulate the wealth of others. As Hume expressed it:

> There is certainly an original satisfaction in riches deriv'd from that power, which they bestow, of enjoying all the pleasures of life; and as this is their very nature and essence, it must be the first source of all the passions, which arise from them. One of the most considerable of these passions is that of love or esteem in others, which therefore proceeds from a sympathy with the pleasure of the possessor. (*Treatise*, 414)[12]

It was as if, looking at their wealthy neighbour over the border, the Scottish intelligentsia were determined that their culture too could profit from the exchange-value of sympathy in a new expanding empire.

If the cordial influence of sympathy was pre-eminent among the responses of the Scottish Enlightenment to integration within the Union, Burke's theory of the sublime, with its emphasis on terror and the threat of self-annihilation, articulated a less optimistic Irish response to the embrace of empire. That Burke's Irish origins hovered in the background of the reception accorded in England to the *Enquiry* is clear from the comments of contemporary observers, such as Richard Payne Knight's patronizing dismissal of its central concern with terror and pain as 'a stout instance of confusion even with every allowance that can be made for the ardour of youth in an Hibernian philosopher of five and twenty'.[13] As Nicholas Robinson writes of Burke, the rhetoric of excess and wildness associated with the sublime linked it irrevocably with the extremes of his Irishness:

> For some years the words 'Sublime and Beautiful' (offered as an alternative to phrases like 'arrah' and 'by Jasus' and the depiction of that Irish icon, the potato) would suffice to identify him [i.e. Burke] in caricature. Nor would this reference be intended as flattering: there was a strong anti-intellectual element in society which would see such pretentious flights of fancy as adding to Burke's crime of Irishness and adventurism.[14]

This tone is evident in what is perhaps the first mention of Burke in public life. In 1763, when his employment as private secretary to the Irish Chief Secretary at Dublin coincided with the first outbreak of agrarian unrest in the form of the Whiteboy agitation in Munster, the robustly Protestant *Freeman's Journal* had occasion to link Burke's aesthetics to his support for the Catholic cause, pointing out that had the Lord Lieutenant not laid the basis for 'refining our language in a certain pension to a certain author':

the Roman Catholics, the Body of the Nation, would have lost a zealous Advocate and Private Agent with G[overnment] and our young S[enators], tho' desirous of distinguishing themselves in Oratory, would have lost the Opportunity of improving from those delicate touches of the Sublime and the Beautiful, with which some particular speeches were bespangled in the last S[ession]...[15]

In what follows, I will argue that the travails of 'the Roman Catholics, the Body of the Nation', the milieu of Burke's own upbringing in the Nagle country of Co. Cork, were indeed abiding, albeit submerged, concerns in the formulation of his aesthetic theory. The attacks on clarity and direct communication in his aesthetic thought may themselves be an apologia of sorts for the effulgence of his own powerful, figurative language, emanating from the kind of unresolved cultural concerns that were often veiled by the force of rhetoric of his political speeches and writings. As we shall see, while Adam Smith's *Theory of Moral Sentiments* was instrumental in negotiating the moral and psychological grounds for a civic investment in colonialism, Burke's *Enquiry* was less sure of its own ground, its concern with terror laying the basis for a fraught engagement with the anxieties of empire, whether generated by religious bigotry of Ireland, the plunder of Warren Hastings in India, or the sordid excesses of British military policy during the American Revolution.

DAVID HUME AND THE COLONIAL SELF

The philosophical theory of sympathy, first given currency by David Hume but receiving its most influential expression in Adam Smith's *The Theory of Moral Sentiments*, was one of the most lasting contributions made by the Scottish Enlightenment to European intellectual culture. In its initial formulation, it may be seen as a peripheral variant of the cult of sensibility which swept France and metropolitan Europe, and the more low-keyed doctrine of benevolence associated with Shaftesbury, Butler, and the British 'moral sense' school of philosophy in the early eighteenth century. The newly found emphasis on feeling, emotion and sensibility represented the first systematic attempt to ground ethics in a psychological or materialist outlook on life. The secularization of morality was prefigured in the work of political theorists such as Machiavelli, Hobbes, and Mandevillle, but in their *realpolitik* versions of a fallen universe, goodness was at most on the side of the angels, and was all but absent from the human world. Without God, life was indeed, as Hobbes feared, 'nasty, brutish and short' – unless, that is, the strong arm of Leviathan, and the awesome power of the state, intervened. In marked contrast to this, the cult of sensibility presented, for the first time since antiquity, a prospect of a human agent untainted by original sin, whether in a traditional religious form, or in its new mechanistic, self-interested guise, the unsatiated force of egoism.[16] The importance of the theory of sympathy was that it gave a pronounced social inflection to the inner-directed, individualist orientations of sensibility: instead of feeling, it stressed 'fellow-feeling', a form of experience which did not exist in isolation but depended on a relationship with others.[17] If the eighteenth century, as John B. Radner has observed, was pivotal in developing modern concepts of psychology, moral philosophy, and literary criticism, 'few concepts were as central as sympathy to what is most original and enduringly significant about eighteenth-century British thought in all these areas'.[18] The question that concerns us here is why the theory of sympathy and the particular aesthetic version of the sublime which derived from it were not just British but, in very different forms, distinctively *Scottish* and *Irish* contributions to modern philosophy.

Tom Nairn has remarked that in laying the intellectual foundations for what later came to be known as the social sciences, it is no coincidence that the great figures of the Scottish Enlightenment such as Adam Ferguson, John Millar, William Robertson, and Adam Smith, were preoccupied with theories of social development, making immense contributions to our understanding of 'how society in general can be expected to progress out of barbarism into refinement':

Scottish Enlightenment thinkers were capable of this astonishing feat because, obviously, they had actually experienced much of the startling process they were trying to describe. Not only that: the old 'barbaric' world was still there, close around them.[19]

I would suggest that for similar reasons, the theory of sympathy came to the forefront of Scottish (and as we shall see, later 'Celtic') social theory. It derives from a profound cultural experience of displacement and a lived experience of the continual presence of another within one's own sphere of existence. The Act of Union of 1707, and the devastation of Highland culture after the Battle of Culloden in 1746, are the main political factors which presided over this renegotiation of cultural identity in Scotland. Pared down to its essentials, the theory of sympathy involves a denial of the boundaries of the isolated self, and an intense awareness of, and susceptibility towards, the experiences of another. Though directed mainly at resolving the antinomies of personal identity, there is a sense in which the theory of sympathy also expressed the profound cultural predicament of Scottish culture as a whole. Undue pressure from the influence of another, particularly an imperial other, threatened to erode rather than to strengthen a sense of identity in a new political and economic dispensation.

It is perhaps in this light that we should consider the nervous speculations on the self and personal identity which break through the surface equanimity of David Hume's 'common sense' philosophy. In a well-known passage in *A Treatise of Human Nature*, Hume asserts that

> There are some philosophers, who imagine we are every moment intimately conscious of what we call our SELF; that we feel its existence and its continuance in existence; and are certain, beyond evidence of a demonstration, both of its perfect identity and simplicity... Unluckily all these positive assertions are contrary to that very experience, which is pleaded for them, nor have we any idea of *self*, after the manner it is here explain'd. (*Treatise*, 299)

As many commentators have pointed out, Hume here is not so much denying the existence of the self as the possibility that we may entertain an *idea* of it, or enjoy privileged access to it through the immediacy of inner experience. Hence his famous declaration that consciousness can never catch itself off guard: it is always aware of something in particular, but never aware of itself:

> Self or person is not any one impression, but that to which our several impressions and ideas are suppos'd to have a reference... For my part, when I enter most intimately into what I call *myself*, I always stumble on some particular perception or other, of heat or cold, light or shade, love or hatred, pain or pleasure. I can never catch *myself* at any time without a perception, and can never observe anything but the perception. (*Treatise*, 299–300)

By denying that introspection of the Cartesian sort is the ultimate source of our knowledge of ourselves, and hence of personal identity, Hume lays the basis for his argument that the self is socially constituted and mediated through our understanding of others. The problem of discerning continuity and persistence among the 'bundle of perceptions' that comprises the self is no different in principle from the difficulties we face in attributing identity to others: it is not that we infer their inner life from first-hand experience of our own but that we discern in ourselves *the same things* we recognize in them. This is facilitated by the operation of *sympathy*, which establishes a natural affinity between ourselves and others: 'nature has preserv'd a great resemblance among all human creatures, and that we never remark any passion or principle in others, of which, in some degree or other, we may not find a parallel in ourselves' (*Treatise*, 368).

In support of his argument that 'identity' can persist while its constituent 'bundle of perceptions' or ideas change, Hume draws upon the telling analogy of political identity:

> In this respect, I cannot compare the soul more properly to any thing than to a republic or commonwealth, in which the several members are united by the reciprocal ties of government and subordination, and give rise to other persons, who propagate the same republic in the incessant changes of its parts. And the same individual republic may not only change its members, but also its laws and constitutions; in like manner the same person may vary his character and disposition, as well as his impressions and ideas, without losing his identity. (*Treatise*, 309)

In his otherwise illuminating discussion of this passage, Joel Weinsheimer contends that the political entity Hume has in mind is England,[20] but it would seem that Scotland and its ambiguous role in the emerging commonwealth of Great Britain is the more likely candidate. The fear of losing one's political identity in the kind of 'incessant changes' that transform not only individuals but 'laws and constitutions' calls to mind the Williamite Settlement, but given Hume's acute uneasiness over his Scottishness, the aspects of the settlement with which he was most concerned were those which pertained to the Act of Union between Scotland and England in 1707. An Enlightenment figure who acquired notoriety for his breezy irreverence towards religion and who evinced outright hostility to 'papist superstition', Hume was nevertheless torn both personally and politically between his progressive Whig principles and a lingering Tory affection for the Stuart family.[21] It was perhaps the uncertainty of his own deepest political allegiances which led him to confide to his friend Gilbert Elliott during the height of anti-Scottish sentiments sparked off by the *North Briton* controversy and the Wilkes campaign of the mid-1760s:

> I do not believe there is one Englishman in fifty, who, if he heard that I broke my Neck to night, would not be rejoic'd with it. Some hate me because I am not a Tory, some because I am not a Whig, some because I am not a Christian, and all because I am a Scotsman. Can you seriously talk of my continuing an Englishman? Am I, or are you, an Englishman? Will they allow us to be so? Do they not treat with Derision our Pretensions to that Name, and with Hatred our just Pretensions to surpass & to govern them?[22]

These considerations should lead us to question John Mullan's observation that while Hume's essays and historical writings are clearly influenced by his national context, this does not extend to his philosophical works, on account of their generalized and more abstract nature.[23] Kenneth Simpson is more forthright in his judgement when he avers in relation to Hume that 'the Philosopher's abiding concern with identity (like that of Smith and Hutcheson) is a reflection at least in part of the national crisis of identity',[24] and that his structuring of the self in terms of the body politic was more than simply a casual analogy. The mention of Adam Smith in this context, moreover, is salutary, for in his *The Theory of Moral Sentiments*, a work heavily indebted to Hume, we encounter perhaps the most sustained contribution by the Scottish Enlightenment to bring the concept of the self into line with what might be termed, to borrow Freud's phrase,[25] 'the psychic economy' of colonialism.

STRANGER ON THE SHORE: ADAM SMITH AND THE EMPIRE OF SENTIMENTS

The pleasure of a stranger, for whom we have no friendship, pleases us only by sympathy. (David Hume, *A Treatise of Human Nature*)

It is true, of course, that the progress and optimism which characterized the Scottish Enlightenment should make us very wary of one-dimensional versions of cultural domination and imperial control. It was indeed an Enlightenment, and the sense of progress was far from being an illusion, even if it was, at times, qualified in the writings of Adam Ferguson and, indeed, Smith himself.[26] But even those who benefited most from the rapid social and economic development that followed the Union, and who were willing to trade political sovereignty (in Shapiro's terms outlined above) for the benefit of economic exchange, still ran the risk of a loss of cultural face and an exposure to ridicule, instead of the growth in status and esteem that might have been expected to accompany social advancement. In other words, they still had to cope, as Robert Crawford and others have pointed out, with the question of prejudice and cultural condescension, and a marked discrepancy between economic success and social prestige.[27] The aspirations of upwardly mobile Scots to Britishness, and their visibility in high places at the metropolitan centre, were bitterly contested by powerful interests within English society, most notably those factions within the Whigs who, mobilizing in the 1760s under the popular leadership of John Wilkes, looked to Englishness, and the proud tradition of the 'free-born Englishman', as the true guardian of liberty. It was not too difficult to see the grounds for complaint. Following the Act of Union, and particularly the brutal suppression of the Jacobite uprising in 1745–6, a successful policy of integrating Scotland into the Union had to deploy the carrot as well as a stick. As Linda Colley expresses it:

> This was to be the other side of forcible integration: allowing Scots to compete for advancement in the state on a wider scale and on more favourable terms than ever before. And it was the recognition that this was happening, in fact, that made English outsiders like John Wilkes and his followers so furious. In their prejudiced but not unperceptive eyes, more opportunities for Scots meant fewer perks for Englishmen.[28]

Framed against this background of a double-edged Enlightenment, an experience of both loss and gain, the theory of sympathy adumbrated in Adam Smith's *The Theory of Moral Sentiments* may be seen as a cultural manifesto, however modest its own perception of its political importance. On the face of it, the notion of sympathy would appear to be the ideal means of understanding other societies, and conducting cross-cultural dialogue. As we have observed above, one of the signal achievements of the Scottish school was to shift moral philosophy away from its grounding in inner experience towards social interaction. Hence Hume's and Smith's insistence that sympathy, as a social relation of 'fellow-feeling', be distinguished from benevolence, pity, or compassion which, for all their concern with others, are still located in the psychology of our make-up as individuals. Sympathy, then, is not just one form of moral sentiment but is the underlying principle of all moral feeling: in Glenn Morrow's succinct formulation, it

> is not the object, but the basis of moral approbation... It is only through the capacity of thus overleaping the bounds of our own individuality that a moral judgement is possible. Sympathy, or this participation in the feelings of others, is the basis of the moral life.[29]

But the question then arises: does sympathy really extend the horizons of an individual person or specific culture, allowing us to view the world through other eyes in a way that positively enriches our own experience? If we attend to the celebrated example which Smith uses to set the scene for his argument at the beginning of *The Theory of Moral Sentiments*, it would seem that even fellow-feeling has clearly defined limits:

> Though our brother is upon the rack, as long as we ourselves are at our ease, our senses will never inform us of what he suffers. They never did, and they never can, carry us beyond our own person, and it is by the imagination only that we can form any conception of what are his sensations. (*Moral Sentiments*, 9)

We cannot actually experience what he is going through: the most we can hope to do is, by an act of imagination, to put ourselves in his situation:

By the imagination we place ourselves in his situation, we conceive ourselves enduring all the same torments, we enter as it were into his body, and become in some measure the same person with him, and thence form some idea of his sensations, and even feel something which, though weaker in degree, is not altogether unlike them. His agonies, when they are thus brought home to ourselves, when we have thus adopted and made them our own, begin at last to affect us, and we then tremble and shudder at the thought of what he feels. (*Moral Sentiments*, 9)

The most salient part of Smith's analysis for our present purposes, however, is when he points out that the operation of sympathy is not all one-way. Just as the feelings of the spectator are modified, so crucially are the feelings of the person on the receiving end of the act of sympathy. He attempts to put himself in our shoes, though with what success when he is stretched out on the rack remains to be seen. However, in the case of sorrow, for example, Smith is right to insist that there is a genuine sense in which an extension of sympathy eases the burden:

The cruelest insult... which can be offered to the unfortunate, is to appear to make light of their calamities. To seem not to be affected with the joy of our companions is but want of politeness; but not to wear a serious countenance when they tell us their afflictions, is real and gross inhumanity. (*Moral Sentiments*, 15)

So the victim at least benefits in this way from an expression of regret or condolence. But what does the person who offers sympathy get out of it? Smith relies here on the acute psychological observation that whatever its unsettling effect, it is always disagreeable to find that we cannot sympathize with an afflicted person, for

instead of being pleased with this exemption from sympathetic pain, it hurts us to find that we cannot share his uneasiness. If we hear a person loudly lamenting his misfortunes, which, however, upon bringing the case home to ourselves, we feel, can produce no such violent effect upon us, we are shocked at his grief. (*Moral Sentiments*, 16)

Likewise, Smith points out, it rankles when we see someone too happy over 'a little piece of fortune', or more tellingly, where humour is concerned, 'when our companion laughs louder or longer at a joke than we think it deserves' – especially when it is his own joke. What grates here is that the self-indulgence of the other person shuts us out, preventing the expression of fellow-feeling. It is at this point that stoicism, perhaps the single most important philosophical influence on Smith's intellectual formation, makes its presence felt. To facilitate the two-way flow of sympathy, it is vital that the object of concern, the wounded party in the case of pain, temper his or her emotions, bringing them into line as much as possible with the more detached feelings of the spectator. This, indeed, is how the expression of sympathy affords relief:

> To see the emotions of their hearts, in every respect, beat time to his own, in the violent and disagreeable passions, constitutes his sole consolation. But he can only hope to obtain this by lowering his passion to that pitch, in which the spectators are capable of going along with him. He must flatten, if I may be allowed to say so, the sharpness of its natural tone, in order to reduce it to harmony and concord with the emotions of those who are about him. (*Moral Sentiments*, 22)

In this, it is possible to see in microcosm the dilemma of Scottish culture in the mid-eighteenth century: it has to adjust itself and curb its excesses so as not to give offence to its more temperate, civilized neighbour. It is fitting that *The Theory of Moral Sentiments* opens with a section 'On Propriety', for Smith was to the forefront of that anxious strain of Scottish patriotic sentiment which sought to remove the impurities of their own native culture in order to present a more acceptable face to English polite society. This period in the mid-eighteenth century saw an intensification of the project of cultural 'improvement' in Scottish intellectual circles, leading to a proliferation of courses on elocution, rhetoric, and belle lettres. Smith's own Lectures on Rhetoric and Belle Lettres delivered at Glasgow in 1751 were pioneering in this respect, and, according to Robert Crawford, lend weight to his claim to be considered not just the founder of modern economics, but also of English literature as an academic discipline.[30] For Smith, an appreciation of the English language brought with it the need to take on board 'Englishness' as part of one's own cultural identity:

> Our words must not only be English and agreeable to the custom of the country but likewise to the custom of some particular part of the nation. This part undoubtedly is formed of the men of rank and breeding... It is the custom of the people that forms what we call propriety, and the custom of the better sort from whence the rules of purity of stile be drawn. As those of the higher rank generally frequent the court, the standard of our language is therefore chiefly to be met with there.[31]

In arguing thus, Smith was at one with other leading members of the Scottish Enlightenment such as Hume, Smollett, and Boswell who also found themselves drawn by the powerful gravitational pull of the high road to London. As John Dwyer has dryly observed of this trend among the Scottish literati:

> Unless it came from the pretty lips of a desirable lass, Boswell regarded the Scottish dialect with disdain. His well-known praise of Scotland in *Humphrey Clinker* notwithstanding, Smollett proposed a scheme for a purified English language that may be viewed as the fulfilment of a long-standing imperialist agenda. If Hume's

acute anxiety over his own Scottish 'impurities' was marginally less xenophobic, it too represented the negative side of the Scottish Enlightenment. The erstwhile champions of forbearance and humanity could be extremely intolerant of anything, including their own heritage, that stood in the way of the advancement of the concept of a polite British community.[32]

If we return to the argument of Smith's *Theory of Moral Sentiments*, we can see that the standards of propriety which it so assiduously endorsed were precisely those belonging to the decorum of polite British society. Not the least important of the psychic mechanisms which effected this was Smith's famous theory of 'the impartial spectator', for an understanding of this goes some way towards explaining how lingering attachments to hearth and homeland are prised loose from their traditional moorings. According to Smith, though sympathy as the language of feeling might appear to be most amenable to personal and intimate relationships, to immediate ties of family, friends, and community, this, in fact, is not how the secret springs of sympathy work their influence through society. If the moral purpose of sympathy is to achieve that self-command and composure that is the true hallmark of virtue, then there is a sense in which this resolve and 'coolness about [our] own fortune' may be jeopardized by local and affective ties, by being too attached, as Burke would have it, to 'our little platoon'. If we revert to the case of our brother on the rack, or someone in the throes of grief, a mere acquaintance, according to Smith, may be of more assistance than a friend, since 'we cannot open to the former all those little circumstances which we can unfold to the latter: we assume, therefore, more tranquillity before him, and endeavour to fix our thoughts on those general outlines of our situation which he is willing to consider' (*Moral Sentiments*, 23). With our friends we are not so worried about losing face and thus have less compunction about offloading our troubles, moaning and groaning about our misfortunes. With a detached spectator, by contrast, we have to stand back and compose ourselves, the prerequisite, Smith contends, for coming to terms with our situation. In this recourse to a seemingly disinterested third party, we have surely the germ of 'the talking cure' involving the offices of a 'stranger' which lies at the basis of psychoanalysis, or psychotherapy in general. It is significant, in this respect, that Smith proceeds to further extend the remit of sympathy to embrace what we would now see as mass society, the comfort of strangers:

We expect still less sympathy from an assembly of strangers, and we assume, therefore, still more tranquillity before them, and always endeavour to bring down our passion to that pitch, which the particular company we are in may be expected to go along with. Nor is this only an assumed appearance: for if we are at all masters of ourselves, the *pretence* of a mere acquaintance will really compose us still more than that of a friend; and that of an assembly of strangers, still more than that of an acquaintance. (*Moral Sentiments*, 29)

The emphasis here is not on what we can do for strangers, but what strangers can do for us.

Hence the emergence of the 'impartial spectator', the 'stranger within' who allows us to stand back and pull ourselves together. The association of this mechanism with the anonymity of mass society helped to develop the economic rationality without which the impersonal forces of the market could not function: as Richard Teichgraber comments, 'Smith observed that in the minds of ordinary people in the eighteenth century, the processes of sales and exchange had yet to be disentangled from personal and concrete social relationships', and the impartial spectator was on hand to ease the pain of this transition to a new commodified social order.[33] Smith's signal achievement at a cultural level was to show how economic progress also brought with it the refinement necessary for the cultivation of the arts, thus laying the basis for what could truly be considered a 'polite and commercial society'. The internalization of the protocols of polite society in this manner transforms the 'native' into 'a man of the world', enabling him to escape the limiting horizons of his own community. As James Macpherson wrote of Highlanders like himself:

Many have now learned to leave their mountains, and seek their fortunes in a milder climate; and though a certain *amor patriae* may sometimes bring them back, they have, during their absence, imbibed enough of foreign manners to despise the customs of their ancestors. Bards have been long disused ... consanguinity is not so much regarded.[34]

There is a certain irony in the fact that the discourse of sympathy, which presents itself initially as an ideal medium of cross-cultural dialogue, ends up through the distancing device of the impartial spectator erasing the identity of one, if not both, parties to the transaction. This, of course, is not as Smith would see it – though the loss of one's culture and political sovereignty might appear to be a high price to pay, the long-term perspective of the impartial spectator prevents a situation arising in which 'the loss or gain of a very small interest of our own, appears to be of vastly more importance ... than the greatest concern of another with whom we have no particular connection' (*Moral Sentiments*, 135). Though this 'other' may in fact reduce us to a subordinate position, it is still in our long-term interest 'to enter by sympathy into the sentiments of the master' and to view matters 'under the same agreeable aspect'. In what could be taken as a gloss on these passages, Smith wrote elsewhere, of Scotland's acquiescence to the Act of Union, that:

> The union was a measure from which infinite Good has been derived to this country. The Prospect of that good, however, must then have appeared very remote and very uncertain. The immediate effect of it was to hurt the interest of every single order of men in the country... No wonder if at that time all orders of men conspired in cursing a measure so hurtful to their immediate interest. The views of their Posterity are now very different; but those views could be seen by but few of our forefathers.[35]

In bringing about this apparently felicitous concord between both parties to the Union, the role of 'impartial spectator' merges imperceptibly with Britishness, in its colonial guise as a synonym for progress, civility, and humanity itself. That the assimilative thrust of Smith's treatise was not confined to the 'Celtic' periphery of Britain in this regard, but extended to the farthest reaches of the empire, is clear from its formative role in fashioning colonial subjects in India into very models of modern British gentlemen. As Gauri Viswanathan points out, when Lord Macauley in his official capacity as a member of the Council of Education set about reforming the Indian school curriculum, pride of place was given to the 'noble Christian sentiments' of Smith's *Moral Sentiments*, alongside Shakespeare, Addison, Bacon, Locke, and others, on the grounds that it was 'the best authority for the truest science of morals which English literature could supply'. Viswanathan adds that Smith's treatise 'remained a central text in the Indian curriculum throughout the nineteenth century, both in government and missionary institutions – the Calcutta University Commission Report of 1919, for instance, still listed it as part of its prescribed course of studies'.[36] In its realignment of the inner life of the subject, the 'impartial' readily evolved into the 'imperial' spectator.

EDMUND BURKE AND THE SYMPATHETIC SUBLIME

> Shall I then vapour in a stoic strain,
> Who, while I boast, must writhe myself for Pain.
> (Burke, 'Epistle to Dr Nugent')

When Adam Smith writes of personal identity that true 'self-government' is that mode of propriety which takes its command from the impartial spectator, acting, as he tellingly puts it, as a 'vicegerent' for a higher authority (*Moral Sentiments*, 130),[37] it is difficult to avoid the conclusion that therein lies a message for any colonized culture stretched on the cultural equivalent of the rack. The importance of detachment and a stoic-like bearing, for Smith, is that it ultimately absolves the spectator of the need to intervene: impartiality provides a rationale for that 'spectatorial aloofness' which, according to John Mullan,[38] is the governing principle of Smith's theory of sympathy. For Edmund Burke, by contrast, it was precisely such restrained expressions of sympathy from those in a position to alleviate distress, and endless passivity among the victims of suffering, which reduced colonized cultures to a state of abjection.[39] In the rapidly deteriorating political circumstances of Ireland in the 1790s, Burke's eye for the exemplary event, particularly as it involved the relapse of the state itself into barbarism, fastened on to the vindictive punishment meted out in 1795 to an Irish soldier, Private James Hyland, who received 100 lashes for refusing as a Catholic to attend Protestant church services at Carrick-on-Suir in Co. Tipperary, where he was quartered. Inveighing against those timorous leaders in the Catholic community who were unmoved by the plight of someone who, after all, shared and suffered for their own cause, Burke fulminated:

If these leading men have so Little Sympathy with those, whose heads are thrust into the Pillory of a Ladder, and whose bodies are torn with whips in their common cause, they well deserve, what most certainly they will feel, to have their own backs well disciplined with the protestant Cat o'nine tails, in order to make some impression on their unsocial and unfeeling Breasts. All the miseries of Ireland have originated, in what has produced all the miseries of India, a servile patience under oppression, by the greatest of all misnomers called prudence.[40]

Whereas the stricken figure of Philoctetes was taken to task by Smith for entreating the sympathies of the spectator and refusing to stifle his complaints, Burke had no compunction about highlighting the agony of suffering, all the more so when it was due to colonial oppression or injustice. This, in his view, was the condition of the native population in Ireland and India, and though in both cases he sought to attribute misrule to the iniquity of the local colonial garrison rather than to the British connection,[41] he was nevertheless clear that fortitude and equanimity on the part of its victims were not the answer to their cruel maltreatment. As if the lacerated body of the soldier Hyland had become an emblem of the entire Catholic nation, Burke argued that his scourging was not just an isolated case, but part 'of the systematic ill-treatment of Catholics'. He concedes that his censures of government oppression may have the effect 'of exciting the people to sedition and revolt', but this would only be reprehensible if the oppression in question was exceptional, rather than the rule:

If [the] oppression... be nothing more than the lapses, which will happen to human infirmity at all times and in the exercise of all power, such complaints would be wicked indeed... but, whenever a hostile spirit on the part of the Government is shewn the Question assumes another form. – This is no casual Errour, no lapse, no sudden surprise...[42]

Some years earlier, in the immediate aftermath of the French Revolution, the image of the lash had been used by one of Burke's closest Irish associates, the Rev. Thomas Hussey, to illustrate the limits of moderation in the face of extreme provocation:

Sublimated however as men's minds are by the *french disease* (as it is not improperly called) one cannot foresee what a continuation of oppressive laws may work upon the minds of people: and those of the Irish Catholics are much altered within my own memory; and they will not in future bear the lash of tirranny and oppression which I have seen inflicted on them, without their resisting or even complaining.[43]

Burke concurred with these sentiments, and as late as December 1796, he was still consumed by the Hyland incident. In a letter to Hussey, he reminds him: 'You remember with what indignation I heard of the scourging of the Soldier at Carrick for adhering to his religious Opinions', and protests that it is impossible to get a hearing for the Irish question in the British Parliament, adding that only 'if the people of Ireland were to be flayed alive by the predominant faction', would their plight receive any notice.[44] The callousness of the authorities in the Hyland affair made it all the more imperative that the leaders of the Catholic cause avoid 'that false and adulterate moderation, which is nothing else but a mode of delivering deluded men, without a struggle, to the violence and intemperance of their enemies'. For this reason, it was vital for the victims of oppression not to 'pass by in Silence any one act of outrage, oppression, and violence that they may suffer, without a complaint and a proceeding suitable to the nature of the wrong'.[45] If this amounted to sedition, Burke pointed out that this was only because the grievances themselves were not exceptional but were inextricably bound up with the overall corruption of the body politic.

These shrill denunciations of the abuse of power, which have more in common with Tom Paine than with Adam Smith, date from the Ireland of the 1790s, and may be seen as responses to a wave of political insurgency that placed the entire countryside on the verge of revolt. As against Adam Smith's ascetic call for the injured party to stifle his or her cries and to put themselves in the place of the impartial spectator, Burke's sympathies were in the reverse order, insisting that there could be no dispassionate gaze in the face of genuine suffering. Referring again to the Hyland incident, he wrote to Hussey:

I am, (you will believe, whatever others may) beyond all men perhaps, a friend to a lenient Course; but my lenitives are, not for pride, cruelty, and oppression, but for those, who are likely to suffer from these vices, in action, under Royal, or Aristocratick or Democratical power. I would not put my Melilot Plaster, on the back of the Hangman, but upon the Skin of the Person who has been torn by his Whips.[46]

In considering suffering through the agitated response of the victim rather than through the eyes of impartial spectator, Burke is drawing on the aesthetics of excess outlined in the *Enquiry*, with its emphasis on terror and scenes of real distress or pain. It is clear that notwithstanding his reputation as a founder of the aesthetics of sensationalism,[47] Burke's unease with the staging of spectacles of pain was already evident, as we have observed, in his earliest writings, particularly as it concerned the aesthetic detachment afforded by the mimetic powers of art. This repudiation of aesthetic distance was carried forward into the *Enquiry* where Burke remarks:

I imagine that we shall be much mistaken if we attribute any considerable part of our satisfaction in tragedy to a consideration that tragedy is a deceit, and its representations no realities. The nearer it approaches the reality, and the further it removes us from all idea of fiction, the more perfect is its power. (*Enquiry*, 47)

What Burke is distancing himself from here is the *sentimental* notion of sympathy, the indulgence in the pathos of distress, which came to be established as a norm of refinement in eighteenth-century bourgeois sensibility.[48] As D. D. Raphael points out, this new aestheticized form of sympathy, which received its full philosophical underpinning in Smith's work, differed in an important sense from its more interventionist, ethical counterpart. This latter corresponds to

sympathy in its most common meaning of compassion; when one feels compassion for the sorrow or the need of another, one is moved to give comfort or help. Sympathy of this kind, serving as a motive of action, promotes a sense of responsibility to share the burden of others. [By contrast] Sympathy in Adam Smith's sense is a socializing agent in a different way,[49]

and is directed towards a third party, towards eliciting the approval or, as it may turn out, the disapproval, of others. Sympathy of this latter sentimental variety lends itself to spectatorial relations, for the onlooker tendering sympathy is not just aware of the victim, but also of the fact that he or she is, in turn, perceived by others, and is subject to their invigilation. When their approval is forthcoming, the expression of sympathy becomes a source of pleasure, if not an end in itself – which is why, to revert to one of Smith's examples cited above, the sentimentalist feels at a loss when deprived of the opportunity to indulge in such displays of refinement. Even when others are not actually present to give their approbation – indeed, this is the ideal situation for Smith – we internalize the gaze of a 'generalised other',[50] thus giving rise to the inner, impartial spectator – 'this abstract man, the representative of mankind' (*Moral Sentiments*, 130) within the breast. The self is thus divided into two components: 'the first, is the spectator [within]... the second, is the agent' engaging in acts of sympathy or charity (*Moral Sentiments*, 113).

This provides the rationale for the 'privatization' of charity or philanthropy ushered in by the age of sentimentalism, in which expressions of sympathy set out to draw attention to the plight of others in need, but end up drawing attention to themselves. This shift in sensibility was not without its critics, however, not least David Hume, who argued somewhat cynically that if sympathy proved so agreeable, then a 'Hospital wou[l]d be a more entertaining Place than a Ball'.[51] Hume is pointing to the danger of solicitations of sympathy being so pleasurable that sensitive souls actively pursue them, becoming connoisseurs of pain in the process. To forestall this criticism, Smith incorporated into the second edition of his *Theory of Moral Sentiments* an explanation to the effect that sympathy was a two-tiered process, the first stage, the apprehension of distress, leading perhaps to discomfort, but the second stage, when there is concord between our response and that of others (if necessary, in the form of 'the spectator within'), leading to pleasure, the glow that radiates from moral righteousness. In this hierarchy of moral sentiments, it is clear that the role of detached spectator takes precedence over the need to engage in remedial action. As John Mullan concludes, sympathy and sociability are thus 'moderated – a product of distance carefully maintained, self-control cannily preserved... [Smith] seeks, in fact, to remove sympathy from the realm of contending passions and interests: a willed uninvolvement precedes sympathetic identification'.[52]

As against Smith's 'willed uninvolvement' and its deference to the stranger, whether without or within, Burke had little doubt that the only genuine solace in times of affliction was that to be had from the ministrations of those closest to us. In one of his earliest surviving letters, he writes to his morose confidant and friend, Richard Shackleton, who was undergoing an acute personal crisis:

If to sympathize with you in all your afflictions and to bear a friendly part in your Sorrows could in any measure alleviate 'em I believe I might claim the merit of being no indifferent Comforter but alas! we every day feel how little that avails and how much greater we will find the number of those that will insult us in our miseries than those will pity us.[53]

This is elucidated in a later letter to Shackleton, in which he emphasizes the importance of sharing our sorrows with friends: 'It may be some Consolation to you, to impart them [i.e. Shackleton's tribulations] and their cause to a friend who tho' he could not remove might partake them – Solamen miseris socios habuisse doloris [i.e. 'A solace to the unhappy to have had companions in grief'].'[54] Burke is sceptical about exhortations to seek reassurance in times of need from 'the Sayings of Philosophers', particularly those of the stoics,[55] and this leads to his expressing reservations about stoic responses to distress in general:

Not that I am a bit displeas'd at your manner of writing I only lament the Cause of it, the Stile of the heart tho ever so melancholy is more agreeable to me than a forc'd Calmness, which only serves to aggravate your own affliction and keep me ignorant of it – indulge then your Sorrows I beg you in what you write, to me... I cannot thoroughly sympathize with you, I cannot make your Case my own 'till I am informed of its Cause.[56]

Some years later, when Burke was facing rejection from some of his closest friends following his bitter quarrel with Lord Hamilton, he wrote that one of Hamilton's greatest faults was that 'he never in reality did comprehend even in Theory, what Friendship or affection was; being, as far as I was capable of observing, totally destitute of either friendship or enmity; but rather inclined to *respect* those who treat him ill'. Burke certainly could not be reproached on this account. With regard to those fastidious friends who sought to be impartial throughout the whole acrimonious episode, he wrote that 'I should be just as well pleased that they totally condemned me, as that they should say that there were faults on both sides, or that it was a disputable Case, as I hear is[,] I cannot forbear saying, the affected Language of some persons.' By the same token, he wrote to Monck Mason, he could not affect an air of diffidence, for such calmness under duress could be taken as a tacit acceptance of one's own guilt: 'You will excuse me for this heat, which will in spite of me attend and injure a just cause whilst Common judgments look upon coolness, as a proof of innocence though it never fails to go along with guilt and ability.'[57] It was only in the face of what he considered utter betrayal by his friends that Burke espoused calmness and 'cold neutrality' as the lesser of two evils, for to do otherwise would contaminate the very idea of friendship, as happened in the case of his painful breach with Charles Fox in the aftermath of the French Revolution.[58]

In Burke's 'anguish of spectatorship', as Sara Suleri describes it,[59] an impassive response to distress in others is not a sign of impartiality or 'stoic self-command', but rather of complicity in the face of suffering. Burke saw 'absolute indifference and tranquillity of the mind' (*Enquiry*, 93) as the domain of abstract inquiries such as mathematical speculation, but placed in those precarious situations which confront us with the terrors of the sublime, we are 'alarmed into reflexion' (*Reflections*, 175), and convulsed into action. Hence his protest, in the speech on Fox's East India Bill, against those who sought to play down the atrocities committed in India by reporting them in an even-handed, dispassionate manner:

> I am sensible that a cold style of describing actions, which appear to me in a very affecting light, is equally contrary to the justice due to the people, and to all genuine human feeling about them... It has been said (and, with regard to one of them, with truth) that Tacitus and Machiavel, by their cold way of relating enormous crimes, have in some sort appeared not to disapprove them; that they seem a sort of professors of the art of tyranny, and that they corrupt the minds of their readers, by not expressing the detestation and horror, that naturally belong to horrible and detestable proceedings.[60]

Though a considerable part of the rhetorical force of Tom Paine's powerful attack on the *Reflections* in *The Rights of Man* lay in the imputation that Burke had reduced ethics to mere aesthetic effects – 'He is not affected by the reality of distress touching his heart, but by the showy resemblance striking his imagination'[61] – in fact, Burke's aesthetics of engagement questioned the very basis of detached, spectatorial responses to tragedy. As Frans de Bruyn succinctly describes it, writing of the related question of the response to landscape, Burke's aesthetic paradigm demands 'full engagement in society as a regulator of its "infinitely diversified combinations of men and affairs"; nor does he regard such engagement as compromising the gentleman's capacity for impartiality and disinterest'.[62]

These are the considerations which lie behind one of the arguments in the *Enquiry* which drew most criticism from Burke's contemporaries, namely, that words have a greater expressive power than images in conveying the emotional intensity of the sublime. Images, for Burke, as we have observed,[63] allow for a mode of representation which is at one remove from reality, and which thus lend themselves to the detached stance of the spectator, in marked contrast to the capacity of words to capture vivacity and emotion: 'I know several who admire and love painting, and yet who regard the objects of their admiration in that art, with coolness enough, in comparison of that warmth with which they are animated by affecting pieces of poetry or rhetoric. Among the common sort of people, I never could perceive that painting had much influence on their passions' (*Enquiry*, 61). It is in this sense that the sublime goes beyond representation, in that it cannot be mapped out by the mimetic strategies involved in conventional, literal descriptions of the world. Language, therefore, shares with sympathy the capacity to generate a form of animated solidarity that picks up where dispassionate 'description' leaves off: 'We yield to sympathy, what we refuse to description... by the contagion of our passions, we catch a fire already kindled in another, which probably might never have been struck out by the object described' (*Enquiry*, 175–6). Burke proceeds to point out that 'very polished languages, and such as are praised for their clearness and perspicacity' are deficient in this quality, whereas 'the oriental tongues, and in general the languages of the most unpolished peoples' are fired by it. The irony in the case of the *Enquiry* is that, notwithstanding its abstract intellectual tone, the logic of its arguments, at least where Ireland and India are concerned, is to sympathise with 'the languages of the most unpolished peoples'.[64] As he expresses it, there is always 'a moving tone of voice, an impassioned countenance, an agitated gesture, which affect independently of the things about which they are exerted' (*Enquiry*, 175).

This has important consequences for what may be termed 'the sympathetic sublime', for contrary to the primitivist tendency to construe feelings as raw, untutored responses to nature, Burke espoused what has been described as a 'Baroque' theory of the passions, in which feelings relate in an almost allegorical fashion to the situations that give rise to them.[65] Though his use of the word 'contagion' seems to denote a direct, unmediated transfer of sentiments, akin to a natural, physiological process, in fact the opposite is the case, for obscurity, artifice and incompleteness – the language of 'metaphors, and allegories' (*Enquiry*, 18) – are the conditions of such intense communion. The shock of the sublime is not simply to induce intense sensation; it is to ensure that 'we are alarmed *into reflexion*' (*Reflections*, 175: my italics). The sublime is that which disrupts custom in the sense of unthinking, 'sluggish' habit (*Reflections*, 140, 181), and thus contains a reflective and critical element from the outset, notwithstanding its charged, almost visceral impact.[66] As in Herder's description of Philoctetes noted above,[67] language becomes more, rather than less, mediated in moments of sympathetic contagion, and it is this mediation which also militates against spectatorial aloofness.[68] Crucially, this element of 'reflexivity' or mediation which disrupts the continuum of our own culture also facilitates the extension of sympathy from our own familiar circles to societies and peoples different from ourselves, as in Burke's own impassioned identification with the distant culture of India. In this case, the 'contagion' of the sympathetic sublime enabled vital expressions of cross-cultural solidarity without recourse to the abstract rationality of universal rights, the ethical projections of an 'impartial spectator'.[69] It is as if, paradoxically, looking through a glass darkly becomes the means of drawing closer to the objects of our deepest concern.

The disjointed, convulsive aesthetics of shock precipitated by the sublime allows sympathy to cut across radical cultural differences, in what might be seen as a proto-modernist version of montage. For Burke, the sublime consists in abrupt or 'quick transition(s)', since 'whatever either in sights or sounds makes the transition from one extreme to the other easy, causes no terror, and consequently can be no cause of greatness' (*Enquiry*, 83):

Thus are two ideas as opposite as can be imagined reconciled in the extremes of both; and both in spite of their opposite nature brought to concur in producing the sublime. And this is not the only instance wherein the opposite extremes operate equally in favour of the sublime, which in all things abhors mediocrity. (*Enquiry*, 81)

This could be a description of the 'pathos' or emotional intensity of Eisenstein's theory of montage, as described by Gilles Deleuze:

It is no longer a case of the formation and progression of the opposites themselves, following the twists of a spiral, but of the transition from one opposite to the other, or rather into the other, along the spans: the leap into the opposite. There is not simply the opposition... [but] the transition of the one into the other, and the sudden upsurge of the other out of the one. There is not simply the organic union of opposites, but the pathetic passage of the opposite into its contrary.[70]

This then is the collision of opposites, the 'spark' in Burke's terminology, which 'transfuses their passions from one breast to another' (*Enquiry*, 44), and which generates the imaginative leap, at an ethical or sympathetic level, across two radically different cultures. It is possible to see this, perhaps, as a development of the idea of 'transport', a force which carries us beyond or outside ourselves, which featured prominently in Longinus's characterization of the sublime.[71] In keeping with Burke's reading of sympathy, this did not necessarily involve the eclipse of the self but by a dual process may even invigorate it, the mind appropriating to itself some of the power of the force – the originally incommensurable 'other' – which challenged it. It is in this sense, as Sara Suleri observes, that sympathy across a colonial divide 'is a dynamic of alienation rather than of association, in that it constitutes the empowerment of the spectator at the expense of the spectacle, unleashing an economy of gain and loss at the centre of aesthetic experience'.[72]

In its classic formulations in Scottish Enlightenment ethics, the operation of sympathy presupposes communal boundaries and a common culture, or, if it extends beyond this, a renunciation of local or national allegiances in favour of a 'generalized other', or 'impartial' standard of humanity.[73] In both cases it involves homogeneity and sameness, either of our own community or that of a universal human nature. Burke's procedure, by contrast, is to prevent the absorption of the (concrete) particular into the (abstract) universal by bringing two particulars into contact through the sympathetic shock of the sublime. Hence the passion of local allegiances – the love of 'our little platoon' – is not restricted to our own community but brought to bear on our concern for justice in other cultures, by virtue of their particularity or difference from us. The need for this sympathetic contagion is especially evident in the case of those societies in which difference itself is endangered, and in which the survival of their own culture is threatened by the advance of 'progress' or 'modernity', conceived in hierarchical, stadial terms. Unlike the cosmopolitanism of the Scottish Enlightenment, this cross-cultural solidarity does not require detachment from, or a renunciation of, one's local habitation, but in fact presupposes deep, and in Burke's own case, virtually clandestine cultural allegiances. Though alien and remote, India was not totally foreign to him. In his letter to Sir Hercules Langrishe in 1792 about the state of Ireland, he alludes to the Whiteboy agitation in the early 1760s: 'my heart goes with what I have written. Since I could think at all, those have been my thoughts. You know that thirty-two years ago [i.e. 1760] they were as fully matured in my mind as they are now.' But then, he explains, in recent years he has been 'interrupted' by an undertaking 'which I have not yet finished, in favour of another distressed people, injured by those who have vanquished them, or stolen a dominion over them' – that is, his crusade against the East India Company.[74] It is as if the energies of one were transferred to the other, and then used in turn to revitalize the original, a form of sympathetic contagion in which, true to Burke's own fervour, the 'opposite extremes operate equally in favour of the sublime, which in all things abhors mediocrity' (*Enquiry*, 81). There is, of course, a universal of sorts implied here, in the sense of a shared experience of suffering but, as we shall see below, Burke was concerned to invest even this common standard with a radical particularity, discerning in the most elemental experiences of pain the inscriptions of cultural difference.

AESTHETICS AND ENGAGEMENT: THE CRITIQUE OF DETACHMENT

Though Burke's *Enquiry* has often been taken as simply a further, empiricist refinement of this aesthetic of terror, its main thrust is, in fact, to question some of its most basic assumptions. For one thing, Burke seeks at the outset to dissociate firmly the idea of enjoyment from scenes of distress by introducing an important distinction between 'pleasure' and 'delight'. Pleasure is a positive feeling, bound up with the agreeable experience of 'the beautiful', while delight is a 'relative' or negative feeling which follows the removal or easing of pain, and is thus constitutive of the experience of the sublime:

> Whatever is fitted in any sort to excite the ideas of pain, and danger, that is to say, whatever is in any sort terrible, or is conversant about terrible objects, or operates in a manner analogous to terror, is a source of the *sublime*; that is, it is productive of the strongest emotion which the mind is capable of feeling... When danger or pain press too nearly, they are incapable of giving any delight, and are simply terrible: but at certain distances, and with certain modifications, they may be, and they are delightful, as we every day experience. (*Enquiry*, 39–40)

From this it may seem that the removal of pain bears solely on self-preservation and the removal of personal danger, an aspect of Burke's argument that has led some commentators to discern in his theory of the sublime a self-centred aesthetics of individualism indifferent to the welfare of others.[75] This reading derives from the early sections of the *Enquiry*, in which Burke contends that the three basic social passions, 'the three principal links' in 'the great chain of society', are *sympathy*, *imitation*, and *ambition*. 'Imitation', and its related ideas of repetition and copying, is associated with the concept of the beautiful (setting limits, incidentally, to the range of what can be represented or 'imitated'), and 'ambition', with its emphasis on emulation and going beyond what was there before, lends itself clearly to the heroic striving of the sublime.

It is, however, in relation to the key concept of 'sympathy' that the dichotomy between the sublime and the beautiful breaks down. For almost all commentators on the *Enquiry*, sympathy is seen is the sole preserve of the social domain of the beautiful, which would indeed have the effect of confining the sublime to an individualist aesthetic characterized by 'safety' and 'self-preservation'. Hence, for example, having made the accurate observation that the theory of sympathy provides 'an important link between Burke's aesthetics and his political philosophy', Burleigh T. Wilkins proceeds to argue that 'the idea of beauty [in the *Enquiry*] finds its origin in those passions which relate to society, in love, affection, sympathy, and tenderness', thereby excluding the sublime from the socializing effects of sympathy.[76] This point is elaborated from a different perspective by Tom Furniss:

> Although Burke argues that the three principal links in 'the great chain of society' are *sympathy, imitation,* and *ambition*, he adds that sympathy and imitation (which are associated with the beautiful) could never in themselves lead to social improvement... Progress comes, rather, through individual ambition and the 'satisfaction [a man feels] arising from the contemplation of his excelling his fellows'... The sublime, then, is experienced not through sympathy with, but in competition against, and at the *expense* of, other human beings.[77]

While the striving and restlessness associated with ambition are correctly identified with the sublime, it is not clear why sympathy should be seen solely as a stabilizing force and an attribute of the beautiful, rather than a potential source of disruption and social change. As we have seen, Burke initially defined sympathy in the *Enquiry* as that passion whereby 'we enter into the concerns of others', or 'are put in the place of another man, and affected in many respects as he is affected' (*Enquiry*, 44), but he is careful to extend its remit to include the sublime as well as the beautiful: 'this passion [of sympathy] may either partake of the nature of those which regard self-preservation, and turning upon pain may be a source of the sublime; or it may turn upon ideas of pleasure...' (*Enquiry*, 44).[78] The infusion of sympathy with the volatile contagion of the sublime is, in fact, the basis on which Burke takes issue with a pictorialist aesthetic, for while the latter is clearly linked, as we have seen above, to imitation, and hence to the beautiful, the sympathetic sublime gestures beyond pictorial description towards the obscurity and indeterminacy of language:

> Poetry and rhetoric do not succeed in exact description so well as painting does; their business is, to affect rather by sympathy than imitation; to display rather the effect of things on the mind of the speaker, or of others, than to present a clear idea of the things themselves. (*Enquiry*, 172)

Burke is levelling his criticisms here not just at imitation or representation, but at the optical basis of spectacle which, as we have observed, above, treats reality itself as a representation, giving the illusion of presence without participation. For Burke, this voyeuristic detachment is unacceptable: it is through sympathy, he writes, 'that we enter into the concerns of others; that we are moved as they are moved, and *are never suffered to be indifferent spectators of almost anything which men can do or suffer*' (*Enquiry*, 44: my italics). Burke is clearly aware that there is a difference between beholding suffering and suffering ourselves, but his reworking of the sublime in terms of sympathy attempts to close the gap between the two, rather than to open it up. Thus, for example, he acknowledges that immunity from danger is intrinsic to the sublime, but is adamant that this is not due to a self-centred assurance about our own security. It is at most a necessary condition of being able to approach danger in the first place:

> If a man kills me with a sword, it is a necessary condition to this that we should have been both of us alive before the fact; and yet it would be absurd to say, that our being both living creatures was the cause of his crime and of my death. So it is certain, that it is absolutely necessary my life should be out of any imminent hazard before I can take a delight in the sufferings of others, real or imaginary, or indeed in any thing else from any cause whatsoever. But it is a sophism to argue from thence, that this immunity is the cause of my delight either on these or on any other occasions. (*Enquiry*, 48)

The point of undergoing the shock of the sublime, therefore, is not just to alleviate our own suffering, but also that of others. If scenes of distress were too painful to behold, we would shun them and turn our backs on the plight of fellow human beings, 'as, some who are so far gone in indolence as not to endure any strong impression actually do' (*Enquiry*, 46). But if sympathy is brought to bear on the terrors of the sublime, our response to the sufferings of others need not take the form of physical repulsion, callous indifference, or aesthetic enjoyment conceived as an end in itself:

> as our Creator has designed we should be united by a bond of sympathy, he has strengthened that bond by a proportionable delight; *and there most where our sympathy is most wanted, in the distresses of others*... This is not an unmixed delight, but blended with no small uneasiness. The delight we have in such things, hinders us from shunning scenes of misery; and *the pain we feel, prompts us to relieve ourselves in relieving those who suffer*. (*Enquiry*, 46: my italics)

We experience enough 'delight', in other words, to draw closer to the scene, but enough discomfort to do something about it rather than simply stand back and let it happen.

Burke is advocating here an aesthetics of intervention rather than of disengagement. His strictures about the limits of representation in drama come to the fore here, for part of the pleasure in fictive representations is that it absolves us of the need to intervene. This is the basis of his contention in the *Enquiry* that real executions are a source of greater emotional intensity than the 'most sublime and affecting tragedy' (*Enquiry*, 47), for the horror of the actual event elicits genuine sympathy on our part, rather than simply gratifying our senses through the lure of spectacle. By thus demonstrating the 'the comparative weakness of the imitative arts, and proclaim[ing] the triumph of real sympathy (*Enquiry*, 47), Burke concludes that 'we delight in seeing things, which so far from doing, *our heartiest wishes would be to see redressed*' (*Enquiry*, 47: my italics). While mimetic strategies of artistic representation may confirm the detachment of the spectator, Burke is keenly aware that the mass psychology of audiences need not always operate in this forensic way. Through the 'triumph of real sympathy', and a profound identification with the sufferer, the multitude may be galvanized into doing something to redress what they consider a travesty of justice. One of Burke's main achievements as a critic of colonialism in both Ireland and India was to give political expression to this 'triumph of real sympathy', removing the safety barriers of aesthetic distance in order to expose the true horror presented by the colonial sublime.

SORRY FOR YOUR TROUBLE: BURKE, SMITH, AND CROSS-CULTURAL SOLIDARITY

When punishments are inflicted, it is not just the lash they feel, but the disgrace.
(Burke, 'Speech in the Impeachment of Warren Hastings')

Though the sublime is concerned with self-preservation in the face of danger, the relationship with pain may also be bound up with the emulation and striving that attends heroism, particularly as it addresses great public causes.[79] This is the 'patriotic' interpretation of sublimity invoked by Richard Stack against the background of the mobilization of the Volunteer movement in Ireland in the 1780s:

Suppose our country were invaded by a powerful enemy, against whom there was little hope of making a successful stand; and that in this season of public calamity, we should hear a man expressing his fears lest he might be involved in the general ruin which threatened: The most vehement pathos could excite no ideas but those of contempt and disgust. But the noble and disinterested patriot, who at such a crisis should be seen alarmed and terrified, not for his own personal safety, but the salvation of his country, is one of the most glorious objects that can be presented to view; and the passion excited in such a subject, and by such an occasion, might be uttered in language truly sublime.[80]

It is striking that whereas Stack, writing in a patriotic Irish context, sees in resistance to invasion a heroic expression of the sublime, John Baillie, in his earlier treatise on the sublime, written in Britain's 'Augustan age', looks to the ravages of conquest as an ennobling ideal:

The affections unexceptionably sublime, as heroism, or desire of conquest, such as in an Alexander or a Caesar... generally arise... from a desire of power, or passion for fame; or from both... It is not every power which is the ambition of a hero, nor every power which carries the idea of the sublime. A Caligula commanding armies to fill their helmets with cockle-shells, is a power mean and contemptible, although ever so absolute; but suppose an Alexander laying level towns, depopulating countries, and ravaging the whole world, how does the sublime rise, nay although mankind be the sacrifice to his ambition.[81]

For Burke, as we have seen, the rapid transitions which characterize the volatility of the sublime entail that even in the face of overwhelming odds, powerlessness may often be transformed into empowerment ('the mind always claiming to itself some part of the dignity and the importance of the things which it contemplates' (*Enquiry*, 50–1)).[82] The ravages of the conqueror, as Burke was all too aware, may provoke his victims into acts of resistance, their original torpor or quietude being precipitated into violence or fury. It is this sense of foreboding which informs Burke's elaboration of the colonial sublime, particularly as it affected the outrages perpetrated by British misgovernment in India.

Contrasting the different moral and political orientations of Adam Smith's and Edmund Burke's theories of sympathy, Steven Bruhm remarks that the Scottish philosopher ultimately gravitates towards an individualist conception of 'fellow-feeling', whereas Burke is drawn in the opposite direction, towards a communalist sense of sympathy and the self:

Whereas Smith locates individualism at the limits of the imagination, Burke envisions an almost limitless imagination that can create community... Despite his optimism, Smith has brought Enlightenment scepticism [about the extent to which we can imaginatively identify with others' sufferings] to its peak, resulting in individualism; Burke, conversely, overwrites the limited imagination with intersubjective capability.

Bruhm's perceptive analysis is to the point, as we shall see, but it is the far-reaching conclusions he draws from it that are open to question. 'With this new aesthetic' that 'proclaimed the potential imaginative transference of self into other', he writes, a fundamental shift in European intellectual currents took place: 'the unified, sympathetic body was invested with power to close the subject–object gap, and it heralded the migration from what we call the Enlightenment to what we call the Romantic'.[83] There is little doubt that Burke's desire to endow his notion of sympathy with an aesthetic component adds a powerful, imaginative leavening not found in Smith, but it remains to be seen why this should exclude it from the Enlightenment. The assumption here is that Burke exemplified, if not inaugurated, a trend whereby Romantic aesthetics acted as a countervailing current against the Enlightenment, but in the concluding section of this chapter, I hope to show that the logic of Burke's position is in fact to extend the ethical basis of the Enlightenment, bringing the imaginative reach of sympathy to regions excluded from mainstream Enlightenment thought. For Burke, this involved a profound, troubled engagement with the plight of colonized peoples whether in Ireland, India, or America, an extension of cross-cultural solidarity to those cultures that were doomed, according to Enlightenment theories of progress, to the dustbin of history.

According to Adam Smith, since 'we can have no immediate experience of what other men feel', we 'can form no idea of the manner in which they are affected, but by conceiving what we ourselves should feel in the like situation' (*Moral Sentiments*, 9). The result of this is that there will always be a shortfall between the intensity of our own experience of pain, and our capacity to feel for others:

> the emotions of the spectator will still be very apt to fall short of the violence of what is felt by the sufferer. Mankind, though naturally sympathetic, never conceive, for what has befallen another, that degree of passion which naturally animates the person principally concerned. The imaginary change of situation, upon which their sympathy is founded, is but momentary. The thought of their own safety, the thought that they themselves are not really the sufferers, continually intrudes upon them. (*Moral Sentiments*, 21)

It is instructive to compare this not so much with Smith's thought experiment of the prisoner on the rack but with a more vividly realized theatre of pain that impinged directly on British colonial policy, the sufferings of people in India as presented by Burke in his impassioned opening speech on the impeachment of Warren Hastings. On 18 February 1788, in the course of his opening speech, Burke drew on all his powers of rhetoric to recreate for an astonished audience a grotesque picture of the refinements of British cruelty in India. Central to Burke's indictment was his contention, based on the imaginative transfer of sympathy, that, in certain cases, the experience of even the most intense physical pain is not as unbearable as our exposure to the sufferings of those we love. Having described in graphic detail the hideous tortures inflicted on Indians who hid grain for their own subsistence, he continues in an extended passage:

> There are persons whose fortitude could bear their own suffering; there are men who are hardened by their very pains; and the mind rises, strengthened even by the torments of the body, rises with a strong defiance against its oppressor.[84] They were assaulted on the side of their sympathy. Children were scourged almost to

death in the presence of their parents. This was not enough. The son and father were bound close together, face to face, and body to body, and in that situation cruelly lashed together, so that the blow which escaped the father fell upon the son, and the blow which missed the son wound over the back of the parent. The circumstances were combined by so subtle a cruelty, that every stroke which did not excruciate the *sense*, should wound and lacerate the *sentiments* and *affections* of nature. ('Impeachment: Fifth Day', vii, 189, my italics)

As in his rhetorical exploitation of the ultimate transgression of sexual violation in his speech on the murder of Jane McCrea during the American Revolution, and the more famous *mise-en-scène* of the invasion of Marie Antoinette's bedchamber during the French Revolution, Burke then invokes the spectacle of 'virtue in distress',[85] the despoliation of innocent virgins, to bring home to his listeners the literal rapacity of Hastings' rule in India:

On the same principle, and for the same ends, virgins, who had never seen the sun, were dragged from the inmost sanctuaries of their houses; and in the open court of justice, in the very place where security was to be sought against all wrong and all violence (but where no judge or lawful magistrate has long sat, but in their place the ruffians and hangmen of Warren Hastings occupied the bench), these virgins, vainly invoking heaven and earth, in the presence of their parents, and whilst their shrieks were mingled with the indignant cries and groans of all the people, publicly were violated by the lowest and wickedest of the human race. Wives were torn from the arms of their husbands, and suffered the same flagitious wrongs, which were indeed hid in the bottom of dungeons in which their honour and liberty were buried together. ('Impeachment: Fifth Day', vii, 189)

With an outraged eye, Burke then outlined in lurid detail the sadistic tortures inflicted on these vulnerable and sheltered young women, before invoking the wilful obscurity of the sublime to hide the most barbarous obscenities, and draw a veil over the horror:

Often they were taken out of the refuge of this consoling gloom, stripped naked, and thus exposed to the world, and then cruelly scourged; and in order that cruelty might riot in all the circumstances that melt into tenderness the fiercest natures, the nipples of their breasts were put between the sharp and elastic sides of cleft bamboos... Growing from crime to crime, ripened by cruelty for cruelty, these fiends, at length outraging sex, decency, nature, applied lighted torches and slow fire – (I cannot proceed for shame and horror!) – these infernal furies planted death in the source of life, and where that modesty, which, more than reason, distinguishes men from beasts, retires from the view, and even shrinks from the expression, there they exercised and glutted their unnatural, monstrous, and nefarious cruelty. ('Impeachment: Fifth Day', vii, 189–90)

At this point in his catalogue of cruelty, Burke then shifts the argument to explain that there are greater torments than even physical pain, and these involve the systematic humiliation and ostracization of the young women in question as a result of contravening the most basic taboos of Gentoo society. This is a critical move in his intellectual (or rhetorical) strategy, for while physical pain cannot literally be shared, mental or 'imaginative' pain that comes from the breaking of common social or cultural codes can be (as they are 'mental' constructs in the first place). The disgrace and shame is not confined to the victim but extends to his or her family and community, which compels them to ostracize the hapless victim from society, removing them to the lowest, untouchable caste. In a passage that echoes, albeit with greater vehemence, his account of the destructive effects of the Penal Laws in Ireland on family loyalties, Burke claims that in such cases of humiliation:

All the relations of life are at once dissolved. His parents are no longer his parents; his wife is no longer his wife; his children no longer his, are no longer to regard him as their father. It is something far worse than complete outlawry, complete attainder, and universal excommunication. It is a pollution even to touch him; and if he touches any of his old caste they are justified in putting him to death. Contagion, leprosy, plague, are not so much shunned. ('Impeachment: Fifth Day', vii, 190–1)[86]

As the physical language of 'touching', 'pollution', and 'contagion' indicate, certain kinds of mental or 'cultural' suffering bound up with shame or disgrace are depicted here as having the same somatic intensity as bodily illness or physical torture. Because they are imaginatively conceived, however, a result of cultural codes engendered by society itself, the pain in question in principle can be shared by others. Sympathy involving the breach of cultural norms, then, may acquire the physical force of 'contagion' as it spreads throughout society, a form of intersubjectivity which instead of having negative effects (the usual implication of contagion) may be the source of some of our most primordial (as against primal) social ties. Indeed, it is at a primordial, formative level that the deepest cultural allegiances acquire 'natural' propensities facilitating their transmission through 'contagion', for, Burke observes, 'besides such things as effect us in various manners according to their natural powers, there are associations made at that early season [in our formative years], which we find it very hard afterwards to distinguish from natural effects' (*Enquiry*, 130).[87]

It is in this context that we should view the claim in the *Enquiry* that sympathy works by a 'contagion of the passions' *(Enquiry,* 175), and is evoked by certain dispositions of the body – 'a moving tone of voice, an impassioned countenance, an agitated gesture' (*Enquiry*, 175) – rather than the descriptive powers of language. Two kinds of sympathy thus emerge in Burke's account of 'fellow-feeling' or shared moral sentiments. The first has to do with 'the common condition of humanity which belongs to us all', and which concerns the kind of suffering caused by 'famine, degradation and oppression',[88] or the excruciating physical tortures endured by the young Indian women described above: 'These, my lords, were sufferings which we feel all in common in India and in England, by the general sympathy of our common nature' ('Impeachment: Fifth Day', vii, 190). But, as he proceeded to explain, 'it was not corporal pain alone that these miserable women suffered':

Men are made of two parts, the physical and the moral. The former he has in common with the brute creation. Like theirs, our corporal pains are very limited and are temporary. But the sufferings which touch our moral nature have a wider range, and are infinitely more acute, driving the sufferer sometimes to the extremities of despair and distraction ... This is a new source of feelings that often make corporal distress doubly felt; and it has a whole class of distresses of its own. ('Impeachment: Seventh Day of Reply', viii, 274)

Burke's radical extension of Enlightenment thinking sought to arouse our sympathies not just for (corporal) violations of our human nature, that which is shared by everyone, but also for fundamental breaches of cultural integrity which address questions of cultural difference, and which thus challenge the parochial emphasis on 'sameness' which often passes for cosmopolitanism. By a form of radical 'contagion' which crosses cultural boundaries, members of other cultures can be induced to feel a sense of moral outrage with an intensity not unlike the members of the aggrieved society themselves. Though possessing the particular codes of the local, in that it is grounded in attachment to our own culture, it is nonetheless transferable onto a wider global or world stage by means of the galvanic, montage effects of the 'sympathetic sublime'.

Burke's reasoning here is that deeply felt cross-cultural sympathy is possible while speaking out of one's own culture, rather than transcending it in the name of an undifferentiated, 'common' humanity. This is the equivalent, at a cultural level, of the 'spark' or 'contagion' which enables an intersubjective sharing of pain between individuals. For Adam Smith, this is impossible because of the barriers posed by the physicality of the body, but Burke sees the mind and body as so interrelated that one can enter into the interiority of another's body by simulating their outward expressions. In an aesthetic version of Pascal's dictum that 'if we kneel down often enough, we will begin to pray', Burke cites the practice of the 'celebrated physiognomist Campanella':

> When he had a mind to enter into the inclinations of those he had to deal with, he composed his face, his gesture, and his whole body, as nearly as he could into the exact similitude of the person he intended to examine; and then carefully examined what turn of mind he seemed to acquire by this change. So that, says my author, he was able to enter into the dispositions of others and thoughts of people, as effectually as if he had been changed into the very men. I have often observed, that on mimicking the looks and gestures, of angry, or placid, or frighted, or daring men, I have involuntarily found my mind turned to that passion whose appearance I endeavoured to imitate; nay, I am convinced it is hard to avoid it; though one strove to separate the passion from its correspondent gestures.[89] (*Enquiry*, 133)

One is tempted here to recall the extraordinary passion of Kafka's beloved Milena Jesenska, whose 'subterranean conversation' and identification with his suffering from consumption was such that she actually coughed up blood.[90] Burke expands on this solidarity in the face of suffering by drawing attention to the fact that, even under intense pain, Campanella was still capable of 'projecting' himself beyond the limits of his body, thus, in a sense, conquering his own pain:

> Campanella, of whom we have been speaking, could so abstract his attention from the sufferings of his body, that he was able to endure the rack itself without much pain; and in lesser pains, every body must have observed, that when we can employ our attention on anything else, the pain has been for a time suspended. (*Enquiry*, 133)

The logic of this argument is that since physical pain is not the ultimate threshold of suffering, the sympathetic imagination is not constrained by it and thus we can enter into the woes of others while in the midst of our own suffering – or, indeed, prefer our own suffering to that of others, so intensely is it possible to feel their pain (as in the case of the Indian natives described by Burke above who were 'assaulted on the side of their sympathy' for their children when it was found they could bear their own pain). The contrast with Adam Smith could not be greater.[91] As Bruhm summarizes it:

> For Smith, 'we have no immediate experience of what other men feel'; there is never enough feeling. For Burke, on the other hand, sympathetic pain can 'press too close'; we can feel it too much... aesthetic distance is necessary [for Burke] because the ability to feel another's pain is all too strong: for that reason, the experience of another's pain must be regulated and diminished.[92]

As we have seen, Burke considers the emotional release of the sublime to consist not so much in taking pleasure from the spectacle of pain, but experiencing 'delight' from its removal or regulation. This adds a crucial caveat to Richard Stack's concept of disinterested heroism cited above, in which self-preservation and the experience of pain rules out any public identification with the plight of others. So far from our own pain precluding this kind of sympathetic identification, it may be that alleviating our own suffering often requires helping others in distress: 'The delight we have in such things, hinders us from shunning scenes of misery; and the pain we feel, *prompts us to relieve ourselves in relieving those who suffer*' (*Enquiry*, 46: my italics).

For Burke, the exercise of sympathy, as a rule, is addressed to members of our own society, however conceived, and thus operates within the ambit of the familiar or, in terms of his aesthetic theory, 'the beautiful'. It is in this context that, in his *Tracts Relative to the Laws on Popery*, he castigates the tendency to 'transfer humanity from its natural basis – our legitimate and homebred connections' and 'meretriciously to hunt abroad after foreign affections' as 'a disarrangement of the whole system of our duties' ('Popery Laws', vi, 27). Home may be where the heart is, but yet in his speeches and writings on India, the extension of our deepest sympathies to the other side of the globe is what is uppermost in his mind:

The Tartar invasion was mischievous: but it is our protection that destroys India. It was their enmity; but it is our friendship. Our conquest there after twenty years, is as crude as it was the first day ... Young men (boys almost) govern there, without society and without sympathy with the natives. They have no more social habits with the people, than if they still resided in England. ('East India Bill', ii, 194)

Burke's hearers and readers on this occasion resided in England, and the purpose of his heightened rhetoric and dramatic oratorical performances was to bring home to them a kind of sympathy more in keeping with a first-hand engagement with Indian civilization. Burke pours scorn on Warren Hastings's reliance on testimony from 'those young men (boys almost)' who have at most a superficial knowledge of the culture – 'these wild, loose and silly observations of travellers and theorists [and] every stranger who had been hurried in a palanquin through the country'.[93] The irony here is that Burke himself had not even visited the country, and the vivid, imaginative flights of the sympathetic sublime which he launched at Westminster may have been designed as much to transport himself to India as his listeners.

The most noticeable aspect of Burke's rhetorical performance is his resolute Swiftian refusal to invoke abstract principles devoid of cultural mediation, such as those of the 'rights of man', to promote the kind of long-distance solidarity or identification that is required to alleviate the sufferings of those in societies other than our own. As we have seen, human nature, for Burke, furnishes not so much natural rights as a kind of basic, general sympathy which addresses itself, in all but the most flint-hearted, to natural or social disasters and physical pain. The difficulty with this general sympathy is that while obviously in a position to address physical torture or distress, it is not sufficiently modulated to gauge the enormity of the crimes that violate the most deeply ingrained social taboos (or values) in a society, those forms of humiliation or shame, 'mental' or 'imaginative' pain, arising out of cultural difference, or the specificity of other cultures. Outrage against such transgressions comes easily in our own society, because of our familiarity with its moral codes and customs, but proves much more difficult in the case of other societies, whose values come across to us as strange, exotic or even incomprehensible. The sublime, with its emphasis on difficulty, incongruity, and the unknown, helps us to negotiate this dark continent of the unrepresentable, our imaginations 'yield[ing] to sympathy what we refuse to description' (*Enquiry*, 175).

In the end, however, the problem faced by Burke with regard to the sympathetic sublime is that it may bridge the gap all too effectively between the familiarity of home, and the kind of horrors of colonial rule that are best kept at a distance to avoid contaminating the heartlands of the empire. In an initial attempt to map the unyielding strangeness of India, Burke sought to compare it to a disordered country closer to home, Germany, so that it:

might be approximated to our understandings, and if possible to our feelings, in order to awaken something of sympathy for the unfortunate natives, of which I am afraid we are not perfectly susceptible, whilst we look at this very remote object through a false and cloudy medium. ('East India Bill', ii, 183)

But in fact this strategy proved too successful, and Burke's ultimate fear was that the corruption of India would find its way back from the outposts of empire to those in 'England [enjoying] the comforts of their morning and evening tea'.[94] The Nabobs, with the booty of empire, 'pour in on us every day', but 'they not only bring with them the wealth they have acquired, but they bring with them into our country the vices by which it was acquired'. The sympathetic contagion is in danger of emitting the foul odours of corruption, bringing pestilence in its wake:

I have opened it [the prosecution of Hastings] that a quarantine might be performed; that the sweet air of heaven, which is polluted by the poison it contains, might be let loose upon it, and that it may be aired and ventilated before your lordships touch it.[95]

In marked contrast to Smith, who expects the sufferer to approximate to the condition of the impartial spectator, Burke's theatre of terror effects a shift in the opposite direction. The sympathetic sublime runs the risk of removing the aesthetic barriers from the spectacle of pain, thus allowing the sufferings of the victim to unsettle the composure of the spectator: 'When danger and pain press too nearly, they are incapable of giving any delight, and are simply terrible' (*Enquiry*, 40). Instead of Smith's stoical self-control, the body may be convulsed into action, giving rise to what Burke ominously refers to as 'sympathetic revenge' – 'revenge transferred from the suffering party to the communion and sympathy of mankind'. This needs to be tempered by the forces of culture and the 'beautiful', so that 'its harsh quality becomes changed' and 'laying aside its savage nature it bears fruits and flowers'. Still, this is 'revenge regulated, but not extinguished' by the insipid refinement of sensibility: 'This is the revenge by which we are actuated, and which we would be sorry if the false, idle, girlish, novel-like morality of the world should extinguish in the breasts of us who have a great public duty to perform' ('Impeachment: First Day of Reply', vii, 471).[96] As we shall see in the next chapter, this could well have been the nature of Burke's response had he lived to witness another catastrophe which was redressed in the imperial heartlands through the refinement of private charity and benevolence rather than the 'great public duty' of 'sympathetic revenge': the Irish Famine.

4

Did Edmund Burke cause the Great Famine? Commerce, culture, and colonialism

> If there were a doubt in any reflecting man's mind on the correctness of 'Burke's Thoughts and Details on Scarcity', he need only come to Ireland to have it removed and be satisfied that the greatest evils may arise from Government being depended upon for the subsistence of the people, or meddling with it if it can be avoided.
> Deputy Commissary-General Dobree to Charles Trevelyan, Waterford, 24 April 1846

> If Burke had spoken of the Irish famine in the same terms as Thoughts and Details, it would have been a manifestation of the rigid, doctrinaire ideological thinking that he spent his life denouncing... We should not lightly assume, then, that Burke would have been an insane reasoner in the face of a major famine.
> Francis Canavan, *The Political Economy of Edmund Burke*

Protesting against the ruin of India in his opening speech in the impeachment of Warren Hastings, Edmund Burke summed up for his listeners a scene of apocalyptic devastation:

the face of an utterly ruined, undone, depopulated country, and saved from literal and exceptionless depopulation only by the exhibition of scattered bands of wild, naked, meagre, half-famished wretches who rent heaven with their cries and howling.[1]

For Burke such cries in the wilderness were all the more harrowing because the wilderness was man-made, the product of unchecked economic avarice and colonial misrule. Asking his hearers to place themselves in the position of an Indian peasant 'when he sees everything in the world seized, to answer an exaggerated demand', Burke argued that passivity and quietude have their limits even under protracted servitude: 'Let the mind of man be ever so inured to servitude, still there is a point where oppressions will rouse it to resistance' ('Impeachment: Fifth Day', vii, 194–5). One may wonder, in the light of this, what Burke's response would have been in the face of

121

the catastrophe of the Great Famine in Ireland, which unfolded in all its terrible consequences in 'Black '47', exactly fifty years after his death. Certainly, there were important contrasts between Ireland and India: famine had different ecological causes, for one thing, and it was not so much corruption in Ireland as rigid economic orthodoxy which presided over the calamity. For this reason, the doctrinaire political economists with their unyielding dogma of economic rationality which, in effect, legitimated the Great Famine, would have corresponded in Burke's eyes not so much to Warren Hastings and his minions but to what he considered the ideological despots of the French Revolution, the 'geometers' who proposed to carve up even the countryside itself in the shape of political and economic abstractions. As he wrote of such 'improving' zealotry:

I confess to you that I have no great opinion of that sublime abstract, metaphysic reversionary, contingent humanity, which in *cold blood* can subject the *present time*, and those we *daily see and converse with*, to *immediate* calamities in favour of the *future and uncertain* benefit of persons who *exist only in idea*.[2]

Burke, as we shall see, could be numbered among the most advanced proponents of political economy in the late eighteenth century, but market laws were only in a position to take their course in countries with sufficient material abundance and which had attained the 'age of commerce' – such as England, 'the most flourishing country that exists'.[3] One of the symptoms of the reign of 'sophisters [and] oeconomists' (*Reflections*, 170) was the mechanical application of a template from one culture to another, very different one, regardless of the exigencies of time and place. Not least of the tragic ironies of the Great Famine was that Burke's own writings on scarcity in the relatively advanced economy of England in the 1790s were used to justify the ruination that reduced Ireland itself to the condition of a howling wilderness under the iron laws of economic rationality.

BURKE, SCARCITY, AND FAMINE

In October 1845, a deputation from Achill Island, led by the parish priest Fr Monaghan, pleaded for assistance from the British government at the onset of the famine that was eventually to sweep away 2,000 of the islanders. In his withering reply to Fr Monaghan, Sir Randolph Routh, the Chairman of the Relief Commission, sought to pre-empt one of the main charges levelled against government handling of the crisis by nationalist critics: 'I told him that we had a little more respect for his illustrious countryman Burke, than to despise the rules of political economy, where they really tended to their own advantage.'[4] As against John Mitchel's accusation that while God may have sent the potato blight, *English* political economy caused the Famine, Routh is here insisting that the Irish have only themselves to blame for the catastrophe in the form of the economic doctrines of 'their illustrious countryman', Edmund Burke. Routh is in good company here for as Peter Gray has observed, the tendency to blame the victims, placing responsibility for the famine 'squarely on the moral failings of Irishmen of all classes', became a sounding note of the highly influential Providentialist school of political economy during the Famine.[5]

Sir Randolph Routh's rejoinder to the hapless Achill deputation clearly followed on his correspondence with Sir Charles Trevelyan a week earlier, in which Trevelyan had sent him extracts from Edmund Burke's 1795 *Thoughts and Details on Scarcity*, invoking Burke's authority for his rigid implementation of *laissez-faire* doctrines:

> It may be added [wrote Trevelyan], as applicable in an especial manner at the present time, that any unusual interference with the freedom of trade must have a general bad effect ... we have already gone to the utmost limits which the circumstances of the case justify ... if we go beyond this, to adopt further restrictive measures which are not obviously and immediately necessary for putting food into the mouths of starving people, sudden and violent interference with the regular course of trade will be regarded by the mercantile community *as the habit of government*, and the effect upon our social system, the present crisis of our country, will be disastrous indeed.[6]

So enamoured was Trevelyan of Burke's missive that in the spring of 1846 he arranged for copies of the publication to be sent to various relief officers, urging them to read it and comment on it.[7] That Burke was the ultimate source of the economic policies which presided over the Famine, as against the more obvious examples of Adam Smith and his later disciples, recurs in a number of modern commentaries. In her wide-ranging study *The Idea of Poverty*, Gertrude Himmelfarb contrasts Adam Smith's and Edmund Burke's commitment to *laissez-faire* principles, all the more to underline Burke's implacable and insensitive opposition to any form of state intervention:

> In fact Smith never carried out that principle as rigorously as Burke did ... [Burke] allowed no qualification of his earlier prohibition of any 'meddling' with subsistence, even on the occasion of famine or great distress.[8]

Burke's alleged hardhearted response to the appalling suffering of famine is given a specific Irish twist in Nigel Everett's criticism of Conor Cruise O'Brien's thematic biography of Burke, *The Great Melody* (1992).

Everett takes O'Brien to task for his uncritical adulation of 'Burke's genius and consistency' and in particular for glossing over his harsh economic views: a critic of Burke's *Thoughts on Scarcity*, he writes,

> might feel that Burke bears some moral and intellectual responsibility for the treatment of his native Ireland during the Great Famine. Charles Trevelyan's simple economic certainties were far more reminiscent of Burke than of Adam Smith.[9]

What are we to make of these attempts to portray the Irish as the authors of their own calamities where the Famine was concerned, shifting the burden of 'moral and intellectual responsibility' away from English or Scottish authorities? Gertrude Himmelfarb has written of the difficulties in reconciling Burke's economic thought with his unremitting attack on 'sophisters, economists and calculators' in the *Reflections on the Revolution in France*, but the incongruity with his views on Ireland is even more starkly apparent. It was, after all, Burke who described the operation of the Penal Laws in the eighteenth century as:

> a machine of wise and elaborate contrivance; and as well fitted for the oppression, impoverishment, and degradation of a people, and the debasement in them, of human nature itself, as ever proceeded from the perverted ingenuity of man. ('Langrishe', iii, 343)

This was the kind of state intervention which colonial Ireland could have well done without. As an Irish speaker raised in the household of one of the most distinguished Catholic families in Ireland, his maternal relatives being the Nagles of Cork, Burke was the most resolute and highly placed defender of the beleaguered Catholic cause in eighteenth-century Ireland.[10] It was largely through his influence and his writings, both published and unpublished, that the dismantling of the Penal Laws was effected, though he never realized his ultimate ambition of full Catholic emancipation. How then are we to entertain the proposition that Burke would have stood idly by in the face of a famine that not only oppressed but threatened to extinguish a substantial proportion of the Catholic population whose cause he espoused so consistently – and courageously – in the eighteenth century? So far from his writings providing a rationale for the Famine, such a fundamental breakdown in the social order would, on Burke's terms, have undermined the whole basis and legitimacy of the government that let it happen. In this respect, the true successors of his political and economic writings, at least with regard to abuses of colonial rule, were not to be found in the communications of Sir Charles Trevelyan and his colleagues at the British Treasury but rather in the pages of *The Nation* newspaper and similar publications. Notwithstanding his importance as an architect of empire, Burke was adamant that in certain circumstances Britain could be deemed to have abrogated its right to rule in American colonies and, more pertinent to the Irish case, in India. The Famine, I will argue, represents such a set of extreme circumstances where Ireland was concerned, and proved indeed a turning point for the legitimacy of the colonial administration. As Francis Canavan has surmised, 'one may wonder whether Burke should have repeated the advice he gave in *Thoughts and Details* if he had been born several decades later and had lived to see the Irish famine of 1845–1849'.[11]

POLITICAL ECONOMY AND PROGRESS

Writing about the food crisis in the southern counties of England in early 1795 which precipitated Burke's *Thoughts and Details on Scarcity*,[12] E. P. Thompson advises caution in generalizing from the various alarmed responses to what was a highly abnormal situation in English political life, given the forebodings already generated by the war with France:

> generalisations ... are risky if taken only from these war years, since they are a special case: both the climax and the terminus of the [food] riot tradition, in a context of war and invasion fears, with the gentry and their retainers under arms (as Yeomanry) and in a state of anti-Jacobin panic.[13]

This is the backdrop against which we should view the shrillness of Burke's opposition to state intervention in English food markets of the mid-1790s. We must remember at the outset that in this period espousal of free trade principles could only be seen as beneficial from an *Irish* point of view. The lifting of the crippling economic constraints placed on the Irish economy as part of its colonial subjugation was one of the main objectives of Grattan's Parliament. It was, indeed, Burke's defence of free trade with Ireland, as against the protectionist measures sought by the merchants of Bristol, which was partly responsible for his losing his seat as MP for Bristol in 1780. What Burke would have thought of the version of free trade which prevailed in the midst of the Great Famine is the key question, but we can be reasonably sure that he would not have been impressed by claims that it was just and equitable, benefiting all the Irish people.

Burke's opposition to state intervention was given an extra edge in the mid-1790s by the war with revolutionary France. The severe food shortages of 1795 led to serious rioting in London, with attacks on the King's carriage at the opening of the session of parliament being accompanied by shouts of 'No war!', 'No King!', 'Down with George!', and 'No Famine!'[14] In order to alleviate the crisis, the Justices of the Peace in Speenhamland, Berkshire, determined that wages should be subsidized to bring them up to a minimum subsistence level, thus setting a precedent for extending poor relief to the employed as well as to the unemployed. It was this which provoked the ire of Burke in the adjoining county of Buckinghamshire. For Burke, to allow the state to arrogate to itself functions which belonged to civil society was to follow the insidious example of revolutionary France. in which the all-pervasive state assumed responsibility for promoting the public good.[15] Burke's main fear was that raising expectations with regard to the provision of food by central government would prove gravely detrimental to public order, for 'there is nothing on which the passions of men are so violent, and their judgement so weak, and on which there exists such a multitude of ill-founded popular prejudices' ('Thoughts and Details', v, 83). When popular demands are not met, the finger is pointed at government and it becomes a casualty of its own good intentions: food riots, in the volatile political climate of 1795, could lead to full-scale revolutionary upheavals. Hence, he writes of the events which precipitated the French Revolution:

the leading vice of the French monarchy... was in good intention ill-directed, and a restless desire of governing too much. The hand of authority was seen in everything, and in every place. All, therefore, that happened amiss in the course even of domestic affairs, was attributed to the government; and as it always happens in this kind of officious universal interference, what began in odious power, ended always, I may say without an exception, in contemptible imbecility. ('Thoughts and Details', v, 108–9)

These contextual points aside, Burke then goes on to evince a callous attitude towards the poor at a time of scarcity that has mystified many commentators who have sought to integrate his economic thinking into his overall political philosophy.[16] Burke first begins by even questioning the very category of the 'labouring poor':

Nothing can be so base and so wicked as the political canting language, 'The labouring *poor*.' Let compassion be shown in action, the more the better, according to every man's ability; but let there be no lamentation of their condition. It is no relief to their miserable circumstances; as it is only an insult to their miserable understandings. ('Thoughts and Details', v, 84)

'Hitherto', he writes elsewhere, 'the name of poor (in the sense that it is used to excite compassion) has not been used for those who can, but for those who cannot labour – for the sick and infirm; for orphan infancy; for languishing and decrepit age; but when we affect to pity as poor, those who must labour... we are trifling with the condition of mankind.'[17] The fact that someone is an ablebodied labourer is sufficient by itself to exclude them from the category of the poor, for labour is a commodity which can be exchanged for other goods. Moreover, the reality of the market is such that it is not the need of the labourer, great as it may be, that determines the price, but the demand of the buyer. In fact the more pressing the need of the labourer to sell his or her labour, the less value will be placed upon it, for he or she will be prepared to sell it at any price: 'labour is a commodity like every other, and rises and falls according to the demand. This is the nature of things...' ('Thoughts and Details', v, 85). It is at this point that Burke raises the question that was to weigh ominously on government responses to the Irish Famine:

But what if the rate of hire comes far short of his necessary subsistence, and the calamity of the time is so great as to threaten actual famine? Is the poor labourer to be abandoned to the flinty heart and griping hand of base self-interest, supported by the sword of law, especially when there is reason to suppose that the very avarice of the farmers themselves has concurred with the errors of government to bring famine on the land? In that case, my opinion is this. Whenever it happens that a man can claim nothing according to the rules of commerce, and the principles of justice, he passes out of that department, and comes within the jurisdiction of mercy. In that province, the magistrate has nothing at all to do: his interference is a violation of the property which it is in his office to protect. ('Thoughts and Details', v, 92)

This must indeed have commended itself to those officials in the Treasury who sought to absolve themselves of all responsibility for alleviating distress during the famine. But it is important to realize the precise context in which this statement was made, and above all to understand what Burke means by mercy here, before applying it as a template to the very different economic circumstances which prevailed in Ireland during the 1840s.

Burke's opposition to state intervention in the economy applies primarily to wages, and is based on the presupposition that a fully commercialized labour market exists, underpinned by formal freedom of contract. For such a market to operate, it is vital, as Burke optimistically envisages it, that 'in the case of the farmer and the labourer, their interests are always the same, and it is absolutely impossible that their free contracts be onerous to either party' ('Thoughts and Details', v, 88). For a labourer to enter a contract under conditions that would leave him or her materially worse off is, according to the tradition of contract theory Burke is drawing on here, tantamount to slavery; by the same token, and on an even more benign view of class relations under the market, while it is in the farmer's interest to increase his profits, this can only be done if the labourer is as well nourished 'as may keep his body in full force, and the mind gay and cheerful' ('Thoughts and Details', v, 88).[18] So far from condoning famine, therefore, as Himmelfarb and Everett allege above, Burke's argument against overt state interference in the labour market rests precisely on a belief, which was the ruling orthodoxy of the day, that commercial progress within English agriculture was such that famine was unlikely, even in times of scarcity. This, indeed, lay at the basis of western, and specifically British claims, that economies ruled by the laws of the market were superior to all other economic systems. As Nassau Senior wrote later in the aftermath of the Great Famine, 'famine [was] a calamity which cannot befall a civilized nation', and to acknowledge such a fundamental breakdown within one's own borders was, in effect, to describe a relapse into a barbaric state.[19]

Burke is explicit about this, arguing that scarcity and poverty are relative categories, and that the distress in England in the 1790s is far less severe than the type of destitution which was common early in the century, or, as we shall see, in Ireland:

Even now, I do not know of one man, woman, or child that has perished from famine; fewer, if any, I believe, than in years of plenty, when such a thing may happen by accident. This is owing to a care and superintendence of the poor, far greater than any I remember... Not only very few (I have observed that I know of none, though I live in a place as poor as most) have actually died of want, but we have seen no traces of those dreadful exterminating epidemics which, in consequence of scanty and unwholesome food, in former times, not infrequently wasted whole nations. ('Thoughts and Details', v, 107)

It is clear then that Burke's strictures on tampering with the market rested on a conviction, however misplaced, that there was no famine, nor was it likely to occur. As T. P. O'Neill points out, one of the most serious consequences of following Burke's analysis to the letter, and applying *Thoughts on Scarcity* uncritically as a formula for dealing with the Irish Famine, was that it allowed the government to diminish the scale of the horror, and to delude themselves that only a situation of scarcity obtained in Ireland. Hence minimalist measures were all that were called for:

The British government treated the Irish crisis as if it came within the definition of 'scarcity' rather than 'famine'. In all official correspondence and speeches, the more euphemistic term 'distress' is used, instead of 'famine', and the policy followed was that laid down for a minor rather than a major crisis.[20]

Through a perverse logic, Burke's pamphlet may indeed have contributed to the sequence of events that culminated in the Great Famine, but precisely because it was *mis*read for doctrinaire ideological purposes inimical to his own political philosophy, and grossly misrepresenting his response to poverty under the new dispensation of political economy.

BURKE AND THE CRITIQUE OF POVERTY

When we speak of Poverty we must speak of something comparative. Ireland when compar'd with England in the time of her most prosperous State was a distresssed Country... Causes of it obvious – though misrepresented by Writers. Above 400 years of continual War... The introduction of a new religion by Force, not as in England and other places... (Burke, Sheffield Papers, Bk. 8, 173)

The debate over the ambivalence of Burke's attitude to poverty is further fuelled by a controversial section in his first published book, *A Vindication of Natural Society* (1756), which appears initially to be a violent condemnation of the misery to which the mass of the labouring poor are doomed in society. 'Power', he suggests, 'gradually extirpates from the mind every humane and gentle Virtue. Pity, benevolence, friendship are things almost unknown in high Stations.' On account of this insensitivity, the toiling masses 'are considered as a mere herd of cattle' by their superiors. In a revealing change of metaphor from an Irish point of view, he castigates the aristocracy for treating 'their Subjects as the farmer does the Hog he keeps to feast upon. He holds him fast in his Stye, but allows him to wallow as much as he pleases in his beloved Filth and Gluttony.' Burke then proceeds to describe in graphic detail the worst excesses of exploitation in mines and menial occupations, where

unhappy wretches... work at a severe and dismal Task, without the least Prospect of being delivered from it; they subsist upon the coarsest and worst sort of Fare; they have their Health miserably impaired, and their Lives cut short... If any Man informed us that two hundred thousand innocent Persons were condemned to so *intolerable Slavery*, how should we pity the unhappy Sufferers, and how great would be our just Indignation against those who inflicted so cruel and ignominious a Punishment?... To say nothing of those other Employments, those Stations of Wretchedness and Contempt in which Civil Society has placed the numerous *Enfans perdus* of her Army.

'This is an instance', he concludes, 'of the numberless things which we pass by in their common dress, yet which shock us when they are nakedly represented' (*Vindication*, 88, 49, 54, 85–6).

The extent to which this scathing indictment of oppression represents Burke's sincere views is rendered problematic, however, by a preface appended to the second edition of the work in 1757 which explains that his intent was satirical all along, and that the *Vindication* was, in fact, a parody of the egalitarian ideas of Lord Bolingbroke and other apologists for 'natural society' such as Rousseau. Burke's irony seems to have been too sophisticated for its own good, for many later radical thinkers took its critique of injustice to heart, including the young William Godwin, on whom it may have been a major formative influence.[21] For the most part, however, critics have accepted Burke's version that it was an ironic composition, intending to subtly undermine the views which were so passionately enunciated. Yet, in recent years, Isaac Kramnick has challenged this orthodoxy by showing, incontrovertibly, that certain of the views expressed in the work appear elsewhere in Burke's writings, without any satirical strings attached.[22] The most germane aspect of this argument for our present purposes is that the expressions of outrage over the oppression of the poor in the *Vindication* are prefigured in his outraged descriptions of poverty in Ireland,[23] which depict a society clearly at odds with the benign view of agricultural progress in the English countryside that informed his *Thoughts on Scarcity*.

While a student at Trinity College, Burke made frequent journeys to his old school at Ballitore, Co. Kildare, and perhaps to his maternal home at Ballyduff, Co. Cork, where he was reared. The destitution of the Irish countryside made a discernible impression on him, for in No. 7 of *The Reformer*, a periodical which he wrote and published in 1747–8, he rails against the indifference of the rich, and more particularly the government, to the plight of the Irish poor. Declaring roundly at the outset that 'It is the Care of every wise Government to secure the Lives and Properties of those who live under it', he continues: 'Whoever travels through this Kingdom will see such Poverty, as few Nations in *Europe* can equal. In this City Things have the best Face; but still, as you leave the Town, the scene grows worse, and presents you with the utmost Penury in the Midst of a rich soil' ('Reformer', 96). Money, he writes, is a stranger to the people, and

> As for their food, it is notorious that they seldom taste Bread or Meat; their Diet, in Summer, is Potatoes and sour Milk; in Winter, when something is required comfortable, they are still worse, living on the same Root, made palatable only by a little Salt, and accompanied with Water: Their Cloaths so ragged, that they rather publish than conceal the Wretchedness it was meant to hide; nay, it is no uncommon Sight to see half a dozen Children run naked out of a Cabin, scarcely distinguishable from a Dunghill, to the great disgrace of our Country with Foreigners, who would doubtless report them Savages, imputing that to Choice which only proceeds from their irremediable Poverty. ('Reformer', 97)

On entering, or rather creeping into, a cabin, he continues, in terms which prefigure the *Vindication*, 'you see (if the Smoke will permit you) the Men, Women, Children, Dogs, and Swine lying promiscuously; for their

Opulence is such that they cannot have a separate House for their Cattle, as it would take too much from the Garden, whose produce is their only Support' ('Reformer', 97).

It is difficult to imagine the writer of this providing an alibi for the British Treasury's inhumane and doctrinaire approach to the suffering of the Irish poor during the famine. In view, moreover, of the attempts by Providentialists and others to project responsibility for the disaster onto the destitute themselves, it is worthwhile reading Burke's response to a similar situation. 'That some should live in a more sumptuous Manner than others, is very allowable', but 'that those who cultivate the Soil, should have so small a part of its Fruits... is a kind of Blasphemy on Providence, and seems to show, as our Motto finely expresses it, "the Heavens unjust"' ('Reformer', 98). As for the question of the landowner's unqualified rights to property, Burke is adamant that they are not absolute but are instead 'for promoting the Public Good; And when, by the use they make of their Fortunes, they thwart that End, they are liable to the same or a greater reproach than a Prince who abuses his power'. But, he adds:

there are some People who shut their Hearts to Charity, and to excuse their want of compassion, throw all the Fault as well as Misfortune on the unhappy Poor. Their Sloth, say those, is the cause of their Misery. 'Tis pleasant to observe, that this objection frequently comes from those who in all their lives have not been as serviceable to their Country, as the idlest of these creatures in one day. ('Reformer', 98)

In an uncanny presentiment of the misapplication of his own recommendations for the English market onto Irish conditions, Burke concludes that the main difficulty for Irish agriculture lies in the facility with which the landlord class take English conditions as the norm – a ruinous tendency that could push the Irish system to the verge of catastrophe:

Gentlemen perceiving that in *England* Farmers pay heavy Rent, and yet live comfortably, without considering the Disproportion of Markets and every Thing else, raise their Rent high, and extort it heavily. Thus none will hold from them but those desperate creatures who ruin the Land (in vain) to make their Rent; they fly; the Landlord seizes, and to avoid the like Mischance, takes all into his own hands; which being unable to manage, he turns to grazing; thus one part of the Nation is starved, and the other deserted. ('Reformer', 99)

It is not easy to account for the vehemence of Burke's assault on the privileges of the landed gentry at this early juncture, but the mention of the prospect of mass starvation and desolation in the countryside suggests that Burke may have been talking from first-hand experience of famine. This is indeed likely, for as David Dickson has shown, the devastating

'Arctic Famine' of 1740–1, which lasted for almost two years and annihilated a fifth of the population, ravaged Munster and particularly north Cork where Burke was living with his maternal relatives.[24] Writing from Cork in May 1741, Bishop Berkeley remarked that 'the havoc of mankind in the counties of Cork and Limerick, and some adjacent places has been incredible. The nation probably will not recover the loss for a century.'[25] The young Burke was perhaps one of those who found it difficult to recover, for he was removed from Cork to Ballitore in Kildare in the same month, April 1741, that the thaw finally set in after the unremitting harshness of the winter. This suggests that he was frozen in for the duration of the famine in that region of north Co. Cork. While it may be argued that there are many differences between Burke's opinions in the 1740s and the 1790s,[26] one view did not change, and that is his implacable opposition to the supremacy of Protestant landed interests in Ireland, and their indifference to the well-being of the mass of the Catholic population. In 1792, he commented acidly to Sir Hercules Langrishe:

> Sure I am, that there have been thousands in Ireland, who have never conversed with a Roman Catholic in their whole lives, unless they happened to talk to their gardener's workmen, or to ask their way, when they had lost it, in their sports; or at best, who had known them only as footmen, or other domestics, of the second and third order. ('Langrishe', iii, 335)

'SUBLIMED INTO MADNESS': FAMINE AND COLONIALISM

In this respect, and in view of Burke's belief about the greater availability of 'care and superintendence' for the poor in Britain due to the progress in agriculture, the caveats registered by the ominously named Commissary-General Pine-Coffin in a memo to Sir Charles Trevelyan in April 1846, are of interest in determining the relevance of Burke's *Thoughts on Scarcity* to the Great Famine. Discussing Burke's pamphlet in the context of the disintegrating Irish agrarian economy, he writes candidly of the Irish labouring classes:

> But those only can participate in this result [i.e. the putative mutual benefits of the market] who have an interest in the struggle, and the unfortunate Irish cottier has none. His condition excludes him from the circle in which commerce revolves, and his labour avails him only for the direct production of food on which he depends for subsistence, the failure of that food leaves him incapable of profiting by the resources of the market, and consequently liable to starve in the midst of plenty. Not having the legal claim to support of the English labourer, his only refuge is in the care of Government, and in such circumstances is it possible for the Government to refuse it?[27]

What Pine-Coffin is drawing attention to here is one of the key anomalies of forced 'modernization' under colonial rule, namely, that the integration of the underdeveloped Irish economy into the market in such adverse circumstances operated systematically to the detriment of native producers and, in particular, the labouring cottier class.[28] The Penal Laws, which Burke had inveighed against for over half a century, had seen to it that Catholics were not equal under the law, and had little or no legal security for engaging in agricultural enterprises. For the dominant landlord class, on the other hand, maximum profits in an economy where the majority of producers were in no position to benefit from, or indeed to engage in, improvements, entailed a direct and absolute immiseration of the labouring poor. Productivity could only be enhanced by increasing the number of labourers, a process facilitated by the subdivision of holdings, but as the quantity of land does not increase proportionately, access to the means of subsistence diminishes. Accordingly, increased productivity brought with it increased competition for access to land. This led to a steady rise in rent, which was accompanied, in a vicious downward spiral, by a gradual lowering of the threshold of subsistence, and increased dependence on the potato. Instead of benefiting, even relatively speaking, from integration into a market economy, as Burke argued, cottiers ended up much worse off to the point where they eventually faced extinction. Moreover, as Eamonn Slator and Terrence McDonough have argued in relation to the 'market distorting consequences of the dispossession and re-entry of the Irish peasantry in relation to the land':

We must be mindful here that the existence of this competition by the whole population for access to the land is initially conditioned by the conquest of Ireland by the British. This conquest began a process of the elimination of the customary access to the land of the indigenous peasantry. While the peasantry remained, the Gaelic tribal chief was replaced by the new landlords who could treat the land as their private property, having no traditional obligations to the actual occupiers of the land.[29]

This has crucial consequences for Burke's seemingly heartless comment that charity and mercy take over when the market fails to cater for the well-being of all. What Burke emphatically does *not* mean here is voluntary and optional relief, the 'privatization' of charity characterized by the rise of philanthropy and the cult of benevolence in the eighteenth century. Going to the aid of others is entirely discretionary under this dispensation, so much so, indeed, that only those of superior moral worth are deemed to possess this advanced form of sympathy.[30] Hence the Pharisee-like tones of self-congratulation in Sir Charles Trevelyan's encomium to the sacrifices made by the British empire to help the Irish in their hour of need:

> A painful and tender sympathy pervaded every class of society. From the Queen on her throne to the convict in the hulks, expenses were curtailed, and privations were endured, in order to swell the Irish subscription. The fast was observed with unusual solemnity, and the London season of this year was remarkable for the absence of gaiety and expensive entertainments. The vibration was felt through every nerve of the British Empire. The remotest stations in India, the most recent settlements in the backwoods of Canada, contributed their quota.[31]

It may have been with these good vibrations in mind that Burke wrote contemptuously of the kind of 'benevolence to the whole species, and want of feeling for every individual with whom the professors come in contact, [which] form[ed] the character of the new philosophy'.[32] The nature of the sympathy described by Trevelyan may be gauged from the fact that even the satirical magazine *Punch*, not noted for its tenderness towards the Irish, managed to donate £50.

The moral approbation and personal virtue accruing from charity of this kind derives from the fact that it is gratuitous and hence not obligatory. But for Burke, concern for the well-being of others is not a mere social accessory, the moral equivalent of costume jewellery. In his *Thoughts on Scarcity*, he emphasizes that:

> without all doubt, charity to the poor is a *direct and obligatory duty* put upon all Christians, next in order after the payment of debts, full as strong, and by nature made infinitely more delightful to us. Puffendorff, and other casuists, do not, I think, denominate it quite properly when they call it a duty of imperfect obligation. ('Thoughts and Details', 92: my italics)[33]

The forthright nature of this statement has not prevented some commentators from appropriating Burke to the ranks of a latter-day *laissez-faire* apologist by misreading it as suggesting that he *endorses* the concept of 'imperfect obligation', rather than questioning it. As Norman Barry formulates it:

> The fact that Burke had good, pragmatic reasons for not enjoining the state to perform a welfare role ... does not mean that we are all absolved from that responsibility. The duty to relieve suffering may be one of 'imperfect obligation', ranking below the duties to keep promises, respect property and so on, but charity is a feature of Christian morality.[34]

But this is precisely what Burke does not say: 'Puffendorf, and other casuists, do *not*, I think, denominate it quite properly when they call it a duty of imperfect obligation' (my italics). The seemingly throwaway reference to Pufendorf, the great seventeenth-century German jurist, is crucial in this respect, for in dissenting from the view that the duty to relieve suffering is merely a secondary 'imperfect' obligation, Burke is questioning one of the most important tenets of *laissez-faire* economic philosophy. As succinctly expressed by Adam Smith, it stipulates that while 'a man shuts his breast against compassion, and refuses to relieve the misery of his fellow sufferers', he may still 'often fulfil the rules of justice by sitting still and doing nothing' (*Moral Sentiments*, 81, 82) – a dictum echoed in Lord Clarendon's rueful comment during the Great Famine that he was unable 'to shake Charles Wood and Trevelyan that the right course was *to do nothing* for Ireland'.[35] Burke's expression of outrage in 1774 over the draconian measures taken against the American colonies by the British government is apposite here: protesting that they threatened to strip away the most basic judicial rights, he charged: 'You sentence...to famine at least 300,000 people in two provinces, at the mere arbitrary will and pleasure of two men.'[36]

The relegation of compassion and concern for the poor to the domain of voluntary 'imperfect obligation' derives from the natural rights tradition in political philosophy associated with the great early modern jurists, Grotius and Pufendorf – a tradition which passed into British political economy through the writings of Hobbes and Locke, and, more particularly, through the influence of Gershom Carmichael and Francis Hutcheson in Scotland. The problem which these natural rights theorists sought to address was one that was becoming increasingly acute in an era of both commercial expansion and the centralization of state power: how to reconcile the natural right to property with the conflicting claims of the 'right of necessity', i.e. a right to subsistence based on the fundamental right of self-preservation. The right to subsistence had an historical and religious dimension, deriving from the original patrimony to the earth, and 'the fullness thereof', granted by God to *all* mankind. The difficulty then became one of explaining the origins of both private property and the state, and the emergence of a system in which most of humanity was excluded, or allowed themselves to be excluded, from the right to subsistence. How could the mass of people, short of acting irrationally or being subjugated by force, abrogate their common right to subsistence, and, in effect, contract themselves into inequality or, at worst, slavery and starvation?

One immediate response to this quandary by early natural rights theorists underlines the importance of the term 'scarcity' in the title of Burke's

1795 missive. So far from inducing a sense of fellow-feeling and altruism, scarcity in an original state of nature was identified as the fatal flaw in the scheme of things which gave rise to property, providing the pretext for self-interest and exclusivist demarcations between 'mine' and 'thine'. But as even the rationale for this primal form of appropriation rested on a right to self-preservation, Grotius argued that in cases of acute crisis such as starvation or famine, the original communal right could be activated, hence subordinating private property to the common good (albeit defined in this minimalist subsistence form).[37] A lot of the ingenuity, or what Burke referred to as 'casuistry', in subsequent natural rights philosophies was devoted to closing off this crucial 'opt out' clause of the original social contract, which was accurately perceived as undermining the absolute right to property. Burke was correct, moreover, in identifying Pufendorf as the key figure in this ideological shift, a manoeuvre effected by his denial that natural rights ever existed in the first place, whether communal or private.[38] All rights for Pufendorf could only be established through prior social agreement, so that no positive rights existed in a state of nature. This cut off the escape route of primordial communal rights, but unfortunately for subsequent theorists in the British tradition, it also vitiated a natural right to private property, in effect rendering null and void any grounds of resistance to a monarch for violating this right. Pufendorf had no difficulty with this, being committed, in the last instance, to a defence of royal absolutism, but clearly this did not lend itself to apologists for the Glorious Revolution.

However, the need to secure the stability of private ownership in an era of protracted religious wars and civil conflict was vital to Pufendorf's project, and it was in this context that he attached central importance to a distinction, derived from Grotius, between perfect and imperfect rights or obligations.[39] Before the contract, human beings enjoy only negative or imperfect rights: but after the pact, positive or perfect rights are established, ownership of property being pre-eminent among them.[40] As our sense of humanity or fellow-feeling belongs to the former state, it is therefore not subject to the ordinances of duty or obligation in the latter positive sense. As Pufendorf himself puts it: 'Perfect rights nearly always involve a pact, but not imperfect rights. Since imperfect rights are left to each person's sense of decency and conscience, it would be inconsistent to extort them from another by force except when a grave necessity compels it.'[41] In *On the Duty of Man and Citizen*, Pufendorf elaborates on this dissociation of the moral sensibility, declaring that whereas perfect rights involve specific pacts:

One must also take note that what is due on the basis of the duty to humanity alone, differs from what is due on an agreement or a perfect promise, above all in the following point. It is indeed right to make requests on the basis of humanity and honourable to grant them, but I may not compel the other party to performance by force either on my own part or on the part of a superior, if he neglects to perform of his own accord; I may only complain of his inhumanity, of his boorishness or insensibility. But I may resort to compulsion when what is due by a perfect promise or agreement is not freely forthcoming. Hence we are said to have an imperfect right [*jus imperfectum*] to the former, a perfect right [*jus perfectum*] to the latter.[42]

– as in the case of someone denying me access to my own property, or refusing to pay a debt.

This would appear to be the conception of imperfect obligation which, contrary to Norman Barry, Burke dissents from in *Thoughts on Scarcity*, for by insisting that charity, especially in times of scarcity and distress, is a '*direct and obligatory duty* put upon all Christians, next in order to the payment of debts' (my italics), Burke is clearly intent on giving it the force of a perfect rather than an imperfect obligation.[43] There is, however, an important caveat to this, for he does not go so far as to say that the state should enforce this duty: it is involuntary not through coercion but by virtue of the fact that we are governed by rules and norms arising from our participation in a common culture – a form of 'virtual obligation as binding as that which is actual' in Burke's eyes. This point is taken up in his *Appeal from the New to the Old Whigs* where he argues that whatever about the voluntary nature of the putative original contract, human beings now enter society encumbered with duties and obligations that derive 'in great measure' from 'the ancient order into which we are born':

Men come in that manner into a community with the social state of their parents, endowed with all the benefits, loaded with all the duties of their situation. If the social ties and ligaments... in most cases begin, and all cases continue, independently of our will; so, without any stipulation on our part, are we bound by that relation called our country, which comprehends (as it has been well said) 'all the charities of all'.[44]

From this it follows that 'charity has its own justice, and its own Rules' and 'there is nothing in these things voluntary but the beginning of them'.[45]

The forms of compassion which extend beyond 'imperfect obligation' for Burke are among the 'duties imposed upon us by the law of social union' (*Reflections*, 205). They impress themselves upon us not through private discretion or benevolence, but through tradition, custom, and common law, the constituents of what E. P. Thompson refers to as the 'moral economy'. This matrix of inherited rights, obligations, rituals, and cultural practices, extending over centuries, forms the underlying connective tissue of society for Burke, without which even economic contracts would not have the binding force they possess in civil society. It is for this reason, Burke writes, that it is incumbent on us 'to reconcile our economy with our [pre-existing] laws, than to set them at variance: a quarrel which in the end must be destructive to both'.[46] The polity, he elaborated elsewhere, ought not to be confined to government, in the abstract *laissez-faire* sense, but should embrace 'the whole commonwealth' and the different orders in society ('Langrishe', iii, 302–3). What Burke took particular exception to in the French Revolution was the attempt by the state to arrogate to itself the functions of the moral economy, in so much as paper money was substituted for the metallic money which formed the basis of a stable and thriving fiscal policy.

It was in fact through reckless financial speculation and the growth of an uncontrollable national debt that the state was able to consolidate its power in the first place. The animus which Burke displayed towards state intervention in the economy, and its related violations of property, was motivated by a concern for a particular version of the moral economy, exemplified by the integral role of religious orders in attending to the poor and alleviating social distress in a Christian polity. 'While we provide first for the poor', he writes, religion will not be relegated to the margins of society, but will 'be mixed throughout the whole mass of life, and blended with all classes in society':

It is true, the whole church revenue is not always employed, and to every shilling, in charity; nor perhaps ought it; but something is generally so employed. It is better to cherish virtue and humanity, by leaving much to free will, even with some loss to the object, than to attempt to make men mere machines and instruments of a political benevolence. (*Reflections*, 203)

In attempting to convert the state into a machine of 'political benevolence', and to offset the public debt, the French revolutionaries took it upon themselves to abolish religious orders and to confiscate church property. In so doing, they attacked the very foundations of both property and welfare in society, converting land into paper money and thus eroding the power of the landed gentry, the main counterweight, in Burke's eyes, to both the limitless expansion of the monied interest, and the centralization of state (or, indeed, monarchical) power. According to J. G. A. Pocock, this is the rationale for the feudal rhetoric of 'chivalry' and 'manners' which Burke deployed in the *Reflections*, but it would be mistaken, he goes on to argue, to portray this as merely the politics of nostalgia, a genuflection towards an anachronistic social order. For Burke, modern commerce can only flourish when the power of the state and the city is curtailed, and for this reason, the critique of both excessive court influence and financial speculation was central to Whig ideology, particularly its landed, country variant.

Moreover, the affinities between this appeal to the past and the popular constitutionalism of the moral economy as envisaged by E. P. Thompson, should make us wary of construing the politics of retrospection as entirely reactionary in character, a monopoly of conservative ideology. As the very language of Chartism in the early nineteenth century showed, it could equally be associated with a form of radical antiquarianism, tracing its pedigree from Magna Carta, and indeed from King Alfred.[47] For the most part, this was associated with the Protestant heritage of the 'free-born Englishman' and a residual puritan republicanism. In some notable instances, however, it extended beyond this to a critique of the prejudice that liberty was a Protestant preserve, seeking to develop more expansive concepts of liberty that addressed religious prejudice itself, and, in particular, the plight of the majority Catholic population in Ireland under English rule. The issue which prompted this re-appraisal of the conventional radical hostility to Catholicism (and, by extension, to the Irish) was the growing controversy over Poor Law reform. In his *History of the Protestant Reformation* (1829), published in the same year as the granting of Catholic Emancipation, William Cobbett argued that the 'right of necessity' to poor relief was grounded historically in the welfare system of the Catholic Church, before the systematic suppression of the monasteries by Henry VIII. Echoing Burke, though from the other side of the political spectrum, Cobbett wrote that though large tracts of land were legally in the hands of the clergy, the diffusion of wealth to the poor saw to it that 'tithes, and every other species of income of the clergy, were looked upon, and were in fact and in practice, more the property of the poor than of the Monk, nuns, priests, and bishops'.[48] Idealized as this image of the past was, it was taken up by one of the most radical early socialists, the Irish labour activist James Bronterre O'Brien, who argued that the destitute and uprooted possessed historical rights to poor relief, given to them in exchange for the confiscation of the church lands that were used to support them before the English Reformation.[49] Nor is this invocation on the part of the Left of powerful extended networks of institutional relief entirely anachronistic in today's new world order for, as Michael Hardt and Antonio Negri suggest, what are humanitarian non-governmental organizations (NGOs) such as Amnesty International and Oxfam but 'the charitable campaigns and mendicant orders' of the global economy, operating outside direct governmental control but significant political players in their own right.[50]

In embracing a concept of the political beyond the totalizing designs of the state, 'the Whig Burke', as Pocock observes, 'had placed himself at a point from which Tory and Radical argument could take off'.[51] The implications of this imaginary transfer of communal rights for the Irish situation did not need to be spelled out, and it was Burke who made the explicit connection, linking the 'tyrant' Henry VIII with Cromwell, and other avatars of destruction in Ireland. But whereas the violence of the suppression of the monasteries, and Catholicism in general, in England could be masked over to maintain the fictive continuity of the English constitution, in Ireland it was more difficult to draw the 'decent drapery of life' over the scars inflicted by conquest. The mass of the Irish population were indeed reduced, in Burke's graphic terminology, to their 'naked shivering nature', without even the rudiments of a moral economy – except that of their own native Rundale land system – to protect them against hardship and oppression. The basic substratum of political legitimacy in England rested 'on our *antient* indisputable laws and liberties, and that *antient* constitution of government which is our only security for law and liberty' (*Reflections*, 117). Hence the appeal to a moral economy in which, notwithstanding the persistence of conflict and inequality, 'there is a communion of interests, and a sympathy of feelings and desires between those who act in the name of any description of people, and the people in whose name they act' ('Langrishe', iii, 334). The central difficulty with colonial rule in Ireland – and Burke explicitly refers to it in these terms – is that no such common culture or even union of sentiments exists. 'The colonial garrison', as he described it in 1792,

divided the nation into two distinct bodies, without common interests, sympathy, or connexion. One of these bodies was to possess *all* the franchises, *all* the property, *all* the education; the other was to be composed of drawers of water and cutters of turf for them... What was done was not in the spirit of a contest between two religious factions; but between two adverse nations. ('Langrishe', iii, 301, 320)

'There is a relation in mutual obligation', he adds, but it was certainly not evident in the relations between the native population and their colonial masters in Ireland.

It was the absence of this fundamental layer in the polity, of 'mutual obligations' and sympathies deeper than laws and contracts, and of forms of solidarity more lasting than the mere caprice of private charity, which became so starkly apparent in the attitudes shown by the British ruling establishment to the Irish during the famine. The problem, in fact, was that where the mass of the labouring population were concerned, the law itself was as arbitrary as charity, and 'perfect obligation', in Burke's and Pufendorf's terms, degenerated into 'imperfect obligation', and indeed into no obligation at all. As Kevin O'Neill describes it, the increased commercialization of agriculture did not even bring about the mythic commonality of interest envisaged by Burke in contractual relations, but led to a total breakdown in communal ties:

> There were no recognized community rights, no commons, and no village decisions regarding land distribution, crop choice, or crop rotation. There was no legally recognized preventative check on the use of land other than economic restraints. This made the Irish peasant, however reluctant, the most market oriented peasant in Europe and helps to explain the extreme nature of Irish economic and social developments as agriculture moved painfully into a fully capitalized system.[52]

These may form the basis of commercial relations in an advanced market economy, but even then, for Burke, they did not provide the lineaments of the state, or provide the model for all social relations. The state, he wrote, 'ought not to be considered as nothing better than a partnership agreement in a trade of pepper and coffee, calico or tobacco, or some other such low concern' (*Reflections*, 194), but is based on a civic culture grounded in tradition (customs and manners), the arts, and religion. 'Even commerce and trade, and manufacture', Burke points out, 'the gods of our oeconomical politicians, are themselves but creatures; are themselves but effects' of these principles. He then goes on to ask:

> how well a state may stand without these fundamental principles, what sort of a thing must be a nation of gross, stupid, ferocious, and at the same time, poor and sordid barbarians, destitute of religion, honour, or manly pride, possessing nothing at present, and hoping for nothing hereafter? (*Reflections*, 174)

This is the core of Burke's argument, however deluded, that a famine would not have been permitted in the polite and commercial society of eighteenth-century Britain, the most advanced economy in the world, with all its improved measures for 'the care and superintendence of the poor' ('Thoughts and Details', v, 107). When Pine-Coffin notes that the 'unfortunate Irish cottier' is excluded from the benefits of 'the circle in which commerce revolves', does not even have 'the legal claim to support of the English labourer', and hence is forced to fall back on central government, he is, in effect, conceding that it is only central government, and the coercive apparatus of colonial rule, which holds the Union in place. In these circumstances, as Burke himself conceded in other colonial contexts, the state is obliged to step in, and give imperfect duties the force of perfect obligations. Notwithstanding the seemingly rigid application of *laissez-faire* principles in *Thoughts on Scarcity*, Burke was careful not to rule out entirely the possibility of state intervention: 'nothing, certainly, can be laid down on the subject that will not admit of exceptions, many permanent, some occasional' ('Thoughts and Details', v, 107). The 1795 food crisis itself proved such an exception, and within a month of committing his thoughts on scarcity to paper, Burke expressed strong support for government measures to send ships to Africa, South America, Canada, and mainland Europe to purchase grain to ease the shortage. Ten years earlier, when the depredations of the East India Company had brought the Carnatic region in India to the verge of economic collapse, the people were plunged into 'the jaws of famine': 'all was done by charity that private charity could do', Burke writes, 'but it was a people in beggary; it was nation which stretched out its hands for food':

> Every day seventy at least laid their bodies in the streets, or on the glacis of Tanjore, and expired of famine in the granary of India. I was going to awake your justice towards this unhappy part of our fellow-citizens, by bringing before you some of the circumstances of this plague of hunger. Of all the calamities which beset and waylay the life of man, this comes nearest to our heart... but I find myself unable to manage it with decorum; these details are of a species of horror so nauseous and disgusting; they are so humiliating to human nature itself; that, on better thoughts, I find it more advisable to throw a pall over this hideous object, and to leave it to your general conceptions.[53]

Burke then asks his listeners to imagine what their response would be if 'the sweet and cheerful country' of England was reduced to such a scene of desolation: 'what your thoughts would be if you should be informed, that they [the authorities] were computing how much had been the amount of the excises, how much the customs, how much the land and malt tax, in order that they should charge (take it in the most favourable light) for public service... What would you call it? To call it tyranny sublimed into madness, would be too faint an image' ('Nabob', iii, 161–2). One wonders in the light of this how Burke himself would have responded to the attempts by the Treasury in London to make the destitute Irish economy responsible for relief measures during the Famine. Burke explicitly charged the state with the responsibility for restoring the economic infrastructure of the region which depended on a system of over 10,000 reservoirs to irrigate the fields,[54] but concludes ruefully:

> A ministry of another kind would have first improved the country, and have thus laid a solid foundation for future opulence and future force. But on this grand point of the restoration of the country, there is not one syllable to be found in the correspondence of our ministers, from the first to the last; they felt nothing for a land desolated by fire, sword, and famine. ('Nabob', iii, 165)

In an instructive gloss on the principles underlying the Act of Union, Lord John Russell declared early in 1846:

> My opinion is... that Irishmen ought to have the same privileges as both Englishmen and Scotchmen. I consider that the Union was but parchment, an unsubstantial Union, if Ireland is not to be treated in the hour of difficulty and distress as an integral part of the United Kingdom, and unless we are prepared to show that we are ready to grant to Irishmen a participation in all our rights and privileges, and to treat them exactly as if they were inhabitants on the same island... For myself, I think I could do no greater benefit than to endeavour to cement betwixt all parts an affection both in peace and war.[55]

But no sooner had he assumed the office of Prime Minister later in the year than he turned his back on this imaginary union of sentiments, in effect conceding that Ireland was not integral to the United Kingdom. For Charles Trevelyan, the Famine seemed both providential for British interests, and a fortunate fall for the 'undeserving poor' who constituted the bulk of the Irish nation:

> The uniting power of a common misfortune has also been felt throughout the British empire. Those who never before exchanged words or looks of kindness met to co-operate in this great work of charity... In the hour of her utmost need, Ireland became sensible of a union of feeling and interest with the rest of the empire.[56]

But to replace the ancient fabric of the British constitution with the threadbare ties of private benevolence would have rendered the Union null and void in Burke's terms, exposing it as a barely concealed system of tyranny. When Trevelyan goes on to note that 'the most wholesome symptom of all' arising from the Famine 'is that the plan of dependency or external assistance has been tried to the utmost and has failed; that people have grown worse under it than better; and that an experiment ought now to be made of what independent exertion will do', he said more than he perhaps intended. *The Nation* newspaper picked up on this kind of rhetoric, arguing that if 'independent exertion' was being forced upon the Irish, why not follow the logic of this to full political independence and self-government? Giving a more radical turn to the usual providential argument that good might come out of evil, it declaimed at the outbreak of the Famine:

> Without a Government that can govern – without a Legislature to legislate on our own soil, our fate may become whatever blind chance determines, if there be not native energy in the country to bring order out of chaos, and give a positive direction to its own future... Gracious Heaven, to think that these evils, threatening us on the angry horizon, might be mitigated or turned aside, or, haply, transformed into the occasion of great public virtue, if this country were governed by its own

people... These things a child may see; but the far result, the great opportunities won or lost, or the goal missed or found – this is what it asks some seer of the future – a BURKE, a MIRABEAU, or an O'CONNELL – to see and tell.[57]

Burke and Mirabeau may make strange bedfellows, but in associating the alleged counter-revolutionary with the revolutionary fervour of his great antagonist, *The Nation* showed a better understanding than Treasury officials of how Burke would respond to a cataclysm such as the Great Famine.[58]

PART III

Colonialism and the Enlightenment

5
'Tranquillity tinged with terror': the sublime and agrarian insurgency

> Not able long to exist here, pressed at once by wild beasts and famine, the same despair drove them back; and seeking their last resource in arms, the most quiet, the most passive, the most timid of the human race, rose up in an universal insurrection.
> Edmund Burke, 'Speech on the Impeachment of Warren Hastings'

> Pain and fear consist in an unnatural tension of the nerves... this is sometimes accompanied with an unnatural strength, which sometimes changes into an extraordinary weakness... these effects often come on alternately, and are sometimes mixed with each other. This is the nature of all convulsive agitations, especially in weaker subjects.
> Edmund Burke, *Enquiry into the Sublime and Beautiful*

Describing the terror produced by the wave of agrarian disturbances which swept Munster in the 1780s, Dominic Trant had occasion to cite one of the most famous classical examples of the sublime, Lucretius's image of a shipwreck in a storm, watched in safety from the shore.[1] In the original example, the security of the spectator is assured, but such conditions did not obtain in the political turbulence of Munster:

> No private man is so secure in his fortunes or establishment, as not to be within the vortex of general calamity, nor is he in the situation described by the poet... as, in fact, he does not view the shipwreck from a lofty cliff, *himself safe from the effects of the storm*, but is *actually involved in the danger*, and a *mariner* on board the *unfortunate vessel* which is threatened with immediate destruction.[2]

The image of a shipwreck was regularly evoked in the eighteenth century to describe the privation and danger experienced by Catholics under the Williamite settlement,[3] and it was perhaps with the sense of foreboding of one such ancient mariner that Edmund Burke experienced at first hand the approaching storm that signalled the initial outbreak of agrarian disturbances in the south of Ireland in the early 1760s.

In late 1761, as noted in Chapter 1 above, the first official communication to Dublin Castle of serious agrarian unrest in Ireland, in the form of an alleged treasonable Whiteboy conspiracy in Munster, found its way on to Burke's desk in his capacity as private secretary to William Gerard Hamilton, Chief Secretary to the Lord Lieutenant. It must have been with some alarm that Burke noticed the names of his childhood friends, the Hennessys, and, even closer to home, his own maternal relatives, the Nagles, among those mentioned in the dispatch as organizing the Whiteboys. In the round-ups that followed this initial outbreak of Whiteboy activity, a kinsman, Garret Nagle, was among those imprisoned on suspicion of aiding the insurgents. Nor did the unsettling connection of the Nagles with the Whiteboys end there. In 1766, in the aftermath of the execution of Fr Nicholas Sheehy, Burke was entreated privately by his uncle Patrick Nagle to use his influence on behalf of a distant relative, James Nagle, who was charged with treason and engaging in Whiteboy activities. Burke took an unusual degree of interest in these proceedings, for among his private papers were found a series of documents relating to the executions of three more Whiteboys, Edmund Sheehy, James Farrell, and James Buxton in May 1766. While awaiting execution, Buxton was promised a pardon if he incriminated certain leading Catholic gentlemen, among them James Nagle.[4] Such was Burke's personal involvement in the proceedings that he arranged for his last extended visit to Ireland in the second half of 1766 in order to organize a powerful defence council for the remaining Catholics due for arraignment. In this, as Louis Cullen suggests, he was successful, for the first wave of persecutions seems to have ended with this initiative.[5]

That Burke's association with the Whiteboy agitation pursued him in London is clear from the fact that the *Public Advertiser* could taunt him as a 'Whiteboy, a Native of a Bog in Ireland' who had come to reside in England.[6] Burke's reaction to these events betrays the nervous intensity of someone looking over the edge of a political abyss. In a sombre account of the political polarization which led to the escalation of agrarian unrest in nineteenth-century Ireland, Henry Giles wrote:

There is but one step from the aristocracy to the peasantry in Ireland, and that step is over a fearful precipice into the abyss of indescribable, of unimaginable desolation. There are but few intermediate grades to break the view, or to soften the contrast; it is a yawning gulf, exposed in all its horrors, from which the gazer shrinks back affrighted, with a reeling head and with quivering nerves.[7]

This is akin to the passage in the *Enquiry* in which Burke uses Virgil's description of the mouth of hell to convey 'that state of the soul, in which all its motions are suspended, with some degree of horror' (*Enquiry*, 57): 'before he unlocks the secrets of the great deep, he seems to be seized with religious horror, and to retire astonished at the boldness of his own design' (*Enquiry*, 71). Burke makes much of the absence of boundaries or 'intermediate grades to break the view' in his description of the sublime, and, for some contemporaries, it was as if the Whiteboys in their destruction of fences and boundaries were engaged in improving the view at the most crude material level, laying themselves open to the charge that they were converting the landscape into a wilderness. As one pamphlet expressed it, comparing in rapid succession the wild abandon of the insurgents to a riderless horse leaping fences at will, to primitive savages and to prostitution:

he leaps the adjoining Fences, flies wantonly abroad, tears up the Meadows and Corn-fields that were intended for his own sustenance, and becomes the companions of the wild and bleak Elements... no worse could be done or attempted by any Hottentots or Savages that ever inhabited the Wild of Africa, who never entered a court of justice, or heard the Toll of a Bell... But, what is to be done? The chaste name of LIBERTY, through the Country and Capital, is profaned and vilely strumpeted by an outrageous rabble.[8]

AESTHETICS, POLITICS, AND THE SUBLIME

In recent years, several commentators have drawn attention to the manner in which Burke's early writings on aesthetics foreshadowed his later condemnation of the terrors unleashed by the East India Company in India, and by the Jacobins in revolutionary France. If any lesson is to be learned from recent trends in scholarship, according to Stephen K. White, 'the most prominent... may be that political theorists can no longer afford to think that the aesthetic or literary aspects of a major figure's work are something that can be safely set to one side while "serious" analysis is done' on the more overt political writings. Given that Burke's main contribution to the aesthetics of the sublime was to invest it with the morbidity of terror and horror, White continues, 'the question that arises rather quickly is why did Burke persist in this refiguring of the sublime?'[9]

But the question also arises: why did Burke place such emphasis on the aesthetics of terror and darkness in the first place? If Burke's aesthetics and politics are in a complex and, at times, strained dialogue with each other, to what extent, then, were both part of a sustained critical engagement with the forces of terror and fear that presided over his early personal formation in Ireland? To the degree that Burke considered agrarian unrest as primarily concerned with economic grievances, narrowly defined, the injustices the

Whiteboys and their associates sought to redress could perhaps have been remedied within the existing political system – or, aesthetically speaking, within Burke's stabilizing category of the beautiful. It is for this reason that some contemporary historians, intent on distancing agrarian protest from forces that challenged the whole system of colonial representation in the eighteenth century, have tended to stress its immediate economic objectives, as against its wider political or cultural context. Hence, for example, S. J. Connolly's observation that in the outbreaks of popular violence which disturbed twenty-two out of Ireland's thirty-two counties in the eighteenth century: 'Protest... was in all cases defensive in character, arising in response to changes in existing patterns of land use or economic relationships, and seeking to preserve what were seen as existing rights within the agrarian system.'[10] But the question immediately arises: *whose* agrarian system? That of the colonizer – informed by the 'improving' ideology of the landed Protestant elite – or that of the colonized, also concerned with improvement but permeated by the very different cultural and landholding ethos of the old Gaelic order and the majority Catholic population? The fact that there was no unified system, no 'shared' consensus governing both ruler and ruled – such as E. P. Thompson identifies as the 'moral economy' in English society – was the basis of Burke's sustained critique of colonial rule in eighteenth-century Ireland. Writing to Sir Hercules Langrishe in 1792 in terms that prefigure Henry Giles's depiction of the utter polarization of Irish society, he pointed out, as noted above, that the systematic exclusion of Catholics from the public sphere through the imposition of the Penal Laws had 'divided the nation into two distinct bodies, without common interest, sympathy, or connexion – in effect, dispensing with any notion of a common, overarching culture ('Langrishe', iii, 301). Because of this clash between conflicting cultures, and competing modes of agricultural production within a commercial agrarian economy, demands for economic or social reform of the kind that could normally be accommodated within the existing political order tended to acquire a disruptive dimension that challenged the system itself. As agrarian insurgency in the form of Defenderism intensified on the eve of the 1798 rebellion, Burke noted that if its grievances could be contained at a purely economic level, they would be far more amenable to social control than when they were motivated by more deeply rooted, subterranean impulses:

That Jacobinism... which arises from Wantonness and fullness of bread, may possibly be kept under by firmness and prudence... But the Jacobinism which arises from Penury and irritation, from scorned loyalty, and rejected Allegiance, has much deeper roots. They take their nourishment from the bottom of human Nature, and the unalterable condition of things, and not from humour and caprice, or the opinions of the Day about privileges or Liberties.[11]

In this, it is possible to discern one of the most important reasons for Burke's alarm at the magnitude of the French Revolution. In his estimation, the extent of the upheaval was such that it not only concerned itself with the top-soil of 'privileges or liberties' but was a 'total revolution in all the principles of reason, prudence, and moral feeling',[12] seeking to restructure the individual psyche from the inside out. By including culture within its remit, it became 'a complete revolution', one that seemed 'to have extended even to the constitution of the mind of man'.[13] This represented an unprecedented degree of social change in the annals of conquest and revolution, as is clear from his observation elsewhere that notwithstanding the upheavals wrought by colonization in India, the 'venerable' English constitution was still unable to penetrate the innermost core of Indian culture – those aspects cut off from western values 'by manners, by principles of religion, and [by] inveterate habits as strong as nature itself':

Even English judges in India, who have been sufficiently tenacious of what they considered the rules of English courts, were obliged to relax on many points... as the civil and political government has been obliged to do in several other cases, on account of insuperable difficulties arising from a great diversity of manners, and what may be considered as a diversity even in the constitution of their minds.[14]

This view is clearly at odds with Stephen K. White's contention that Burke 'simply is unable to entertain the possibility that second nature [i.e. tradition and custom] goes "all the way down"', into the deepest recesses of the personality.[15] The obduracy of local custom in India derives precisely from the fact 'that they have stood firm on their ancient base – they have cast their roots deep in their native soil' ('Impeachment: Third Day', vii, 47). As such, they are impervious to complete foreign cultural domination – unless it manifests itself in the most thoroughgoing and brutal forms of colonial conquest.[16] Though Burke was willing to concede that radical social changes may be required in the interests of progress and 'improvement', or to remedy serious grievances in the system, these should never be so far-reaching as to disturb the structure of society itself, the dense filigree of custom and tradition that had evolved over the centuries. This was ultimately the cement of society without which even laws and commerce could not function: 'customs operate... better than laws, because they become a sort of Nature to the governors and the governed'.[17] Though Burke frequently uses geological and natural metaphors in these contexts, it is important for his view that structures are not simply foundations, but rather spread throughout the system: 'These are ties which, though light as air, are as strong as links of iron.'[18] This dispersal throughout the system – Burke also uses the metaphor of rays of light being refracted through a prism – means that connective links may even be concentrated in small details, or, as we have seen, 'exemplary events'. To destabilize the system is to attack it at one of these nodal points, however marginal or incidental they appear to the untutored eye. It is this profound inability to even recognize the intricate political filaments threaded through other cultures which characterizes the insensitivity of colonial rule in Ireland, India, and America, whether in the execution of Fr Nicholas Sheehy or the lashing of Private Hyland in insurgent Tipperary, the execution of Nundcomar in Bengal, or, as we shall see in Chapter 7, the murder of Jane McCrea in revolutionary America. Hence Burke's insistence, as noted in Chapter 1, that there was a categorical difference between the English 'Glorious Revolution' of 1688–9 and the French Revolution, and his strenuous objections to those political radicals, like Dr Richard Price and Joseph Priestley, who sought to blur the boundaries between the two. The Glorious Revolution did not snap the vital connection with the past or disturb the underlying substratum of society but rather sought to *re-connect* with tradition – in this case, the principles of the ancient constitution which had been suspended during the reign of James II. This is in stark contrast to the destructive innovations of the French Revolution, which set out to liquidate the past and to abolish the entire social order which pre-dated the Revolution.

But if these are the grounds for distinguishing between a just and an unjust revolution, what then are we to make of the devastating effects of the Williamite settlement on the pre-existing social order in seventeenth- and eighteenth-century Ireland? Does it not conform more to the unjust French model than to its benign English counterpart? Burke himself was acutely aware of the enormous disparity between the 'progressive' effects of the Revolution in England, and its calamitous consequences for Irish society:

In England it was the struggle of the *great body* of the people for the establishment of their liberties against the efforts of a very *small faction*, who would have oppressed them. In Ireland, it was the establishment of the power of the smaller number, at the expense of the civil liberties and properties of the far greater part; and at the expense of the political liberties of the whole. It was, to say the truth, not a revolution, but a conquest; which is not to say a great deal in its favour.[19] ('Langrishe', iii, 319)

That Burke was not quite sure of the status of the Glorious Revolution as it affected Ireland is further evident from the prevarications in his *Speech for Conciliation with America* [1775] and his earlier *Tracts on the Popery Laws* [*c*. 1765]. In the former, he attempted to subsume Ireland under the English model by arguing that 'almost every successive improvement in constitutional liberty, as fast as it was made here, was transplanted thither ... [T]he roots of our primitive constitution, were early transplanted into that soil; and grew and flourished there' ('Concilation', i. 483). From this it followed that the changes which had been effected in Irish society by successive conquests were no different in principle from those transitions which had taken place in England. Departing, as we shall see below, from his earlier indictments of the seventeenth-century expropriations in Ireland, Burke writes that the turmoil which followed the Cromwellian and Williamite wars must be seen as irregularities, as exceptions to a colonial rule which remained intact:

> The irregular things done in the confusions of mighty troubles, and on the hinge of great revolutions, even if all were done that is said to have been done, form no example. If they have any effect in argument, they make an exception to prove the rule. None of your own liberties could stand a moment if the casual deviations from them, at such times, were suffered to be used as proofs of their nullity.[20] ('Concilation', i, 484)

In arguing that the effects of conquest, 'the confusions of mighty troubles', can be mitigated to the extent that they are seen merely as exceptions that reinforce the rule, deviations from a larger, more stable system, Burke is drawing not only on his political philosophy but also on some of the most complex strands of his aesthetic theory. In the *Enquiry*, he notes that such is the lethargic effect of custom and conformity on both the mind and body that:

> when any organ of sense is for some time affected in some one manner, if it be suddenly affected otherwise there ensues a convulsive motion; such a convulsion as is caused when anything happens against the expectance of the mind. And though it may appear strange that such a change as produces a relaxation, should immediately produce a sudden convulsion; it is most certainly so, and so in all the senses. (*Enquiry*, 147–8)

The assumption here is that there is an in-built mechanism preventing the body from lapsing into the kind of torpor and 'relaxation' that could endanger its well-being: 'Whence does this strange motion arise; but from the too sudden relaxation of the body, which by some mechanism in nature restores itself by as quick and vigorous an exertion of the contracting power of the muscles?' (*Enquiry*, 148). There is no attempt here to conceal the fact that the abrupt adjustment required to restore vigour from the enervating effects of habit and familiarity may involve quite an unpleasant or even a painful sensation, an argument that extends to the steps required to counter the mediocrity induced in the social sphere by the operation of custom and 'prejudice':

> For as use [i.e. custom] at last takes off the painful effect of things, it reduces the pleasurable effect of others in the same manner, and brings both to a sort of mediocrity and indifference. Very justly is use called a second nature; and our natural and common state is one of absolute indifference, equally prepared for pain or pleasure. But when we are thrown out of this state, or deprived of anything requisite to maintain us in it . . . we are always hurt. It is so with the second nature, custom, in all things which relate to it. (*Enquiry*, 104)

This is the thinking – and indeed the vocabulary ('convulsions', 'relaxation', 'second nature') – which informs Burke's theory of revolution and conquest. No political grievance, as we have noted in Chapter 3 in relation to colonial rule, is felt more deeply than that which offends against the most ingrained customs and mores of a society: 'The dominion of manners and the law of opinion', as Burke observed of India, 'contributes more to their unhappiness and misery than anything in mere sensitive nature can do' ('Impeachment: Fifth Day', vii. 190). It is in this connection that the adversarial but strangely symbiotic relationship between the categories of the sublime and the beautiful in his aesthetic theory is brought to bear on his political concerns. Burke's central argument is that just as the rigours and 'convulsions' of the sublime are needed to jolt the body, or body politic, out of the familiarity and tranquillizing effects of the beautiful, so is the emollient influence of the beautiful required in turn to soften the asperity of the sublime, to prevent the disruption of the system from becoming too painful or unmanageable. Custom, he argues, 'reconciles us to everything' (*Enquiry*, 148), and in this lay the basis for the great ameliorating forces in society, for 'the soft collar of social esteem . . . which made power gentle, and obedience liberal, which harmonised the different shades of life, and which, by a bland assimilation, incorporated into politics the sentiments which *beautify* and soften private society' (*Reflections*, 171; my italics).

At one point in the *Enquiry*, Burke explicitly distinguishes beauty from custom, on account of its possessing novelty and originality: 'beauty is so far from belonging to the idea of custom, that in reality what effects us in that manner is extremely rare and uncommon' (*Enquiry*, 103). Yet, as Tom Furniss notes and as the previous quotation from the *Reflections* indicates, beauty and custom are equated as ameliorating influences in his response to the French Revolution.[21] Frances Ferguson traces this connection between beauty and custom back to the *Enquiry* itself, notwithstanding Burke's own attempts to suggest otherwise:

The beautiful, insofar as it represents the virtues of custom and civilized behaviour, is a near relation to the law that, of course, continually functions to support the force of custom and civilization; the sublime, which is cut off from custom inasmuch as it is associated with novelty and surprise, quite simply overruns the claims of legality.[22]

The connection here has to do with the socializing and familiarizing effects of beauty, its smooth and tranquillizing qualities which resemble the operation of custom in 'mollify[ing] the rigour and sternness of terror' (*Enquiry*, 157). To the extent that the silent operation of custom and 'the beautiful' is capable of absorbing the shocks of 'corrective' violence induced by the sublime, and is able to restore the stability of the system, revolution and conquest may be justified in Burke's eyes. Hence, for all his supposed veneration of tradition and 'time immemorial', Burke disagreed with those 'nativists' who sought to ground the antiquity of the British constitution in the myth of the free-born Englishman, in so far as this denoted an idyllic period of Anglo-Saxon liberty before the imposition of the Norman yoke.[23] Rather than violating 'the purity of the primitive constitution', Burke saw the Norman Conquest as delivering English law from an era in which it was 'involved in superstition and polluted with violence'. For this reason:

The Norman Conquest is the great era of our laws. At this time the English jurisprudence, which had hitherto continued a poor stream, fed from some few, and those scanty, sources, was all at once, as from a mighty flood, replenished with a vast body of foreign learning, by which, indeed, it might be said rather to have been increased than much improved: for this foreign law, being imposed, not adopted, for a long time bore strong appearances of that violence by which it had been first introduced.[24]

But the traces of this violence eventually disappeared: 'Time has, by degrees, in all other places and periods, blended and coalited the conquered with the conquerors. So, after some time, and after one of the most rigid conquests that we read of in history, the Normans softened into the English' ('Langrishe', iii, 319). By the same token, 'because we commenced with reparation, not with ruin', the Glorious Revolution worked eventually to revitalize and enrich a virtually comatose body politic, despite the initial discontinuity and instability which it introduced:

Instead of lying as dead, in a sort of trance, or exposed, as some others [i.e. France in 1790], in an epileptic fit, to the pity or derision of the world, for her wild, ridiculous, convulsive movements... Great Britain rose above the standard even of her former self. An era of a more improved domestic prosperity commenced, and still continues not only unimpaired, but growing, under the wasting hand of time. All the energies of the country were awakened. England never presented a firmer countenance, nor a more vigourous arm, to all her enemies and to all her rivals.[25]

Burke was willing, therefore, to recast certain forms of revolution and conquest in aesthetic terms, as a series of dramatic convulsions whose initially painful effects were subsequently cauterized by the healing powers of time and oblivion. Though his political ambition, in his official persona as an ideologue of empire, was somehow to tailor the colonization of Ireland and India to fit this model, his abiding fear in both cases was that they prefigured a more malign alternative, that of revolutionary France, where the seismic upheavals of the sublime were not ground down by custom but had disturbed even this cumulative deposit of experience. The difficulty with mapping Burke's work in aesthetics too readily on to these illicit forms of conquest or violence, as Sara Suleri notes,[26] is that his treatise on the sublime and the beautiful clearly predates his writings on India and France, and thus could not be influenced by them. But his early foray into aesthetics does not, as we have seen, predate his formative years in Ireland, which suggests that his preoccupation with terror, in both art and politics, had indeed a source nearer home, impinging on his closest ancestral ties.

The avatar of destruction in Burke's historical imagination, prefiguring later manifestations of terror in France and Ireland, was Oliver Cromwell, not so much on account of his usurpation of power in England but more particularly because of the ferocity of his campaign in Ireland, and the reign of terror perpetrated against Catholic landowners through his plantation policies. The legacy of Cromwell surfaces in the *Reflections* when Burke is seeking to discredit the radical Whig claim, advanced by Richard Price, that the French Revolution could look to the Williamite settlement as its legitimate precursor. Burke angrily responded that the revolutionary zeal shown by the Jacobins had 'not been heard in this kingdom, in any of the pulpits which are encouraged or tolerated in it, since the year 1648', and the sectarian harangues of the Solemn League and Covenant. Though describing Cromwell as 'one of the great bad men of the old stamp' (*Reflections*, 136), Burke conceded (if only to maintain his own belief in the essential continuity of the British constitution) that the 'corrective' violence he administered to a country torn by civil war 'was to be sure somewhat rigid, but, for a new power, no savage tyranny'.[27] However, from the visible evidence of his own surroundings in the Cork countryside, and from the scars left on Catholic popular memory as relayed through his own maternal cousins, the Nagle family, Burke was under no illusion but that it was indeed 'a savage tyranny' that Cromwell had inflicted on Ireland. Recent commentators such as Peter J. Stanlis and Stephen K. White are correct, therefore, in identifying the wrath of Cromwell as the only true precursor of the French Revolution in Burke's chamber of horrors, but are mistaken in laying the emphasis solely on his English reputation (which Burke was, in fact, inclined to excuse).[28] Conor Cruise O'Brien's diagnosis of Burke's inner demons is more accurate when he traces the animus against Cromwell to the traumatic repercussions of his notorious Irish campaign. In invoking the spectre of 1648 in his condemnation of Richard Price, moreover, it would not have escaped Burke's notice that Lord Shelburne, Price's most influential patron, was himself a Cromwellian upstart, the direct descendant of the infamous Sir William Petty who advocated mass transportation as the means of divesting Ireland of its surplus native population, and introduced the incubus of 'political economy' into the Irish body politic.[29]

THE CURSE OF CROMWELL

In an exchange of letters at the height of the Whiteboy disturbances in 1762, one of Burke's closest confidants in Ireland, the patriot MP, Charles O'Hara, wrote to him 'that too much of the pleasure one has in improving a place of one's own is from vanity' – until, that is, O'Hara's servants rudely reminded him, by tearing up his shrubs, that everyone did not share his progressive approach to agriculture. O'Hara then proceeds to give an absorbing first-hand account of a visit to Inismurray, a remote island off the coast of Sligo, in terms that would have elicited the approval of some later purist strands of cultural nationalism:

The race of Inhabitants now there are by their tradition of many hundred years' standing. If ever they come to our Continent [i.e. the mainland], they call it going into the great world. They are an unmixd people, Their Irish purer than our people speak and many of their stories I am told, have all the natural beauty so well *counterfeited* in Fingal. They have ruins very singular and of great antiquity. But the innocent simplicity of their lives is extraordinary. Extremely hospitable to any stranger that goes among them; and miraculously chaste; whatever disputes may arise, are settled among themselves; they are never known to carry a complaint into *the great world*.

O'Hara is convinced that the image of such a community would greatly appeal to Burke: 'When I go to London, I shall try to get this island. I think you'd pay me a visit there; tho' you wont here' (referring to his country residence on the Sligo mainland). There is no doubt that the island would have indeed appealed to Burke as a site of uninterrupted tradition, an oasis of calm and continuity. But then O'Hara strikes a discordant note in relation to this idyllic community:

I went yesterday to divide a very large mountain farm among its inhabitants, who according to their own tradition have lived under *me* there 500 years; tis their phrase. With great difficulty I divided them into four villages, for twas an innovation; but I told them they must be moderniz'd... I have a desire to make them industrious, and to preserve them. You'd hardly expect this from a man you usd to accuse last winter as being as bad as any Cromwellian.[30]

What we are witnessing here in microcosm is perhaps the break-up of the native moral economy, based on the 'rundale' agricultural system (the collective mountain farm) and the clustered settlement or 'clachan', and its transformation into a new agrarian capitalist order.[31] The reference to Burke's use of 'Cromwellian' as a term of abuse is revealing in this context, for in his reply by return post to O'Hara, Burke ventilates his barely suppressed rage at the mention of Cromwell by portraying him as the personification of the worst excesses of colonialism in the New World and Ireland. Burke then goes on to equate this form of rapine with the contemporary response of the Munster landlords to the agrarian unrest in which, as we have seen, he had such a deep, personal stake:

You charm me with this account of your Little New World, which you have described so near home. Of what size is this Island, or is it described in the Map? I wish you may get it with all my heart; for I know that you will be no Cortez, Pizarro, Cromwell or Boyle to the Natives. Happy and wise are these poor Natives in avoiding your great World; that they are yet unacquainted with the unfeeling Tyranny of a mungril Irish Landlord, or with the horrors of a Munster Circuit. I have avoided this subject whenever I wrote to you; and I shall now say no more of it; because it is impossible to preserve ones Temper on the view of so detestable a scene. God save me from the power (I shall take care to keep myself from the society) of such monsters of Inhumanity.

The kind of modernization which lends itself to agricultural improvements and Whig ideas of progress takes on, in Burke's imagination, the dark contours of the sublime when it is applied to the Irish countryside. Proceeding to note that only hangmen are fit company for the gentlemen of Munster who are tyrannizing the Catholic population, Burke then breaks abruptly from this disturbing train of thought to enquire: 'Can you get drawings of any of the ruins on Inis Moray?'[32]

It is almost as if Burke looks for solace from the horrors of improvement, Irish style, in the contemplation of ruins. The references to Cromwell and Roger Boyle endow ruins with a very specific local habitation in Burke's memory: we may surmise that the several Roche castles in the vicinity of the Nagle country, systematically devastated by Cromwellian forces, influenced his perception of ruins, and, more particularly, Monanimy Castle, under whose shattered walls he had attended a roofless hedge school taught by an outlawed schoolmaster, O'Halloran.[33] Monanimy also housed the Knights of St John of Jerusalem and in a characteristic astute observation, William O'Brien remarks of Burke's unfinished work on English history, written two years after the *Enquiry*:

We need, however, be at no loss to understand the origin of his sympathetic references to the monasteries in his Abridgement of English History, if we remember the impressions that must have been stamped upon his young mind by the sight all over the valley of those devastated shrines, whose very silence gave tragic witness of the confiscations and persecutions that were pressing to the earth his kinsmen of the old faith of his mother.[34]

In the *Tracts on the Popery Laws*, Burke discerns in the ruins of Ireland the history of the vanquished, an indictment of those sectarian accounts of the Cromwellian period which often provide little more than apologias for confiscation. Expressing his contempt for 'those miserable performances which go about under the name of Histories of Ireland', he adds, in a telling passage: 'But there is an interior History of Ireland, the genuine voice of its records and monuments, which speaks a very different language from those histories, of Temple and Clarendon; these restore nature to its just rights, and policy to its proper order' ('Popery Laws', vi, 45). For Burke, ruins are a kind of inner speech within a culture, disjointed and fragmented expressions of what is suppressed in official discourse. Indeed, it is possible to detect a similar form of inner speech in the hesitations and anxieties of his own texts, dividing them at a number of critical conjunctures against themselves. Burke's avowed aim in the *Tracts on the Popery Laws* is to admit Catholics to the benefits of the British constitution, and to give them access to the edifying rewards of industry and improvement. Ireland, he claims, 'is a country wholly unplanted': the lands are for the most part without 'fences and communications; in a word, in a very unimproved state' ('Popery Laws', vi, 44). He inveighs in particular against the short tenure allowed to Catholics under the Penal Laws:

A tenure of 30 years is evidently no tenure upon which to build; to plant; to raise enclosures; to change the nature of the ground; to make any new experience which might improve agriculture... Confine a man to momentary possession, and you at once cut off that laudable avarice which every wise State has cherished as one of the first principles of its greatness. ('Popery Laws', vi, 43)

The problems with this presentation of the case for progressive agriculture arise when Burke elucidates the grounds for extending its remit to Catholics. The Penal Laws, he points out, exclude Catholics from citizenship for subscribing to a principle which lies at the heart of the British constitution, namely, 'an implicit admiration and adherence to the establishments of their forefathers' ('Popery Laws', vi, 32). However, the difficulty with allowing Catholics to defer 'to the wisdom of times past' ('Popery Laws', vi, 33), particularly in the case of his own maternal family, the Nagles, was that it would uncover an adherence to Jacobitism and to the errors of 'monkish superstition' – the very forces which both Cromwell and the Glorious Revolution sought to expunge from English history through the harsh retribution of the untrammelled sublime. 'It is true', writes Burke:

that bigotry and fanaticism may, for a time, draw great multitudes of people from a knowledge of their true and substantial interest. But... if such a spirit has been at any time roused in a society, after it has had its paroxysm it commonly subsides and is quiet, and is even the weaker for the violence of its first exertion; security and ease are its mortal enemies. ('Popery Laws', vi, 46)

This, he believes, is the case in mid-eighteenth-century England where the originary violence unleashed by the sublime in the turbulent seventeenth century has been tamed and domesticated by the beautiful, by the 'soft collar' of tradition and social esteem. The disruption of hereditary succession by William's accession to the throne was discreetly covered by placing 'a politic, well-wrought veil over every circumstance tending to weaken the rights, which in the meliorated order of succession they meant to perpetuate' (*Reflections*, 103). In a letter written thirty years later to his son Richard in Ireland, Burke picks up once more the threads of this argument, asserting that custom and habit often step in where history fears to tread, helping to resolve energies and hatreds which escape the nets of reason or religious disputation:

Strange it is, but so it is, that men, driven by force from their habits in one religion, have, by contrary habits, under the same force, often quietly settled in another. They suborn their reason to declare in favour of their necessity. Man and his conscience cannot always be at war. If the first races have not been able to make a pacification between the conscience and the convenience, their descendants come generally to submit to the violence of the laws, without violence to their minds.[35]

But, as he ruefully remarks in the *Tracts on the Popery Laws*, such a situation only obtains when old animosities are laid to rest: 'if anything can tend to revive and keep it up [i.e. the initial resistance to violence], it is to keep alive the passions of men by ill usage' ('Popery Laws', vi, 46). It is this possibility above all which torments Burke, and sees to it that Irish politics is racked by the convulsions of the perpetual sublime. Instead of following the English example, letting 'Time draw his oblivious veil over the unpleasant modes by which lordships and demesnes have been acquired' ('Richard Burke', vi, 75), the ideologues of the Protestant Ascendancy in Ireland constantly return to the violence of their original conquest like criminals revisiting the scene of a crime:

One would not think that decorum, to say nothing of policy, would permit them to call up, by magic charms, the grounds, reasons, and principles of those terrible confiscatory and exterminatory periods. They would not set men upon calling from the quiet sleep of death any Samuel, to ask him, by what act of arbitrary monarchs... by what fictitious tenures, invented to dispossess whole unoffending tribes and other chieftains! They would not conjure up the ghosts from the ruins of castles and churches, to tell for what... the estates of the old Irish nobility and gentry had been confiscated. They would not wantonly call on those phantoms, to tell by what English acts of parliament, forced upon two reluctant kings, the lands of their country were put up to a mean auction in every goldsmith's shop in London; or chopped to pieces, and cut into rations, to pay the mercenary soldiery of a regicide usurper. They would not be so fond of titles under Cromwell, who, if he revenged an Irish rebellion against the sovereign authority of the parliament of England, had himself rebelled against the very parliament whose sovereignty he asserted full as much as the Irish nation, which he was sent to subdue and confiscate, could rebel against that parliament... ('Richard Burke', vi, 77)

Burke's heightened language here has shifted into a Gothic register, as if the excess of hatred unleashed by successive waves of conquest can no longer be contained, but may in fact be exacerbated by the sullen operation of habit and custom. Instead of providing stable foundations, tradition in Ireland builds up a 'bank of discontent, every hour accumulating, upon which every description of seditious men may draw at pleasure' ('Langrishe', iii, 336). As Frances Ferguson points out, it is 'when Burke introduces properties of sublimity which he allies with habit and custom that the sublime begins to appear threatening – largely because habit and custom operate to obscure the threat'.[36] In a key section of the *Enquiry*, Burke contends that the sublime is never as threatening as when it ceases to be transient, and acquires the constancy of the beautiful. In certain extreme circumstances, he points out, the body may be placed under such duress that 'The senses strongly affected in some one manner, cannot quickly change their tenor, or adapt themselves to other things; but they continue in their old channel until the strength of the first mover decays' (*Enquiry*, 74). The disorienting effects of such repetition leads to the kind of obsession which can even convert love – the repository of 'the beautiful' – into its opposite, the violent rapture of the sublime. Hence the 'violent effects produced by love, which has sometimes been even wrought up to madness': 'When men have suffered their imaginations to be affected with any idea, it so wholly engrosses them as to shut out by degrees almost every other, and to break down every partition of the mind which would confine it' (*Enquiry*, 41). Taken to its extreme, such an agitated condition can degenerate into the behaviour of madmen who 'in the constant repetition of some remark, some complaint, or song; which having struck powerfully on their disordered imagination, in the beginning of their phrensy, every repetition reinforces it with new strength; and the hurry of their spirits, unrestrained by the curb of reason, continues it to the end of their lives' (*Enquiry*, 74). For Burke, the equivalent of this contagion at a public level is to be found in the tumult of the mob during political unrest, which 'so amazes and confounds the imagination, that in this staggering, and hurry of the mind, the best established tempers can scarcely forbear being borne down, and joining in the common cry, and common resolution of the crowd' (*Enquiry*, 82). It is striking how echoes of these descriptions find their way into Burke's unfinished report on the origins of the Whiteboy disturbances in Munster. As a result of his own investigations, he concluded that the disturbances owed their origins to an unstable individual, one Mr Fant, who growing 'visionary, restless, and unquiet' and 'disordered in his senses':

assembled at night many of the meaner people of Kilmallock, and having warmed them with liquor, he harangued them on the grievances which the poor in general suffered from the rich; and telling them that their town-common had been illegally enclosed . . . they completely demolished all the fences which enclosed their reputed common.[37]

It was as if the frenzied resistance to enclosures bore out Burke's worst fears of the failure of 'the beautiful' – with its civilizing fences and 'partitions' – to contain the destructive energies of 'the sublime'.

'DREADFUL DEFENDERISM': FROM THE 1760S TO THE 1790S

Just as custom can combine in a lethal manner with its opposite, the disruptive violence of the sublime, so Burke feared that the veneration of the past in the Catholic peasantry would fuse with the revolutionary fervour of

Jacobinism. In a letter written to William Smith during the intensification of agrarian conflict in 1794/5, he recalled his own memories of the vicious repression of the Whiteboys thirty years earlier, again having recourse to the language of pathology to account for the spasmodic outbreaks of violence among the peasantry:

I remember but one period in my whole life, (I mean the savage period between 1761 and 1767) in which they have been more harshly or contumeliously treated, than since the last partial enlargement. And thus I am convinced it will be by paroxysms, as long as any stigma remains on them, and whilst they are considered as no better than half citizens. If they are kept such for any length of time, they will be made whole Jacobins. Against this grand and dreadful evil of our time (I do not love to cheat myself or others) I do not know any solid security whatsoever.[38]

The most instructive feature of Burke's alarmist, and in the end prophetic, reading of the deteriorating political situation in Ireland was his recognition that custom, the very bedrock of the constitution in England, could also turn out to be the fault-line in the colonial system elsewhere. In a letter to his son Richard in late 1792, he wrote that 'the Question is not, as the Hucksters of Ascendancy think, of dealing with a credulous Mob, soon inflamed, soon extinguished. No such thing, as you know as well as I. The igneous fluid has its Lodging in a solid mass.'[39] The very subsoil of society, the strata of stability and security in the colonial centre, turns out to be explosive and a source of seismic upheavals in a colonized culture. Custom indeed may reconcile us to everything but when it is infused with the sublime, it is not so much a reconciliation of opposites which is effected but a volatile juxtaposition which may leave both extremes intact and even revitalized:

Thus are two ideas as opposite as can be imagined reconciled in the extremes of both; and both in spite of their opposite nature brought to concur in producing the sublime. And this is not the only instance wherein the opposite extremes operate equally in favour of the sublime, which in all things abhors mediocrity. (*Enquiry*, 81)

It may be that even Burke himself was affected by these revolutionary tremors. In November 1792, he mentions that he has been reading the newspapers of the United Irishmen, and he finds them 'rational, manly and proper' in every respect but their tendency to ascribe to the British connection ills that emanate, as he sees it, from the 'jobbing Ascendancy'.[40] The attempt to infuse the 'manly' energy of the sublime into the propagation of the Catholic cause is a recurrent note in his writings of this period and though he stopped short at advocating violent resistance, by

1796 even this had changed as if his aesthetic theory was following its logical, or rather pathological, course through Irish history. In a letter to Rev. Thomas Hussey, he claims that there is little left in Ireland but a 'desperate alternative between a thankless acquiesence under grievous oppression, or a refuge in Jacobinism, with all its horrors and all its crimes', but he proceeds to make it clear that by the horror of the Jacobins he does not mean the United Irishmen or the Catholic defenders, but their 'servile imitators', the 'great French empire of pure and perfect Protestantism' that 'apes, at an humble distance, the Tone of its capital [in Paris], to make a crusade against you poor Catholics'.[41] This provides the cue for an admission of political loyalties which leaves little doubt where his allegiance lies if it comes to a choice between 'desperate alternatives':

> I am not at all surprised at it; and consider it as one of the natural consequences of a measure better intended than considerd – that of the Catholick Clergys persuading the Laity to give up their Arms. Dreadful it is: but it is now plain enough, that Catholick *Defenderism* is the only restraint upon Protestant *Ascendency*.[42]

Writing in 1800 after the passing of the Act of Union, Peter Burrowes, one-time friend of Theobald Wolfe Tone, warned against taking the silence of the subjugated Catholic population at face value in the aftermath of the savage reprisals inflicted by the government during the 1798 rebellion:

> No man who has not a general and in some degree a confidential intercourse with the Catholics of Ireland, can imagine what a determined and desperate spirit of counteraction the orange outrages and principally those which have been tolerated since the suppression of the rebellion have spread among that body and their friends of every description. Terror for the present silences all expression of resentment.

Burrowes went on to observe that 'those detailed accounts of their severities exercised since [1793] toward their body...will probably sleep for ever if the country be quiet. Yet if a storm should rise, I dread the effect of such materials in inflaming the public mind.'[43] Burrowes' warning is instructive for those commentators who are willing to read into the silences of the Catholic population for long periods during the eighteenth-century an acquiesence in their own condition. Burke, with his attentiveness to the façades of decorum and civility, was not likely to mistake the mute condition of servitude as evidence of social tranquillity, any more than his own silences are a measure of his acceptance of political oppression. Decrying the lack of conviction in the government's attempts to stamp out corruption in India, he took issue with those who 'would recommend oblivion as the best remedy' so that 'mute despair, and sullen patience, is construed into content and satisfaction' ('Impeachment: Fifth Day', vii, 192). In times of crisis, custom itself becomes a conduit of the sublime, and hence is no longer in a position to run its lethal energies to earth: 'retrospect could have no advantage, and could serve only to irritate and to keep alive animosities' ('Impeachment: Fifth Day', vii, 193).[44] By denying the tranquillizing effects of tradition in a colonial context, Burke was, in effect, drawing a distinction between the restorative violence of the British constitution at home, and its irredeemably destructive character when imposed on Ireland and India – albeit with the rider, as we have seen, that the latter eventually comes home to base and contaminates the former. Though committed in his official public persona to a politics of reform, the sense of foreboding sounded in his aesthetic writings anticipates the kind of crisis in which reform is no longer possible, at least where the colonies are concerned. There may indeed be a surface calm: but the most dangerous form of the colonial sublime, as he reminds us in the *Enquiry*, is precisely that of 'tranquillity tinged with terror' (*Enquiry*, 136).

6
Burke and colonialism: the Enlightenment and cultural diversity

> It should be noted that in claiming that Burke was no less a product of modernity than Paine, I am not equating 'modernity' simply with the Enlightenment – its genealogy was far more complex.
>
> James Vernon, *Re-Reading the Constitution*

> There are other examples of... efforts to articulate a form of modernity that could answer to Irish needs, such as Burke's reinvention of the sublime as an aesthetic experience...
>
> James Livesey, 'Introduction' to Arthur O'Connor, *The State of Ireland*

In his famous Vienna lecture of 1935, *The Crisis of European Sciences*, Edmund Husserl summed up one of the central (if often unspoken) tenets of the Enlightenment by asserting that while all cultures were free to express themselves mythically, religiously, or creatively, only Europe had the capacity to produce theory, or modes of thought consistent with the ordinances of universal reason. Art, religion, and myth can assume vernacular forms, speaking, as it were, in regional accents, but criticism and intellectual enquiry for the most part remain firmly located in the metropolitan centre.[1] Much of what passes for contemporary critiques of the Enlightenment in postmodern theorists such as Foucault and Lyotard is levelled at such universalist designs on the part of western thought,[2] but it may well be that by construing the Enlightenment almost exclusively in advanced metropolitan terms, the postmodern avantgarde is itself guilty of the very Eurocentrism it deplores in others.

Paul Gilroy has remarked that for some black cultures 'the "enthusiasm of 1789" relates more to Port au Prince than it does to Paris',[3] and it this possibility of alternative Enlightenments outside the centre which arises in relation to Edmund Burke's critique of universal reason, and the kind of abstract theorizing about human society that he associated with the French Revolution. According to Burke:

Nothing universal can be rationally affirmed on any moral or any political subject. Pure metaphysical abstraction does not belong to these matters. The lines of morality are not like the ideal lines of mathematics. They are broad and deep as well as long. They admit of exceptions; they demand modifications. These exceptions and modifications are not made by the process of logic, but by the rules of prudence. ('Appeal', iii, 16)

Though Burke's admonitions against universal reason are often attributed to his conservatism and traditionalism, many of them are in fact compatible with another school of advanced European thought, that of the eighteenth-century Scottish Enlightenment, which, as we have seen in Chapter 3, replaced the sovereignty of reason by the civic and moral refinement of the 'man of feeling'. Burke shared David Hume's view that reason is the slave of the passions, or rather of sympathy, but would have emphasized more than Hume that it is as much determined by the cultural circumstances of time and place, as it is by the internal springs of affection. The cult of sensibility and its attendant ethics of sympathy were crucial components of the Enlightenment, and contributed as much to the abolition of slavery, for instance, as the more abstract 'rights of man' espoused by American and French republicanism – though, in the last instance, Adam Smith's and John Millar's arguments about the economic inefficiency of slavery may have carried greater weight with more practical minded apostles of progress in Scotland and elsewhere.[4]

PROGRESS AND PRIMITIVISM

Edmund Burke – and, it might be added, his countryman Richard Brinsley Sheridan – were among the foremost opponents of slavery at this early period, though as with many other Enlightenment thinkers, the question of immediate abolition was not considered politically or economically viable.[5] Where Burke went further than many of his contemporaries, however, was in developing an incipient critique not just of the slave trade, but of colonialism. While helping to abolish slavery, the Scottish Enlightenment did not hold out much hope for African, or any other oppressed cultures, wishing to throw off the shackles of colonialism. Instead, by espousing a philosophy of progress which established a clear hierarchy among cultures, and identifying that progress in turn with the advancement of political economy and British civilization, Scottish versions of liberty offered as little in the long run to the people of Port au Prince as the erstwhile French revolutionaries who suppressed the slaves' rebellion in Haiti.

One of the reasons the Enlightenment – whether in its Scottish, American or French manifestations – has come to be identified with westernization, if not western aggrandizement, is precisely the weakness of its critique of colonialism. Even the abolition of colonial slavery, as we have noted, was motivated more by sentimentalism, Christian philanthropy, and the calculations of political economy, than by a determination to abolish the evils of colonialism itself.[6] Where Burke is unusual among dissident or critical Enlightenment figures is in his heightened awareness of the malaise of colonialism, and, in particular, its violation of *cultural* and *group* rights, whether in Ireland, India or, from a different perspective, America. In this he was no doubt indebted to the emphasis on local circumstances and cultural specificity first adumbrated by Montesquieu,[7] but Burke went further than his French mentor in emphasizing that difference does not necessarily entail inferiority, and that civilization is not a monopoly of European cultures. As Frederick G. Whelan has recently noted:

Burke was one of the first major European thinkers, and one of the first writers in the traditional canon of Western political theory, to have made a serious effort to understand a non-Western civilization and to incorporate his findings into his general political thought... In taking India seriously, Burke was at the same time one of the first major Western thinkers to grapple with the moral and political problems of European empire over non-Western nations.[8]

Under universal conceptions of the rights of man, equality extended to individuals, abstractly conceived, but not to cultures; while all human beings were equal, some cultures were less equal than others, and their destruction was justified in the name of progress. It was precisely Burke's sensitivity not just to custom and tradition but also to the diversity and adaptability of cultures, which made him deeply suspicious of such linear or homogeneous maps of mankind. This conception of cultural diversity made provision for change, reform, and even revolution, but not if it involved the root and branch extirpation of a culture, and still less the usurpation of one culture by another in the name of its superior claim to progress and civilization.

Burke's respect for tradition, his sentimental attachment to the 'age of chivalry' and the values of the old aristocratic order, is often taken as inherently counter-revolutionary. It is for the reason that he has become the patron saint of those strands of conservatism in Britain intent on viewing the glories of a vanished imperial past through the haze of the heritage industry. But was Burke an uncritical worshipper at the altar of tradition? He was undoubtedly against innovation, of the kind which turns the world upside down, uprooting cultures and cutting off all ancestral ties. But he was not against renovation, even if it involved a radical alteration of our relationship with the past. Unlike the contemporary political theorist, Jon Elster, tradition for him was not mindless repetition, nor did it reside in sclerotic rituals impervious to the passage of time.[9] Rather, it was a highly malleable form of life, adaptable to the circumstances of both time and place and answerable to the body and its social needs as well as to the more cerebral demands of reason. In particular – and here we see one of his fundamental disagreements with republican thought of the contractarian variety – Burke warned against the rigidity of forms of tradition which make a cult of their foundational moments, seeking their essence in rational determinations of origins, however unhistorical, rather than in the actual developments of societies over time and place.

Hence his dismissal, in the early unpublished *Abridgement of English History*, of those quasi-republican strands in British thought that looked to the golden age of Anglo-Saxon liberties, before the imposition of the 'Norman Yoke', as laying down the principles of liberty which had subsequently been corrupted or compromised by the passage of time. As we have seen in Chapter 5, Burke saw the Norman Conquest and, indeed, the 'Glorious Revolution' of 1688, not as disrupting the initial purity of principle established at the foundational moments of the state, but as bestowing beneficial effects, often redeeming or palliating the primal acts of violence that attended the origins of the body politic. So far from indulging in nostalgic idylls, Burke had few illusions about a mythic 'Golden Age', and particularly about the foresight, rationality and harmony presupposed by an original social contract.[10] As his anxieties about probing too deep into the foundations of governments show, he was all too aware of the violence and attrition of history, whether in a colonial or any other context. As he wrote of the triumphalist commemorations of the Protestant Ascendancy in Ireland:

One would think they would wish to let Time draw his oblivious veil over the unpleasant modes by which lordships and demesnes have been acquired in theirs, and almost in all other countries upon earth. It might be imagined that when the sufferer (if a sufferer exists) had forgot the wrong, they would be pleased to forget it too; that they would permit the sacred name of possession to stand in place of the melancholy and unpleasant title of grantees of confiscation. ('Richard Burke', vi, 75–6)

In such cases, to celebrate origins was to re-open the scars of conquest and humiliation, to convert the past itself into a pathology.

This argument had far-reaching implications for the associations of progress with sensibility and moral sympathy so central to the refined puritan ethos of the Scottish Enlightenment. Even when the existence of an actual historical original contract had been derided by philosophers such as Hume,[11] there remained in the new ideology of commerce and civility a nostalgia for primitive simplicity, and the rigours of a frugal, rural lifestyle to offset the more enervating effects of progress.[12] This helps to explain what may otherwise seem an anomaly or contradiction in liberal philosophies of progress, that is, the persistence of the myth of a Golden Age in the past, notwithstanding the belief that the best was to come yet. In the writings of John Locke, there is a pathos for a world we have lost with the rise of money and commerce, particularly as exemplified by the austere, almost classical nobility of the American Indians.[13] Whig recriminations against the corruption of commerce became more pronounced after the 1745 Jacobite invasion, when the near military success of the Scottish Highlanders led Adam Smith to observe that

another bad effect of commerce is that it sinks the courage of mankind, and tends to extinguish martial spirit. [As a result of commerce and civility] the minds of men are contracted and rendered incapable of elevation... and heroic spirit is almost utterly extinguished.[14]

To remedy this relapse into luxury and effeminacy, the Scottish Enlightenment made a key distinction between savagery, on the one hand, which could be idealized at the safe remove of 2,000 miles or, even better, years, and on the other hand, barbarism, the state of degeneration into which previously noble savages had subsequently fallen.[15] This led to a search for a noble savage closer to home, and the metropolitan centre was not slow to find its obscure object of desire in the outer fastnesses of the Celtic periphery. Hence the extraordinary cultural investment in the Ossian revival and its attendant cult of Celticism which emerged in the 1760s, following the Scottish militia controversy. If Edinburgh was to be the Athens of the North, then it was fitting that it would have its Homer in the Highlands.

Inspired by Ossian and the stages theory of history, the Scottish intelligentsia demonstrated, as Walter Bagehot remarked in one of his rare humorous asides, 'how from being a savage, man had grown to be a Scotsman' – with nothing in between.[16] For the Enlightenment, what had happened 'in between' – the centuries of Gaelic culture and monkish superstition – were an unfortunate detour on the road to progress (which tended to point in the same direction, as Dr Johnson dryly observed, as the high road to London). It was not the distant but the recent past which proved an embarrassment to the pursuit of a polite and commercial society. Primitivism had the advantage of placing the Golden Age in remote antiquity so that it might function at most as an model, or a set of ideals, rather than a culture in a lived relationship, no matter how fractious, with the present. The clannish Highlanders, with their inveterate communalism and tribal ways, represented a degeneration from this ideal and came in fact not to be seen as Scottish at all, but more akin to the Irish, the true relics of barbarism in the modern age. Seeking to disabuse Herder, in his role as romantic theorist and Celtic enthusiast, of Irish claims on Ossian, James Macdonald wrote from Scotland in 1776:

The tales of the Irish are improbable, extravagant romances, full of enchanted castles, fights, drunkenness, witchcraft and murder. Their *love* is a sort of fury accompanied by half-mad unnatural elopements, stepping over the Irish channel at a bound, and performing other things which even *Irish love* in our own days cannot perform. Their poems... are totally different from those of the ancient Caledonians. The tales of the latter are romantic indeed, but always delighting in sentiments of morality, and in pictures of innocence and nature. Their bravery is human; their actions great, but possible; their love the essence of sensibility and honour... if it were in any doubt that Ossian was really an Irishman, the authenticity of his poems would thereby receive a mortal wound.[17]

As we shall see below, the difficulty with Ireland was that the difference presented by Catholicism and Gaelic culture could not be safely interred in the primitive mists of antiquity, but persisted in an endangered historical continuum which impinged directly on the present.

BURKE, CULTURAL DIVERSITY, AND CONSTITUTIONALISM

Do the conquests of Charlemagne prove his People were more numerous and civilized than others, unless we suppose that none but the most numerous nations make great Conquest[s], which is likewise most false. Does this prove that the conquering Country was of more antiquity than the conquered? (*Edmund Burke* 'Note book')

Considered in this light, the Scottish Enlightenment's concern to redeem the cultural enervation of polite society with the virtue of ancient primitivism may be seen as an attempt to establish a psychic economy of colonialism, according to which civility was the preserve of those willing to break with the inheritance of the recent past, or who removed themselves from their native habitats. For this reason, Burke's reinstatement of the long 'in-between', as represented by the (alleged corrupting) influence of custom, tradition, and vernacular culture, laid the basis for a more culturally sensitive version of the Enlightenment, at least where native or indigenous peoples were concerned – even if in the metropolitan centre, where tradition stood for stability and order, such a position could be construed as an attack on modernity itself.[18] For Burke, the presence of a richly variegated 'in-between', the continuous modification of custom and practice between distant origins and an uncertain present, was necessary to heal the wounds of history, and, in particular, the originary violence through which conquests, or revolutions, established new political regimes. Transferring the concept of sympathy to a cultural and political level from its mainly personal and psychological moorings in Scottish theories, Burke contended that without an underlying stratum of shared sentiments – marked by diversity and tolerance as much as uniformity – laws, contracts, and the other constituents of civil society could not even function: 'Bodies tied together by so unnatural a bond of union as mutual hatred, are only connected to their ruin.'[19] Cultural ties in this extended sense – language, manners, mores, rituals, customs, moral practices – are not only the connective tissue of society, however, but provide its conditions of legitimacy. It followed from this that societies in which culture and tradition were systematically intensifying conflict, rather than, as he hoped, helping to resolve it, were laying the basis for despotism, perpetuating the violence of the original usurpation or conquest. The problem in such societies was not one of diversity but of *domination*, in that one usurping tradition repudiates dialogue in favour of the subjugation and destruction of other cultures or ways of life.

Burke, as we have seen in Chapter 3, was acutely aware of the difficulties in cultivating sympathy across great cultural and geographical distances, between the rulers and the ruled, whether in Ireland or in India. In India, as he explained to the House of Commons, one was dealing with a society thousands of miles away, 'different in language, in manners, and in rites, men separated by every barrier of nature from you' ('Impeachment: Third Day', vii, 16):

We are in general, Sir, so little acquainted with Indian details; the instruments of oppression under which the people suffer are so hard to be understood; and even the very names of the sufferers are so uncouth and so strange to our ears, that it is very difficult for our sympathy to fix upon such objects... All these circumstances are not, I confess, very favourable to the idea of our attempting to govern India at all. ('East India', ii, 196–7)

For reasons more to do with history than geography, such sympathy was also conspicuous by its absence in Irish society, belying the surface tranquillity which seemed to obtain under the harsh regime of the Penal Laws. If the Protestant interest in Ireland was 'to possess all the franchises, all the property, all the education', and the abject mass of the Catholic population 'was to be composed of drawers of water and cutters of turf for them', then one was dealing with a society based not on the legitimacy of consent but on the running sore of conquest:

> The Protestants settled in Ireland consider themselves in no other light than that of a sort of a colonial garrison to keep the natives in subjection to the other state of Great Britain. The whole spirit of the Revolution in Ireland was that of not the mildest conqueror. In truth... [w]hat was done was not in a spirit of a contest between two religious factions, but between two adverse nations. ('Langrishe', iii, 320)

Notwithstanding its proximity to Britain, Ireland was in a worse condition than India for two reasons. Firstly, as we have already noted, conquest was attended not only by arbitrary power but by classic colonial patterns of confiscation and plantation – 'the total extirpation of the interest of the natives in the soil' ('Langrishe', iii, 321). This was not attempted in India, if only because the magnitude of the task and the deep-rootedness and resilience of diverse cultures on such a vast scale made it virtually impossible. Secondly, although there was a profound communicative gulf between the rulers and the ruled in India, it did not extend to systematic and official hostility to Indian civilization of the kind that emerged under the imperialist ideologies of James Mill and Macaulay in the nineteenth century. As has been frequently pointed out, Burke's great adversary, Warren Hastings, was not without his sympathies for the learning and cultural achievements of Indian civilization: he spoke three Indian languages, helped Sir William Jones to establish the important Asiatic Society of Bengal, and sponsored the first major translations of Sanskrit literature, such as Charles Wilkins' pioneering translation of the *Bhagavad Gita* in 1785.[20] As Burke experienced at first hand, this interest in native culture and religion was notably lacking in the more strident Protestant or Anglo-Irish attitudes towards the Gaelic or Catholic Irish in the eighteenth century:[21]

> The penal laws of that unparalleled mode of oppression, which were made after the last event [of 1691], were manifestly the effect of national hatred and scorn towards a conquered people, whom the victors delighted to trample upon, and were not at all afraid to provoke. ('Langrishe', iii, 321)

In seeking to redress this situation, Burke did not simply invoke the liberal Enlightenment principle that native peoples, whether in Ireland or in India, should be admitted to civil society, having proved themselves worthy by meeting various (imposed) standards of rationality, propriety or, indeed, amusement. This is the logic of assimilation, in which difference is divested of its material force (its political, economic, and cultural expressions) and recreated as an 'aesthetic imaginary', restricted to literary, artistic or creative activity, or else removed from power to the emotional solace of the private or domestic sphere. The full ideological underpinning for this project was provided in the nineteenth century by a reformulated ideology of Celticism, which, under the influence of writings by Matthew Arnold and others, attempted to extend the integrationist aesthetic inspired by the Ossianic cult in eighteenth-century Scotland and later Scottish romanticism to the more intractable political landscape of post-Famine Ireland.[22] Arnold's thinking on this was deeply influenced by Burke in that he recognized that an Act of Union effected by legislation only, in which Ireland was little more than bolted on to Britain, was not a true union at all, since it lacked precisely a shared sense of sympathy, a union of affections and sentiments.[23] This hardly needed spelling out after the Famine for, as Isaac Butt, Aubrey de Vere, John Mitchel, and others protested vigorously at the time,[24] the fact that the Irish were not treated equally as British subjects in Yorkshire or Cornwall would have in similar catastrophic circumstances, effectively excluded Ireland from the much-vaunted benefits of the English constitution.

Arnold's solution to this was to allot the Irish a vicarious role in public affairs, enabling the Celt, as it were, to provide the saving grace of culture (if not quite of refinement) in an age of commerce, venality, and philistinism. The Celt was granted an unlimited poetic licence as a consolation for the loss of political power, in keeping with the elegiac note in Romanticism where communities excluded from the march of progress – Orientals, Africans, native Americans, or, closer to home, an idealized peasantry – enjoyed an afterlife in the realms of the imagination, or, in the case of women, in the confines of home or the libidinal economy. This added a much-needed spiritual and imaginative leavening to the sober industriousness of Victorian economic and political life, the feminization of the Celt, in common with other colonial subjects, also ensuring that this aestheticized version of culture did not seriously encroach on the business of public life. Hence Husserl's argument, cited at the outset, that while non-European peoples or obsolete cultures may assume a creative or imaginative voice, this does not extend to the exercise of reason, the use of theory and criticism, which are still very much the preserve of the metropolitan European Enlightenment.

The most striking aspect of Burke's recognition of cultural difference is his refusal to construe it solely in aesthetic terms, thereby bringing the economic and political order, the domain of philosophy and the social sciences, into the contested zones of cross-cultural influence. Civilization did not proceed along a one-way street, bringing the Enlightenment from the centre to the periphery, but travelled in both directions, with each side standing to gain from an encounter with 'the other'. Attacking the myths of Oriental tyranny and despotism, Burke declared:

I assert that their morality is equal to ours, in whatever regards the duties of governors, fathers, and superiors; and I challenge the world to show, in any modern European book, more true morality and wisdom than is to be found in the writings of Asiatic men in high trust, and who have been counsellors to princes. ('Impeachment: Fourth Day', vii, 114)

Undoubtedly, this version of cultural equality is elaborated under an imperial aegis, but for Burke, it was incumbent on the colonial administration in India to acknowledge Hindu customs, to 'govern them upon their own principles and maxims and not upon ours':

We must not think to force them into the narrow circle of our ideas; we must extend ours to take in their system of opinions and rites, and the necessities which result from both: all change on their part is absolutely impracticable. We have more versatility of character and manners, and it is we who must conform. ('Impeachment: Third Day', vii, 44)

The problem for Burke was not diversity but domination: the sympathetic sublime, as we have seen, allows for considerable degrees of discord and even cacophony in cultural dialogue, but this is jeopardized by a descent into ethnocentrism, and the destructive righteousness of those who are convinced they have God – or his Enlightenment equivalents, reason and progress – on their side.

In the cross-cultural dialogue between Europe and India, Burke had little difficulty conceding that so far from being an inferior culture, the people of India were 'for ages civilized and cultivated; cultivated by all the arts of polished life, while we were yet in the woods' ('East India', ii, p. 182). In some respects, Asian civilization was even superior to its counterparts in the West. Rejecting Warren Hastings's imputations of uniform despotism to Tartar systems of government, Burke enlisted the publication of *Institutes Political and Military... by the Great Timour* (1783), and some characteristic hyperbole, to support his account of the reign of Tamerlane:

There is no book in the world, I believe, which contains nobler, more just, more manly, more pious, principles of Government than this book, called Institutions of Tamerlane. Nor is there one word of arbitrary power in it, much less of the arbitrary power which Mr. Hastings supposed himself justified by. ('Impeachment: Fourth Day', vii, 108)

In arguing thus, Burke was not unaware of the pitfalls of relativism, in which respect for other cultures is stretched to the point where they become a law unto themselves, immune to any criticism or influence. This was certainly the problem presented to him by Hindu culture: 'these people are, of all nations, the most unalliable to any part of mankind. They cannot – the highest orders of them, at least, cannot – come into contact with any other' ('Impeachment: Third Day', vii, 43). Yet, as we have noted above, the 'contagion' generated by the sympathetic sublime was invoked precisely by Burke to permit cross-cultural influence and interaction between seemingly alien and incommensurable ways of life. For this reason, it was crucial that tradition did not function as an ossified, self-contained continuum, but allowed for renovation and even substantial upheavals, as in the Glorious Revolution of 1688.[25] Ethnic absolutism or fundamentalism was more in keeping, in Burke's eyes, with the dogmatism and 'metaphysics' of the Jacobins than with the practical reason of societies ruled by the accumulative deposits of custom and practice.[26] His opposition to the East India Company was not based on the premise that Warren Hastings failed to respect local traditions in India, but that he availed himself only of the worst of their customs, invariably exploiting them for his own gain. In keeping with Enlightenment thought, Burke had no difficulty in holding what he considered negative aspects of native cultures up to opprobrium, and so far from subscribing to an uncritical 'whatever is, is right' version of tradition, was prepared to concede that injustice may even be aggravated by its consolidation over the centuries:

What can be conceived so monstrous as the Republick of Algiers? and that no less strange Republick of the Mamalukes in Egypt? They are of the worst form imaginable, and exercised in the worst manner, yet they have existed as a nuisance on the earth for several hundred years.[27]

The very fact that a society was unable to throw 'a politic well-wrought veil' (*Reflections*, 103) of custom and tradition over the violence involved in state formation, and was instead in a condition of chronic, irresolvable conflict, was sufficient to undermine its legitimacy: 'a nation is not governed, which is perpetually to be conquered' ('Conciliation', i, 463). In the case of America, and more particularly the protracted political struggle in Poland, Burke accepted that incremental reform was out of the question, and that violent revolution – 'bold enterprize and desperate experiment' – was inevitable.[28] Gradual reform may have been consistent with the slow evolution of the ancient constitution (though even this was not without its 'convulsions'), but under the grim conditions of colonial misrule in Ireland or India, or subjugation by an imperial power, 'desperate experiments', however regrettable, may be the only weapons left to the weak.

Burke's main departure from conventional Enlightenment thought lay not in his rejection of universalism, but in his reluctance to invoke abstract or 'metaphysical' standards of evaluation, whether of reason or justice, in understanding other cultures. The very recourse to such allegedly neutral standards deprives other cultures of their specificity, often requiring them to shed their most distinctive features to come under the rubric of 'civilization'. In arguing thus, Burke, as we have seen, was not necessarily eschewing 'external' critiques of culture, but was insisting, in keeping with his mentor Montesquieu, on a more embedded, socially grounded approach to political rights and cultural difference:

> These metaphysic rights entering into common life, like rays of light which pierce into a dense medium, are, by the laws of nature, refracted from their straight line. Indeed in the gross and complicated mass of human passions and concerns, the primitive rights of men undergo such a variety of refractions and reflections, that it becomes absurd to talk of them as if they continued in the simplicity of their original direction. (*Reflections*, 152)

In this, Burke can be seen as anticipating some of the co-ordinates of contemporary, postmodern or post-colonial revisions of the Enlightenment,[29] as in the rediscovery of the sublime in aesthetic criticism; the political and cultural theories of writers as diverse as James Tully and Will Kymlicka (political thought), Frank Ankersmidt (historiography/political philosophy), Bruce Robbins and Timothy Brennan (cultural theory); the rethinking of the concept of tradition and rationality in the moral philosophy of Alasdair MacIntyre, or the critique of 'impartiality' in the feminist political theory of Iris Marion Young.[30] According to Iris Marion Young's influential intervention, liberal and republican conceptions of citizenship in the West persist in defining the public good, or justice, 'as a realm of generality in which all particularities are left behind': 'the idea that citizenship is the same for all translate[s] in practice to the requirement that all citizens be the same'. As against this, Young argues for an alternative theory of group rights in which:

> It is possible for persons to maintain their group identity and to be influenced by their perceptions of social events derived from their group-specific experience, and at the same time to be public spirited, in the sense of listening to the claims of others and not being concerned for their own gain alone... A repoliticization of public life should not require the creation of a unified public sphere in which citizens leave behind their particular group affiliations, histories and needs to discuss a general interest or common good. Instead of a universal citizenship in the sense of this generality, we need a group differentiated citizenship and a heterogeneous public.[31]

This echoes the recognition of difference and belonging which informs Burke's accounts of cross-cultural interaction, encounters with the new and the strange which are all the more challenging because they resist the standardizing civic ideals of 'universal' cosmopolitanism. The distinctive features of Hindu culture, Burke writes, 'renders it difficult for us to enter with due sympathy into their concerns, or for them to enter into ours, *even when we meet on the same ground*' ('Impeachment: Third Day', vii, 43). Genuine pluralism or diversity, for Burke, transcends the search for sameness which prevails in abstract cosmopolitanism, and is willing to encounter the shock of the strange, without the safety-nets of familiarity or civic uniformity. As Uday Singh Mehta argues, it is not that Burke is rejecting reason, but rather his purpose is 'to enlarge its ambit, to make it social and more passionate, and more informed by the uncertain vagaries that attend and inform experience'. This provides for a more grounded, alternative cosmopolitanism in that

> it holds out the possibility, and only the possibility, that through the understanding of what gives experiences their meaning two strangers may come to converse with each other, perhaps befriend each other, perhaps disagree with each other, along with the myriad other eventualities that structure where a conversation may lead and end up.[32]

For Burke, the appeal to impartiality and even-handedness in indictments of injustice and treachery often masks the fact that 'there is no middle point in which the Commons of Great Britain can meet tyranny and oppression':

> A compromising, balanced, neutralized, equivocal, colourless confused report [of injustice]; in which the blame was to be impartially divided between the sufferer and the oppressor... this kind of equitable, candid, and judge-like proceeding... [would only ensure] that the whole complaint would calmly fade away; the sufferers remain in the possession of their patience, and the tyrant of his plunder. ('Impeachment: Fifth Day', vii, 193)

Indeed for Burke, it may have been precisely the 'impartiality' of justice, the new abstract formulations of the common good bequeathed by the natural rights school associated with Pufendorf, Locke and the Scottish Enlightenment, that facilitated an imperceptible transition from 'impartiality' to 'detachment', and ultimately to the 'indifference' of *laissez-faire* morality in the public sphere. Abstracted from communal concern and sympathy, the new 'disinterested' metaphysics of justice placed no obligation on the citizen or the state to alleviate social distress, even, as we have seen, in the face of catastrophes such as famine. It was not just romantic nostalgia, but his acute awareness of the shadows thrown by the dark side of the Enlightenment, which led Burke to argue that 'pre-modern' – or, for that matter, non-European – conceptions of justice, which placed the right of necessity and life over the right to property and the market, had still something to offer to the modern, market driven world.[33]

Burke's writing on Ireland, India, and colonialism generally contain important lessons for contemporary debates on multiculturalism, 'federalist' moves towards economic integration, and globalization. Much of what passes for cultural diversity and regional identity is motivated by what James Clifford has termed the 'salvage paradigm', the romanticization of cultures or minority groups in so far as they do not impinge on the serious business of political power and economic progress, or are not contaminated by the impurities of actually lived history.[34] In this new primitivism, difference and distinctiveness are projected onto those aspects of a culture that have been left behind by modernity, in the name of 'authenticity' and 'nativism', while tourism, the heritage industry, and the creative arts are pressed into service to act as comfort blankets for political and economic disenfranchisement in the real world. Hence the trend in many restrictive versions of multiculturalism to give cultural recognition, in the narrow aesthetic sense, to various minorities, but to prevent this as far as possible from intruding on civic space, in the sphere of law, education, politics, or commerce. As James Tully has observed of the siphoning-off of difference to the margins of society, it has become increasingly difficult in modern constitutionalism:

to conceptualize the people as agreeing to establish a constitutional association that recognizes and accommodates cultural diversity by arrangements of legal and political pluralism so that citizens can relate to government in culturally different ways or participate in different political institutions.[35]

The 'salvage paradigm', as Clifford describes it, presents a contemporary, commodified version of eighteenth-century primitivism, a putative, desocialized 'state of nature' that purports to pre-date modernity and civil society but is in fact produced by it. The most attractive feature of the Golden Age for modernity is that it is indeed dead and gone, and is all the more idealized because of its readiness to facilitate a similar idealized view of modernity, freed from all the encumbrances of the past. But, for Burke, this collusion between progress and primitivism gives rise to a more sinister development, a new form of modern barbarism in which societies were 'subtilized ... into savages' (*Reflections*, 181), and were recreated in the image of the very primal hordes they sought to purge with the march of civilization.

This, in Albert Hirschman's terminology, is the 'perversity thesis' among theoretical critiques of the Enlightenment, according to which 'reason attempts to create a new set of institutions that would realize the ideas of the Enlightenment but succeeds in creating an unmitigated disaster... [and] bringing about results diametrically opposed to what was intended'.[36] For Hirschman, this is 'the single most popular and effective weapon in the annals of reactionary rhetoric' but the fact that Burke shares the company of Hegel and later, Max Horkheimer and Theodor Adorno, in developing this critique indicates that it may also be considered as an attempt to bring the 'alienation effects' of the Enlightenment to bear on a critical engagement with its own ideals.

PART IV

Progress and primitivism

7

'Subtilized into savages': Edmund Burke, progress, and primitivism

> From cruel men they are transformed into savage beasts, with no other vestiges of reason left but what serves to furnish the inventions and refinements of ferocious subtlety for purposes, of which beasts are incapable, and at which fiends would blush.
>
> Edmund Burke, 'Opening Speech in the Impeachment of Warren Hastings'

> ...a fatal union [:] the manners of savages were the Luxury of Civilized...
>
> Edmund Burke, notes for 'Speech on the Use of Indians' (1777)

> I am very sorry to say that I have those engaged with me in service, whom are more savage than the savages themselves.
>
> Thayendenega (Joseph Brant), the Iroquois chief, on Loyalist troops under his command

In one of the more notorious polemical passages in his *Reflections on the Revolution in France*, Edmund Burke equates the modernizing zeal of the French Revolution, and its enthusiastic supporters in Britain such as Richard Price, with its own perceived historical opposite, the 'primitivism' and 'savagery' of American Indians. Using his shrillest powers of invective, Burke excoriates the march which escorted the royal family in triumph from Versailles on the 6 October 1789, as the 'most horrid, atrocious, and afflicting spectacle, that perhaps ever was exhibited to the pity and indignation of mankind':

It was (unless we have been strangely deceived) a spectacle more resembling a procession of American savages, entering into Onondaga, after some of their murders called victories, and leading into hovels hung round with scalps, their captives, overpowered with the scoffs and buffets of women as ferocious as themselves, much more than it resembled the triumphal pomp of a civilized martial nation. (*Reflections*, 159)

In discerning a dark shadow on the underside of the Enlightenment in its moment of triumph, Burke can be seen as prefiguring the sense of hubris that has characterized many critiques of modernity in the twentieth century, particularly in the wake of the unprecedented barbarism of the Holocaust. For critics such as Zygmunt Bauman, the mass industrialization of death perpetrated by Nazism was not a corruption of European civilization but a virulent strand secreted within it from the very outset.[1] The very demonization of 'the other', or past ages, under the rubric of 'savagery', concealed a logic of extermination that was integral to the rise of western expansionism, and the fact that civilization itself was capable of perpetrating atrocities on an unimaginable scale. In Walter Benjamin's terms, 'there is no document of civilization which is not at the same time a document of barbarism', and the more advanced the society, the greater its tragic potential for depravity, and descent into the vortex of violence.[2]

The extravagance of Burke's language in the earliest days of the Revolution may seem far removed from the nemesis of the Enlightenment in the mid-twentieth century, but, even at this early stage, Burke was intent on counting the cost – and the casualties – of modernity, and not always from what his critics have considered a regressive, counter-Enlightenment position. In marked contrast to Adam Smith and the more optimistic currents within the Scottish Enlightenment, the main thrust of Burke's anxiety as a progressive Whig was that commerce, the most advanced stage of civilization, did not necessarily 'improve' or bring out the best in societies it embraced, but might, in fact, impel them towards their destruction. Burke's obsession with the depredations of the East India Company under the tutelage of Warren Hastings had already sown deep misgivings about the beneficial effects of the invisible hand as a modernizing agency, unaided by wise government or, indeed, Providence. In the destructive fury of the events unfolding in France, these earlier fears extended to the political domain and had emerged fully grown in Burke's imagination as the dragon's teeth of revolution.

Burke's rhetorical conversion of the threat presented by the French Revolution into the menacing savagery of American Indians was not based entirely on analogy, but drew on an earlier repertoire of beliefs and prejudices, contrasting the French rapprochement with 'the savage other' in America with the more hostile attitudes adopted by British colonial settlers. As Francis Parkman described it later in his monumental *France and England in North America* (1865–92), 'Spanish civilization crushed the Indian, English civilization scorned and neglected him, French civilization embraced and cherished him.'[3] But Burke's choice of the Iroquois Confederacy of Six

Nations, based at Onondaga, near Syracuse, New York, as precursors of the excesses of the French Revolution brought the accommodation with the 'savage' uncomfortably closer to home. While the British may have 'scorned and neglected' Indians in general, this was not so in their relations with the Iroquois. Of all the Indian nations, the Iroquois were regarded as the most advanced politically and economically: but they were also the most ruthless and refined practitioners of cruelty. As Bacqueville de La Potherie observed in his *History of North America* (1722):

> When one talks of the Five Nations in France, they are thought, by a common Mistake, to be meer Barbarians, always thirsting after Human Blood; but their true character is very different: They are the fiercest and most Formidable People in North America, and at the same time as Politick and Judicious as well can be conceiv'd.[4]

Famous for their sophisticated political ideas of confederacy, which impressed founders of the new American republic such as Benjamin Franklin, they were also greatly feared for their finesse in the arts of war and torture.[5] In bringing the Iroquois directly within the ambit of republicanism in its revolutionary French guise, Burke was, in effect, exploding the foundational myth of the Enlightenment that primitivism was only to be found in a 'state of nature', at a safe remove in time or space from the comforts of civility. The problem with closing the gap between the 'primitive' past and the present, however, was that it was not only the French but the British who were contaminated by association with 'the savage other'. From the seventeenth century, the Iroquois were assiduously courted and cultivated as Britain's most steadfast allies, the jewels in the crown of British interests in America. Burke's abiding fear, however, was that instead of being tamed by the guiding hand of progress, 'primitive' peoples would be transformed into grotesque travesties of the violence and aggression used by their civilized masters to subdue them – and, by the same token, that their masters would be corrupted by this intensified violence in turn, becoming grim parodies of the brutish heathens they vilified and demonized.

BEAUTY AND THE BEAST: REVOLUTION AS 'CAPTIVITY NARRATIVE'

Given the comparison of the revolutionary mob with Indians, it is not surprising that the threat presented by the march to Versailles, culminating in the violation of Marie Antoinette in her boudoir, should re-enact the early Gothic genre of the 'captivity narrative' that haunted the colonial experience in America from the late seventeenth century. The props and stage-setting for this rhetorical tableau had already been put in place ten years earlier when, before a shocked House of Commons, Burke first seized on the gory details of an incident that captured the public imagination during the opening salvos of the American Revolution, the murder of Jane McCrea on 27 July 1777, by Indians aligned to the British cause. That atrocity became an emblematic event in the early days of the Revolution, contributing, in the eyes of some historians, to a shift in the balance of forces that led to the defeat at Saratoga, one of the major turning points in the war.[6] Such was its impact that it projected the captivity narrative onto the political stage at a national level, becoming the subject of poems, novels and, in a dramatic painting by John Vanderlyn, 'Murder of Jane McCrea' (1804), one of the most famous artistic representations of the Revolution (Fig. 8).[7] Part of Burke's polemical strategy in invoking the Indian captivity narrative as a shadow text in his assault on the French Revolution may have been to emulate the propaganda success of the Jane McCrea episode, thus galvanizing public opinion against the fatal fascination exerted by events in France on Dissenters, radical Whigs, and other enlightened circles in Britain. The difficulty with this manoeuvre was that it implicated British policy itself, or, more particularly, the excesses of British colonialism, in the reign of terror associated with the revolutionary fervour of the Jacobins.

On 6 February 1778, during a debate in the House of Commons on the losses suffered by British forces during the war, Burke made an impassioned speech, considered by those present to have been 'the best Mr. Burke ever delivered'.[8] Burke's speech was an attack on the military incompetence that led to the defeat of the British at Saratoga, but he directed his most caustic criticism at the deployment of Indians and blacks to fight Britain's dirty war: 'a war of distress and intimidation was to take [the] place of a war of conquest, which had been found impracticable' ('Indians', iii, 355–6):

Whole nations of savages had been bribed to take up the hatchet, without a single regular officer or soldier amongst them. This he instanced in the case of the Cherokees, who were bribed and betrayed into war... and for want of the support promised, were nearly exterminated, and the remains of that people now lived in a state of servitude to the Carolinians. ('Indians', iii, 358–9)

According to Linda Colley, the vehemence of Burke's attack on the deployment of Indians and blacks in the war should help to dispel any illusion that he had sympathy with the plight of indigenous peoples who fell victim to colonialism: 'How do we reconcile these outbursts, which struck even his admirers as excessive, with Burke's abolitionism, or his well known campaign against British injustices in India?' For Burke, she continues, 'those

Fig. 8 John Vanderlyn, 'Murder of Jane McCrea' (1804)

Native Americans who allied themselves with the British Army... were "banditti", "barbarians", remnants of a savage past with no place in what America should be: "there was no occasion for holding any political connection with them as nations".[9] But as Burke's comments on the Cherokees indicate, he was not entirely without sympathy for the plight of the Indians, manipulated as they were by competing colonizing forces into disastrous alliances that almost led to their destruction. The Indians' savagery was not entirely of their own making, but may have been one of the consequences of their succumbing to white civilization, as they themselves degenerated from a former, pre-colonial culture. As Burke saw it, the reason Indians could no longer be considered as nations was due to their decline from an earlier period in which they were much more powerful, and enjoyed greater parity with the settlers on account of their unrivalled knowledge of the wilderness. Now, however,

> the savages were so reduced in number, that there was no necessity of any connection with them as nations. They were only formidable from their cruelty; *and to employ them was merely to be cruel ourselves in their persons*; and to become chargeable with all the odious and impotent barbarities, which they would certainly commit, whenever they were called into action. ('Indians', iii, 357: my italics)

In the more heightened passages of his speech, Burke dwelt on the details of Indian cruelty 'with a Pathos', according to one newspaper account, 'which melted the Auditory almost to tears and filled them with the utmost Horror'.[10] Nonetheless, he was insistent that his objections to the deployment of Indians in war were not based on racial grounds, on 'their being one colour or another' ('Indians', iii, 356). As he expressed it on another occasion, in relation to his prosecution of the East India Company: 'I know what I am doing; whether the white people like it or not.'[11] The implication here is that barbarism for Burke is not so much an inherent characteristic of Indian life as a state into which they have fallen due to historical circumstances, which in their case meant the corrosive influence of colonization. In his notes for his parliamentary speech, Burke observed that there were once 'two great Empires – The Hurons and Iroquois. The French would not subsist without the One nor we without the other' ('Indians', iii, 365) – an interdependency between settler and native that militated against any suggestion of a primordial state of aggression and violence on the part of the Indians. The notes then gloss their descent into savagery: 'They [were once] a great[,] we a little people involved and entangled in their affairs – by a course of Events reduced – Now only bodies of banditti of the most cruel and atrocious Kind' ('Indians', iii, 362).

Burke reserved his most scathing criticisms for official justifications of the British policy in deploying Indians in terror tactics against the rebel patriots, heaping scorn on General Burgoyne's lame excuse that they encouraged the Indians to exercise restraint, and 'that care had been taken to prevent mischief' ('Indians', iii, 358). What were the Indians used for, Burke remonstrated, but to excel in the survival strategies of terror to which they had been reduced under successive waves of conquest? Expecting them to exercise restraint in these circumstances was, in his estimation, equivalent to the keeper of the zoo at Tower Hill in London addressing the animals during a break-out: 'my gentle lions, my sentimental wolves, my tenderhearted hyenas, go forth, but take care not to hurt men, women, or children'.[12] Burke then recited the litany of horrors perpetrated by Burgoyne's and Colonel St Leger's expeditions

> to shew, that the savages did in effect, indiscriminately murder men, women and children, friends and foes; and that particularly the slaughter fell mostly on those who were best affected to the King's government, and who for that reason had been lately disarmed by the provincials. Here he painted in very strong colours the horrid story of Miss Mac Ray [*sic*], murdered by the savages on the day of her marriage with an officer of the King's troops. ('Indians', iii, 358)

Though the discretion of the parliamentary reporter spared us the lurid details of the murder of Jane McCrea,[13] Burke's draft notes for his speech, however abbreviated and disconnected, give some idea of the macabre *mise-en-scène* he recreated for the benefit of his listeners. Recounting Jane McCrea's preparations for her marriage on the eve of her death, Burke exploited to maximum effect the set-pieces that had become the staple of sentimental fiction:

> Suppose a Virgin of an honourable place, that had grown up in the delight and comfort of a family... In that moment of blessing that God[,] who meant the union the relation and continuance of his Creatures[,] has made the highest point of human felicity and is indeed a part of pleasure and innocence which Angels might look down and Envy, when this poor Creature dressed up in those pretty little ornaments which ingenious poverty with which we make the most of our condition... surrounded with tender parents, and sympathising kindred, and holy Priests and happy Lovers just in that moment <of momentary> anxiety of love – and those with that hair dressed for other purposes that morning torn from her head to decorate the infernal habitation of cruelty and barbarism and there left a naked and <foul scale> her body a mangled ghastly spectacle of blood and horrour, crying through a hundred mouths to that whose image was defaced for Vengeance. Is it to be wondered that the whole Country with a general insurrection rose to exterminate the <savages>. ('Indians', iii, 363–4)

But then, having vented his spleen against the 'savages', he added a contemptuous throwaway remark laying responsibility directly with Burgoyne and British policy: 'Those who have ordered have done it.'[14]

The murder of Jane Mc Crea is still shrouded in controversy due to the propaganda wars that quickly subsumed the event, but the main outlines are reasonably clear.[15] Jane McCrea, the 23-year-old daughter of a Scots–Irish Presbyterian minister based in New Jersey, came north for her impending marriage to meet with her betrothed, Lieutenant David Jones, an officer in Burgoyne's army. On the way, she stayed at the home of Mrs McNeal, a widowed cousin of General Simon Fraser near Fort Edward, in upstate New York, until she could cross British lines safely nearby. Accounts differ on whether Indians were actually sent to escort her or whether they raided the home of the widow, but, in any case, as she was being led through the woods, a dispute arose among different Indian parties as to who should receive the reward for delivering her to Lieutenant Jones. In the ensuing fracas, Jane McCrea was butchered to death and was immediately scalped by a Wyandot Indian, Panther, to collect the bounty for scalps offered by British authorities.[16] In one of the more grisly accounts, her fiancé, waiting at the camp, recognized the scalp: 'He knew the long golden tresses of Miss McCrea, and in defiance of all danger, flew to the spot to realize the horrid tale.'[17] The feelings of outrage over the murder were compounded by Burgoyne's granting a pardon to the offending Indian, due to a threat of a mass walk-out by the British force's Indian allies. This prompted a vitriolic public rebuke to Burgoyne by General Horatio Gates, the commander of the American rebel forces in the region, which was, perhaps, one of Burke's sources in his accounts of the incident:

Miss McCrea, a young lady lovely to the sight, of virtuous character and amiable disposition, engaged to an officer of your army, was, with other women and children, taken out of a house near Fort Edward, carried into the woods, and then scalped and mangled in a most shocking manner... The miserable fate of Miss McCrea was particularly aggravated by her being dressed to meet her promised husband; but she met her murderer employed by you.[18]

Gates went on to suggest that there was nothing 'new nor extraordinary' in savages acting thus,

but that the famous Lieutenant-General Burgoyne, in whom the fine gentleman is united with the soldier and scholar, should hire the savages of America to scalp Europeans and descendants of Europeans, nay more, that he should pay a price for each scalp so barbarously taken, is more than will be believed in Europe, until authenticated facts, in every gazette, confirm the truth of the horrid tale.

Though there is no firm evidence that Jane McCrea was 'lovely to the sight' (Gates) or possessed 'the bloom of beauty' (Burke) – indeed, one surly contemporary described her looks as being singularly undistinguished[19] – her murder lent itself to a powerful national allegory of beauty and the beast, in which chastity and national virtue were pitted against the forces of lust and imperial evil. These were the resonances, with all their potential for sentiment and pathos, that were exploited by Burke and others. According to Mrs Mercy Warren, in a passage that fused Burke's expression of outrage over the young American woman with his later panegyric on Marie Antoinette, the Indians who massacred Jane McCrea 'made the blooming beauty, shivering in the distress of innocence, youth, and despair, the victim of their fury'.[20] Central to this allegory of innocence and evil was the act (or threat) of sexual ravishment, a highly charged transgressive tableau imported into the captivity narrative from popular English sentimental novels such as Samuel Richardson's *Pamela* and *Clarissa*. As Michelle Burnham points out, though such forms of violation featured in earlier captivity narratives, most notably in Hannah Dustan's of 1697, they did not become part of an attempt to enlist sympathetic readers in an imagined moral community of outrage until the American Revolution. Hence, for example, in a fictionalized narrative sympathetic to the rebel cause, *The Affecting History of the Dreadful Distresses of Frederic Manheim's Family* (1800), twin daughters are abducted by Indians, stripped naked by their captors and tortured while tied to a tree (Fig. 9).[21]

By the same token, though rape was not actually part of the horror in the Jane McCrea incident, reports of the case were embellished with graphic sexual details from the outset. In a memoir of his travels through the colonies during the early phase of the war that formed the basis for his novel on the incident, the French writer, René Michel Hilliard d'Auberteuil, noted of the incident that the Indians 'seized this young victim, carried her into the woods, and stripped her of her garments; and having performed on her all that their fury and brutality would suggest, they scalped her'.[22] In what may be the first American novel, Hilliard d'Auberteuil worked these notes up into a prose fiction, *Miss McCrea* (1784), and extended the sexual violation to Jane's travelling party in a scene that prefigures the lurid Mannheim woodcut. The Indians, we are told

> who had received a double ration of brandy this day, surrounded Jane and those who accompanied her. The Indians stripped them completely naked, tied them to trees, and divided their clothes and baggage among themselves... The opinions of the savages were divided concerning Jane. The most important of them, taken with her beauty, stared desirously at her charms... Her anguish added to her beauty; her hair, long enough to serve as a veil for her modesty, made the whiteness of her skin appear lustrous.[23]

This coyness regarding Jane's modesty is also suggested in Vanderlyn's painting through a depiction of her bare breast, and exposed nipple, set against her torn bodice. In Joel Barlow's turgid epic poem, *The Columbiad* (1807), Jane's reaction to her Mohawk assailants is rendered in a kind of purple poetic diction that added to the prurience of the spectacle:[24]

Fig. 9 'The Affecting History of the Dreadful Distresses of Frederic Manheim's Family' (1800)

> She starts, with eyes upturned and fleeting breath,
> In their raised axes views her instant death,
> Spreads her white hands to Heaven in frantic prayer,
> Then runs to grasp their knees and crouches there.
> Her hair, half lost among the shrubs she pass'd,
> Rolls in loose tangles around her lovely waist;
> Her kerchief torn betrays globes of snow
> That heave responsive to her weight of woe.
> Does all this eloquence suspend the knife?
> Does no superior bribe contest her life?[25]

These scenes of sexual ravishment derive their political shock-value from an underlying topos in the literature of the period that depicted the rebel colony's relationship with the parent culture as that of a beleaguered young woman or daughter.[26] 'I am returning under the banners of General Burgoyne', writes Jane's British lover, somewhat tactlessly, in *Miss McCrea*, 'to conquer your country and you in order to possess you forever' (50). As Jay Fliegelman has suggested, General Burgoyne's failure to punish the assassins of Jane McCrea on the eve of her wedding came to be seen, in the popular imagination, as 'a tyrannical parent sending his ferocious minister to deny his child, his loyal Tory child, the sacred nuptial rites'.[27] This rhetorical figure is evident in Thomas Paine's justification in *Common Sense* for rebellion on the grounds that there are 'certain injuries which nature cannot forgive; she would cease to be nature if she did. As well can the lover forgive the ravisher of his mistress, as the continent forgive the murders of Britain.'[28] In Paine's emotionally charged analogy, the suffering of the heroine is augmented by her helplessness, a situation in which she can rely for protection and defence only on her virtuous male lover. That many such virtuous males were sworn to the cause as a result of the murder of Jane McCrea is clear, as we have noted, from the fact that it acted as a powerful recruiting agent for Gates's army in the northwest corridor of war.[29] In Vanderlyn's painting, moreover, it is not too difficult to see why, for, in a flagrant departure from the few agreed-upon facts of the case, the helpless male spectator in the background is transformed from a British redcoat to a soldier decked in American blue. Though barely discernible, he holds an empty scabbard in his right hand, and raises a sword in his left hand, as he vainly tries to rescue his doomed sweetheart. It was as if, in the real-life theatre of war, male gallantry attempted to make amends for Jane's hapless lover, since many not only joined the rebel forces to avenge her death but went into the momentous battle of Saratoga, in October 1777, with her name on their lips.[30]

PURITY AND PRIMITIVISM

Part of the sentimental appeal of the captivity narrative was that it transferred the powerlessness of the victim to others present at the scene, and, by extension, to viewers or readers outside the picture or text, alerting them to their vulnerability as unwilling, passive spectators.[31] In the pathetic raised sword and empty scabbard of the diminutive figure of the forlorn lover in the background of Vanderlyn's painting, it is difficult not to discern echoes of Edmund Burke's famous lament over the death of chivalry in the desecrated bedchamber of Marie Antoinette:

> It is now sixteen or seventeen years since I saw the queen of France, then the dauphiness, at Versailles; and surely never lighted on this orb, which she hardly seemed to touch, a more delightful vision... Little did I dream that I should have lived to see such disasters fallen upon her in a nation of gallant men, in a nation of men of honour and of cavaliers. I thought ten thousand swords must have leaped from their scabbards to avenge even a look that threatened her with insult. – But the age of chivalry is gone. – That of sophisters, oeconomists, and calculators, has succeeded; and the glory of Europe is extinguished for ever... It is gone, that sensibility of principle, that chastity of honour, which felt a stain like a wound, which inspired courage whilst it mitigated ferocity, which ennobled whatever it touched, and under which vice itself lost half its evil, by losing all its grossness. (*Reflections*, 169–70)

Considered in the light of his earlier speech about Jane McCrea, it would seem that Burke's fear here is not of the savage without but the savage within, the impossibility of 'mitigating ferocity' under new untrammelled modes of modernity: 'We have not (as I conceive) lost the generosity and dignity of thinking of the fourteenth century: nor as yet have we subtilized ourselves into savages' (*Reflections*, 181). As several critics have pointed out, Burke was Hobbesian not so much in his dark view of human nature but in his acknowledgement of the violence and pain involved in the civilizing process, the passage from nature to culture.[32] The ordeal of the captivity narrative, including its liminal position between nature and culture and the recurring possibility of 'reverting' in the wilderness to a savage state, was a more accurate, chilling metaphor of the foundations of society than the harmonious progressive fiction of the social contract. Such latter 'pleasing illusions' were, at most, the product of civility for Burke, its destination rather than its source.

The most disconcerting aspect of the captivity narrative as applied to the violation of Marie Antoinette is that it is not confined to the wilderness but has invaded the garden itself, the hallowed precincts of Versailles. It is striking that to achieve maximum emotional effect, Burke converts Marie Antoinette into a virgin queen, the 'dauphiness' or daughter of 'sixteen or seventeen years' earlier. Virginity is used, in time-honoured fashion, to emphasize purity and innocence, but in marked contrast to primitivist thinking, it is not construed as a 'tabula rasa', a pristine body awaiting the inscriptions of culture or, for that matter, colonialism.[33] For Burke, innocence – 'the quiet innocence of shepherds' (*Reflections*, 123) – belongs to the garden, to the moral refinement of a state of grace rather than the presocial condition of a state of nature. Accordingly, it is equated with the clothed, rather than the naked, body, consisting in the 'well-wrought veils' thrown over the baser instincts of our human nature. Costume, in this scheme of things, is the sartorial equivalent of custom, the fabrication of manners and social codes which, in Sir John Davies's graphic description of the 'Ancient Constitution', evolves naturally from society 'like a silk-worm that formeth all her web out of herself onely'.[34] In the *Enquiry*, Burke takes this a stage further by construing beauty, and by extension the innocence of femininity, as the underlying connective tissue of the body politic, the outer plumage without which society would indeed expire like a dying bird.

Set against this fabrication of power, the sexual defilement of the female body is transformed into an attack on the foundations – or, perhaps, more appropriately for Burke, the foundation garments – of society itself. 'At the very heart of the *Reflections*', Ronald Paulson shrewdly observes, 'the metaphoric stripping of society has become the literal stripping of the Queen.'[35] But with the rapacity of the French Revolution, in Burke's famous threnody over the passing of the old order,

all the pleasing illusions, which made power gentle, and obedience liberal, which harmonized the different shades of life, and which, by a bland assimilation, incorporated into politics the sentiments which beautify and soften private society, are to be dissolved by this new conquering empire of light and reason. All the decent drapery of life is rudely torn off. All the super-added ideas, furnished from the wardrobe of a moral imagination, which the heart owns, and the understanding ratifies, as necessary to cover the defects of our naked shivering nature, and to raise it to dignity in our own estimation, are to be exploded as ridiculous, absurd, and antiquated fashion. (*Reflections*, 171)

Hence the obsessiveness with which Burke returns at key rhetorical moments to such primal scenes of transgression: the murder of Jane McCrea; the humiliation of young daughters, or the dowagers of Oudh, in India; the molesting of daughters in the privacy of their own homes by the 'dancing masters, fiddlers, pattern-drawers, friseurs, and valets de chambre' given a free hand in revolutionary Paris;[36] and, of course, the ultimate degradation of Marie Antoinette. In a characteristic example of what Adam Phillips calls the 'erotic empiricism' of the *Enquiry*, Burke reminds us that 'beauty in distress is much the most affecting beauty', but in a subsequent passage, it is hinted that the distress is not the sole preserve of the victim but may unsettle the composure of the spectator.[37] As if with the ambiguous allure of Vanderlyn's painting in mind, he writes:

> Observe that part of a beautiful woman where she is perhaps the most beautiful, about the neck and breasts; the smoothness; the softness; the easy and insensible swell; the variety of the surface, which is never for the smallest space the same; the deceitful maze, through which the unsteady eye slides giddily, without knowing where to fix, or whither it is carried... (*Enquiry*, 115)

This passage suggests that erotic disorientation extends beyond the decorous confines of beauty and is more on a continuum with the terrors 'and great power of the sublime, that far from being produced by them, it anticipates our reasonings, and hurries us on by an irresistible force' (*Enquiry*, 57). As Frances Ferguson has argued, Burke is gesturing here towards the deeply disturbing category of 'fatal beauty' (*Enquiry*, 171), a deadly combination of the sublime and the beautiful associated at the end of the *Enquiry* with the seductive charms of Helen of Troy (*Enquiry*, 171) or, more ominously in the *Reflections*, to the frenzied femininity of 'harpies' or 'furies'.[38]

One of the areas where the captivity narrative diverged from the sentimental romances of Richardson and others was in the propensity of the heroine to resort to violence to achieve freedom, and escape from her captors. In 1697, in one of the most celebrated cases, Hannah Dustan, her child and her child's nurse effected their escape in the middle of the night by taking a tomahawk to the heads of the Indian braves, squaws, and children sleeping beside them:

> Only one *Squaw* escaped sorely Wounded from them in the Dark; and one *Boy*, whom they reserved asleep, intending to bring him away with them, suddenly wak'd and Scuttled away from this Desolation. By cutting off the *Scalps* of the *Ten Wretches*, they came off, and received *Fifty Pounds* from the General Assembly of the Province, as a Recompence of their Action; besides which, they received many *Presents of Congratulation* from their more private Friends; but none gave 'em a greater Taste of Bounty than Colonel *Nicholson*, the Governour of Maryland, who hearing of their Action, sent 'em a very generous Token of his Favour.[39]

The hearty congratulations extended to Hannah Dustan must have been tinged with some disquiet at the erosion of the boundaries between civility and savagery in the very act of escaping from Indian perfidy. It was precisely the fear of this relapse into – or perhaps, more accurately, a *recourse to* – brutish behaviour that troubled Burke, not least because one of the consequences of such 'reversions' was to raise questions about where exactly civility ends and barbarism begins. The placing of a 'well-wrought veil' over such violence was certainly advisable where female behaviour was concerned, and such unbecoming aspects of captivity narratives were relegated to the margins of received interpretations of the ordeal in the wilderness throughout the eighteenth century. The more acceptable, official versions dictated that the rescue of helpless women be accomplished by their God-fearing male protectors but, as Burnham shows, in the ideological ferment of a revolutionary crisis, these gender roles were destabilized.

The escalation of violence in the early 1770s following the Boston Massacre of 1770 was accompanied by an unprecedented interest in the republication of captivity narratives, as if the patriotic rebels were learning their lines to plot their escape from their own colonial captors. The most famous narrative and foundational text of the genre, that of Mary Rowlandson in 1682, went through seven editions in the 1770s alone, having been reprinted only once previously since its original date of publication. But one noticeable feature of the avid interest in these texts during the revolutionary era was the transformation of the passive female victim of the official version to the problematic 'fatal beauty' of the active, violent woman. Thus, the woodcut used for the frontispiece for the 1773 Boston edition of Rowlandson's story showed the protagonist confronting her Indian captors with a rifle (Fig. 10).[40] The allegorical resonances are unmistakable here for as Greg Sieminski has demonstrated, the pictorial format of the woodcut directly parallels the compositional structure of Paul Revere's famous engraving of the 1770 Boston Massacre (Fig. 11).[41] The empowerment of the 'rebel daughter' figure – in effect, the radical transformation of the helpless Jane McCrea into a precursor of Marianne, or Liberty, at the Barricades – operated as both a symptom and a cause of the revolutionary energies released in a time of acute political crisis. The problem facing the Founding Fathers of the American Revolution was how to contain and domesticate this turbulence in the postrevolutionary period, and it was to this end that the evocative allegorical emblem of the 'Republican Mother' was directed, signifying the mode of reproduction in the new social order.[42]

For Burke, however, the defilement of the female body perpetrated by revolution is irredeemable and reproduces not beauty but terror. This perversion of reproduction extends to the act of nurturing itself, the umbilical cord that sustains the birth of the next generation, for instead of feeding a new life, it turns back on its own body, cannibalizing and devouring its very existence. Following the logic of the captivity narrative, the Jacobins

Fig. 10 'A Narrative of the Captivity, Sufferings and Removes of Mrs. Mary Rowlandson' (1773)

Fig. 11 Paul Revere, 'Bloody Massacre Perpetrated in King-Street, Boston' (1770)

keep the king captive, but only to add legitimacy to their own regime by representing themselves as his progeny:

They only held out the royal name to catch those Frenchmen to whom the name of the king is still venerable... They used it as a sort of navel-string to nourish their unnatural offspring from the bowels of royalty itself. Now that the monster can purvey for its own subsistence, it will only carry the mark about it, as a token of its having torn the womb it came from. ('Assembly', ii, 532)

This display of savagery was exemplified for Burke, above all, by women taking power into their hands, or indeed, taking to the streets, as in the march to Versailles. As he describes it, with the invasion of the royal palace by the mob, the king and queen

> were then forced to abandon the sanctuary of the most splendid palace in the world, which they left swimming in blood, polluted by massacre, and strewed with scattered limbs and mutilated carcasses. Thence they were conducted into the capital of their kingdom... [and] were slowly moved along, amidst the horrid yells, and shrilling screams, and frantic dances, and infamous contumelies, and all the unutterable abominations of the furies of hell, in the abused shape of the vilest of women. (*Reflections*, 164–5)

The Grand Guignol of this impassioned outburst linking the female mob with the 'furies' of Greek mythology as well as hysterical savages is obviously indebted to the 1778 speech on Indian atrocities, but can be traced back to an earlier neglected work co-written with his kinsman William Burke, *An Account of the European Settlements in America*, published in 1757, the same year as the *Enquiry*.[43] Though often dismissed as derivative and of little importance for Burke scholars, the *Account* is in fact of considerable interest, demonstrating Burke's thorough familiarity with the vast range of ethnographic and travel writing charting the shock of the colonial encounter with the other.[44] Although it is based entirely on English and French sources, the arrangement of the material is given a highly original cast by being filtered through categories drawn from the *Enquiry* and from Burke's first book, *The Vindication of Natural Society*, published a year earlier in 1756. Not least of the merits of the *Account* is that it throws valuable light on the problematic fusion of sociability and ferocity noted above in relation to the Iroquois, what Gordon M. Sayre has described as the 'enigma of the Noble Savage's merciless cruelty and familial tenderness'.[45] The derivativeness of the *Account* was nothing new, for borrowing liberally from each other, ethnographic travelogues of Indian life in the seventeenth and eighteenth centuries tended to follow similar plot-lines, culminating in a sensational torture scene where the unmitigated savagery of the Indian was exposed in all its chilling detail.

The *Account* adheres to this convention, giving Burke ample scope to rehearse the masque of terror that would be brought to bear on his denunciation of the murder of Jane McCrea, and on his full-scale polemical assaults on the French Revolution. Thus the impassioned references to cannibalism and the depravity of women under the Jacobins, which we have noted above, and the outrage expressed in his 1778 speech over Indian practices of 'torturing, mangling, roasting alive by slow fires and frequently even devouring their captives', are prefigured in the *Account* by a gruesome description of the treatment meted out to enemies by their Indian captors:

> They pull off this flesh, thus mangled and roasted, bit by bit, devouring it with greediness, and smearing their faces with blood, in an enthusiasm of horror and fury... The women, forgetting the human as well as the female nature, and transformed into something worse than furies, act their part and even outdo the men in this scene of horror. (*Account*, i, 190–1)[46]

The true horror of this scene resides in the fact that it does not belong to an original state of nature, as theories of 'primitivism' would have it, but is a condition coexisting with progress, albeit in the guise of colonialism. Burke's animadversions against Indians might better be seen as an extension of his critique of primitivism, noted in Chapter 6 above, or of any attempt to see the essence of human nature in its origins in a putative pre-social state of nature. Hence he insists, in the *Account*, that the cruelties with which Indians treat their enemies are not pre-social but exist alongside deep communal bonds that are grounded in expressions of care and humanity and that give cohesion to tribal life. Burke can scarcely conceal his admiration for the fact that their 'kings' rule by persuasion and eloquence rather than coercion and, in marked contrast to the Hobbesian state of nature, they have no need of prisons, guards, or officers of justice. Describing a network of social ties that would not be without its appeal for his own later writings, the *Account* notes that the Indian way of life is regulated by manners and customs, not by laws:

> Governed as they are by manners, not by laws, example, education, and the constant practice of their ceremonies, gives them the most tender affection for their country, and inspires them with most religious regard for their constitution, and the customs of their ancestors... Family love, rare amongst us, is a national virtue of which all partake.[47] (*Account*, i, 175)

For Burke, the most unsettling aspect of the dark side of human nature was that it did not belong solely to 'primitive' peoples, and hence could not be conveniently projected back into the distant past, or childhood, of civilization. This was the reassuring message of the dominant strains in the Scottish Enlightenment, but as we have seen, like some of the dissident voices among the Scottish intelligentsia, Burke was acutely aware of the recurring cost of progress.[48] In the *Vindication of Natural Society*, he proposed that the true scandal of history is not that primordial origins are bathed in blood, but that such violence is a permanent feature of the march of civilization. The blood-stained history of ancient Sicily, to cite one of his many examples, only differs in degree from that of other nations: 'You will find every Page of its History dyed in Blood, and blotted and confounded by Tumults, Rebellions, Massacres, Assassinations, Proscriptions, and a Series of Horror beyond the Histories perhaps of any other Nation in the World; though the Histories of all Nations are made up of similar matter' (*Vindication*, 28–9). The annals of destruction perpetrated in the name of civility and improvement conclude in the *Vindication* with the 'Torrents of silent and Inglorious Blood' that have 'fed the savage Forest of America for so many Ages of continual War':

What has been done since, and what will continue to be done whilst the same inducements to War continue, I shall not dwell upon. I will only in one word mention the horrid Effects of Bigotry and Avarice, in the Conquest of Spanish America; a Conquest on a low estimation effected by the murder of ten Millions of the Species. (*Vindication*, 36, 35)

While commentators, as we have seen in Chapters 3 and 4, have repeatedly drawn attention to the parodic nature of the *Vindication*, with its avowed aim of satirizing Lord Bolingbroke's espousal of 'natural' religion and society, the ironic intent of this example is far from clear, for it also appears unequivocally in Burke's own voice in the *Account*, and twenty years later in his review of William Robertson's *History of America*. Inveighing against Pizarro's ruthless extermination of the Indians, he writes:

These inhuman subverters of the Empire of the Incas, destitute of the genius and greatness of mind of Cortes, exceeded him so far in cruelty, that their barbarous actions, if they cannot lessen the enormity, at least take away from the effect produced by the worst parts of his conduct. These cruelties appear all the more lamentable, as the manners, disposition, government, the civil and religious institutions of the Peruvians, were moderate, mild, and equitable; far removed from the harshness of government, fierceness of disposition, gloomy superstitions, and bloody rites of the Mexicans.[49]

In a similar fashion, the passages in the *Vindication* that castigate the inhumanity of mining are echoed in the *Account* where the Spanish enslavement of over 60,000 natives in the mines is equated with genocidal attempts to depopulate the country but with even more devastating effects than disease or the sword. The harshness of tone that Linda Colley discerns in Burke's fulminations against the barbaric practices of the American Indians may derive less from an animus against primitive society than from an underlying anxiety that such depravity thrived due to the harsh imperatives of commerce and the ruthless scramble for world trade in the earliest phases of colonialism.

The prospect of decay and ruin recurs in Burke's philosophy of progress, betraying an abiding fear that the passage from lower to higher forms of society, enshrined in the Scottish Enlightenment's four stages theory of social development, may not be at all the inevitable product of civilization.[50] Whereas figures such as Adam Smith, William Robertson, and John Millar envisaged a steady rise from primitive hunting and pastoral (or 'shepherd') stages of society to agriculture, commerce, and civility, Burke was acutely aware of the possibility of 'regression', in which higher stages merged with archaic, 'primitive' forms of savagery. In the *Annual Register* of 1760, he purported, somewhat sardonically, to give an account 'of a famous nation improved, if we may say so, by one stiled a Philosopher, into brutes' and followed this up a year later by publishing 'as a suitable companion to it, that of a considerable number of men transformed by necessity into downright savages'.[51] This related to the systematic destruction by Spanish colonizers of the way of life enjoyed by the Buccaneers on the island of Hispaniola in the West Indies. The possibility of such a descent into darkness recurs in his famous 'Speech on Conciliation with America', in which he envisages the oppressive policies of the Crown prohibiting an increase in the grants of lands and driving the settlers at the frontier back into a nomadic state of nature:

> Over this they would wander without a possibility of restraint; they would change their manners with the habits of their life; would soon forget a government by which they were disowned; would become hordes of English Tartars; and pouring down upon your unfortified frontiers a fierce and irresistible cavalry...[52] ('Conciliation', i, 473)

This apologia for colonial expansion is not without a certain irony for it corresponds almost exactly to Burke's explanation of how the American Indians themselves were driven into savagery by previous misguided colonial policies. In a marginal gloss to his draft notes for his 1778 'Speech on the Use of Indians', he observes that while Europeans were 'little struggling Settlements [on] the [banks] of brooks and the mouths of rivers', the Indians constituted 'innumerable Nations of which now no trace remains – great Empires – now shrunk to nothing... The Indians are no longer a *people* in any proper acceptation of the Word – but several gangs of Banditti, scattered along a wild of a great civilized empire' (WS, iii, 365).[53] These sentiments carry unmistakable echoes of the ominous passage from Tacitus's lament for the Roman despoliation of Britain that testifies to the power of empire itself to create the wilderness it purports to conquer. As Burke quotes it in the *Vindication*:

Vastum ubique silentium, secreti colles; fumantia procul tecta; nemo exploratoribus obvius [Everywhere a vast silence, lonely hills; smoking roofs, no one is met by scouts], is what *Tacitus* calls *facies Victoriae* [The face of victory].[54] (*Vindication*, 34)

That these sentiments were close to his own heart is clear from their recurrence in his powerful evocation of the laying waste of India under the slash and burn campaigns of Warren Hastings and the East India Company. As Frank N. Pagano notes of the Tacitus quotation, not least of its disturbing implications for Burke lay in its suggestion that 'there was no difference between the wars that destroyed the empire and those which created it. Implicitly it raises the question of whether conquests of uncivilized peoples by more civilized peoples are not more justified than the reverse' (*Vindication*, 34)

'THAT FATAL BEAUTY'

In an unusually candid passage in the *Account* Burke enunciates a particularly stark version of 'the law of unintended consequences' to account for the injustices of history. As far as the benefits of colonialism are concerned, it is not the meek who shall inherit the earth but the avaricious and ruthless adventurers who trample on the rights of others. In a character sketch of the mentality of the colonizer that anticipates his scathing attack on the ambitious youths entrusted with power by Warren Hastings in India, he writes: 'Thus we have drawn from the rashness of hot and visionary men; the impudence of youth; the corruption of bad morals; and even from the wretchedness and misery of persons destitute and undone, the great sources of our wealth, our strength and our power' (*Account*, ii, 104). Expanding on this profane equivalent of the fortunate fall, he cites different examples from medicine, religion, and even climate to explain how good may come paradoxically out of evil:

There are humours in the body, which contained may be noxious to it, yet which sent abroad are the proper materials for generating new bodies. Providence, and a great minister who shall imitate providence, often gains their ends by means, that seem most contrary to them; for earthquakes, and hurricanes, and floods, are as necessary to the well being of things, as calm and sunshine; life and beauty are drawn from death and corruptions; and the most efficacious medicines are often found united with the most deadly poisons. This, as it is well known, is the order of nature, and perhaps it might not unwisely be considered, as an example of government. (*Account*, ii, 105)

This coexistence of the most 'efficacious medicines' with the most 'deadly poisons' might help to explain how, in Burke's view, the admirable qualities of sociability may be combined in Indian societies with ferocity and cruelty. But under conquest and colonization, it is precisely this social fabric, equated in Burke's aesthetics with the beautiful and the ameliorating influence of custom and tradition, that is torn unceremoniously from the body politic.[55] The link between primitivism and the republicanism that stalked the streets of Paris lay, for Burke, in their common obsession with disinvestiture, with stripping away the raiments of culture in a misguided attempt to uncover human nature in its original, uncontaminated condition. It was this possibility of removing the trappings of history accumulated over the ages that gave rise to the myth of natural liberty, in which republicans found common cause with American Indians and other primitive societies. The heroic ethos of classical antiquity, the cradle of civilization, resembled to this extent the warrior ethos of the 'noble savage', leading the American painter Benjamin West to exclaim, on first encountering the famous Apollo Belvedere: 'My God, how like it is to a Mohawk warrior!'[56] Similar sentiments inform Vanderlyn's painting of the murder of Jane McCrea, influencing not only his conspicuous choice of Mohawks, with their shaven heads, as the assailants in the picture but also the pronounced muscular physiognomy of the idealized male body. By contrast, female hair, the erotic zone in which, according to Burke's logic, culture and grooming become flesh – at once both natural and artificial – is subject to scalping, thus leading to the ultimate violation of the female body.

For Burke, the projection of origins onto a 'state of nature' provides less an image of a 'pristine people' than a pretext for depravity and degeneracy. Reviewing William Robertson's *History of America* in 1778 against the backdrop of the revolutionary wars, he noted acidly that Robertson had incontrovertibly debunked the myth of the Golden Age: 'That age, which was supposed to be golden, we now behold; and discover it affords only a state of weakness, imperfection, and wretchedness, equally void of innocence, and incapable of happiness.'[57] It is striking how this description echoes Burke's notorious account of women in the *Enquiry*, according to which the 'female sex, almost always carries with it an idea of weakness and imperfection. Women are very sensible of this; for which reason, they learn to lisp, to totter in their walk, to counterfeit weakness, and even sickness' (*Enquiry*, 110). As the term 'counterfeit' indicates, this state of weakness is not an original condition but, in Steven Blakemore's words, 'an infantile regression of learned female behaviour' instilled by a patriarchal value-system to promote female inferiority.⁵⁸ As Mary Wollstonecraft acutely pointed out, however, this duplicitous beauty is far from innocent, for it evokes Adam's description of Eve in *Paradise Lost* – 'this fair defect' – and is thus linked to death and destruction, the 'fatal beauty' that Burke discerned in Helen of Troy.⁵⁹ The danger of being seduced by such cosmetic appearances prompted Burke to inveigh against peaceful overtures from France in the mid-1790s, warning Parliament against proceeding as if that 'dire goddess... with a murderous spear in her hand, and a gorgon at her breast, was a coquette to be flirted with' ('First Letter', v, 203). Or again, as he put it in his 'Letter to a Noble Lord' (1796), quoting Virgil's *Aeneid* in a tirade against 'obscene harpies', both mothers and daughters, who have 'sprung from night and hell':

> They have the face of virgins; from their bellies
> Flows out the vilest discharge, and their hands
> Are talon-like, their features always pallid
> With hunger.⁶⁰

For Burke, the 'great fear' presented by the French Revolution lay in the prospect of civilized savagery, of beauty itself – the socializing impulse which forms the basis of our deepest loyalties – being implicated in terror, as in the spectacle of the 'Amazonian' women unleashing their fury on the streets of Paris ('Third Letter', v, 273). This is the gender equivalent of the Gothic scenario of the 'perpetual sublime' outlined in relation to Irish culture in Chapter 5, according to which the social expressions of beauty as a stabilizing force – custom, tradition, 'second nature' – are themselves infused with terror under colonial rule.⁶¹ In the case of France, Burke sought to distance himself from this drive towards entropy by projecting it onto a demonic alliance between primitivism and republicanism, both intent on tearing the 'decent drapery' off life and reducing it to its 'naked shivering nature'. The tragic circumstances surrounding the murder of Jane McCrea, however, and Burke's invocation of the Iroquois settlement at Onondaga to condemn the march back to Paris from Versailles, raised the grim possibility that the depredations of the Indian buck stopped, as it were, closer to home, with British colonial policy. In his 'Address to the Colonists', drawn up in 1777, before the full horror of the war unfolded, Burke warns of the possibility that coming into contact with 'civility' may have intensified rather than palliated Indian savagery. He apologizes to the American colonists for 'letting loose upon you, our late beloved Brethern, those fierce tribes of Savages and Cannibals, in whom the traces of human nature are effaced by ignorance and barbarity'. He continues:

We rather wished to have joined with you, in bringing gradually that unhappy part of mankind into civility, order, piety, and virtuous discipline, than to have *confirmed* their evil habits, and *encreased* their natural ferocity... We should think that every barbarity, in fine, in wasting, in murders, in tortures, and other cruelties too horrible and too full of turpitude for Christian mouths to utter or ears to hear, if done at our instigation... *to be, in all intents and purposes, as if done by ourselves.*[62]

The ultimate responsibility for the 'natural' ferocity of the Indians lay not with the savages themselves but with their civilizing masters: 'their vices <ours>', as he notes in his marginal comments.[63] These rueful observations were borne out by one of Burgoyne's officers, Lieutenant James Hadden, who reported from first-hand experience the fatal encounter between civility and savagery: 'the... most mischievous and treacherous Nations are those who are nearest & mix most with the Europeans: they acquire only our Vices & retain their ferocity'.[64] This was the appalling vista opened by the colonial sublime: terror lay not only unredeemed but also perverted by the fatal power of beauty.

8

'The return of the native': the United Irishmen, culture, and colonialism

> We will not buy or borrow liberty from America or France, but manufacture it ourselves, and work it up with those materials which the hearts of Irishmen furnish them with at home...
> *Address of the United Irishmen to the Scottish Convention, 1793*

On 20 June 1789, as members of the newly formed National Assembly were taking the revolutionary oath in a tennis court in Versailles, another strange, if less epochal, ceremony was taking place at Detroit, in the heartlands of the Iroquois nation, admitting a new member to the famous Indian confederacy:

I, David Hill, Chief of the Six Nations, give the name of *Eghnidal* to my friend Lord Edward Fitzgerald, for which I hope he will remember me as long as he lives. The name belongs to the Bear Tribe.[1]

'I have been adopted by one of the Nations', wrote Fitzgerald to his mother, 'and am now a thorough Indian' (*Lord Edward Fitzgerald*, i, 147). The distinction conferred on the errant aristocrat came towards the end of an extended visit to America in 1788–9 which brought him into contact with the rigours of life in the wilderness. In the grip of a Canadian winter, he charted a new route, 'never before attempted, even by the Indians',[2] which halved the distance between New Brunswick and Quebec, before proceeding south through the woods to Niagara and the United States. Though arduous in the extreme, the whole undertaking proved exhilarating to the young, unsettled adventurer:

There is something in a wild country very enticing; taking its inhabitants, too, and their manner into the bargain. I know Ogilvie [i.e. his foster-father] says I ought to have been a savage, and if it were not that the people I love and wish to live with are civilized people, and like houses, &c., &c., I really would join the savages; and, leaving all our fictitious, ridiculous wants, be what nature intended we should be. Savages have all the real happiness of life, without any of those inconveniences, or real obstacles to it, which custom has introduced among us. (*Lord Edward Fitzgerald*, i, 91)

Fitzgerald's encounter with the American Indians came at a time when the eighteenth-century fascination with the myth of the noble savage was slowly succumbing to the new, emergent ideologies of romanticism and racism. As the Enlightenment moved into a triumphant phase following the American and French Revolutions, the radical diversity presented by other non-Western or 'primitive' cultures became a pressing political concern, and not just something to be idealized at a distance. In this new political dispensation, as we have observed in Chapter 6, it gradually became apparent that universal declarations of human rights extended with greater ease to individuals than to cultures. Thus the remit of the American Declaration of Independence did not extend to Indians (not to mention others such as women and slaves) and, in fact, the obdurate presence of native peoples in the 'wilderness' came to be construed as the greatest single obstacle to the untrammelled pursuit of liberty and happiness. By the same token, the treatment meted out to the peasants of the Vendee or, as noted above, the black Jacobins in the slave insurrection in Haiti, left no doubt as to the limits of the Enlightenment where other 'peoples without history' were concerned. Not only did the metropolitan Enlightenment exclude 'primitive' cultures, but its whole rationale was built on their exclusion from the public sphere. It was left to Romanticism, then, to pick up where the Enlightenment left off, offering an imaginary realm of myth and nostalgia as a consolation for those excluded from the material benefits of citizenship and progress in the real world.

THE REPUBLIC OF NATURE

In its most benign form, this romantic out-take from the Enlightenment promulgated the cult of the noble savage, and related ideologies of primitivism. These offered to radical thinkers in the West an image of 'natural liberty', a journey back in time to bear witness to the origins of natural rights. Notwithstanding the unmistakable traces of colonial condescension, native Americans were portrayed as the modern counterparts not only of primitive peoples at the dawn of European history, but also of the proud freemen of ancient Greece and Rome. The first extensive ethnographic accounts of the native Americans by the French writers, Baron de Lahontan and Joseph-François Lafitau, saw much to admire in the Indian way of life and were enormously influential on subsequent commentators, among them, as we have seen, Edmund Burke. As several recent writers have noted, such favourable accounts did not feature so prominently in the work of British officials and soldiers, but among the most sympathetic observers of the native Americans were two from an Anglo-Irish background, Cadwallader Colden (1688–1776), Surveyor-General and Lieutenant-Governor of New York, who played a conspicuous role in the events leading up to the War of Independence, and Sir William Johnson (1715–74), Superintendent of Indian Affairs in North America and perhaps the most important strategist in bringing about the fateful alliance between Indian and British forces in their various conflicts with the colonial settlers.[3]

In his pioneering *The History of the Five Indian Nations of Canada, which are Dependent on the Province of New York* (1727), the first systematic account of the Iroquois in English, Colden showed that while he was not blind to their negative qualities, such as the hideous torments which they inflicted on their enemies, native Americans had no monopoly on cruelty:

Whoever reads the History of so famed ancient Heroes, will find them, I'm afraid, not much better in this respect. Does Achilles' Behaviour to Hercules [*sic*] dead body in Homer, appear less savage? ... witness the Carthaginians and Phoenicians burning their children alive in Sacrifice, and several Passages in Jewish History; and witness, in later Times, the Christians burning one another alive, for God's sake.

But the analogies with classical antiquity were not entirely negative, and Colden proceeded to strike a note that accentuated the nobility of the Iroquois warrior, and lent itself particularly to subsequent idealizations of indigenous peoples by republican and Enlightenment theorists:

The Five Nations are a poor and, generally called, barbarous People, bred under the darkest Ignorance; and yet a bright and noble Genius shines through these black Clouds. None of the greatest Roman Heroes have discovered a greater Love to their country, or a greater contempt of death, than these people called Barbarians have done, when Liberty came in competition. Indeed, I think our Indians have outdone the Roman in this Particular; some of the greatest of those have we know murdered themselves to avoid Shame or Torments; but our Indians have refused to die meanly, or with but little Pain, when they thought their Country's Honour would be at Stake by it; but have given their Bodies willingly to the cruel Torments of their Enemies, to shew, as they said, that the Five Nations consisted of Men, whose Courage and Resolution could not be shaken.[4]

The stoical demeanour of the Indians, in conjunction with their indomitable courage and martial valour, contributed to their image as exemplars of natural rights, of humanity in its original Edenic state of nature. But as Virgil reminded those who searched for a paradise on Earth, even death is present in Arcadia.[5] The fatal flaw in the primitivist love affair with the Indian was that it was essentially nostalgic and elegiac, in effect paying homage to the simple austerities of a vanished social order. Under theories of progress adumbrated by the Scottish Enlightenment, this myth of origins was elaborated into a stages theory of history, with justice and natural rights being transferred through a process of abstraction from their primordial 'natural' state to those societies at the highest stage of civilization.

While few theorists went so far as to discern in the Indian way of life the putative condition of humanity before the 'original' social contract, none the less the alleged freedom enjoyed by the Indian lent itself to fantasies of the abolition of society, with individuals enjoying freedom devoid entirely of social or communal obligations. Traces of this pre-lapsarian dream are evident in Lord Edward Fitzgerald's reflections on his life among the Iroquois, but unlike some of his latter-day *laissez-faire* counterparts, he recognized that the absence of society also means the absence of property and money. Comparing the economic worries and vanities of polite society to a simple, primitive existence, he speculated that if he were brought up among the Indians there would be 'no cases of looking forward to the fortune for children – of thinking how are you to live: no separations in families, one in Ireland, one in England; no devilish politics, no fashions, customs, duties, or appearances to the world, to interfere with one's happiness' (*Lord Edward Fitzgerald*, i, 92). But no sooner has he expressed these sentiments than he reveals that his utopian lifestyle is not quite so devoid of duties and obligations; rather, it possesses different and more deep-rooted social commitments than those found in corrupt commercial societies. Indian freedom does not consist in an atomized individualism but its opposite, a society permeated by mutual obligations and care for others, as against the instrumental exchanges that pass for civil society in the West:

They enjoy the love and company of their wives, relations and friends, without any interference of interests or ambition to separate them. To bring things home to oneself, if *we* had been Indians, instead of its being my duty to be separated from all of you, it would, on the contrary, be my duty to be with you... Instead of being served and supported by servants, everything here is done by one's relations – by the people one loves; and the mutual obligations you must be under increase your love for each other. (*Lord Edward Fitzgerald*, i, 91–2)

In drawing attention to these contrary ideals – a society that is at once without duties and custom, and yet is even more saturated with mutual obligations than Western societies – Fitzgerald is exposing one of the main fault-lines in the appropriation of 'primitive' tribes as foundation myths for Western societies. On the one hand, they are pre-social, existing in a state of nature; on the other, they are *too* social, living permanently in 'the shadow of each other'. The source of the confusion has to do with the ambivalence itself of the Golden Age: a form of life idealized and venerated at a distance, but denied and indeed actively suppressed as it approximated reality, or came closer to home in the metropolitan centre. The key consideration here was distance, in both its spatial and temporal senses. For many contemporaries as well as subsequent scholars, the opening up of the New World marked a Copernican revolution in culture, de-centring the self-image of the Old World which equated humanity with Europe and its various hinterlands. As many commentators observed, epic and ethnography fused as the scale of the New World required a voyage of discovery as fundamental in redrafting the contours of the Western imagination as Homer's *Odyssey*.[6] This had far-reaching consequences for perceptions of time as well as space during the Renaissance, for it gradually undermined cyclical theories of history driven by a desire to restore the grandeur of classical antiquity in a modern age. New forms of the past now presented themselves which were not so amenable to restoration, opening up the possibility that history was carried forward by an irreversible flow, a river of no return.

THE SPATIALIZATION OF TIME

The initial response to this disruption of the genealogy of the world was to integrate the Indians into existing accounts, even at the cost of breaking up the narrative coherence of the 'great chain of being' which had held medieval Christendom in place. American Indians were variously linked with the Lost Tribes of Israel, or with ancient Asian peoples such as the Phoenicians and the Scythians, and came to be seen as 'degenerate examples of human regression planted in their new continent after the flood and the dispersal of nations following the fall of the Tower of Babel'.[7] This facilitated another momentous shift in European sensibility, as the elaboration of natural rights and contractarian theories of society encouraged political theorists to look for evidence of precontractual formations to justify their models of human evolution. It is at this conjuncture that the conflicting images of precontractual society present themselves, oscillating from the anarchic freedom of isolated individualism to the close interdependence of archaic communalism. For Grotius, there was little difficulty in reconciling primitive, precontractual society with the accounts outlined in Genesis, for both shared communal property and the absence of government which made the original general contract necessary. It was left to Thomas Hobbes to link these conceptions directly to the American Indians, relating his famous picture of the state of nature, in which 'the life of man, is solitary, poore, nasty, brutish, and short', to the New World:

It may peradventure be though, that there never was such a time, nor condition of war as this; and I believe it was never generally so, all over the world: but there are many places, where they live so now. For the savage peoples in many places of America, except the government of small Families, the concord whereof dependeth on natural lust, have no government at all; and live at this day in that brutish manner, as I said before.[8]

Hobbes' formulation is of note in that he still does not discern in the condition of the Indians the template for the origin of *all* mankind. It is this latter step, traced by Ronald Meek to the late seventeenth century, and particularly to the four stages theory of history promulgated by the French and Scottish Enlightenments in the eighteenth century, which introduced the 'spatialization of time', the equation of distance in time with distance in space, which was so amenable to colonial ideology. Boundaries and frontiers in space became the equivalent of stages and epochs in history. This is the notion of origins which informs John Locke's important modification of Hobbes' account: 'In the beginning all the world was *America*.'[9] The universality of the 'state of nature' was attributed at first to a common ancestry, as in the biblical story, but by relocating origins in different geographical settings, with no direct relation between them, time was given a new spatial differentiation. As the Scottish historian William Robertson expressed this recasting of the origins of society in his landmark *History of America* (1777):

A tribe of savages on the banks of the Danube must nearly resemble one upon the plains washed by the Mississippi. Instead then of presuming from this similarity, that there is any affinity between them, we should only conclude, that the dispositions and manners of men are formed by their situation, and arise from the state of society in which they live... In every part of the earth, the progress of man hath been nearly the same; and we can trace him in his career from the rude simplicity of savage life, until he attains the industry, the arts, and the elegance of polished society. There is nothing wonderful, then, in the similitude between the Americans and the barbarous nations of our continent.[10]

As is clear from Robertson's formulation, the influence of Montesquieu was crucial in promoting awareness of the effects of climate, environment and modes of subsistence on the determination of national character and cultural diversity. This new current in Enlightenment thought throws a less favourable light on the tendency, endemic in homages to the noble savage, to establish affinities between native American and other distinguished – and not so distinguished – ancient societies, for it was by virtue of this temporal dislocation that Indians were cast in the mould of obsolete cultures, peoples who had essentially outlived their usefulness in the modern world.

As early as 1609 native Americans were being compared to ancient Sparta in French writings, thus establishing a trope linking their freedom to ideals of virtue in ancient Rome (as in Colden's account above) or, in more radical political tracts, to republican concepts of liberty. But instead of conferring cultural prestige on the Indians and elevating them to the position enjoyed by the Romans in Western thought, the universalizing thrust of primitivism served to divest them of all cultural specificity, in effect, denying that they were cultures at all. Time and again, the image of the solitary Indian silhouetted against the horizon, or of individual hunters wandering through the wilderness oblivious to each other, recurred in the Western imagination. 'The life of a fisher or a hunter', wrote Lord Kames, 'is averse to society, except among the members of single families. The shepherd life promotes larger societies, if that can be called a society, which scarce hath any other than a local connection.'[11] Likewise, William Robertson observed: 'In America, man appears under the rudest form in which we can conceive him to subsist. We behold communities just beginning to unite, and may examine the sentiments and action of human beings in the infancy of social life.'[12]

THE SAVAGE ON ONE'S NATIVE SHORE

It is striking that throughout Scottish attempts to apply a developmental model to the state of nature, converting it from a state to a process, there is a recurrent anxiety about the nature of sociability, and the transition to social interaction. This is particularly noticeable in the tendency, evident in Kames's pronouncement above, to collapse the family, and related local affections, into a pre-social state, at odds with the prerequisites of civil society. What is at stake is not so much the New World and distant lands as a more immediate menace, the residual Gaelic culture and clan system of the Highlands and, of course, Ireland.[13] Roy Harvey Pearce has observed that 'American theorizing about the Indian owed its greatest debt to a group of eighteenth-century Scottish writers on man and society',[14] but as we have observed in Chapter 3 above, it may be that this concern with primitivism was motivated by matters closer to home, the threat presented by the Scottish Highlands and Ireland to new conceptions of Britishness being forged in this century. 'Resemblances in time', as Hugh Blair liked to call them, between native Americans and native Scottish culture date to the end of the sixteenth century, when Theodor de Bry, in Part I of his *America*, included illustrations of ancient Picts to accompany John White's famous ethnographic drawings of Indian life in Virginia.[15] But these at least were reassuringly removed in time from contemporary discontents in Scotland. What was less comforting, and what the whole discourse of primitivism sought to prevent, was the presence of the savage on one's native shore.

Following the logic of the new realignment of time and space, the native savage was accordingly projected back into antiquity. Instead of posing a challenge for cultural diversity in the present, Gaelic culture was presented as something superseded in the past: the Highlanders appeared, in Peter Womack's description, as 'no longer as different from ourselves, but *as what we once were*'.[16] To exorcize the ghosts of Culloden, the lived experience of the recent past – the connective tissue of custom and clan society – was dispelled, and replaced by the unattainable aura of a distant past. Everything that happened in between was construed as corruption and decay, as a once glorious epoch fell into decline. A cultural legacy extending over centuries, incorporating early Christianity, the middle ages and the early modern period, was declared waste, the temporal equivalent of the Atlantic Ocean, opening up a void between then and now. As David Hume wrote to his friend David Wilkes in 1754:

If your time had permitted, you should have gone into the Highlands. You would have seen human Nature in the golden Age, or rather, indeed, in the Silver: For the Highlanders have degenerated somewhat from the primitive Simplicity of Mankind. But perhaps you have so corrupted a Taste as to prefer your Iron Age.[17]

For Hume and for other members of the Scottish Enlightenment there was little doubt that the source of the contamination lay not only with feudalism but with tradition and the persistence of vernacular culture (both shorthand for Catholicism and Gaelic culture). In the section on 'Rude Nations' in his *Essay on the History of Civil Society*, Adam Ferguson argued that accounts of antiquity lack sufficient authority since they 'are made to bear the stamp of the times through which they have passed in the form of tradition, not of the ages through which their pretended descriptions relate':

We therefore willingly quit the history of our early ancestors, where Caesar and Tacitus have dropped them; and perhaps, till we come within the reach of what is connected with present affairs, and makes a part of the system on which we now proceed, have little reason to expect any subject to interest or inform the mind.[18]

It is in this context that the dim figure of Ossian emerged from the mists of the Highlands, mildewed with age but somehow transporting himself across the centuries to come within the reach of 'present affairs'. Much of the difficulty experienced by James Macpherson in vouching for the authenticity of his alleged translations derived from his reluctance to admit that such originals as existed had more to do with the vagaries of oral tradition than with the purity of manuscript sources. Howard Gaskill rightly points out, as a corrective to Dr Johnson's throwing down the gauntlet to Macpherson to 'produce the manuscripts', that on no occasion did Macpherson make the absurd claim that his originals were texts dating from Ossian's own era, or even that they were based exclusively on manuscripts.[19] Nevertheless it is clear that Macpherson was less than happy with having to rely on the debased medium of oral culture: 'Probability is all that can be established on the authority of tradition, ever dubious and uncertain.'[20] The invocation of oral tradition had its advantages, however, for it provided Macpherson with a pretext for 'improving' his raw materials or, as he preferred to describe it, restoring them to the original. As Andrew Gaillie, who worked with Macpherson on the Gaelic poems for *Fingal*, expressed it:

It was, and I believe still is well known, that the broken poems of Ossian, handed down from one generation to another, got corrupted. In the state of the Highlands, and its language, this evil, I apprehend, could not be avoided; and I think great credit is due, in such a case, to him who restores a work of merit to its original purity.[21]

As to the source of the corruption, Macpherson had little doubt that the rot set in with the advent of the bardic tradition. The bards and the Gaelic order they embodied summoned up the bogey of the recent past in Scotland, but were also a painful reminder of the obduracy of Irish culture, which could not so easily be consigned to oblivion as its counterpart in the Highlands. For this reason, it was vital that their role as custodians of a distinguished culture be discredited, and ultimately destroyed:

I have shewn how superior the probability of this system is to the undigested fictions of the Irish bards, and the more recent and regular legends of both Irish and Scottish historians... It was chiefly for this reason, that I have rejected wholly the works of the bards in my publications.

Irish historians fared no better than the bardic order, as Macpherson proceeded to pour scorn on 'the improbable and self-condemned tales of Keating and O'Flaherty. Credulous and puerile to the last degree, they have disgraced the antiquities they were wont to establish.'[22]

It was not just the 'undigested fictions' of the bards, but also their native allegiances and sense of belonging which caused offence to primitivist ideology. They celebrated – or excoriated – what they knew best, but never lifted their eyes above their immediate horizons, which made them of little interest to other cultures: 'Their ideas, it is confessed, are too local, to be admired in another language; to *those who are acquainted with the manners they represent, and the scene they describe*, they must afford pleasure and satisfaction.'[23] In this statement, we can see one of the key contributions made by primitivism to Enlightenment thought, namely, the imputation that any kind of cultural specificity or local mode of address prevents cross-cultural communication – and, by extension, citizenship, the capacity to become a citizen of the world. Under this dispensation, as Johannes Fabian has argued, knowledge of the other can only take place across a lapse of time, so that the more distant the culture is from the here and now, the greater the appeal to cosmopolitan sensibilities.[24] Hence, as against the mere provincialism of the bards, Macpherson is at pains to point out that Ossian 'acted in a more extensive sphere, and his ideas ought to be more noble and universal; neither gives he, I presume, so many of those peculiarities, which are only understood in a certain period or country' ('Dissertation', 198). This, as it happened, was highly convenient for Macpherson's muse, for it released him from the onerous task of having to attend to the kind of topographical details and local knowledge which were noticeably missing from the poems.

This rarefaction of the past was also bound up with another major lacuna in Macpherson's Ossian that goes to the heart of the contradictions we have earlier noted in primitivist ideology. Historians of 'rude nations' had struggled with the difficulty of reconciling the excessive sociability of savage peoples with their isolated, pre-social condition, but the relocation of the noble savage in Scottish antiquity circumvented this problem. As Hugh Blair noted in his influential treatise on Ossian, one of the most distinctive features of the poems

is the entire silence which reigns with respect to all the great clans and families, which are now established in the Highlands. The origins of these several clans is known to be very ancient: And it is well known, that there is no passion by which a native Highlander is more distinguished, than by attachment to his clan, and jealousy for its honour.[25]

So far from detracting from its authenticity, moreover, this was taken as a clear demonstration that Macpherson had got it right – politically, if not historically. In laying down the cultural conditions for the transition from previous stages to the highest phase of social development, that of civility and commerce, Adam Smith had noted that the obstinacy of familial and communal attachments constitutes a formidable barrier to the abstract, impersonal relations of the market. In his *Theory of Moral Sentiments*, he recalled:

> It is not many years ago that, in the Highlands of Scotland, the Chieftain used to consider [i.e. show consideration] the poorest man of his clan, as his cousin and relation. The same extensive regard to kindred is said to take place... I believe among all other nations who are merely in the same state of society in which the Scots Highlanders were about the beginning of the present century. (*Moral Sentiments*, 223)

The anxiety induced by the dense layers of filiation in Highlands society is nowhere more evident than in Smith's agitated response to the Jacobite uprising of 1745, in which the army of invading Highlanders are stripped, in his imagination, of the raiments of society and reduced to a primal horde of savages. Decrying the lack of 'courage' and 'martial spirit' in an advanced, commercial age, he observed ruefully:

> This is confirmed by universal experience. In the year 1745 four or 5 thousand naked unarmed Highlanders took possession of the improved parts of this country without any opposition from the unwarlike inhabitants. They penetrated into England and alarmed the whole nation, and had they not been opposed by a standing army they would have seized the throne with little difficulty.[26]

As we have seen in Chapter 3, theories of sympathy adumbrated by the Scottish Enlightenment are based on the premise that the experience of suffering, or the expression of grievances in general, are incompatible with Enlightenment ideals of citizenship and fraternity, still less with human or universal solidarity. According to David Hume, though sympathy can be extended to those in need, it is pre-eminently directed at the rich and the powerful:

> Upon the whole, there remains nothing, which can give us an esteem for power and riches, and a contempt for meanness and poverty, except the principle of sympathy, by which we enter into the sentiments of the rich and poor, and partake of their pleasure and uneasiness. (*Treatise*, 411)

The 'uneasiness' generated through sympathy with the poor is little short of repulsion, and Hume anticipates Smith's neo-stoical repudiation of the right to complain, arguing that the poor, or the 'misfortunate', only deserve sympathy when they look for it least: 'a man who is not dejected by misfortunes, is the more lamented on account of his patience; and if that virtue extends so far as utterly to remove all sense of uneasiness, it still further increases our compassion' (*Treatise*, 419).[27] Adam Smith extends this to a principle that the ventilation of grievances in the public sphere is an affront to propriety which, in Smith, is shorthand for the discipline and refinement of the body required by a polite, commercial age. According to Smith, 'it may be laid down as a general rule' that the kind of 'affections which tend to unite men in society' are those 'more or less agreeable to the person concerned', such as 'humanity, kindness, natural affection, friendship, [and] esteem' (*Moral Sentiments*, 243). By contrast, experiences of pain and duress, as we have noted in Chapter 3 above, tend to shut out fellow-feeling, turning our minds and bodies in on ourselves:

> the passions which the spectator is least disposed to sympathize with, and in which, on that account, the point of propriety may be said to stand low, are those of which the immediate feeling or sensation is more or less disagreeable, or even painful, to the person principally concerned. This general rule, so far as I have been able to observe, admits not of a single exception... We esteem the man who supports pain and even torture with manhood and firmness; and we can have little regard for him who sinks under them, and abandons himself to useless outcries and womanish lamentations. (*Moral Sentiments*, 243–4)

It would seem from this that Smith had not attended a traditional Irish wake, where misfortune and distress brought out sociability, 'useless outcries and womanish lamentations' with all the excess he despised and feared. But behind Smith's stoical imperative is an attempt to sever suffering or grievances of any kind from social interaction or concern for others – thus laying the basis for a market economy in which compassion and the alleviation of distress, even in conditions of crisis, are no longer necessary for social justice. In a revealing observation on appropriate responses to hunger, he writes:

> It is indecent to express any strong degree of those passions from a certain situation or disposition of the body; because the company, not being in the same disposition, cannot be expected to sympathize with them. Violent hunger, for example, though upon many occasions not only natural, but unavoidable, is always indecent, and to eat voraciously is universally regarded as a piece of ill manners. (*Moral Sentiments*, 27)

In a 'Digression Concerning the Corn Trade and Corn Laws' in *The Wealth of Nations*, this is given political expression in what might be seen as a foreshadowing of the government's response, based on Smith's authority, among others, to the Great Famine in Ireland: 'Famine has never arisen from any other cause but the violence of government attempting by improper means to remedy the inconvenience of a dearth.'[28]

The underlying assumption for Smith, as for Hume, is that sympathy, in the new, refined moral sense, requires the age of commerce to bestow its benefits on society. According to the natural right theories of Grotius and Pufendorf, to which Hume and Smith owed much of their intellectual formation, scarcity and want did not produce a sensitivity towards the plight of others but rather selfishness and possessiveness. For this reason, it is only in conditions of relative comfort and abundance that the refinement of the passions which permit morality takes place. This involves a conquest of physical appetite and a purging of the body from the public sphere, a form of psychic discipline considered impossible in primitive societies. Hence the paradox that for all their sociability and 'clannishness', primitive societies are incapable of sympathy, as defined in Smith's moral lexicon, on account of their constant struggle for survival. In the case of the American Indians, he asserts that 'circumstances not only habituate him to every sort of distress, but teach him to give way to none of the passions which that distress is apt to excite. He can expect from his countrymen no sympathy or indulgence for such weakness' (*Moral Sentiments*, 205). This lays the basis for the critical argument that adversity forces us to look after ourselves:

Before we feel for others, we must in some measure be at ease ourselves. If our own misery pinches us very severely, we have no leisure to attend to that of our neighbour; and all savages are too much preoccupied with their own wants and necessities to give much attention to those of the other person. (*Moral Sentiments*, 205)

The implications of this argument are far reaching. 'Primitive' societies, and 'the other' within – Gaelic culture, the poor – are disenfranchised at the outset from the Enlightenment project as being incapable of thinking beyond themselves, or attaining that generosity of vision that comes so effortlessly to citizens of the world. Insult is added to injury as there is not only the actual experience of hardship or suffering, but the added indignity of ostracization or isolation. Solidarity among the oppressed, particularly across cultural boundaries or between different societies with shared experiences of colonialism, is ruled out *a priori* as being beyond the reach of the primitive mind. It became imperative for this reason to widen the gap between civility and savagery – a process facilitated greatly by clearly defined 'stages' of history – to prevent primitive societies from aspiring to traits that could qualify as modern, rendering them eligible for the notions of liberty, justice, and equality that were the sole preserve of advanced Western societies.

THE SOLIDARITY OF THE OPPRESSED

On every lump of sugar, I see a drop of blood. (Thomas Russell, United Irishman, on slavery)

If we return to Lord Edward Fitzgerald's sojourn in America in the light of these observations, it can be seen that his acknowledgement of the dense networks of social ties, duties, and obligations which underlie the 'natural simplicity' of primitive societies marks off the Iroquois as a fully constituted culture, not merely the denizens of a putative state of nature. For Adam Smith, as we have seen, refinements of the passions such as sympathy, not to mention the delicacy of feeling that characterizes sentimental love, are not to be found among 'the savages in North America': 'The weakness of love, which is so much indulged in ages of humanity and politeness, is regarded among savages as the most unpardonable effeminacy' (*Moral Sentiments*, 205). But Fitzgerald, not without a certain amount of wishful thinking on his part, saw the Indians as very much his contemporaries, and revelled in flirtatious exchanges with the females who accompanied him:

> They are delightful people; the ladies charming, and with manners that I like very much, they are so natural. Notwithstanding the life they lead, which would make most women rough and masculine, they are as soft, meek and modest as the best brought up girls in England. At the same time, they are coquettes *au possible*. Conceive the manners of Mimi in a poor *squaw*, that has been carrying packs in the woods all her life. (*Lord Edward Fitzgerald*, i, 145–6)

Thomas Moore correctly notes, in his biography of Fitzgerald, that 'much of the colouring' which he gave to 'savage life' was 'itself borrowed from civilization', but what is of interest here is the impulse (however misguided in terms of gender and ethnography) to bring native Americans into the modern world. For Moore, this aligns Fitzgerald's republicanism with that of Thomas Jefferson, whom he cites as paying homage to 'such societies (as the Indians) which live without government' and who accordingly enjoy greater happiness than 'those who live under the European governments' (*Lord Edward Fitzgerald*, i, 102). But notwithstanding their admiration and enthusiasm for the American Enlightenment, leading figures in the United Irishmen expressed profound misgivings over the treatment of slaves and Indians in the new land of liberty. Following the efforts of future United Irishmen such as Thomas MacCabe to prevent Belfast becoming a centre of the slave trade, James Hope took Jefferson to task in his poem, 'Jefferson's Daughter'. 'As ye trample the rights of your dark fellow men':

> Do you boast of your Freedom! peace, babblers be still,
> Unfetter your slaves, and the goddess will hear.
> Have ye power to unbind, are you wanting the will.
> Must the groans of your bondsman still torture the ear,
> The daughter of Jefferson sold as a slave.[29]

During his protracted stay in the United States, Archibald Hamilton Rowan expressed the same romantic longings for life in the wilderness as Lord Edward Fitzgerald, but also shared with him the determination to include oppressed minorites with his pastoral vision. Responding to conflicting advice to settle down in Philadelphia, or to buy a small farm, he writes:

I will do neither; I will go to the woods; but I will not kill Indians, nor keep slaves. Good God! if you heard some of the Georgians, or the Kentucky people, talk of killing the natives! Cortes, and all that followed him, were not more sanguinary in the South, than they would be in North America.[30]

As noted in Chapter 6, one of the reasons the Enlightenment – particularly in its revolutionary Paineite form – was unable to develop a universal vision which genuinely addressed cultural diversity, and which clearly distinguished progress from colonialism and cultural domination, was its overriding concern with primitivism and the question of origins. Revolutionary upheaval called not so much for a break with the past, as with the lived experience of recent history, conveyed by custom, tradition and other forms of precedent. Thomas Paine's intention was to push aside this cultural inheritance – characterized, as it was, by monarchy, feudalism, and other vestiges of privilege and inequality – to recover the true foundations of rights in their original, pristine integrity. In effect, this meant sweeping away the accumulated deposits of time and place, the distinctive features of a particular culture, in order to embrace a universal brotherhood in nature. The difficulty with worshippers of the past, such as Edmund Burke, was not that they went back in time but that they did not go back far enough:

[The] error of those who reason by precedents drawn from antiquity, respecting the rights of man, is that they do not go far enough into antiquity. They do not go the whole way. They stop in some of the intermediate stages of an hundred or thousand years, and produce what was then done as a rule for the present day. This is no authority at all.[31]

The ultimate source of authority, for Paine, is not in history at all, but in nature.

For the United Irishmen, however, lifting 'the fog of time and antiquity' that hung over the intermediate stages revealed not so much a prospect of Nature as of a hidden culture, an alternative social order. In a number of declarations, they set their faces firmly against the past, but this has been erroneously taken to mean the old Irish or Gaelic order.[32] In fact, it was the *British* past which was the target of their invective, particularly the record of strife and conflict caused by the imposition of British rule in Ireland over the centuries. In the crucial years 1793–6, the pressures of the revolutionary war forced British radicals into a patriotic retrenchment, moving away from Paineite declarations of universal rights to embrace versions of liberty derived from the heritage of the 'free-born Englishman'. At the same time, Irish radicals were travelling in the opposite direction, questioning the capacity of the British constitution to treat Irish people as equal subjects, let alone citizens. Defending Archibald Hamilton Rowan at his state trial in 1794, John Philpot Curran argued that 'England is marked by a natural avarice of freedom, which she is studious to engross and accumulate, but most unwilling to impart': 'In order to confirm that observation... I should state the case of the invaded American, and the subjugated Indian, to prove that the policy of England has ever been to govern her connexions more as colonies, than as allies.'[33] In the same year, Rev. James Porter, Thomas Russell, and William Sampson published anonymously a scathing satire on the revered British constitution, *Review of the Lion of Old England*, which professed to be a critical exegesis of a mock-heroic epic poem on English law, and its current war policy. The target of their satire was Edmund Burke in his role as High-Priest of the 'ancient constitution' in England which had by then come to be seen by the more radical United Irishmen as the main bulwark against revolution in Ireland and in Britain.

The centrepiece of this squib takes the form of a visit to a glorious temple with the priest or 'prophet Edmund', arrayed in 'sooth-saying attire... in which was inserted his parliamentary dagger', acting as guide.[34] As the prophet explains to the visitor 'the sublime and mysterious beauties of this venerable edifice' (*Review of the Lion*, 31),[35] the lion adorning the temple is so overcome 'that he involuntary [*sic*] threw his paws around the neck of the prophet, and in this manner, both one and t'other remained motionless, speechless and suspended for the space of many minutes' (*Review of the Lion*, 38) (Fig. 12). While 'the beautiful' and 'the picturesque' are the aesthetic styles most in evidence in the hallowed precincts of the building,

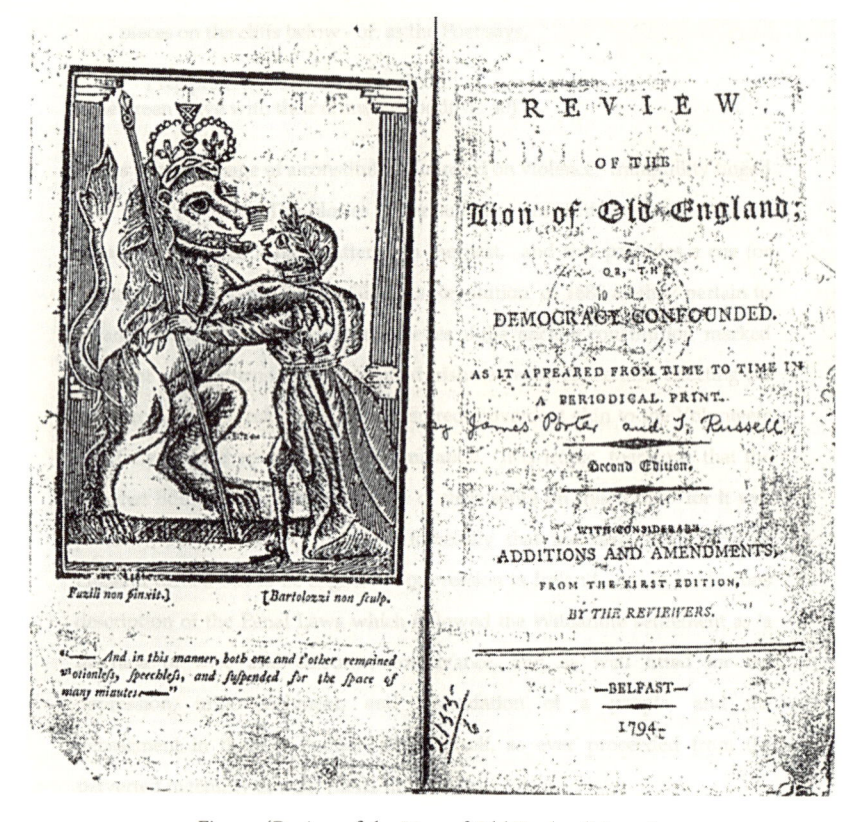

Fig. 12 'Review of the Lion of Old England' (1794)

a sense of terror and foreboding makes its presence felt on entering the Tudor rooms. This intimation of the sublime casts an ominous gloom over another neglected corner of the building, where, in 'rugged niches were disposed the mouldering statues of the ANCIENT DRUIDS', or precursors of the bards. These, the prophet informs his visitors:

are the most ancient of all our historians. Although ignorant of letters, they possessed, according to Caesar, all the learning of the Western world – with those harps which you perceive in their hands, which are indeed much decayed and disfigured by the cankering tooth of time; they were used to accompany the sweet melody of their voices, and to carol forth the praises of the virtuous and the brave... so might they have escaped the disgraceful punishments inflicted on them in after times, by the royal mandates of the conquering EDWARD. He [i.e. the prophet] then pointed to the rude sculpture which represents the throwing them down the tremendous cliffs, where their mangled bodies were either dashed to pieces on the cliffs below – or, as the Poet says,

> Precipitated headlong in the flood
> The green wave with their crimson blood.
> (*Review of the Lion*, 40)

This is Burke's image of a constitution founded on violence, 'tranquillity tinged with terror' (*Enquiry*, 136). The glories of the ancient constitution are built on the remains of cultures it has shattered in the past, and this provides a cue for the authors of the pamphlet to debunk the benefits of 'the Glorious Revolution' of 1688 as they pertain to Ireland. This radical break with the pieties of the 'ancient constitution' marked the point of no return for the United Irishmen, effecting the shift from being a reformist, Whig-inspired movement, akin to the Volunteers, to a fully fledged revolutionary organization. It is ironic, therefore, that the 'prophet Edmund' should be the butt of their satire on this count, for it was precisely Burke who argued most forcefully that measures for liberty in England turned out to be engines of oppression in Ireland – as in his famous description of the Penal Laws which followed the Williamite settlement as 'a machine of wise and elaborate contrivance, and as well fitted for the oppression, impoverishment, and degradation of a people, and the debasement in them of human nature itself, as ever proceeded from the perverted ingenuity of man' ('Langrishe', iii, 343).

In fact, the radical transformation in the thinking of the United Irishmen at this juncture, renouncing the imperial remit of the English constitution and turning their attention to the rights of endangered, native cultures, can be seen as giving a specific Burkean inflection to what were otherwise Paineite conceptions of the universal rights. In the Enlightenment tradition derived from the 'Social Contract', freedom was envisaged as an original 'state of Nature', a universal realm which transcended all cultures. Culture, and by extension tradition, was seen as a fall from grace, a series of constraints upon liberty which entailed that the very concept of cultural freedom, or cultural rights, was a contradiction in terms. Hence the romantic appeal of the wilderness in which natural rights merged with the image of humanity at the dawn of creation, divested of all its cultural accretions. For metropolitan radicalism, the republic of nature presented itself as the only utopian space existing outside the constitution, as if no other cultures or societies had anything to offer in re-drawing the map of mankind.

Not least among the contradictions of primitivism, therefore, was the fact that radically different cultures, such as those of the American Indians, were valued as an alternative to Western civilization precisely because they were not treated as cultures at all; 'the particular language', as Helen Carr writes, even when it is positive, 'ignores the Indians' own social organization'.[36] This romantic impulse, as the main vocabulary of radicalism, undoubtedly influenced the thinking of the United Irishmen, but by the mid-1790s, it was not Nature but *another culture*, the endangered inheritance of Gaelic Ireland and of the majority Catholic population, which provided a zone of critical engagement with the pieties of the English constitution. The British constitution was found wanting, in their eyes, not simply from the abstract standard of natural rights, but also in comparison to other allegedly inferior cultures such as that which they found around them, and which they also identified in America and Africa. Writing in 1796, Thomas Russell inveighed against the policies of press-ganging up to 150,000 Irishmen – directed mainly at conscripting Catholic Defenders – into the British army in the war against France, arguing that such forms of tyranny would put so-called savage societies to shame:

Consider beside the number of these your countrymen who have themselves perished by disease, famine and the sword; think of the men torn, without even the form of legal process, from their destitute innocent families under the name of defenders, by a set of detestable ruffians; crammed on board ships of war, and there to fight in a cause which, perhaps, they thought wrong. The North American savages are superior to such a practice. When they go to war, every man of the tribe who disapproves of it is at liberty to remain at home or peaceably follow his avocations of hunting... Are the Irish people aware that this contest involves the question of the slave trade, the one of the greatest consequence on the face of the earth?... Do they know that by it thousands and hundreds of thousands of these miserable Africans are dragged from their innocent families like the miserable defenders, transported to various places, and there treated with such a system of cruelty, torment, wickedness and infamy, that it is impossible for language adequately to express its horror and guilt.[37]

For Russell, the cause of the Defenders is on a continuum with that of African slaves; and the standards of civility against which English tyranny is found wanting derive not from nature but from other cultures on the receiving end of colonialism, including that of the native Americans.

This kind of argument, cognizant of the rights of other cultures or religious traditions, had to await the ambivalent freedom of political exile in the United States to receive its fullest articulation in the writings of New York United Irishmen, such as William Sampson, one of Russell's co-authors on the *Review of the Lion of Old England*. In 1812, in a landmark case in American legal history centring on the secrecy of the Catholic confessional, Sampson, in his professional capacity as a lawyer, helped to establish the constitutional basis for the free exercise of religious worship in the United States. As Walter J. Walsh describes it:

[This] event ranks as perhaps the earliest recorded instance of impact litigation in American constitutional history – a test case in which an insular minority deliberately sought to appropriate the courts to transform the political structure of American society.[38]

Sampson's argument was that the discrimination against Catholicism in American law was a residue of the kind of colonial repression permitted in Ireland under the British constitution in Ireland, but which had no place in a republican constitution truly devoted to liberty. This was part of the sustained campaign, commenced during the 1790s in Ireland, against those who worshipped at the shrine of the British constitution. Ridiculing English imputations of barbarism to the Irish language and Gaelic culture, Sampson proposed that the clotted language of the British legal system, as eulogized by Sir William Blackstone and Sir Edward Coke, put the Irish language in the shade:

Indeed, [he wrote] some of the very acts of parliament, enacting penalties against those that spake Irish, or dwelt among the Irishry, are such a queer compound of Danish, Norman, hog-latin and I know not what, as to be the most biting satires upon the *Englishry*, and those that spake English.

And as for those who, like Coke, saw in the longevity of the ancient constitution proof of its divine status, Sampson remarks:

All I can say of it is this, that the same panegyric will apply *totidem verbis* to the institutions of our red brethren, the *Iroquois*. The league of the five nations is similar to that of the heptarchy [into which ancient Britain was divided]...The five nations think themselves, by nature, superior to the rest of mankind, and call themselves *Ongue honwee*...ONGUE HONWEE, then say I and away with your old barons, kings, monks, and druids...If we look to antiquity the red men have it. If we regard duration, they have it still more, for the *Picts* and the Britons have long ceased to dye themselves sky-blue. The *Indian* paints himself for war, even to this day.[39]

What we have here is a radical appropriation of some of the key tropes of primitivism and colonialism encountered earlier in this chapter. In a conscious inversion of the Enlightenment equation of native Americans with ancient Picts or Britons, the very survival of the former is taken as a triumph over adversity, and a rejoinder to the myth that they are, like the Picts, doomed to extinction. The Burkean defence of the ancient constitution on the grounds that it has existed 'time out of mind' is turned on its head as applying equally to other ancient peoples, whose very longevity and political organization rivals that of their European counterparts.[40] Sampson makes it clear that his mockery of the ancient constitution is not aimed at British law as such, but at its imperial claims to superiority over others: all he intends to show, he says, is that 'there are other systems as good' ('Speech in Defense', 160). Among these are the legal codes of Scotland and Ireland. Even when the Scots were defeated and brought to heel by English military might, they still would not accept the superiority of English law, for all its divine wisdom:

> If, then, so important a portion of the British island can do so well without any part of the common law, can it be necessary for us to adopt superstitiously every part of it? The Irish had the common law forced on them ... [They] had an ancient code which they revered. It was called the law of the judges, or the Brehon law. What it was, it is difficult to say; for with the other interesting monuments of the nation's antiquity, it was trodden under the hoof of the satyr that invaded her. ('Speech in Defense', 164)

He then argues that so far from disappearing in the mists of time, like the legacy of Ossian in the Highlands, the Brehon Laws kept resurfacing in the Irish political landscape until the policies of extirpation in the early modern period:

> No wonder that the 'wild natives', even in the days of Elizabeth, still kept and preserved their Brehon law, of which [even] its enemies are constrained to say, that it was a rule of right, unwritten, but declared by tradition from one to another, (like the common law), in which oftentimes there appeared great equity, though it was repugnant both to God's laws and man's. ('Speech in Defense', 165)

By reinstating what Paine and the Scottish Enlightenment, in their different ways, dismissed as mere intermediate or degenerate stages in the passage from antiquity to the present, Sampson is, in effect, appropriating Burkean notions of descent for a republican project. True to Burke's vision, moreover, cultural difference is not decanted into a purely aesthetic realm, a romantic out-take, as it were, from the Enlightenment, but is integrated into the public sphere, in the form of the Brehon Laws, or their social and political residues. Instead of being objects of proscription, subaltern cultures are endowed with the rights of prescription, which take on a new critical valency in redressing the injustices of the past. Nor is this account of cultural diversity limited by the solipsism of localism or relativism which led certain strands in romanticism to construe authenticity as isolation, a withdrawal from the outside world. As if infused by the radical sensibility of Burke's sympathetic sublime, Sampson and Russell highlight the predicament of one culture by bringing it into contact with another, recasting what Walter Benjamin has called 'the tradition of the oppressed' in terms of cross-cultural solidarity. The final arbiter of a culture's worth, according to Sampson, is not just the test of time, whether it conformed to the usages of 'Picts, Romans, Britons, Danes, Jutes, Saxons, Norman or other barbarians', but 'whether it is, or is not, an attack, on the rights of man' – as applied to cultures as well as individuals. In marked contrast to the last rites granted in valedictory accounts of primitive societies, native peoples were now entitled to cultural rights, thus laying the basis for a more ethnographic Enlightenment which does justice to the past as well as the present.

Conclusion: towards a post-colonial Enlightenment

> We can feel for others, whilst we suffer ourselves.
> Edmund Burke, *Enquiry into the Sublime and Beautiful*
>
> At one period of his life, too, when he became the disinterested patron of remote and injured nations, who had none to help them, his character was truly sublime...
> Richard Payne Knight on Burke, *An Analytical Enquiry into the Principles of Taste* (1808)

During the Bastille Day celebrations in July 1792, ten infirm harpers – seven of them blind, one almost a hundred years of age – appeared at the Belfast Harp Festival, a display of longevity on stage not perhaps emulated until the Rolling Stones resumed touring in recent years. The Harp Festival, organized by affiliates of the United Irishmen, was a pivotal event in the revival of native Irish music and culture, leading to the publication of Edward Bunting's landmark *A General Collection of the Ancient Music of Ireland* in 1796. 'Have you got the Irish Music', Martha McTier wrote excitedly to her brother, William Drennan, one of the founders of the United Irishmen, 'it is the rage here.'[1]

That the harp had already moved centre stage to the United Irishmen's cultural politics was clear from its adoption as the emblem of the new movement in October 1791, with the rousing motto: 'It is new strung and shall be heard.' According to the manifesto for the Harp Festival, 'the spirit and character of a people are [intimately] connected with their national poetry and music',[2] and the harp was a resonant image of such national sentiment. According to the Scottish Enlightenment, societies were held together at the deepest level by chords of sympathy and sentiment, and the reverberation of strings in an instrument perfectly conveyed the mutual transfer of 'fellow-feeling' among kindred souls: 'As in strings equally wound up', wrote David Hume, 'the motion of one communicates itself to the rest; so all the affections readily pass from one person to another, and beget correspondent movements in every human creature' (*Treatise*, 626–7).

But if the harp figured as an resonant image of social solidarity in an age of Enlightenment, the Gaelic culture from which it sprang, as we have seen, did not. For sure, the fascination with the Celt had already been part of metropolitan sensibility, inspired by James Macpherson's notorious Ossian 'translations' in the 1760s. But Ossian was suitably transported to a remote, ethereal past, a ghostly voice from a Gaelic culture vanquished at the Battle of Culloden. Under the spell of Celticism, Gaelic culture was recast in the image of romantic primitivism and relegated to a twilight zone of nostalgia, a refuge for the losers of history. Culloden was a fortunate fall from the point of view of the Scottish Enlightenment, for it dealt a body blow to a culture which far from being primitive and asocial, was, as we have seen, *too* social for the abstract relations required by a market economy, and the impersonal protocols of civil society. Though the Scottish Enlightenment's investment in ideas of progress and primitivism manifested itself as a fascination with the 'exotic other', whether in America, Africa or India, from the point of view of lived experience the other was within, in the Gaelic outposts of the Highlands and in the underground culture of Ireland during the Penal Laws. As C. R. Fay remarks of Adam Smith:

The Macs in the picture are few. I do not know that he [i.e. Smith] ever visited the Highlands. But the Highland problem occupied his thoughts; for it presented the classic example of a sharp transition from a natural to money economy, and before his death the potato was a factor of social significance both in Ireland and in the Western Isles.[3]

The obstacles of tradition, superstition, excessive sociability and unruly behaviour presented by Gaelic culture to what Gerhard Oestreich has described as the neo-stoical foundations of the modern state were carried over into the realm of culture,[4] where Gaelic eloquence and music were considered not exactly conducive to rational economic calculation and participation in the newly constituted public sphere. In marked contrast to the man who spoke prose without realizing it, Gaels and other primitive peoples were in the habit of conducting their business in poetry, which militated somewhat against their dutiful espousal of a work ethic. As Adam Smith described it:

The Erse poetry as appears from the translations recently published have very great merit but we never heard of any Erse prose. This may indeed appear very unnatural that what is most difficult[y] should be that in which the Barbarous least civilized nations most excell in; but it will not be very difficult to account for it... The

Savage nations on the coast of Africa, after they have sheltered themselves thro the whole day in caves and grottos from the scorching heat of the Sun come out in the evening and dance and sing together. Poetry is a necessary attendant on musick, especially on vocall musick the most naturall and simple of any. They naturally express some thoughts along with their music and these must of consequence be formed into verse to suit with the music.[5]

Set against this backdrop, the spectacle of ten infirm harpers assembled by associates of the United Irishmen at the Harpers' Festival in 1792, marked a radical turning point in the attitude of the Enlightenment towards native or indigenous cultures. The Enlightenment, in its dominant American and French forms, had set its face firmly against 'first peoples' or vernacular cultures, unless, that is, they were brought within the remit of Romanticism, where they enjoyed a new, sequestered afterlife in the realms of the imagination. In America, to embrace indigenous culture would have meant acknowledging the social and political heritage of native Americans, but their only mention in the Declaration of Independence is as 'merciless Indian savages'.[6] In France, the Convention in year II of the Revolution declared that minority languages such as Breton and Basque should be 'smashed' or 'obliterated'.[7] The aim in both cases was to transform natives into citizens of the world, freed from the limiting horizons of local culture and the encumbrances of time and place.

It was this insistence on the politics of place, the lived complexity of recent history and the inherited past, that Burke brought to bear on Enlightenment debates, albeit in the guise of its most avid and (true to Smith's stereotype of the Irish) eloquent opponent.[8] It is true that from the point of view of metropolitan – or imperial – culture, the obduracy of tradition, due to the very 'sluggish' and 'inert' qualities commended by Burke (*Reflections*, 140, 181), acted as a major force of conservation, absorbing the shocks of modernity and militating against challenges to the existing order. Insofar as it bore witness to the triumph of order and stability over the centuries, British nationalism's embrace of a secure, enduring tradition, and its ability to mask over the real discontinuities presented by, for example, the convulsions of the Civil War, was indeed counter-revolutionary from this perspective. By contrast, tradition in an Irish context, the volatile legacy of the recent as well as the remote past, was more akin to an 'igneous mass' (as Burke himself noted) and, fused with a radical Enlightenment project, was capable of demolishing the imposing Georgian facades of colonial civility: 'There is a hollow murmuring under ground; a confused movement is felt, that threatens a general earthquake in the political world' (*Reflections*, 265). The tradition of the oppressed is charged with the disruptive force of the sublime, deriving its energies from the fact that the originary violence of conquest has never been put to rest. In these circumstances, as Walter Benjamin wrote in a different context, 'the state of emergency in which we live is not the exception but the rule'.[9] This is the prospect raised by the spectre of the colonial sublime. In the absence of the tranquillizing effects of tradition, Burke's great fear was that the transformative power of terror would pass from master to slave, in keeping with the logic of the sublime whereby the endangered subject appropriated to itself part of the force which threatened to overwhelm it (*Enquiry*, 50–1). As he noted in the *Reflections*, picking up a thread of argument that runs from his earliest letters through the *Enquiry*: 'He that wrestles with us strengthens our nerves and sharpens our skill. Our antagonist is our helper' (*Reflections*, 279).

This lesson was not lost on the United Irishmen who saw that instead of acting as a brake on innovation in Ireland, 'tradition', in the form of an emergent cultural nationalism and an alliance with the agrarian underworld of the Defenders in the mid 1790s, might help to transform a constitutional reform movement into a revolutionary organization. In this sense, their greatest antagonist, Burke, was indeed their helper. There was nothing inevitable about this process, however. The United Irishmen, like their Scottish counterparts, might have limited their version of the Enlightenment to a civic integrationist project: in keeping also with the Scottish example, the revival of interest in Irish culture might have been innoculated against its radical political components, and quarantined in the Irish equivalent of Sir Walter Scott's imaginary Highlands. However, in the turbulent political environment of the 1790s in Ireland, native culture – the Irish language, Irish music, and the resurgence of a subjugated social order – became integral to a republican Enlightenment project. The bard and the culture he (or she – one of the harpers in Belfast was woman) embodied was no less the survivor of a shattered past than was Gaelic culture after Culloden, but 'bardic nationalism' (in Katie Trumpener's phrase) was still a vital presence, a force to be reckoned with.[10] The Harp Festival may be seen from one point of view as the end of an era, a valediction to the old Gaelic order, but amid the revolutionary strivings of the 1790s, it also presaged a new beginning, a resurgent alternative vision of Irish society. While Celticism in Scotland languished in antiquity under the spell of Ossian, the cult of the bard in Ireland shifted from ancient to living memory, as Turlough O'Carolan (1670–1738), the so-called 'last of the bards', became the focus of national sentiment. Much is made of Wolfe Tone's alleged indifference to the Harpers' Festival – '*Strum Strum* and be hanged', as he noted in his journal[11] – but it is generally overlooked that on the eve of his departure with his family for America, O'Carolan's music provided the inspiration for the radical melancholia of Tone and his fellow United Irishmen. Gathering at Lough Neagh for the last time, they returned to Belfast for what was to be, in effect, an American wake. As R. R. Madden describes the occasion:

> Everything that good taste and kind feeling could suggest to shew civility to Tone and his family was done. The celebrated Dr Bunting, who has accomplished so much for his country, was present, and played... one of the most touching of his own mournful and powerful airs – [O'Carolan's] 'The Parting of Friends' – when the wife of Tone [Matilda], one 'albeit unused to the melting mood', burst into tears.[12]

But as in Yeats's elegy on Parnell – 'Mourn – and then Onward!' – even lamentation did give way to despair. Ever hopeful, Martha McTier wrote to William Drennan that if O'Carolan's air was supplied with words, it might bring about a change of heart in British attitudes towards Ireland: 'To me they are sounds might make Pitt melt for the poor Irish... Miss Clarke perhaps can do them justice, and if when she plays The Parting of Friends, you should be inspired with words as tender as the tune, you might be immortal.' Fifty years later, the lament still haunted the memory of Matilda Tone, as she wrote in a letter to a New York newspaper: 'I live in complete retirement, and, to use Carolan's words, "Lonely and Desolate I Mourn the Dead".'[13]

Within the cultural logic of the Scottish Enlightenment, the sense of unrequited justice that accompanied defeat or cultural catastrophe found its expression in fatalism, the dark, disabling side of the sensitive Celt: 'They went forth to the war, Ossian says most truly, *but they always fell*.'[14] The self-absorption of the injured body, whether projected onto the outcast Philoctetes on his lonely isle, or the endless sighing of Ossian, became a fitting symbol for the colonial stereotype of the insular Celt, or other cultures doomed to extinction by the march of western civilization. 'Nobody can suppose', wrote the great liberal thinker, John Stuart Mill, 'that it is not more beneficial to a Breton, or a Basque' to be assimilated into the superior culture of France:

> than to sulk on his own rocks. the half savage relic of past times, revolving in his own little mental orbit, without participation or interest in the general movement of the world. The same remark applies to the Welshman or Scottish Highlander as members of the British nation.[15]

Mill was careful to exempt the Irish from his strictures and this is precisely the cultural juncture in which Enlightenment republicanism intersected with an emergent cultural nationalism in Ireland, thereby parting company with the integrationist logic of its 'Celtic' counterparts in Britain, that this study set out to examine.

For Adam Smith, as we have seen, cosmopolitanism, universalism or cross-cultural solidarity are the preserve of advanced western societies. They are, moreover, compatible with local or national affiliations, but only in the context of affluent societies with secure and stable identities, at least by comparison with non-European or 'pre-Enlightenment' cultures. By contrast, Burke's theory of the sublime links the body in pain not just to self-preservation, but also embraces an explicit social dimension, extending to a capacity to sympathize with others, both within and beyond one's own culture. Hence in Sophocles's *Philoctetes*, the complex negotiation of sociability and pain is such that the sympathetic impulse is only paralysed when consciousness itself is extinguished, as when Philoctetes falls unconscious on the ground from extremes of pain as he prepares to leave the island. Even at that, Burke mentions in the *Enquiry* that Thomas Campanella under torture could still 'abstract his attention from any sufferings of his body, [so] that he was able to endure the rack itself without much pain; and in lesser pains, every body must have observed, that when we employ our attention on any thing else, the pain has been for a time suspended' (*Enquiry*, 133). The crucial phrase here is 'lesser pains': if pain is entirely incapacitating, then there is little we can do to help ourselves or others (exceptional cases such as martyrs and heroes, notwithstanding). But the presence of pain by itself does not vitiate the sympathetic impulse:

> When we do not suffer any very acute pain, nor are exposed to any imminent danger of our lives, *we can feel for others, whilst we suffer ourselves*; and often then most when we are softened by affliction; we see with pity even distresses which we would accept in the place of our own. (*Enquiry*, 48, my italics)

These are the grounds on which Burke's (often first-hand) experience of the plight of Catholic and Gaelic culture in eighteenth-century Ireland enabled him to extend the hand of solidarity to the victims of Warren Hastings' regime in India thousands of miles away. In the neo-stoical philosophy of liberalism, the aim of the conquest of pain was to achieve self-control, and independence from others: for Burke, by contrast, the point in helping others is to alleviate our own distress, and vice versa – 'to relieve ourselves in relieving those who suffer' (*Enquiry*, 46).

In bringing his aesthetics to bear on the politics of sympathy, Burke is tracing the lineaments of what might be seen in contemporary debates as a post-colonial ethics, one that relates to the universalism of human rights not through a process of abstraction from one's own culture but rather by means of a shared solidarity and a history of oppression, however variegated. For Burke, as for the radical cultural currents in the United Irishmen, international solidarity did not consist in the relation of one abstract human being to another, divested of their cultural differences, but in the affiliations between individuals who saw in their own histories and attachments a way of reaching out to others. The issue here is not a commitment to universal human rights, but the capacity to pursue them through different routes: what counts as tolerance, diversity and cosmopolitanism looks different when cast through a post-colonial optic, thus bringing a wider range of human beliefs and experience within the ambit of international justice. A more ethnographically sensitive Enlightenment is thus not confined to the task of looking for 'sameness' and commonalities across cultural boundaries, deriving, for example, from an undifferentiated human nature. Much more demanding in Burke's eyes was that difficult form of sympathy which addressed cultural difference, for such was the strangeness of some customs in other cultures that they ran the risk of eliciting ridicule rather than understanding, *'even when we meet on the same ground'* ('Speech on the Impeachment of Warren Hastings', vii, 43). As he observed of Western alienation from Muslim customs:

It is our nature and we cannot help it; it is the most difficult thing in the world to bring ourselves to a proper degree of sympathy when we are describing those circumstances which are not engrafted in our nature by custom. I believe that the first thing that creates laughter throughout mankind by general sympathy is distress which arises not from our [human] nature but from local institution.[16]

True parochialism in such situations is evinced by the complacent cosmopolitanism that cannot imagine alternative civic codes, or moral values, to the political orthodoxies of the West. Much of the Enlightenment discourse of human rights has rightly concerned itself with victims of torture or physical pain, whose plight we can understand by virtue of our common humanity; it takes greater moral imagination, however, to empathize with what, for Burke, might be the deeper psychological wounds inflicted by shame, humiliation or the crushing of the one's cultural values, however alien they may seem to uncomprehending eyes. Oppression in this latter case may result in the slow strangulation of 'social death', the sapping of the dignity and resolve of a people that may in the long run prove as destructive as attempts at physical extermination.[17]

Nor is it a case of seeing other customs as sacrosanct, or beyond criticism: it is, after all, cross-cultural communication and solidarity that is at issue, and the very notion of the sympathetic sublime militates, as we have seen, against self-absorption, or its cultural extension, ethnic solipsism. The exercise of sympathy arising from the sublime is a complex, two-way process, made all the more difficult because it tries to establish solidarity in conditions that extend beyond the 'sameness' or common ground of our humanity. For all the emphasis on 'trade' and 'exchange' in neo-stoical models of the self advocated by Adam Smith and others, the aim is to recreate culture (or at least superior cultures) in the image of the self-possessed individual, the citizen at one with herself or himself, and in command of her or his own destiny. By contrast, individuals in a culture racked with conflict, or subject, in Seamus Deane's phrase, to centuries of colonial concussion, are hardly in possession of such self-composure, and have already experienced at home the sense of being elsewhere, of being strangers in their own land. For this reason – and in marked contrast to the abstract ideals of civic cosmopolitanism – identification with the plight of others need not require stepping outside one's own culture, but may be intensified by our very sense of belonging – an intensity, moreover, that may have as much to do with pain and loss as with more abstract, optimistic ideals of emancipation and justice.

Central to Burke's conjunction of ethics and aesthetics was the image of a person who could withstand any amount of physical pain, but could not bear to see his or her loved ones subjected to similar suffering. Evoking the hideous torture of a father and son who were bound together by Warren Hastings' minions in India so that every lash which escaped the body of one fell on the other, Burke imagined that the most excruciating violation of our humanity was when self-preservation – relief from personal pain – was achieved at the expense of the suffering of those closest to our hearts: 'The circumstances were combined by so subtle a cruelty, that every stroke which did not excruciate the *sense*, should wound and lacerate the sentiments and affections of nature ('Impeachment: Fifth Day', vii, 189)'.[18] It was perhaps with such troubled sentiments in mind that Theobald Wolfe Tone, in a journal entry written in Paris in 1797, described how, as a citizen of the world, he nonetheless experienced the acute loneliness of being cut off from his family and loved ones, without even having, as he mused, the consolation of other Irish people to converse with. There was some compensation to be had, however, from his recent introduction 'to the famous Tom Paine...who has done wonders for the cause of liberty, both in America and Europe'. Tone's conversation with Paine ranged over the great revolutionary's views on theology and politics, but then shifted to the topic of Edmund Burke:

I mentioned to him that I had known Burke in England, and spoke of the shattered state of his mind in consequence of the death of his only son Richard. Paine immediately said that it was the *Rights of Man* which had broke his heart, and that the death of his son gave him occasion to develop the chagrin which had preyed upon him ever since the appearance of that work. I am sure, the *Rights of Man* have tormented Burke exceedingly, but I have seen myself the workings of a father's grief on his spirit, and I could not be deceived. *Paine has no children!*[19]

In this exchange, Tone seems to be playing Burke to Paine's Rousseau, in the latter's persona of an individual who could love humanity but who could not understand the loss of a child, or the personal grief involved in such a loss. Tone's political sympathies are still emphatically with Paine: but to his radical sensibility, the universalism of the rights of man did not require shutting down all affection for one's 'little platoon', or an insensitivity to the 'obligations written on the heart'.

Notes

INTRODUCTION: EDMUND BURKE, IRELAND, AND THE COLONIAL SUBLIME

1. Jean-François Lyotard, 'The sublime and the avant-garde', trans. Lisa Liebman, in Andrew Benjamin, ed., *The Lyotard Reader* (Oxford: Blackwell, 1989), pp. 198–9, 200.
2. In Christopher Norris's summary of Lyotard's recourse to aesthetic concepts to deal with the enormity of the Holocaust, 'the sublime would offer the most fitting analogy for an event which defies all forms of adequate representation, which reason... is totally unable to assimilate, and which therefore demands that we respond to its summons without falling back on established criteria or protocols of validating judgement'. *Uncritical Theory: Postmodernism, Intellectuals and the Gulf War* (London: Lawrence and Wishart, 1992), p. 76.
3. See Paul Gilroy, '"Not a Story to Pass On": Living Memory and the Slave Sublime', in *The Black Atlantic: Modernity and Double Consciousness* (London: Verso, 1993); Sara Suleri, 'Edmund Burke and the Indian Sublime', in *The Rhetoric of English India* (Chicago: University of Chicago Press, 1992); Ronald Paulson, 'Burke, Paine and Wollstonecraft: The Sublime and the Beautiful', in *Representations of Revolution* (New Haven: Yale University Press, 1983); Francis Spufford, 'The Sublime', in *I May Be Some Time: Ice and the English Imagination* (London: Faber and Faber, 1996); Frances Ferguson, 'The Nuclear Sublime', *Diacritics*, 14 (Summer 1984); Rob Wilson, 'Towards the Nuclear Sublime: Representations of Technological Vastness in Postnuclear America', in *The American Sublime: The Genealogy of a Poetic Genre* (Madison: University of Wisconsin Press, 1981); David B. Morris, *The Culture of Pain* (Berkeley: University of California Press, 1993); Steven Bruhm, *Gothic Bodies: The Politics of Pain in Romantic Fiction* (Philadelphia: University of Pennsylvania Press, 1994). For a recent refiguring of both the sublime and the beautiful in terms of contemporary aesthetics and art practice, see Jeremy Gilbert-Rolfe, *Beauty and the Contemporary Sublime* (New York: Allworth Press, 1999).
4. Lyotard, 'The Sublime and the Avant-Garde', p. 199.
5. Burke was the most influential Irish figure to deal in a systematic fashion with the sublime, but was by no means the only Irish writer to explore this dark side of the aesthetic landscape. Among other important contributions to what

might be termed the 'Irish Sublime', see John Lawson, *Lectures Concerning Oratory* (Dublin: George Faulkner, 1759); James Usher, *Clio: Or, A Discourse on Taste* (London, 1769); James Barry, *Works* (London: Cadell and Davies, 1809); Richard Stack, 'An Essay on Sublimity of Writing', *Transactions of the Royal Irish Academy*, i (Dublin, 1787); George Miller, 'An Essay on the Origins and Nature of our Ideas of the Sublime', *Transactions of the Royal Irish Academy*, v (1794). Andrew Ashfield and Peter de Bolla, eds., *The Sublime: A Reader in British Eighteenth-Century Aesthetic Theory* (Cambridge: Cambridge University Press, 1996), includes a valuable section on 'Irish Perspectives', with selections from Burke, Lawson and Usher, but does not address the specific Irish cultural context out of which these works emerged.

6. There is disagreement over whether the youthful works which Burke mentions in a letter to his school friend Richard Shackleton may have been a preliminary version of the *Enquiry*, but it is clear from the young Burke's familiarity with the works of Francis Hutcheson and the classical author Longinus that he was already interested in aesthetic debates during his college years. See F. P. Lock, *Edmund Burke: 1730–1784* (Oxford: Oxford University Press, 1998), i, pp. 91–4. As we shall see below, several key concepts of the *Enquiry* are prefigured in the letters to Richard Shackleton written during this period, and Burke himself states that it was all but finished by 1753. See Edmund Burke, *A Philosophical Enquiry into the Origin of our Ideas of the Sublime and Beautiful* [1757], ed. J. T. Boulton (London: Routledge and Kegan Paul, 1958), p. vii (subsequent references will take the form of 'Enquiry', followed by page number, in parentheses in the text).

7. For the best short account of Burke's influence on Gothic fiction, see David B. Morris, 'Gothic Sublimity', *New Literary History*, 16 (1985).

8. Edmund Burke to Richard Shackleton, 25 January 1744/45, *The Correspondence of Edmund Burke*, ed., Thomas W. Copeland (Cambridge: Cambridge University Press, 1958), i, pp. 38–9. The idea that the power of the sublime may be transported to the person it threatens to overwhelm is central to Longinus's theory, and was incorporated by Burke into the *Enquiry* (*Enquiry*, 50–1). I discuss the implications of this in Chapter 3 below, pp. 106–7.

9. Edmund Burke, 'Speech on American Taxation' [1774], in *The Works of Edmund Burke*, Bohn's Standard Library, 8 vols. (London: George Bell, 1900), i, p. 433 (subsequent references from the Bohn edition will take the form of the key or lead-word in the title of the particular work, followed by volume and page number, in parentheses in the text).

10. As Terry Eagleton observes, 'there is something alarmingly anti-foundational about the notion [in Burke] that power rests upon nothing but consent, opinion and affection', but then Eagleton goes on to note the method in Burke's madness: 'Political power, then, is in an important sense arational: it is no more open to explanation than filial devotion or erotic love, and perhaps all the more durable for that.' Terry Eagleton, *Heathcliff and the Great Hunger* (London: Verso, 1995), p. 39.

11. Seamus Deane, *Strange Country: Modernity and Nationhood in Irish Writing since 1790* (Oxford: Clarendon Press, 1997), pp. 1–3.
12. Longinus, 'On the Sublime', in *Classical Literary Criticism*, trans. T. S. Dorsch (Harmondsworth: Penguin, 1965), p. 100.
13. The legend of Burke's clairvoyance was already prevalent during his own lifetime, as with Charles Fox's pronouncement that 'whether mad or inspired, fates seems to have determined that he should be an uncommon political prophet'. See 'Burke's Political Predictions', in John Timbs, *Anecdote Biography: William Pitt, Earl of Chatham and Edmund Burke* (London: Richard Bentley, 1860), pp. 251–3.
14. Edmund Burke, *Reflections on the Revolution in France* [1790], ed. Conor Cruise O'Brien (Harmondsworth: Penguin, 1976), p. 175 (subsequent references will take the form of 'Reflections', followed by page number, in parentheses in the text).
15. David Bromwich, *A Choice of Inheritance: Self and Community from Edmund Burke to Robert Frost* (Cambridge, MA: Harvard University Press, 1989), p. 52.
16. Burke, 'First Letter on A Regicide Peace' [1796], *Works*, v, 154 (subsequent references will take the form of 'First Letter', followed by volume and page number, in parentheses in the text).
17. Suleri, *Rhetoric of English India*, p. 36.
18. Paulson, *Representations of Revolution*, pp. 67, 68–9.
19. Michel Fuchs, *Edmund Burke, Ireland and the Fashioning of Self* (Oxford: Voltaire Foundation, 1996), p. 191. Fuchs elaborates on this, pointing out that contrary to later romantic interpretations of the *Enquiry* as a work pre-eminently addressed to the sublime in nature – the wilderness, mountains, oceans – 'in fact, it would seem that when Burke first started thinking about the sublime, the first instances that occurred to him were instances of the "social sublime"' (p. 191). This is already apparent in the letter from his adolescent years cited above (pp. 3–4) in which the description of the flooded Liffey during a thunderstorm is subsumed into a series of political reflections on social indifference to suffering, the contingency of power, and the reversibility of master/servant relationships.
20. Ibid., p. 200.
21. Edmund Burke, 'Speech on the Impeachment of Warren Hastings: Fifth Day', 17 February 1788, in *Works*, vii, p. 192 (subsequent references will take the form of 'Impeachment' and relevant day, followed by volume and page number, in parentheses in the text).
22. S. J. Connolly, *Religion, Law and Power: The Making of Protestant Ireland 1660–1760* (Oxford: Oxford University Press, 1992), p. 217.
23. Thomas Bartlett, 'Review of S. J. Connolly, *Religion, Law and Power: The Making Of Protestant Ireland 1660–1760*', *Linen Hall Review* (Winter 1992), p. 28.
24. Edmund Burke, 'A Letter to Sir Hercules Langrishe, M. P.' [1792], *Works*, iii, pp. 320, 323, 321 (subsequent references will take the form of 'Langrishe',

followed by volume and page number, in parentheses in the text). It is important to note, as Thomas McLoughlin points out, that British perceptions of Ireland also saw it in colonial terms. As Lord North remarked of Ireland in 1779, it was by virtue of the prerogative of colonial rule that free trade was not granted to Ireland: 'The mother country had an exclusive right to trade with and forbid all others from having any intercourse with them [the colonies]. Such an exclusive right was the very essence of colonization.' Cited in Thomas McLoughlin, *Contesting Ireland: Irish Voices against England in the Eighteenth Century* (Dublin: Four Courts Press, 1999), p. 182.

25. Edmund Burke to Dr John Curry, 14 August 1779, in *Correspondence*, ed. John A. Woods (Cambridge: Cambridge University Press, 1963), iv, p. 118.
26. Edmund Burke, 'Speech on Mr. Fox's East-India Bill' [1783], *Works*, ii, pp. 175–6 (subsequent references will take the form of 'East India Bill', followed by volume and page number, in parentheses in the text).
27. Connolly, *Religion, Law and Power*, p. 229. Though Burke is not mentioned, his shadowy presence is implied by the phrase 'judicial murder', which Burke coined in relation to Sheehy's execution and also extended to Warren Hastings' execution of Nundcomar, a key oppositional figure to his power in Bengal. Exceptional transgressions leave the system intact, for Burke, but in these cases, 'whenever the law itself is debauched, and enters into a corrupt coalition with violence, robbery, and wrong, then all hope is gone'. Edmund Burke, 'Speech in Reply (on the Impeachment of Warren Hastings): Sixth Day [1794], *Works*, viii, p. 215.
28. See below, Chapters 1 and 5. Burke's abiding Irish concerns, and his personal connections to the Whiteboy movement, had previously been noted in William O'Brien, *Edmund Burke as an Irishman* (Dublin: M. H. Gill, 1926) and Thomas H. D. Mahoney's, *Edmund Burke and Ireland* (Cambridge, MA: Harvard University Press, 1960), but the centrality of the Whiteboy agitation to his espousal of a political career was not emphasized until Walter D. Love's pioneering article, 'Burke's Transition from a Literary to a Political Career', *Studies in Burke and His Time*, 3, 2 (Winter 1964–5). Burke's shadowy Irish background was given wider circulation in Conor Cruise O'Brien's Introduction to his Penguin edition of the *Reflections* in 1968 (see n. 14 above), and in his *The Great Melody: A Thematic Biography of Edmund Burke* (London: Sinclair-Stevenson, 1992). More recently, Katherine O'Donnell has examined the neglected topic of Burke's Gaelic background in 'Edmund Burke and the Heritage of Oral Culture', Ph.D. dissertation, National University of Ireland, 2000, and in 'The Image of a Relationship in Blood: *Parliament na mBan* and Burke's Jacobite Politics', *Eighteenth-Century Ireland*, 15 (2000).
29. Edmund Burke, 'Tracts Relative to the Laws Against Popery in Ireland' [*c*.1765], *Works*, vi, p. 45 (subsequent references will take the form of 'Popery Laws', followed by volume and page number, in parentheses in the text).
30. For the vitality of this subaltern Gaelic culture, see Breandán Ó'Buachalla, 'Irish Jacobitism and Irish Nationalism: The Literary Evidence', in Michael O'Dea

and Kevin Whelan, eds., *Nations and Nationalism: France, Britain, Ireland and the Eighteenth-Century Context* (Oxford: Voltaire Foundation, 1995), and *Aisling Ghéar* (Dublin: An Clóchomhar, 1996). For the political context, both national and international, see Eamonn Ó'Ciardha, *Ireland and the Jacobite Cause, 1685–1766: A Fatal Attachment* (Dublin: Four Courts, 2001), and for the social and economic milieu, see Kevin Whelan, 'An Underground Gentry? Catholic Middlemen in Eighteenth-Century Ireland', in *The Tree of Liberty: Radicalism, Catholicism and the Construction of Irish Identity, 1760–1830* (Cork: Cork University Press, 1996).

31. Edmund Burke, 'Letter to Richard Burke' [*c.*1792], *Works*, vi, p. 77 (subsequent references will take the form of 'Richard Burke', followed by volume and page number, in parentheses in the text).
32. Edmund Burke, 'Third Letter on a Regicide Peace' [1796], *Works*, v, p. 272 (subsequent references will take the form of 'Third Letter', followed by volume and page number, in parentheses in the text).
33. Albert O. Hirschman, *The Rhetoric of Reaction: Perversity, Futility, Jeopardy* (Cambridge, MA: Harvard University Press, 1991), pp. 14ff.
34. For Burke, this kind of forced modernization from above, carving up the Irish countryside in the image of a providential political economy, would be equivalent to the abstract, desocializing structures that formed the administrative systems of post-revolutionary France: 'When the members who compose these new bodies of cantons, communes, and departments... begin to act, they will find themselves in a great measure strangers to one another... without any civil habits or connections, or any of that natural discipline which is the soul of a new republic' (*Reflections*, 298). For a wide-ranging contemporary critique of modernization from above, see James C. Scott, *Seeing like a State: How Certain Schemes to Improve the Human Condition Have Failed* (New Haven: Yale University Press, 1998).
35. See epigraph above, from R. R. Madden, *The United Irishmen, Their Lives and Times*, 3rd series (Dublin: J. Mullany, 1846), ii, p. 149. Russell discharged himself from the British army on grounds almost identical to Burke's and Richard Brinsley Sheridan's indictment of the worst excesses of colonialism: his leaving in disgust, Madden informs us, 'was due to the unjust and rapacious conduct pursued by the authorities in the case of two native women of exalted rank' (p. 145).
36. See Katie Trumpener, *Bardic Nationalism: The Romantic Novel and the British Empire* (Princeton: Princeton University Press, 1997), ch. 3.
37. Iain McCalman, 'Popular Constitutionalism and Revolution in England and Ireland', in Isser Woloch, ed., *Revolution and the Meanings of Freedom in the Nineteenth Century* (Stanford: Stanford University Press, 1996), p. 140.
38. One of the reasons the rebellion failed was not that the United Irishmen made an alliance with Defenderism, but that the alliance did not go far enough, and revolutionary ideology was not grounded sufficiently in the mass movements of the rural dispossessed. Whether this was due to shortcomings in their own strategies, or whether they were prevented in realizing their programme

through the introduction of a new virulent sectarianism into the political conflict to prevent such an alliance, is the subject of much contemporary historical debate. See Whelan, *The Tree of Liberty*, chs. 2 and 3.
39. Edmund Burke to Rev. Thomas Hussey, 18 January 1796, *Correspondence*, ed. R. B. McDowell and Robert A. Smith, viii, p. 378.
40. 'Reading your Reflections warily over, it has continually and forcibly struck me, that had you been a Frenchman, you would have been, in spite of your respect for rank and antiquity, a violent revolutionist.' Mary Wollstonecraft, 'A Vindication of the Rights of Men' [1790], in *Political Writings*, ed. Janet Todd (Oxford: Oxford University Press), p. 44.
41. Raymond Williams, *Culture and Society, 1780–1950* (Harmondsworth: Penguin, 1971), pp. 24–5.
42. For Smith and republicanism, see Donald Winch, *Riches and Poverty: An Intellectual History of Political Economy in Britain, 1750–1834* (Cambridge: Cambridge University Press, 1996); for British radicalism, see John Belcham's classic discussion, 'Republicanism, Popular Constitutionalism and the Radical Platform in Early Nineteenth Century England', *Social History*, 6 (1981).
43. Bromwich, *A Choice of Inheritance*, pp. 53–4. Bromwich does not see Burke as making much allowance for the 'oppressed and the inarticulate', but for Uday Singh Mehta (*Liberalism and Empire*, pp. 159 ff.), this is the most important animating impulse in Burke's political career, particularly as evinced by his impassioned engagement with the suffering of colonial India.
44. Michel Foucault, 'Entretien sur la prison: le livre et sa méthode' (with J. J. Brochier), *Magazine littéraire*, 101 (June 1975), 33, cited in Patricia O'Brien, 'Michel Foucault's History of Culture', in Lynn Hunt, ed., *The New Cultural History* (Berkeley: University of California Press, 1989), p. 25.

1 'THIS KING OF TERRORS': EDMUND BURKE AND THE AESTHETICS OF EXECUTIONS

1. [Thomas Moore], *Memoirs of Captain Rock, the Celebrated Irish Chieftain, with some Account of his Ancestors* (London: Longman, 1824), pp. 155–1.
2. R. R. Madden, historical appendix to Mrs M. J. Sadlier, *The Fate of Father Sheehy: A Tale of Tipperary in the Olden Times* [1845], new edition (Dublin: James Duffy, n.d. [1881?]), pp. 192–3.
3. Letter from 'A Protestant' to the *Freeman's Journal*, 7 February 1775, cited in John Brady, *Catholics and Catholicism in the Eighteenth-Century Press* (Maynooth: Catholic Record Society of Ireland, 1965), p. 170.
4. See Sadlier, *The Fate of Father Sheehy*. For historical accounts of the episode, see Thomas Power, 'Fr Nicholas Sheehy', in Gerard Moran, ed., *Radical Irish Priests, 1660–1970* (Dublin: Four Courts Press, 1998); Philip O'Connell, 'The Plot against Father Nicholas Sheehy: The Historical Background', *The Irish Ecclesiastical Record*, 108 (July–December 1967); and Rev. William P. Burke, *History of Clonmel* (Waterford: N. Harvey and Co., 1907).

5. The consensus among historians is that Sheehy was indeed framed for Bridge's murder. There was even doubt on whether Bridge was murdered, as reports that he was living in Newfoundland were rife during the period.
6. Cited in *The Correspondence of Edmund Burke*, i, p. 147, n. 5. The impressionable (or devious) Fant claimed he personally saw the Pretender and that 'Hugh Massy Ingoldsby who is since that dead the Nagles and Hennessys were the Promoters of the meeting.' As L. M. Cullen remarks, however, the fact that a relative of the Nagles was so highly placed in Dublin Castle may itself have contributed to the fears whipped up by the Protestant interests in Cork bitterly opposed to Catholic reform. L. M. Cullen, 'Burke's Irish Views and Writings', in Ian Crowe, ed., *Edmund Burke, His Life and Legacy* (Dublin: Four Courts Press, 1997), pp. 63–4. For Burke's response to Fant, and to the persecution of the Nagles which continued into 1762 when Cork and Dublin newspapers also carried reports of the arrest of another kinsman of Burke's, Garret Nagle, for Whiteboy activities, see Chapter 5 below.
7. Richard Burke, a cousin german of Edmund's, was married to Catherine, Nicholas Sheehy's sister, in 1755. See Basil O'Connell, 'The Rt. Hon. Edmund Burke (1729–1790): A Basis for a Pedigree', *Journal of the Cork Historical and Archaeological Society*, 60, 192 (July–December 1955), p. 74.
8. Edmund Burke to Charles O'Hara, 24 May 1766; 9 June 1768; 30 December 1762, *Correspondence*, i, pp. 255–6. 353, 162.
9. Speaking of the threat presented by the Jacobins in France to conventional politics, Burke describes it as 'so terrible in its nature, and in its manifest consequences, that there is no way of quieting our apprehension about it, but by totally putting it out of sight, by substituting for it, through a sort of periphrasis', a language entirely at odds with reality, which speaks reassuringly of 'peace and amity'. Edmund Burke, 'Second Letter on a Regicide Peace' [1796], *Works*, v, pp. 243–4 (subsequent references will take the form of 'Second Letter', followed by volume and page number, in parentheses in the text).
10. Sara Suleri, *The Rhetoric of English India* (Chicago: University of Chicago Press, 1992), pp. 31–2.
11. For Burke's linking of his emotional ties with Ireland directly with his maternal affections, see his comment to Charles O'Hara: 'I am sure you will be concerned to hear that my Poor Mother is in a very declining way under a very cruel nervous disorder. There will I fear one of my strongest links to Ireland be snapped off.' Edmund Burke to Charles O'Hara, 30 October 1762, *Correspondence*, i, pp. 152–3.
12. L. M. Cullen, *The Emergence of Modern Ireland, 1600–1900* (London: Batsford, 1981), p. 199. For an extended account, see 'The Letters and Papers of James Cotter Junior, 1689–1720', ed. William Hogan and Liam O'Buachalla, *Journal of the Cork Historical and Archaeological Society*, 68 (January–December 1963), pp. 207–8.
13. See Conor Cruise O'Brien, *The Great Melody: A Thematic Biography of Edmund Burke* (London: Sinclair-Stevenson, 1992), pp. 6–11, and Cullen, 'Burke's Irish Views and Writings', p. 63.

14. *Corke Journal*, 30 May 1757, in John T. Collins, 'Gleanings from Old Cork Newspapers', *Journal of the Cork Historical and Archeological Society*, 69, 209 (January–June 1964), p. 135. Basil O'Connell, in his otherwise meticulous research on Burke's family background, notes that only two records of Richard Burke's legal career – relating to the years 1741 and 1754 – survive, but this later item in a Cork newspaper shows that the connection to the Cotter circle was still present in the years immediately preceding the outbreak of Whiteboy agitation.
15. Cited in T. J. Walsh, *Nano Nagle and the Presentation Sisters* (Monasterevan: Presentation Generalate, 1980), p. 28.
16. Ibid., pp. 29–30. The informer, John Hennessy, who reported Joseph Nagle to the authorities, was a renegade priest, and subsequently disappeared after a visit by what was described as a mysterious body of men.
17. Though the attribution is still questioned (e.g. in F. P. Lock, *Edmund Burke: 1730–1784*, i (Oxford: Oxford University Press, 1998), pp. 6–7), Richard Burke's direct connection with Joseph Nagle attests strongly to the likelihood that he was indeed the 'Richard Burke' who acted as Cotter's attorney.
18. Lord Lovat's execution was covered extensively in the Dublin press in April 1747, and was debated by the Trinity College club of which the young Burke was a founding member. See Boulton's gloss, *Enquiry*, p. 47, n. 17.
19. Edmund Burke, 'Third Letter on a Regicide Peace', *Works*, v, p. 337 (subsequently, 'Third Letter', vol. and p. no. in parentheses in text). Burke also extends these criticisms of spectacle to pompous displays of political power in relation to monarchy and parliament: 'To recommend this system to the people, a perspective view of the Court, gorgeously painted, and finely illuminated from within, was exhibited to the gaping multitude . . . the whole scenery was exactly disposed to captivate those good souls, whose credulous morality is so invaluable a treasure to crafty politicians.' Edmund Burke, 'Thoughts on the Present Discontents [1770]', *Works*, i, p. 320 (subsequent references will take the form of 'Thoughts', followed by volume and page number in parentheses in the text).
20. Frans De Bruyn, 'Theatre and Countertheatre in Burke's *Reflections on the Revolution in France*', in Steven Blakemore, ed., *Burke and the French Revolution* (Athens, GA: University of Georgia Press, 1992), pp. 58–9. De Bruyn traces the inception of this aesthetics of street terror in the *Reflections* to the Wilkes and Gordon riots, but it is likely that Burke's response to these in turn may have been prefigured in his agitated reaction to events in Ireland in the 1760s, and his youthful writings of the 1740s. For a comparison of the scale of state terror in the Gordon Riots and the Whiteboy agitation, see below pp. 247–8, n. 29.
21. *The Reformer*, no. 3, 11 February 1747–8, in *The Writings and Speeches of Edmund Burke*, i, ed. T. O. McLoughlin and James T. Boulton (Oxford: Clarendon Press, 1997), pp. 80–2 (subsequent references will take the form of 'Reformer', followed by page number, in parentheses in the text). In addition to the material contained in his letters noted above (pp. 3–4), the clear affinities between *The Reformer* and arguments later advanced in the *Enquiry* lend credence to the suggestion that his philosophical engagement with aesthetics dates from his

formative period in Ireland. For related sentiments in Burke's writings of the early 1750s, see his condemnation of the hell-fire sermons of some preachers: 'In our colder Climates the Methodist, by painting hell torments in all its [sic] terrors, – like the Rattle-Snake does the Squirrel – terrifies the poor wretch into his Snare. But neither Mahomet nor Methodist have anything to do with the Understanding.' Edmund Burke, 'Several Scattered Hints concerning Philosophy and Learning', in *A Note-Book of Edmund Burke*, ed. H. M. V. Somerset (Cambridge: Cambridge University Press, 1957), pp. 96–7.

22. Edmund Burke, 'Appeal from the New to the Old Whigs', *Works*, iii, pp. 43–4 (subsequent references will take the form of 'Appeal', followed by volume and page number, in parentheses in the text).

23. This was an irony of state repression which advanced republicans in Ireland were not slow to exploit in the political turmoil of the 1790s: as the title of one pamphlet expressed it, to which Arthur O'Connor, the Irish radical and future United Irishman, contributed: *The Measures of a Ministry to Prevent a Revolution Are the Certain Means to Bring it About* (London, 1794), cited in Jim Livesy, 'Introduction' to Arthur O'Connor, *The State of Ireland* [1798] (Dublin: The Lilliput Press, 1998), p. 5.

24. For a perceptive discussion of how the entropy of the 'simply terrible' pervades the *Enquiry*, see William Corlett, 'The Power of Fear in Burkean Traditionalism', in his *Community without Unity: A Politics of Derridean Extravagance* (Durham, NC: Duke University Press, 1989).

25. See Douglas Hay, 'Property, Authority and the Criminal Law', in Douglas Hay, Peter Linebaugh, John G. Rule, E. P. Thompson, Cal Winslow, *Albion's Fatal Tree: Crime and Society in Eighteenth-Century England* (Harmondsworth: Penguin Books, 1977), p. 18, and Peter Linebaugh, *The London Hanged: Crime and Civil Society in the Eighteenth Century* (London: Penguin Books, 1992).

26. 'Mr. Burke's Speech on the Punishment of the Pillory', *The Parliamentary History of England*, xxi, 1814, 3847ff. For accounts of this departure on Burke's part from the conventional prejudices concerning punishment of homosexuals, see Isaac Kramnick, *The Rage of Edmund Burke: Portrait of an Ambivalent Conservative* (New York: Basic Books, 1977), pp. 83–7, and Katherine O'Donnell, 'A Union not to Be Expressed: Burke and the Advent of the Male Homosexual', unpublished paper, ACIS Conference, Albany, New York, 14 April 1997.

27. As E. P. Thompson has argued, 'There is a sense in which rulers and crowd needed each other, watched each other, performed theatre and counter-theatre in each other's auditorium, moderated each other's behaviour' in an 'active and reciprocal', albeit unequal, relation. E. P. Thompson, 'The Patricians and the Plebs', in *Customs in Common* (London: Penguin, 1991), p. 57. Thompson mentions the Sacheverall riots as one of the examples of a show of force dependent on a common culture or moral economy.

28. Burke, 'Speech on the Punishment of the Pillory', pp. 3847ff.

29. Twenty-six agrarian offenders were sentenced to death between 1762 and 1765, and forty-eight between 1770 and 1776 (Connolly, *Religion, Law and Power*, p. 223). By contrast, twenty-five leaders were executed after the Gordon riots.

30. L. M. Cullen, 'The Blackwater Catholics and County Cork Society and Politics in the Eighteenth Century', in Cornelius Buttimer and Patrick Flanagan, eds., *Cork: History and Society* (Dublin: Geographia, 1993), p. 568.
31. See Chapter 5 below for a more detailed discussion of Burke's response to – and involvement in – the fate of the Whiteboys.
32. For a discussion of the manner in which the sectarian fury of the Gordon riots fused the anti-Catholicism of puritan dissenters with the street violence of the French Revolution in Burke's imagination, see Iain McCalman, 'Mad Lord George and Madame La Motte: Riot and Sexuality in the Genesis of Burke's *Reflections on the Revolution in France*', *Journal of British Studies*, 35 (July 1996).
33. Edmund Burke to Richard Shackleton, 13 June 1780, in *Correspondence*, iv, ed., John A. Woods, iv, pp. 245–6.
34. Edmund Burke, 'Letters with Reflections on the Executions of the Rioters in 1780', *Works*, v, 515, 514–15 (subsequent references will take the form of 'Reflections on Executions', followed by volume and page number, in parentheses in the text).
35. For Henry Fielding's contrasting view, see his statement: 'No man indeed of common humanity or common sense can think the life of a man and a few shillings to be of equal consideration... [But] is not the inflicting of punishment more for example, and to prevent evil than to punish?... the terror of the example is the only thing proposed, and one man is sacrificed to the preservation of thousands.' Cited in Stephen Copley, *Literature and the Social Order in Eighteenth-Century England* (Beckenham, Kent: Croom Helm, 1984), p. 190.
36. Michel Foucault, *Discipline and Punish: The Birth of the Prison*, trans. Alan Sheridan (Harmondsworth: Penguin Books, 1979), chs. 1 and 2.
37. Edmund Burke to Richard Shackleton, 26 April 1746, *Correspondence*, i, pp. 62–3. The espousal of such views by William Dennis in the debating club founded by Burke and his friends at Trinity College, Dublin, led Burke, in his role as speaker against the motion to speak 'in favour of lenity for the rebels of the Forty-Five' and to accuse 'Mr. Dennis of disaffection, [saying] he had spoke more like a Rebel than a well wisher to the Government and desire him to clear himself of the charge'. As Conor Cruise O'Brien suggests, Burke here shows a clear awareness of the construction that could be put on his own private views. O'Brien, *The Great Melody*, pp. 34–5.
38. Letter to Richard Shackleton, [24] December 1747, *Correspondence*, i, pp. 100–1. Boulton, in his edition of the *Enquiry*, mentions as another possible source for the section on the loudness of the crowd at a student riot at Black Dog prison in Dublin, May 1747, when Burke was first working on the text that became the *Enquiry* (*Enquiry*, xvii).
39. 'Several Scattered Hints', in Somerset, ed., *A Note-Book of Edmund Burke*, p. 91.
40. Thomas Crofton Croker, *Researches in the South of Ireland* [1824] (Blackrock, Co. Dublin: Irish Academic Press, 1981), pp. 181, 182. Crofton Croker goes on to mention that 'earth from the grave of Father Sheehy' was 'held in great

repute, and taken away so rapidly, on account of its supernatural powers, that the sexton had more than once to renew the covering' (p. 170), and concludes: 'Those criminals whose lives have been forfeited in the cause of rebellion, derive no small consolation from the idea of martyrdom, which they imagine they have attained, and in this way they are encouraged by the popular voice, apostrophizing their shade as that of an hero and a patriot' (p. 182). For an insightful discussion of Irish practices of resuscitation in relation to hanging in Britain, see Linebaugh, *The London Hanged*, ch. 9.

41. For a comprehensive popular account of the Sheehy affair in the nineteenth century, see Major Muskerry, 'Father Sheehy and the Whiteboys: Munster One Hundred Years Since', *The Shamrock*, iv, 84, Saturday, 9 May 1868, pp. 541–4.
42. James Donnelly, 'The Whiteboy Movement: 1761–5', *Irish Historical Studies*, 21, 81 (March 1978), p. 50.
43. *Sleator's Public Gazetteer*, 18 September 1770, cited in Brady, *Catholics and Catholicism in the Eighteenth-Century Press*, p. 40.
44. Thomas Copeland, *Edmund Burke: Six Essays* (London: Jonathan Cape, 1950), p. 90.
45. As he remonstrated in the *Reflections*: 'Do these theorists mean to imitate some of their predecessors, who dragged the bodies of our antient sovereigns out of the quiet of their tombs'. *Reflections*, 107.
46. For the wider implications of Burke's comparison of the Jacobins to 'savages', see below, Chapter 7.

2 'PHILOCTETES' AND COLONIAL IRELAND: THE WOUNDED BODY AS NATIONAL NARRATIVE

1. [Moore], *Memoirs of Captain Rock*, p. 368.
2. Ibid., p. 251.
3. Philoctetes and Prometheus share many affinities: Philoctetes was abandoned on the isle of Lemnos, and it was on this island that Prometheus brought the fire he stole from the gods; likewise, the theme of making fire an elemental sign of civility figures prominently in Sophocles's play, as Philoctetes is forced, in his abandonment, to reinvent the art of lighting a fire. See Charles Segal, *Tragedy and Civilization: An Interpretation of Sophocles* (Norman: The University of Oklahoma Press, 1999), pp. 308, 305–7.
4. Derek Walcott, *Omeros* (London: Faber and Faber, 1990) and Seamus Heaney, *The Cure at Troy* (London: Faber and Faber, 1990).
5. See Simon Richter, *Laocoon's Body and the Aesthetics of Pain: Winckelmann, Lessing, Herder, Moritz, Goethe* (Detroit: Wayne State University Press, 1992), and Mark Roche, *Tragedy and Comedy: A Systematic Study and a Critique of Hegel* (New York: State University of New York Press, 1997).
6. The story of Philoctetes was the subject of plays by at least three of the great classical dramatists, Aeschylus, Euripides, and Sophocles, but only the latter's play has survived. For an influential account of the various treatments of Philoctetes, both ancient and modern, see Edmund Wilson, *The Wound and the Bow* (London: Methuen, 1961).

7. Sophocles, 'Philoctetes', in *The Plays of Sophocles*, trans. Thomas Francklin (London: George Routledge, 1886), p. 138 (subsequent references will take the form of 'Philoctetes', followed by page number, in parentheses in the text). Francklin's popular translation, originally published in 1759, was probably the one used by Barry, though it is not unlikely, given his interest in Swift, that he may have had access to Dr Thomas Sheridan's pioneering translation, discussed below. Francklin, Professor of Greek at Cambridge, was one of the reviewers of Burke's first book, *A Vindication of Natural Society*, in the *Critical Review*, June 1756. Lock, *Edmund Burke*, p. 85.
8. For an outstanding discussion of Philoctetes and the related theme of the wounded warrior in French revolutionary art, see Thomas Crow, *Emulation: Making Artists for Revolutionary France* (New Haven, CT: Yale University Press, 1995), ch. 3.
9. Apart from Sophocles's play, the other classical source which Barry explicitly mentions is Glaucus's epigram to a lost picture of Philoctetes by the Greek painter Parrhasius. Jebb, in his edition of *Philoctetes*, describes a vase painting whose composition seems very close to Barry's painting, and more particularly to his preliminary 1770 sketch and the 1790 engraved version: 'A very beautiful Athenian vase-painting, of about 350 B.C. shows Philoctetes sitting on a rock in Lemnos, under the leafless branches of a stunted tree; his head is bowed as if in dejection; the bandaged left foot is propped on a stone, and the left hand clasps the knee. He wears a sleeveless Doric chiton, girt around the waist; at his right side the bow and arrows rest on the ground. It is probable that the source of this vase-painting was a picture by Parrhasius.' *Sophocles: The Plays and Fragments*, Part IV, 'The Philoctetes', trans. R. C. Jebb (Cambridge: Cambridge University Press, 1890), p. xxxviii.
10. Elaine Scarry, *The Body in Pain: The Making and Unmaking of the World* (Oxford: Oxford University Press, 1985), p. 53.
11. Michael Fried, *Absorption and Theatricality: Painting and Beholder in the Age of Diderot* (Berkeley: University of California Press, 1980) (subsequent references will take the form of 'Fried, *Absorption*', followed by page number, in parentheses in the text).
12. This concise summary of the arguments in *Absorption and Theatricality* is taken from Fried's follow-up study, *Courbet's Realism* (Chicago: University of Chicago Press, 1990), pp. 6–7.
13. For valuable discussions of Fried in this context, see Stephen Melville, *Philosophy Beside Itself: On Deconstruction and Modernism* (Minneapolis: University of Minnesota Press, 1986), and Steven Connor, *Postmodernist Culture: An Introduction to Theories of the Contemporary* (Oxford: Blackwell, 1989), pp. 83–92, 136–43.
14. Fried, *Courbet's Realism*, pp. 7–8. See also Fried, *Absorption and Theatricality*, pp. 82–96.
15. Among the works analysed by Fried are Greuze, *Portrait de Watelat* (c. 1763–4) and *La Tricoteuse endormie* (1759), and Chardin, *The Soap Bubble* (c. 1733) and *The Card Castle* (c. 1737).

16. Scarry, *The Body in Pain*, p. 50.
17. Richard Payne Knight, 'Review of *The Works of James Barry*', *Edinburgh Review*, 16 (August 1810), p. 299. Payne Knight, according to Pressly, was one of many 'professional Barry-hater(s)' who attempted to make the painter's life even more miserable than it was. Pressly, *James Barry*, p. 219.
18. Robert R. Wark, 'James Barry', Ph.D. dissertation, Harvard University, 1952, p. 94 (subsequent references will take the form of Wark, 'James Barry', followed by page number, in parentheses in the text).
19. Fried, *Courbet's Realism*, p. 130. The quotations cited by Fried are from Rudolf Wittkower, *Art and Architecture in Italy, 1660–1750* (London: Penguin, 1965), p. 24.
20. Wark's analysis of Barry's print, *Satan at the Abode of Chaos and Old Night*, may also be applied to the *Philoctetes*: 'There is thus no opportunity for the spectator to let his attention wander away: he must perforce direct it to the principal figures, who are presented almost on top of him'. Wark, 'James Barry', p. 106.
21. Thomas Crow sees in Drouais's version of Philoctetes (1788) an even more explicit address to the viewer than Barry's as the hero directly faces the spectator. It is striking that in both cases, however, tears prevent the warrior from actually 'looking out' from the canvas, even though the body is clearly on display. See Crow, *Emulation*, pp. 80–1.
22. Johannes Joachim Winckelmann, *On the Imitation of Greek Works in Painting and Sculpture* [1755], cited in Gotthold Ephraim Lessing, *Laokoon, and How the Ancients Represented Death* [1756], trans. E. C. Beasley (London: G. Bell and Sons, 1914), p. 7 (subsequent references will take the form of *Laokoon*, followed by page number, in parentheses in the text).
23. This is Lessing's most succinct formulation in an early sketch for the 'Laokoon': see Hugo Blummer's edition, *Lessing's Laocoon* (Berlin: Weidmannsche Buchhandlung, 1880), pp. 358–9, cited in David Wellbery, *Lessing's Laocoon: Semiotics and Aesthetics in the Age of Reason* (Cambridge: Cambridge University Press, 1984), p. 103.
24. James Barry, 'An Inquiry into the Real and Imaginary Obstructions to the Acquisition of the Arts in England' [1775], in *The Works of James Barry, Esq. Historical Painter*, ed. Edward Fryer, 2 vols. (London: T. Cadell and W. Davies, 1809), ii, p. 261 (subsequent references will take the form of 'Inquiry', followed by volume and page number, in parentheses in the text).
25. Denis Diderot, *Salons*, ii, ed. Jean Seznec and Jean Adhemar (Oxford, 1960), p. 145, cited in Fried, *Absorption and Theatricality*, p. 59. Yet for all the 'absorption' of the painting, it does not yield up its meaning at a glance, contrary to Diderot's own demand that the pictorial unity and aesthetic self-sufficiency of such works renders them instantaneously apprehensible. See Fried, *Absorption and Theatricality*, pp. 88ff., and p. 252, n. 27 below. In so far as Greuze's painting is allegorical, it clearly draws on a repertoire of meanings outside the 'aesthetic self-sufficiency' of the work. The implications of the allegorical image in relation to Barry's *Philoctetes* will be explored in greater detail below.

26. Jay Caplan, *Framed Narratives: Diderot's Genealogy of the Beholder* (Manchester: Manchester University Press, 1985), p. 11.
27. Denis Diderot, 'Essais sur la peinture' in *Oeuvres Esthetiques*, ed. Paul Verniere (Paris, 1966), p. 712, cited in Fried, *Absorption and Theatricality*, p. 90. Yet, as we have seen, even the most 'absorptive' painting, such as Greuze's 'Girl with a Dead Canary', may contain 'hieroglyphic', hidden meanings.
28. Maureen Quilligan, *The Language of Allegory: Defining the Genre* (Ithaca, NY: Cornell University Press, 1992), pp. 225–6.
29. Barry, 'Lectures on Painting Delivered at the Royal Academy', in *Works*, i, p. 347 (subsequent references will take the form of 'Lectures', followed by volume and page number, in parentheses in the text).
30. Sir Joshua Reynolds, *Discourses on Art*, ed. Robert W. Wark (New Haven, CT: Yale University Press, 1975), Discourses II and IV. For a valuable discussion of Reynolds in this regard, see John Barrell, *The Birth of Pandora and the Division of Knowledge* (London: Macmillan, 1992), pp. 150ff.
31. Barrell, *The Birth of Pandora*, p. 158.
32. James Barry, 'Fragment on the Story and Painting of Pandora', *Works*, ii, pp. 150–1.
33. Barrell, *Birth of Pandora*, pp. 192, 198ff.
34. See Grimr Jonsson Thorkelin, *Fragments of English and Irish History in the Ninth and Tenth Century* (London: J. Nichols, 1788). Thorkelin was an honorary member of the Royal Irish Academy.
35. Johann Gottfried Herder, 'Essay on the Origin of Language', trans. Alexander Gode, in Jean Jacques Rousseau and Johann Gottfried Herder, *On the Origin of Language* (Chicago: University of Chicago Press, 1986), p. 87 (subsequent references will take the form of 'Herder, "Essay"', followed by page number in parentheses in the text).
36. Richter, *Laocoon's Body and the Aesthetics of Pain*, p. 108.
37. Ibid., p. 108.
38. Segal, *Tragedy and Civilization*, pp. 333, 298.
39. In Philoctetes's eyes, this cynical use of instrumental reason extends also to Ulysses's manipulation of his friend Neoptolemus: 'this poor youth, who, worthier far / To be my friend than thine, was only here / Thy instrument'. *Philoctetes*, 125.
40. Theodor Adorno and Max Horkheimer, *Dialectic of Enlightenment*, trans. John Cumming (New York: Herder and Herder, 1972), p. 51. In a footnote, Adorno and Horkeimer cite anthropological findings that instead of being a mark of 'primitivism', 'the more powerful a nation is, the more significant the practice of sacrifice' (p. 52).
41. Alasdair MacIntyre, *Whose Justice? Which Rationality?* (London: Duckworth, 1988), p. 62.
42. Ibid., p. 59.
43. As Charles Segal observes, 'Heracles' speech, which does finally integrate Philoctetes into both the social and the divine order, exactly complements Neoptolemus'[s], but at a higher level... The friendship that Heracles recalls

44. Adorno and Horkheimer, *Dialectic of Enlightenment*, p. 52.
45. Carole Fabricant, *Swift's Landscape* (Notre Dame: University of Notre Dame Press, 1995), p. xxiii.
46. William Molyneux, *The Case of Ireland Stated* [1698], introduction by J. G. Simms and afterword by Denis Donoghue (Dublin: Cadenus Press, 1977), pp. 21–2.
47. Jonathan Swift, *The Drapier's Letters to the People of Ireland*, Letter iv [1724], ed. Herbert Davis (Oxford: Oxford University Press, 1935), p. 79 (subsequent references will take the form of *Drapier's Letters*, followed by letter number and page number, in parentheses in the text).
48. For the background to the publication, see Oliver W. Ferguson, *Swift and Ireland* (Urbana: University of Illinois Press, 1962), ch. 4.
49. *Mist's Weekly Journal*, 5 Dec. 1724, cited in Ferguson, *Swift and Ireland*, p. 123, n. 139.
50. Dr Patrick Delany, in his prefatory poem to Swift's and Sheridan's remarkable display of wordplay and punning, *The Art of Punning; or the Flower of Languages* [1719], cited in James Woolley, 'Thomas Sheridan and Swift', in Roseann Runte, ed., *Studies in Eighteenth Century Culture*, ix (Madison: University of Wisconsin Press, 1979), p. 101.
51. Woolley, 'Thomas Sheridan and Swift', p. 97.
52. Segal, *Tragedy and Civilization*, p. 294.
53. *The Philoctetes of Sophocles*, trans. Thomas Sheridan (Dublin: J. Hyde and E. Dobson, 1725), p. 41 (subsequent references will take the form of 'Sheridan, *Philoctetes*', followed by page number, in parentheses in the text).
54. 'Am I a *Free-man* in *England*, and do I become a *Slave* in six Hours by crossing the Channel?', asks the Drapier in his third letter (*Drapier's Letters*, iii, 40), addressed 'to The NOBILITY and GENTRY of the Kingdom of IRELAND' – a query echoed in Philoctetes's reduction to slavery in a benighted island off the coast of Greece.
55. See also the passage in which Neoptolemus pretends to help Philoctetes off the island to escape the pursuing Greeks, and queries the afflicted warrior's relapse into physical cries to express his pain, rather than language:

> NEOP. What suff'rings now?
> Why are you silent? For you seem to me
> By Starts and Groans your Torture to confess.
> PHIL. My Son, I'm lost; no longer I conceal
> The malady; it wounds my very Soul;
> It pierces thro' and thro'; O wretched me!
> Murther'd! undone! and lost beyond Redress.
> O dismal, racking, burning, poison'd Pains!
>
> (Sheridan, *Philoctetes*, 27)

56. See e.g. Warren Montag, *The Unthinkable Swift: The Spontaneous Philosophy of a Church of England Man* (London: Verso, 1994), p. 158: 'Swift's Ireland was the first model of the apartheid state and he very directly benefited from the institutional oppression of the Irish people (an oppression, moreover, that was founded and constantly maintained by the might of the British military).' For a rejoinder to Montag's view, see Carole Fabricant, 'Speaking for the Irish Nation: The Drapier, the Bishop, and the Problem of Colonial Representation', *English Literary History*, 66 (1999).
57. Swift's nostalgic evocation of his vists to Sheridan's home in Quilca, Co. Cavan, with its memories of riding and fishing, 'Night Heroics', 'Morning Epics', and 'blind Harpers', leads Joseph McMinn to suggest that 'the combination of domestic ruin and cultural refinement makes Sheridan seem more like one of those Gaelic hedge-schoolmasters than an Anglican clergyman... Whenever Swift is at Quilca, he seems closer to native Ireland than in any other company.' Joseph McMinn, *Jonathan's Travels: Swift and Ireland* (Belfast: Appletree Press, 1994), p. 92.
58. *The Intelligencer*, vi, 18 June, 1728, in Jonathan Swift and Thomas Sheridan, *The Intelligencer*, ed. James Woolley (Oxford: Clarendon Press, 1992), p. 86.
59. Edmund Burke to Marquess of Rockingham, 29 September 1773, *Correspondence*, ii, ed. Lucy Sutherland, p. 468.
60. Cruise O'Brien, *The Great Melody*, pp. 13, 82.
61. Edmund Burke, 'Speech at the Guildhall, in Bristol' [1780], in *Works*, ii, p. 148.
62. Though in debt himself, Burke financed Barry's extended artistic apprenticeship in Italy between 1765 and 1771, during which he painted the *Philoctetes*. Their relationship was often strained subsequently, due mainly to Barry's uncompromising republican principles and his hostility towards Burke's close friend, Sir Joshua Reynolds.
63. For Keating as source, see 'Barry: The Historical Painter', *The Irish Quarterly Review*, 10 (June 1853), 232. Barry's reading of Keating, Charles O'Conor, and other Irish historians is recorded in the notes of his 'Commonplace Book': see William Pressly's thorough account of the painting, 'James Barry's *The Baptism of the King of Cashel by Saint Patrick*', *The Burlington Magazine*, cxviii, September, 1976.
64. For comparisons of ancient Ireland to the 'heroes in arts and in arms' of classical Greece, see Charles O'Conor, *Dissertations on the History of Ireland* [1753] (Dublin: J. Christie, 1812), p. xxi.
65. Crucially, Barry saw this cross-cultural contact as a mode of interaction, not a replacement of one culture by another (superior) one. The pagan past had already, in his eyes, made the transition to letters and civility, albeit in the primitive, republican form which radical writers such as John Toland (1670–1722) projected onto Druidic culture. Toland's influence is discernible in Dermot O'Connor's 1723 translation of Seathrún Céitinn's (Geoffrey Keating's) *Foras Feasa ar Éirinn* [*c*. 1633] (*History of Ireland*), one of Barry's key sources for the painting. Contemporary critics of O'Connor claimed 'that Toland had

assisted in the translation and accused him [Toland] of making suggestions that changed the original in ways that supported his views regarding paganism'. Alan Harrison, 'John Toland's Celtic Background', in *John Toland's Christianity Not Mysterious*, ed., Philip McGuinness, Alan Harrison, Richard Kearney (Dublin: Lilliput Press, 1997), p. 256.

66. For Barry's pioneering efforts to reconcile, on the heroic scale of history-painting, the 'universalism' of republicanism with the 'localism' of romanticism and cultural nationalism, see my '"A Shadowy Narrator" : History, Art and Romantic Nationalism in Ireland, 1750–1850', in Ciaran Brady, ed., *Ideology and the Historians* (Dublin: Lilliput Press, 1992).
67. Edmund Burke, 'A Letter to Thomas Burke, Esq.' [1780], in *Works*, v, p. 492.
68. Charles O'Conor to Charles Ryan, 11 November 1777, in *Letters of Charles O'Conor of Belanagare*, ed. Robert E. Ward, John F. Wrynn, SJ, and Catherine Coogan Ward (Washington, DC: Catholic University of America Press, 1988), p. 358.
69. Matthew O'Conor, *The History of the Irish Catholics from the Settlement in 1691* (Dublin: J. Stockdale, 1813), pp. 246–7.
70. Charles O'Conor to Dr John Curry, 23 June 1758, in O'Conor, *Letters*, p. 55.
71. Charles O'Conor to Denis O'Conor, 16 May 1778, in O'Conor, *Letters*, p. 363.
72. Charles O'Conor to Dr John Curry, 23 October 1778, in O'Conor, *Letters*, p. 370.
73. Thomas Bartlett, *The Fall and Rise of the Irish Nation: The Catholic Question, 1690–1830* (Dublin: Gill and Macmillan, 1992), p. 84.
74. See Webb's encomium to Flood's impassioned speech in defence of Irish legislative independence in 1781, where he alludes to a previous expression of support seven years earlier: 'You have filled up the measure of my most sanguine hope ... I will speak well of you where I can; where I cannot – be silent. The Close [of Flood's speech] was exquisite: it was a perfect accord of voice, sentiment, and gesture. Is not this, that which Demosthenes understood by the word actions? While I triumphed with you, I suffered for another – omnium judicio capex imperandi si nunquam imperasset.' Warden Flood, *Memoirs of the Life and Correspondence of the Right Hon. Henry Flood, M.P.* (Dublin: John Cumming, 1837), pp. 141–2. For Webb's relation to Flood, see also James Kelly, *Henry Flood: Patriots and Politics* (Dublin: Four Courts Press, 1998), pp. 176, 364.
75. Daniel Webb, *An Inquiry into the Beauties of Painting* (London: R. and J. Dodsley, 1761), p. 147 (subsequent references will take the form of *Beauties of Painting*, followed by page number, in parentheses in the text).
76. This might also function as a gloss on Barry's painting of the baptism of King Aongus by St Patrick, where the excited responses of the onlookers contrast with the King's own composure.
77. For Webb's influence on Barry in this respect, see Pressly, *James Barry*, p. 22, and Barrell, *The Birth of Pandora*, pp. 197–8.
78. William Pressly, *James Barry: The Artist as Hero* (London: The Tate Gallery, 1983), p. 126.

79. Ibid., p. 156.
80. Charles Phillips, *Curran and his Contemporaries* (Edinburgh: William Blackwood, 1850), p. 62. Yelverton was a native of Newmarket, Co. Cork, and thus shared Cork associations with both Barry and Burke. He was one of the attorneys hired to defend the last major group of Whiteboys suspects (see below, pp. 00, n. 00).
81. Pressly, *James Barry: The Artist as Hero*, p. 157.
82. [Joseph Pollock], *Letters of Owen Roe O'Nial* [1779] (Dublin, 1779), p. 48. For Pollock, see R.B. MacDowell, *Irish Public Opinion, 1750–1800* (London: Faber and Faber, 1944), pp. 60–1; Neil Longley York, *Neither Kingdom nor Nation*, pp. 118–19; and Thomas Bartlett, 'The Burden of the Present: Theobald Wolfe Tone, Republican, Separatist', in David Dickson, Daire Keogh, and Kevin Whelan, eds., *The United Irishmen: Republicanism, Radicalism and Rebellion* (Dublin: The Lilliput Press, 1993), p. 11.
83. Pressly, *James Barry: The Artist as Hero*, 157.
84. See Siobhán Kilfeather, '"Strangers at Home": Political Fictions by Women in Eighteenth-Century Ireland', Ph.D. dissertation, Princeton University, 1989, pp. 6–7.
85. Edmund Burke to Edmund Sexton Pery, 16 June 1778, *Correspondence*, iii, ed. George H. Gutteridge, p. 457.
86. Burke, 'Speech at the Guildhall, in Bristol', *Works*, ii, p. 145.
87. Payne Knight, 'Review', pp. 322, 321.
88. As Lessing perceptively points out, Philoctetes's sympathies extend not simply to friends but to 'fellow-mourners' (*Philoctetes*, 116), that is, others 'visited with the same calamities as ourselves' (*Laokoon*, 27).
89. Jebb, *Sophocles: The Plays and Fragments*, pp. xxvi.

3 THE SYMPATHETIC SUBLIME: EDMUND BURKE, ADAM SMITH, AND THE POLITICS OF PAIN

1. Adam Smith, *The Theory of Moral Sentiments* (1759), ed. D. D. Raphael and A. L. Macfie (Oxford: Oxford University Press, 1976), p. 29 (subsequent references will take the form of 'Moral Sentiments', followed by page number, in parentheses in the text).
2. Sir Walter Scott, 'General Preface, 1829', in *Waverley* [1814] (London: Penguin, 1985), p. 523.
3. Richard Lovell Edgeworth, *Memoirs*, ii (London: 1820), p. 350. See also William Carleton's related remark in his Preface to *The Black Prophet*, written during the Famine: 'Fiction is frequently transcended by the terrible realities of Truth.' William Carleton, *The Black Prophet* [1847] (Shannon: Irish University Press, 1972), p. viii.
4. Edmund Burke, *A Vindication of Natural Society* [1756], ed. Frank N. Pagano (Indianapolis: Liberty Classics, 1982), pp. 9–10 (subsequent references will take the form of 'Vindication', followed by page number, in parentheses in the text).

5. David Hume *A Treatise of Human Nature* [1739], ed. E. C. Mossner (Harmondsworth: Penguin,1969), II, iii, 3, p. 462 (subsequent references will take the form of 'Treatise', followed by page number, in parentheses in the text). For similar sentiments on Burke's part, see his early animadversions on theory and metaphysical speculation: 'Metaphysical or Physical Speculations neither are, or ought to be, the Grounds of our Duties; because we can arrive at no certainty in them. They have a weight when they concur with our own natural feelings; very little when against them.' 'Religion', in *A Note-Book of Edmund Burke*, p. 71.
6. Frank N. Pagano, 'Introduction' to *A Vindication of Natural Society*, p. xv. Burke also draws attention to the fact that theory often achieves its effects by doctrines 'sometimes concealed, sometimes openly and fully avowed'. *Vindication*, p. 5.
7. William O'Brien, *Edmund Burke as an Irishman* (Dublin: M. H. Gill, 1926), p. 155.
8. As Uday Singh Mehta points out, Burke's purpose here, 'like that of Hume is not to abandon reason but to enlarge its ambit, to make it social and more passionate, and more informed by the uncertain vagaries that attend and form experience'. Mehta, *Liberalism and Empire*, p. 42.
9. Karl Marx, *Grundrisse: Foundations of the Critique of Political Economy*, trans. Martin Nicolaus (Harmondsworth: Penguin, 1973), p. 105. For an incisive discussion of Marx's argument in the context of an argument that theory itself may be European, see Dipesh Chakrabarty, 'Postcoloniality and the Artifice of History: Who Speaks for "Indian" Pasts?' *Representations*, 37 (1992).
10. Fredric Jameson, *The Political Unconscious: Narrative as a Socially Symbolic Act* (London: Methuen, 1981), p. 54 n. 31. See also Dominic La Capra, 'Marxism in the Textual Maelstrom: Fredric Jameson's *The Political Unconscious*', in *Rethinking Intellectual History: Texts, Contexts, Language* (Ithaca: Cornell University Press, 1983), p. 244.
11. Michael J. Shapiro, *Reading 'Adam Smith': Desire, History and Value* (Newbury Park: Sage, 1993), pp. 7, 9.
12. For a brilliant discussion of this aspect of Hume's thought, see Xenos, *Scarcity and Modernity*, pp. 13ff.
13. Richard Payne Knight, *An Analytical Enquiry into the Principles of Taste* (London: T. Payne, 1808), p. 379.
14. Nicholas Robinson, *Edmund Burke: A Life in Caricature* (New Haven: Yale University Press, 1996), p. 10. Robinson goes on to cite another of Payne Knight's jibes, that whatever 'terror' and 'astonishment' might be felt at the prospect of Burke walking up St James without his trousers and armed with a loaded blunderbuss, the sight could hardly be called sublime.
15. *The Public Register or Freeman's Journal*, 4–8 October 1763, cited in *Writings and Speeches of Edmund Burke*, ed. R. B. McDowell, IX (Oxford: Clarendon Press), p. 411.
16. For discussions of the secularization of ethics in the eighteenth century, see Colin Campbell, *The Romantic Ethic and the Spirit of Modern Consumerism*

(Oxford: Basil Blackwell, 1987), chs. 6, 7; Niklas Luhmann, 'The Individuality of the Individual: Historical Meanings and Contemporary Problems', in Thomas C. Heller, Morton Sosna, and David Wellbery, eds., *Reconstructing Individualism* (Stanford: Stanford University Press, 1986).

17. Glenn R. Morrow, 'The Significance of the Doctrine of Sympathy in Hume and Adam Smith', *The Philosophical Review*, 32, 1 (1923), 62ff.

18. John B. Radner, 'The Art of Sympathy in Eighteenth-Century British Moral Thought', in Roseann Runte, ed., *Studies in Eighteenth-Century Culture*, ix (Madison, WI: University of Wisconsin Press), p. 189.

19. Tom Nairn, *The Break-Up of Britain: Crisis and Neo-Nationalism*, 2nd edition (London: Verso, 1981), p. 111.

20. 'If commonwealths are real entities, he [Hume] suggests (and what could be more real than the British Commonwealth?), so are selves. Like England itself, selves are not "self-identical" but exist only hermeneutically, in unity-diversity and permanence-in-change'. Joel C. Weinsheimer, *Eighteenth-Century Hermeneutics: Philosophy of Interpretation in England from Locke to Burke* (New Haven: Yale University Press, 1993), p. 113.

21. See Hume's well-known remark that 'my views of *things* are more conformable to Whig principles; my representations of *persons* to Tory prejudices'. *The Letters of David Hume*, ed. J. Y. T. Greig, 2 vols. (Oxford: Oxford University Press, 1932), i, p. 237.

22. David Hume to Gilbert Elliot, 22 September 1764, *Letters*, i, p. 470. As David Raynor points out, Hume regretted his indiscretion in this letter, and wrote to Elliot eight days later: 'I spoke to you with great Freedom, and am infinitely uneasy lest my letter shoud fall into bad hands': *Letters*, i, p. 471, cited in the Introduction to *Sister Peg: a Pamphlet Hitherto Unknown by David Hume*, ed. David R. Raynor (Cambridge: Cambridge University Press, 1982), p. 35. Hume must have regarded his radical reformulations of the concept of personal identity as a similar 'indiscretion' at a philosophical level for he dropped these sections from the *Treatise* in the popular presentation of his arguments contained in *An Enquiry concerning Human Understanding* (1758).

23. Mullan's judgement is not without its qualifications, however: 'In the *Treatise* at least, standards of judgement and behaviour specific to the ruling class of Hanoverian Britain are only ever implicit. This does not mean that they played no part in determining Hume's project; it does mean that the point of the project was to be the scope of its generalization and abstraction. Unlike the *Essays*, in which the particular historical context of judgement is quite explicit, the *Treatise* is committed to a philosophical description of "human nature".' John Mullan, *Sentiment and Sociability*, p. 23. The concession that the Scottish context is *implicit* is all that is required for my present argument.

24. Kenneth Simpson, *The Protean Scot: The Crisis of Identity in Eighteenth-Century Scottish Literature* (Aberdeen: Aberdeen University Press, 1988), p. 7. Simpson also cites Hume's comments to Benjamin Franklin in 1772: 'I expected, in entering on my literary course, that all the Christians, all the Whigs, and all the Tories, should be my enemies. But it is hard that all the English, Irish and

Welsh, should be also against me. The Scotch likewise cannot be much my friends, as no man is a prophet in his own country.' Hume, *Letters*, ii, p. 258.
25. For a use of Freud's term which is close to the sense employed here, see Perry Meisel's discussion of some of the specific traits of modernity evident in the writings of the Bloomsbury circle: 'From Forster to Strachey, private worlds are a product or function of the public languages to which they are customarily opposed. Bloomsbury's thematic use of "alien associations" [in language] plainly links what James Strachey's translation of Freud (1953–74) calls "psychic economy" with the sphere of real economy as the result of a habitual and strategic identification of the vocabulary or figurations of private life with those of the public.' Perry Meisel, *The Myth of the Modern: A Study in British Literature and Criticism after 1850* (New Haven: Yale University Press, 1987), p. 163.
26. See Adam Ferguson, *An Essay on the History of Civil Society* [1767] (Edinburgh: Edinburgh University Press, 1966), Parts v and vi; Charles L. Griswold, Jr, *Adam Smith and the Virtues of Enlightenment* (Cambridge: Cambridge University Press, 1999), ch. 7; Marvin Becker, *The Emergence of Civil Society in the Eighteenth Century: A Privileged Moment in the History of England, Scotland, and France* (Bloomington: Indiana University Press, 1994), pp. 107–14; John Dwyer, *Virtuous Discourse: Sensibility and Community in Late Eighteenth-Century Scotland* (Edinburgh: John Donald, 1987).
27. Robert Crawford, *Devolving English Literature* (Oxford: Clarendon Press, 1992), especially pp. 55ff.; Linda Colley, *Britons: Forging the Nation 1707–1837* (New Haven: Yale University Press, 1992), pp. 105–32; and Simpson, *The Protean Scot*.
28. Colley, *Britons*, p. 120.
29. Morrow, 'The Significance of the Doctrine of Sympathy in Hume and Adam Smith', p. 69.
30. Crawford, *Devolving English Literature*, pp. 28–9.
31. Adam Smith, *Lectures on Rhetoric and Belles Lettres*, ed. J. C. Bryce (Oxford: Clarendon Press, 1983), pp. 4–5, cited in Crawford, *Devolving English Literature*, p. 29.
32. John Dwyer, 'Introduction – A "Peculiar Blessing": Social Converse from Hutcheson to Burns', in *Sociability and Society in Eighteenth-Century Scotland*, ed. John Dwyer and Richard B. Sher (Edinburgh: The Mercat Press, 1993), pp. 5–6. See also Simpson, *The Protean Scot*: 'The concern of the literati with taste was an aspect of their programme to justify Scotland's partnership in the Union in artistic terms. For them, the development of polite literature was both essential for, and an index to, the refinement of society' (p. 71).
33. Richard F. Teichgraber, *'Free Trade' and Moral Philosophy: Rethinking the Sources of Adam Smith's* Wealth of Nations (Durham, NC: Duke University Press, 1986), p. 160.
34. James Macpherson, 'Fingal: An Ancient Epic Poem in Six Books' [1762], in *The Poems of Ossian and Related Works*, ed. Howard Gaskill, with an introduction by Fiona Stafford (Edinburgh: Edinburgh University Press, 1996), p. 51.

35. Adam Smith to William Strahan, 4 April 1760, in *The Correspondence of Adam Smith*, ed. Ernest Campbell Mossner and Ian Simpson Ross (Oxford: Clarendon Press, 1977), p. 68.
36. Gauri Viswanathan, *Masks of Conquest: Literary Study and British Rule in India* (London: Faber and Faber, 1990), p. 128.
37. Smith uses the metaphor of 'vicegerent' in relation to 'the impartial spectator' acting as God's representative on earth: what is of interest for the present argument is the choice of the metaphor in the first place.
38. Mullan, *Sentiment and Sociability*, p. 43.
39. Alarmed in 1795 at the spread of the revolutionary principles of republicanism in Ireland, Burke expresses the hope that 'some medium may be found between an abject, and for that reason an imprudent Submission, and a contumacious absurd resistance' such as that promoted by the United Irishmen. Edmund Burke to Rev. Thomas Hussey, 18 May 1795, *Correspondence*, viii, p. 249.
40. Edmund Burke to Lord Fitzwilliam, 10 February 1795, ibid., p. 147.
41. Edmund Burke to the Rev. Thomas Hussey, 18 May 1795: 'It is a foolish language, adopted from the united Irishmen, that their Grievances originate from England. The direct contrary. It is an ascendancy which some of their own factions have obtaind here that has hurt the Catholicks with this Government' (ibid., p. 246). The difficulty with Burke's polemical facility to seize upon exemplary events for his own purposes of reform was that their rhetorical force depended on their capacity to implicate an entire system, rather than standing alone as discrete, once-off transgressions. While Hastings took the brunt of Burke's rage against injustices in India, there was no individual to act as a scapegoat in Ireland, and his criticisms embraced the entire Protestant 'Junto' or Ascendancy.
42. Edmund Burke to Rev. Thomas Hussey, post 9 December 1796, *Correspondence*, ed. R. B. McDowell and John A. Woods (Cambridge: Cambridge University Press, 1970), ix, p. 169 .
43. Rev. Thomas Hussey to Richard Burke, 28 August 1790, *Correspondence*, ed. Alfred Cobban and Robert A. Smith, vi (Cambridge University Press, 1967), p. 134. See also quotation from Peter Burrowes below, Chapter 5, p. 164, n. 46.
44. Burke to Hussey, *Correspondence*, ix, pp. 167, 166.
45. Edmund Burke to the Rev. Thomas Hussey, 4 February 1795, *Correspondence*, viii, p. 137. Burke's view contrasts starkly with that of Smith's: 'The greater his [the victim's] patience, his mildness, his humanity, provided it does not appear that he wants spirit, or that fear was the motive of his forbearance, the higher their [i.e. mankind's] resentment against the person who injured him.' *Moral Sentiments*, 34.
46. Ibid. See also the letter to Hussey, 18 May 1795, in which Burke writes about the inflammatory sentiments expressed at a meeting of the Catholics on 9 April at Francis St: 'I am not a man for construing with too much rigour the expressions of men under a sense of ill usage. I know that much is to be given

to passion; and I hope I am more disposed to accuse the person who provokes another to anger, than the person who gives way to natural feelings in hot Language' (ibid., p. 247).
47. See Andrew Wilton, *Turner and the Sublime* (London: British Museum Publications, 1981), p. 29, where 'the common fascination with death (especially violent death), human tragedies and natural disasters, the love of grandiose spectacle and everything grotesquely out of the ordinary' found in modern sensational newspapers is associated with 'Burke and the "terror" school of sublime theorists'. In fact, Burke's aesthetics represents a systematic attack on such sensationalism.
48. For Burke's excoriation of the sentimental trivialization of suffering, see his comments on India, pp. 113ff. below.
49. D. D. Raphael, *Adam Smith* (Oxford University Press, 1985), p. 31.
50. This is George Herbert Mead's term, as adumbrated in his *Mind, Self and Society* (Chicago: University of Chicago Press, 1934). For the affinities between Smith's thought and the social psychology of Charles Cooley and other mentors of Mead's, see Gladys Bryson, *Man and Society* (Princeton: Princeton University Press, 1945).
51. David Hume to Adam Smith, 28 July 1759, *Correspondence of Adam Smith*, p. 43.
52. Mullan, *Sentiment and Sociability*, p. 46.
53. Edmund Burke to Richard Shackleton, 28 December 1745, *Correspondence*, i, p. 59.
54. Edmund Burke to Richard Shackleton, 16 January, 1746, ibid., p. 60.
55. 'A mind at ease may improve, by them, and Seneca will infinitely please in Speculation but Experience will inform you better than I, that in time of affliction they are but Sorry Comforters, the tide of Passion is not to be stopp'd by such feeble dams'. Edmund Burke to Richard Shackleton, 28 December 1745, ibid., p. 59. Burke's generally positive response to Smith's *Theory of Moral Sentiments* contains some barbed praise of the Stoic principles underpinning the work: '[The work] is often sublime too, particularly in that fine Picture of the Stoic Philosophy towards the end of your first part which is dressed out in all the grandeur and Pomp that becomes that magnificent delusion.' Edmund Burke to Adam Smith, 10 September 1759, in *Correspondence of Adam Smith*, p. 47.
56. Edmund Burke to Richard Shackleton, 15 February 1745/6, *Correspondence*, i, p. 61.
57. Edmund Burke to John Hely Hutchinson, May 1765; Burke to John Monck Mason, 29 May 1765, ibid., pp. 199, 196, 197. Perhaps it this aspect of Burke's personality which led Robert Murray to discern in him alleged traits of the Irish national character: 'It is by no means an easy task for an Irishman to repress the vehemence of his nature, and indeed Burke seems to have made very feeble attempts to do so. At all events they failed.' Robert H. Murray, *Edmund Burke* (Oxford University Press, 1931), p. 41.

58. 'Angry friendship is sometimes as bad as calm enmity. For this reason, the cold neutrality of abstract justice is, to a good and clear cause, a more desirable thing than an affection liable to be any way disturbed... [Injustice] is aggravated by coming from lips professing friendship, and pronouncing judgment with sorrow and reluctance. Taking in the whole view of life, it is more safe to live under the jurisdiction of severe but steady reason, than under the empire of indulgent but capricious passion.' Edmund Burke, 'An Appeal From the Old to the New Whigs' [1791], *Works*, iii, p. 3.
59. Sara Suleri, *The Rhetoric of English India* (Chicago: University of Chicago Press, 1992), p. 46.
60. Edmund Burke, 'Speech on Mr. Fox's East-India Bill' [1783], *Works*, ii, pp. 196 (subsequent references will take the form of 'East-India Bill', followed by volume number and page number, in parentheses in the text). Or as Burke put it later with regard to Warren Hastings's outrages: one must not only 'state the fact' but also 'assign the criminality'. Edmund Burke to Philip Francis, 23 December 1785, *Correspondence*, v, p. 245.
61. Paine, *Rights of Man*, p. 73.
62. Frans de Bruyn, *The Literary Genres of Edmund Burke: The Political Uses of Literary Form* (Oxford: Clarendon Press, 1996), pp. 127–8.
63. See above, Chapter 1 and Chapter 5 below.
64. Hence the ambivalent attitudes towards Burke's oratory adopted by commentators more at ease with the clarity and civility of 'polished language'. As one Victorian commentator expresses it, Burke displayed 'an imagination of oriental luxuriance, whose incessant play in tropes, metaphors, and analogies, frequently causes his speeches to gleam on the intellectual eye... But, in all candour, it may be added, that just as a profusion of figure and metaphors sometimes tempted this great orator into incongruous images and coarse analogies, so his passion for irony was occasionally too intense.' Introductory essay to *Selections from the Speeches and Writings of Edmund Burke*, Sir John Lubbock's Hundred Books series (London: George Routledge, n.d.), p. x.
65. See Barbara C. Oliver, 'Edmund Burke's *Enquiry* and the Baroque Theory of the Passions', *Studies in Burke and his Time*, 12 (1970).
66. As David Bromwich points out, the effects of a purely sensational sublime would be to leave us 'alarmed but without reflection' (Bromwich, *A Choice of Inheritance*, p. 52). The disruptive, critical aspect of the sublime is discussed in greater detail in Chapter 5 below, pp. 153–7.
67. See Chapter 2, pp. 59–61.
68. John Mullan (in *Sentiment and Sociability*, pp. 26ff.) correctly traces a shift in eighteenth-century theories of sympathy from earlier theories based on the metaphor of 'contagion' to later, more studied manifestations based on spectatorial relations. However, he overemphasizes the 'natural' or unmediated nature of the sympathy based on contagion: Burke, for one, saw it as more, rather than less, mediated than pictorial representations on account of its reliance on highly wrought, figurative expressions.

69. It was precisely on these grounds that Mary Wollstonecraft took Burke to task, arguing that 'we ought to beware of confounding mechanical instinctive sensations with emotions that reason deepens, and justly terms the feelings of *humanity*' (Mary Wollstonecraft, 'A Vindication of the Rights of Men', *Political Writings*, p. 54). But Burke's approach does not rest on self-validating intuitions or 'instinctive sensations': his theory of sympathy is mediated through language and, indeed, the presence of another (whether another person or another culture). Sympathy may draw on our common humanity, but is filtered through the most distinctive and culturally coded expressions of humanity such as language.
70. Gilles Deleuze, *Cinema 1: The Movement Image*, trans. Hugh Tomlinson and Barbara Habberjam (London: Athlone Press, 1986), p. 35. For some tentative comments linking the eighteenth-century sublime and a modernist 'aesthetics of shock', see Patrice Petro, 'After Shock/Between Boredom and History', in Patrice Petro, ed., *Fugitive Images: From Photography to Video* (Bloomington: University of Indiana Press, 1995), p. 281.
71. Longinus, 'On the Sublime', in *Classical Literary Criticism*, p. 100.
72. Suleri, *The Rhetoric of English India*, p. 38.
73. For a discussion of this aspect of Hume, see Weinsheimer, *Eighteenth-Century Hermeneutics*, ch. 4.
74. The most direct association of oppression in Ireland with that of India occurs in a letter in 1795, in which both are connected in turn to the threat of modernity represented by the French Revolution's attacks on the traditional order: 'I think I can hardly overrate the malignity of the principles of Protestant ascendancy, as they affect Ireland; or of Indianism, as they affect these countries, and as they affect Asia; or of Jacobinism as they affect all Europe, and the state of human society itself.' Burke to Sir Hercules Langrishe, 26 May 1795, *Correspondence*, viii, p. 254.
75. According to Ernst Cassirer, Burke's theory of the sublime represents the apotheosis of individualism: 'Not only the inner freedom of man from the objects of nature and from the power of destiny is expressed in the sense of the sublime but this sense releases the individual from a thousand ties to which he is subject as a member of the community and of the social and civil order. In the experience of the sublime all these barriers vanish; the individual must stand entirely on his own two feet and assert himself in his independence and originality against the universe, both physical and social' (Cassirer, *The Philosophy of the Enlightenment* (Princeton: Princeton University Press, 1951) p. 330). This account of Burke's theory sees it as part of a general shift towards subjectivity and inwardness in pre-romantic sensibility, culminating in what Keats was later to call, in relation to Wordsworth, 'the egotistical sublime'. As we shall see, this emphasis on individual freedom fails to allow for forms of collective or social dissent, which also fall under Burke's description of the sublime.
76. Burleigh T. Wilkins, *The Problem of Burke's Political Philosophy* (Oxford: Clarendon Press, 1967), pp. 145–6.

77. Tom Furniss, 'Edmund Burke: Bourgeois Revolutionary in a Radical Crisis', in *Socialism and the Limits of Liberalism*, ed. Peter Osborne (London: Verso, 1991), pp. 19–20. The severance of the link between the sublime and the 'other-directed', socializing effects of sympathy is central to Furniss's attempt to align Burke's aesthetics with the ideological project of bourgeois individualism in the eighteenth century. For a more detailed discussion, see the same author's *Edmund Burke's Aesthetic Ideology: Language, Gender and Political Economy in Revolution* (Cambridge: Cambridge University Press, 1992), pp. 33ff.
78. Among the few commentators to draw attention to Burke's crucial association of sympathy with the sublime as well as the beautiful, see Joseph Kronick, 'On the Border of History: Whitman and the American Sublime', in Mary Arensberg, ed., *The American Sublime* (New York: State University of New York, 1986), and Fuchs, *Edmund Burke, Ireland and the Fashioning of Self*, p. 176.
79. See Frances Ferguson's acute observation, linking Burke with Kant in this regard: 'Both recognize categories of the beautiful and the sublime, and both link the beautiful with society and the sublime with individuals isolated either by the simple fact of their solitude or *by a heroic distinction that sets then apart even as they participate in social enterprises*' (Frances Ferguson, *Solitude and the Sublime* (New York: Routledge, 1992), 3: my italics). Ferguson's reconciliation of the individualist and social aspects of the sublime in heroism is to the point, though the 'setting apart' may not actually be anti-social, but may be attended by social approbation or fame – or may take the form of the social dissent of the revolutionary. As she states elsewhere: 'For Burke, heroes, though participating in the sublime, are almost incidentally important for their singularity. They are instead essentially important for the contribution their sublimity makes to civilized society; they make the world safe for society.' Frances Ferguson, 'Legislating the Sublime', in Ralph Cohen, ed., *Studies in Eighteenth-Century British Art and Aesthetics* (Berkeley: University of California Press, 1985), p. 134.
80. Richard Stack, 'An Essay on Sublimity of Writing' [1787], *Transactions of the Royal Irish Academy*, p. 8.
81. John Baillie, 'An Essay on the Sublime' [1747], in Ashfield and de Bolla, eds., *The Sublime*, p. 93. It may be that this colonial dimension is required to complete Tom Furniss's picture of aggressive, bourgeois individualism as the driving force of the sublime, and indeed he quotes Thomas Weiskel to this effect: 'we hear in the background of the Romantic sublime the grand confidence of a heady imperialism . . . a kind of spiritual capitalism, enjoining a pursuit of the infinitude of the private self'. Thomas Weiskel, *The Romantic Sublime: Studies in the Structure and Psychology of Transcendence* (Baltimore: Johns Hopkins University Press, 1976), p. 4, cited in Furniss, 'Edmund Burke', p. 32.
82. This, as argued above, is one of the key insights bequeathed by Longinus, and is already evident in Burke's earliest thoughts on the sublime in his adolescent letters. See Longinus, 'On the Sublime', in *Classical Literary Criticism*, p. 107, and 'Introduction' above, pp. 3–4.
83. Bruhm, *Gothic Bodies*, pp. 16–17.

84. It is likely that Burke has in mind here the capacity of native Americans, and perhaps Catholic missionaries martyred by native Americans, to endure and defy the most excruciating pain under torture. This was much commented on in the ethnographic literature of the day, including Burke's own book (co-authored with his kinsman William) *An Account of European Settlements in America* (1757) (see below, Chapter 7, p. 282, n. 43). It is striking that, in this passage, the experience of oppression or pain, instead of turning the victim in on him or herself, empowers the victim to rebel against the oppressor, the servants, as it were, appropriating the power of the master for themelves in the manner described by Burke in his youthful letters (pp. 2–4 above), and consistent with Longinus's depiction of the sublime.
85. See Chapter 7 below. This motif of 'virtue in distress' also presented itself in relation to the notorious practice of *suttee*, the burning of widows in India, which was construed as providing an occasion for Western gallantry – or Burkean chivalry – to rescue the doomed women. See Monika Fludernik, 'Suttee Revisited: From the Iconography of Martyrdom to the Burkean Sublime', *New Literary History* (1999), 30, 412ff.
86. For the relation with the Penal Laws in Ireland, see Frederick Whelan, *Edmund Burke and India: Political Morality and Empire* (Pittsburgh: University of Pittsburgh Press, 1996), p. 185.
87. It is tempting to surmise here that Burke is reflecting on the allegiances of his own formative years, raised in the beleaguered Catholic and Gaelic culture of his maternal family, the Nagles of north County Cork. (See above, Chapter 1, and Chapter 5 below.) For Burke, it is crucial that such primordial, framing narratives in our lives are not just a matter of pre-social, human attachments (maternal or paternal affections), but also involve allegiances to the specific cultural milieu of his upbringing: 'Next to the love of parents for their children, the strongest instinct both natural and moral that exists in man is the love of his country... All creatures love their offspring; next to that they love their homes; they have a fondness for the place where they have been bred, for the habitations they have dwelt in... This instinct, I say, that binds all creatures to their country, never becomes inert in us, nor ever suffers us to want a memory of it.' Impeachment: Fourth Day of Reply', viii, 141–2.
88. Edmund Burke, 'Speech on Impeachment: Seventh Day of Reply', 12 June 1794, in *Works*, viii, p. 264 (subsequent references will take the form of 'Impeachment: Seventh Day of Reply', followed by volume number and page number, in parentheses in the text). See also Whelan, *Edmund Burke and India*, p. 187.
89. See Erasmus Darwin's related 'materialist' account, that if we assume 'the attitude that any passion naturally occasions, we soon in some degree acquire that passion; hence when those that scold indulge themselves in loud oaths, and violent action of the arms, they increase their anger by the mode of expressing themselves; and on the contrary the counterfeited smile of pleasure in disagreeable company soon brings with it a portion of the reality'. 'Of

Instinct', in *Zoonomania* [1794–96], i, pp. 146–7, cited in Walter Jackson Bate, *From Classic to Romantic* (New York: Harper and Row, 1961), p. 139.

90. Franz Kafka, *Letters to Milena*, ed. Willy Hass, trans. Tania Stern and James Stern (London: Minerva, 1992), p. 9.

91. Smith does allow for a certain transfer of emotions though imitation of bodily gestures, but as we have seen, these are considered 'extremely imperfect' (TMS, 11) and are rendered virtually negligible in the kinds of extreme situations which Burke sees as generating sympathetic contagion. In Smith, it is incumbent on the victim to conform to the composure of the spectator; whereas in Burke, the spectator identifies with the agony of the victim.

92. Bruhm, *Gothic Bodies*, pp. 17–18.

93. Edmund Burke, 'Impeachment: First Day of Reply', 28 May 1794, *Works*, vii, p. 489.

94. *The History of the Trial of Warren Hastings* (London, 1796), i, p. 8, cited in Suleri, *The Rhetoric of English India*, p. 61.

95. Edmund Burke, 'Impeachment of Warren Hastings: Speech on the Sixth Charge', *Works*, vii, pp. 448–9.

96. Not least of the ironies here in that one of Thomas Paine's main charges against Burke's defence of the old regime whether in England or France was that he turned a blind eye to their staged spectacles of terror, such as state executions, thus overlooking that 'the effect of those cruel spectacles exhibited to the populace, is to destroy tenderness, to excite revenge'. Thomas Paine, *The Rights of Man*, ed. Henry Collins (Harmondsworth: Penguin, 1971), p. 80.

4 DID EDMUND BURKE CAUSE THE GREAT FAMINE? COMMERCE, CULTURE, AND COLONIALISM

1. Edmund Burke, 'Impeachment: Fifth Day', *Works*, vii, p. 194.
2. Edmund Burke to Adrien-Jean-François Duport, 29 March 1790, *Correspondence*, vi, p. 109.
3. Edmund Burke to Rev. Robert Dodge, 29 February 1792, *Correspondence*, vii, p. 85.
4. Sir Randolph Routh to Sir Charles Trevelyan, 18 November 1846, *Correspondence Explanatory of the Measures adopted by her Majesty's Government for the Relief of Distress arising from the Failure of the Potato Crop in Ireland* (HC 1846 (735), xxxvii, 41, p. 278). The Achill delegation met Routh on 10 October, after Trevelyan had sent him extracts from Burke's 'Thoughts on Scarcity' on 2 October. For an account of the episode, see Rev. J. O'Rourke, *The History of the Great Irish Famine* (Dublin: M'Glashan and Gill, 1875), pp. 222–3.
5. Peter Gray, 'The Triumph of Dogma: Ideology and Famine Relief', *History Ireland*, 3, 2 (Summer 1995), p. 30. For an extended discussion of the colonial imputation of moral and economic failings to the Irish, see Thomas A. Boylan and Timothy P. Foley, *Political Economy and Colonial Ireland* (London: Routledge, 1992), ch. 6.

6. Trevelyan to Routh, 2 October 1846, in *Correspondence Explanatory*.
7. Christine Kinealy, *This Great Calamity: the Irish Famine 1845–52* (Dublin: Gill and Macmillan, 1994), p. 53.
8. Gertrude Himmelfarb, *The Idea of Poverty: England in the Early Industrial Age* (New York: Alfred A. Knopf, 1984), p. 68.
9. Nigel Everett, *The Tory View of Landscape* (New Haven, CT and London: Yale University Press, 1994), p. 37.
10. For Burke's familiarity with the Irish language, see William O'Brien, *Edmund Burke as an Irishman* (Dublin: M. H. Gill, 1926), p. 72, drawing on Robert Bissett's account of Burke's tour of the Highlands in September 1785. On meeting a local antiquarian, Dr M'Intire, 'Burke, who understood the Irish language, spoke to Dr M'Intire in that tongue. He answered in Erse; and they understood each other in many instances, from the similarity of these two dialects of the ancient Celtic.' Robert Bisset, *The Life of Edmund Burke*, 2 vols., 2nd edition (London: George Cawthorn, 1800), ii, p. 248. Burke's knowledge of Irish was also evident in his discovery of a valuable collection of Irish language manuscripts in the library of Sir John Sebright, which were later presented to Trinity College, Dublin. See Walter D. Love, 'Edmund Burke, Charles Vallancey and the Sebright MSS', *Hermethena*, 95 (1961).
11. Francis Canavan, *The Political Economy of Edmund Burke: The Role of Property in his Thought* (New York: Fordham University Press, 1993), p. 137.
12. Originally conceived as a memorandum to the then Prime Minister, William Pitt, in November 1795, Burke's *Thoughts and Details on Scarcity* was not published until after his death in 1800.
13. E. P. Thompson, 'The Moral Economy Reviewed', in *Customs in Common* (London: Penguin, 1993), pp. 291–2.
14. See Thomas H. D. Mahoney, *Edmund Burke and Ireland* (Cambridge, MA: Harvard University Press, 1960), p. 339.
15. 'To provide for us in our necessities is not in the power of government. It would be a vain presumption in statesmen to think they can do it. The people maintain them, and not they the people. It is in the power of government to prevent much evil; it can do little positive good in this, or perhaps in anything else': Edmund Burke, 'Thoughts and Details on Scarcity' [1795], *Works*, v, p. 82 (subsequent references will take the form of 'Thoughts and Details', followed by volume and page number, in parentheses in the text). Burke then goes on to express his fear of state intervention 'leading to the French system of putting corn into requisition' ('Thoughts and Details', v, 97).
16. See e.g. Burleigh T. Wilkins, *The Problem of Burke's Political Philosophy* (Oxford: Clarendon Press, 1967), p. 65: 'One of the greatest oddities in the case of Burke concerns his endorsement of both traditional natural law and the *laissez-faire* economics of Adam Smith, apparently without ever considering their differences.'
17. Edmund Burke, 'Third Letter on a Regicide Peace', v, p. 321.
18. Burke's naïve market optimism here is contradicted by his frank acknowledgement, noted above, that as the labourer's need for work increases, so may his

bargaining power in relation to wages decrease, as the employer's needs take precedence throughout.

19. Nassau W. Senior, *Journals, Conversations and Essays Relating to Ireland* (London: Longmans, Green and Co., 1868), p. 222, cited in Chris Morash, 'Ever under Some Unnatural Condition: Bram Stoker and the Colonial Fantastic', in Brian Cosgrave, ed., *Literature and the Supernatural* (Dublin: Columba Press, 1996), p. 98.

20. As against Himmelfarb's and Everett's charge that Burke condoned famine, O'Neill is one of the few commentators to attend closely to what he actually wrote: 'Edmund Burke, in his *Thoughts and Details on Scarcity*, had propounded the view that, in periods of food shortage, government should not interfere with trade. This was the principle which motivated Lord John Russell's ministry in dealing with Ireland; but Burke had gone on to state that if the calamity was so great as to threaten actual famine, the poor should not be abandoned to the flinty heart and griping hand of self-interest but passed into charity beyond the rules of commerce.' Thomas P. O'Neill, 'The Organisation and Administration of Relief, 1845–52', in R. Dudley Edwards and T. Desmond Williams, eds., *The Great Famine: Studies in Irish History 1845–52* (Dublin: Browne and Nolan, 1956), p. 259.

21. See Isaac Kramnick, *The Rage of Edmund Burke: Portrait of an Ambivalent Conservative* (New York: Basic Books, 1977), pp. 91, 208. For Godwin's own testimony, see his *Enquiry Concerning Political Justice* [1793] (Toronto: University of Toronto Press, 1946), i, p. 13 and ii, pp. 545–6.

22. Kramnick, *The Rage of Edmund Burke*, pp. 88–93. For recent discussions, see Lock, *Edmund Burke*, ch. 3, and Fuchs, *Edmund Burke, Ireland and the Fashioning of Self*, ch. 5.

23. By the same token, sentiments regarding the ruthless exploitation of native Americans under Spanish rule which feature in the *Vindication* also recur in Burke's own voice on several occasions, especially in *An Account of European Settlements in America* [1757], co-authored at virtually the same time he was writing the *Vindication* (see Chapter 7 below, p. 200). Again, this strongly suggests that, at least where indictment of oppression and poverty was concerned, Burke's *Vindication* echoes his own views elsewhere.

24. The extent to which Burke's immediate locality was affected can be seen from a contemporary letter in which it is noted that by the end of January 1739/40, 'the poor' in North Cork were already 'perishing with cold and hunger, notwithstanding great benefactions given'. William Taylor to the Earl of Egmont, 26 January 1739/40, cited in David Dickson, 'An Economic History of the Cork Region in the Eighteenth Century', Ph.D. thesis, 2 vols. Trinity College, Dublin, 1977, ii, p. 622. Dickson points out that in nearby Macroom, burials increased by 342 per cent in 1740, and by 587 per cent in 1741, leading Sir Richard Cox to declare that the devastation was greater than any civil war or plague (pp. 633, 630). For an overview of the 'forgotten' famine, see David Dickson, *Artic Ireland* (Belfast: White Row Press, 1997).

25. Cited in O'Rourke, *History of the Great Famine*, p. 23.

26. But such arguments are themselves selective: conventional readings of Burke's earliest publication, the *Vindication*, have no difficulty in adducing it as evidence of a life-long critique of Rousseau. The counter-reading of the *Vindication* given here establishes a different set of continuities, in this case, his less familiar critiques of Protestant ascendancy and landlordism. This is not to deny that Burke's views may have changed over time but as we shall see below, his bitter indictment of famine in Bengal echoes his earlier indignation against poverty and exploitation. The fact that his early attachments to the Irish countryside, moreover, stayed with him throughout his life make it highly unlikely that he would change his mind fundamentally on these, above all other matters.
27. *Correspondence Explanatory*, p. 99.
28. The contrast with Scotland's prosperity after the Union in 1707 is striking here. As Linda Colley notes: 'Its economy expanded after the 1750s at a faster rate than ever before, in some respects at a faster rate than the English economy. Between 1750 and 1800, its overseas commerce grew by 100 per cent, England's by 200 per cent. In the same period, the proportion of Scots living in towns doubled, whereas England's more substantial urban population increased by only some 25 per cent.' *Britons*, p. 123.
29. Eamonn Slator and Terrence McDonnough, 'Bulwark of Landlordism and Capitalism: The Dynamics of Feudalism in Nineteenth Century Ireland', *Research in Political Economy*, 14 (1994), pp. 71, 70. The fact that there were no mutual obligations throws into question, however, the use of the term 'feudalism' to describe the anomalies of the pre-Famine economy.
30. Due to the moral improvement induced by apprehending scenes of distress, the cult of charity and benevolence in the eighteenth century, according to Carol McGuirk, 'made the presence of an interpreting sensibility seem more important than the wretchedness described'. Carol McGuirk, *Robert Burns and the Sentimental Era* (Athens, GA: University of Georgia Press, 1985), p. 5.
31. Sir Charles Trevelyan, *The Irish Crisis* (London: Longmans, 1848), pp. 116–17.
32. Edmund Burke, 'Letter to a Member of the National Assembly' [1791], *Works*, ii, p. 537.
33. Even though Burke's theology committed him to a Providential view of nature, Adam Smith's theory of 'the invisible hand' was still not sufficient in his eyes to generate public good out of private interest: 'The benign and wise Disposer of things... *obliges* men, whether they will or not, in pursuing their own selfish interests, to connect their general good with their own success' ('Thoughts and Details', v, 89: my italics). Note that there is nothing *automatic* about this: as Peter J. Stanlis observes, the relationship is one of *obligation* rather than of optimistic economic determinism. Peter J. Stanlis, *Edmund Burke, The Enlightenment and Revolution* (New Brunswick, NJ: Transaction Publishers, 1991), p. 29.
34. Norman Barry, 'The Political Economy of Edmund Burke', in Ian Crowe, ed., *Edmund Burke: His Life and Legacy* (Dublin: Four Courts Press, 1997), p. 110.

35. Cited in Cecil Woodham-Smith, *The Great Hunger: Ireland 1845–1849* (New York, 1962), p. 375. For Smith's pitiless response to famine, at least where government intervention was concerned, see Chapter 8 below, pp. 219–20.
36. Cited in Stanlis, *Edmund Burke*, p. 22.
37. As Thomas Horne perceptively argues, this facet of Grotius's philosophy was not motivated by lofty philanthropic impulses, but by the more base considerations of imperial expansion. The assertion of original communal or general rights to the earth allowed European powers – in his case, Dutch imperial interests – 'communal ownership' of the seas, and potential ownership of foreign lands which they then made good by actual possession and occupation. Thomas Horne, *Property Rights and Poverty: Political Argument in Britain 1605–1834* (Chapel Hill: University of North Carolina Press, 1990), pp. 10–21.
38. Burke's reading of Pufendorf dates from his student days at Trinity College, Dublin, where *The Whole Duty of Man* (referred to in the Dublin list as the 'small Pufendorf') was the set text on his fourth year ethics course (Canavan, *The Political Reason of Edmund Burke*, p. 201; Lock, *Edmund Burke*, p. 37). Burke was sufficiently interested to acquire two editions of the larger Pufendorf – the magisterial *Law of Nature and Nations* – for his library. His familiarity with the scholastic and natural law tradition, with its provision for the primacy of the right of necessity over the right to property, may also be derived from the philosophy texts on his course at Trinity College which, with the exception of Pufendorf, were scholastic or neo-scholastic in outlook. Burke's library contained works by the neo-Thomist Jean Domat, and the great jurist Suarez, whom he cites in relation to Ireland in his *Tract on the Popery Laws*. Stanlis, *Edmund Burke*, pp. 9, 16.
39. The contrast derives ultimately from Aristotle's distinction in the *Nicomachean Ethics* between 'universal' and 'particular' justice, the former laying the basis for what was later defined as virtue and goodness, and the latter which corresponded to justice in the later, narrow sense pertaining to property and contractual rights. See Knud Haakonssen, 'Hugo Grotius and the History of Political Thought', *Political Theory*, 13 (1985), p. 254.
40. For Pufendorf, there are two originary contracts, rather than the single contract assumed in most accounts of natural rights theory.
41. Samuel Pufendorf, *On the Law of Nature and Nations*, I, 7, vii, extracted in *The Political Writings of Samuel Pufendorf*, ed. Craig L. Carr, trans. Michael J. Seidler (Oxford: Oxford University Press, 1994), p. 131.
42. Samuel Pufendorf, *On the Duty of Man and Citizen According to Natural Law*, I, 9, iv, ed. James Tully, trans. Michael Silverthorne (Cambridge University Press, 1991), p. 69. This does not rule out the possibility of state intervention attending to a right of necessity – all the more so in view of Pufendorf's absolutist tendencies, and his abrogation of the primacy of the right to property. But Pufendorf's point is that this is at the discretion of those making the contract: it does not emanate from pre-contract natural or primordial rights. See Horne, *Property Rights and Poverty*, pp. 36ff.

43. In arguing thus, Burke fails to acknowledge that he is following Pufendorf himself, who conceded that in exceptional cases, particularly in the event of famine or starvation, we are entitled to assert the right of necessity, and imperfect rights are converted into perfect rights (Pufendorf, *On the Duty of Man and Citizen*, p. 55). Likewise, the Irish moral philosopher, Francis Hutcheson, argued that in the case of famine, needy citizens may take the property of others by force (Alasdair MacIntyre, *Whose Justice?, Which Rationality?* (London: Duckworth, 1988), p. 265).
44. Edmund Burke, 'Appeal from the New to the Old Whigs', *Works*, iii, p. 80. Burke continues, in a manner that seems to combine the endearments of beauty with the awesome power of the sublime: 'Nor are we left without powerful instincts to make this duty as dear and grateful to us, as it is awful and coercive' (ibid.).
45. Edmund Burke to William Windham, 9 June 1795, *Correspondence*, viii, p. 266. The binding nature of the obligation for Burke is clear from his further elaboration: 'if I give a Cottage to a poor man to live in I have no more right to turn him out of it than if I had let it to him for rent' (p. 266). The problem in Ireland was that even rent constituted no contractual obligation, at least where security of tenure was concerned.
46. Edmund Burke, 'Speech on . . . the Economical Reformation of the Civil and other Establishments' [1780], in *Works*, ii, p. 101. As J. G. A. Pocock comments, this marks a major departure from the Scottish Enlightenment's insistence that commerce creates manners and civility: 'Burke is asserting that commerce is dependent upon manners, and not the other way around; a civilized society is the prerequisite of exchange relations, and the latter alone cannot create the former.' J. G. A. Pocock, 'The Political Economy of Burke's Analysis of the French Revolution', in *Virtue, Commerce, and History: Essays on Political Thought and History, Chiefly in the Eighteenth Century* (Cambridge: Cambridge University Press, 1988), p. 199.
47. See, for example, the call by Joseph Gerrald in the immediate aftermath of the French Revolution, for a popular convention which would revive the Anglo-Saxon convention of King Alfred, when the 'Myclegemot, Folk-Mote, or Convention' had met annually on Salisbury plain. (As a reward for this patriotic gesture, Gerrald, a member of the London Corresponding Society, was transported for fourteen years in 1793.) Burke's differences with the radical antiquarians lay, among other sites of contention, in their emphasis on the search for origins and pristine foundations, as against Burke's distrust of primitivism, and contrasting emphasis on the incremental deposits of tradition. For this, and a comprehensive discussion of radical antiquarianism in general, see James A. Epstein, *Radical Expression: Political Language, Ritual and Symbol in England, 1790–1850* (New York: Oxford University Press, 1994), ch. 1.
48. Cobbett, *History of the Protestant Reformation*, 2 vols. (London, 1829), ii, para. 18, cited in Horne, *Property Rights and Poverty*, p. 230.
49. Horne, *Property Rights and Poverty*, p. 249.

50. Michael Hardt and Antonio Negri, *Empire* (Cambridge, MA: Harvard University Press, 2000), p. 36.
51. Pocock, 'Burke's Analysis of the French Revolution', p. 201. Pocock relates Burke to Cobbett in this connection.
52. Kevin O'Neill, *Family and Farm in Pre-Famine Ireland: The Parish of Killashandra* (Madison: University of Wisconsin Press, 1984), p. 34.
53. Edmund Burke, 'Speech on the Nabob of Arcot's Debts', *Works*, iii, pp. 160, 161 (subsequent references will take the form of 'Nabob', followed by volume and page number, in parentheses in the text).
54. 'In order that the people, after a long period of vexation and plunder, may be in a condition to maintain government, government must begin by maintaining them. – Here the road to economy lies not through receipt, but through expense; and in that country nature has given no short cut to your object.' 'Nabob', iii, p. 162.
55. *The Nation*, 17 January 1846, p. 221. Russell was speaking in Glasgow, on the occasion of his being conferred with the freedom of the city, and he began by noting that he was in the city where 'Smith, in his lectures, had laid the foundation of that knowledge which we have since attained respecting the economy of nations.'
56. Trevelyan, *The Irish Crisis*, pp. 191–2.
57. Editorial in *The Nation*, 8 November 1845, p. 56.
58. Burke contributed to the Young Ireland movement's critique of imperialism. As Richard Davis notes: 'An Irish tradition, critical of imperialism, had long existed. Edmund Burke's dictum that the East India never made a treaty which it did not break was quoted ad nauseam in *The Nation*.' Richard Davis, *The Young Ireland Movement* (Dublin: Gill and Macmillan, 1987), p. 200.

5 'TRANQUILLITY TINGED WITH TERROR': THE SUBLIME AND AGRARIAN INSURGENCY

1. See Chapter 3, above, n. 76.
2. Dominick Trant, *Considerations of the Present Disturbances in the Province of Munster* (Dublin, P. Byrne, 1787), p. 4.
3. See, for example, the quotation from Matthew O'Conor in Chapter 3, n. 69 above. O'Conor is probably drawing on the frequent use of the same metaphor – a staple in Gaelic culture after the Williamite conquest – by his grandfather, Charles O'Conor, as in the following letter to Dr John Curry, written when he was in danger of losing his land to a younger brother who had converted to Protestantism: 'After the many shipwrecks which for ages have ruined my family and after the last of all which left but a bare plank to come to shore upon, I am now on the score of my religion called upon to deliver it up to a younger brother by a right of primogeniture in Protestancy.' Charles O'Conor to Dr John Curry, 25 February 1777, in *Letters of Charles O'Conor of Belanagare*, p. 340.
4. For the background to Burke's family connections with the first Whiteboy movements, see *Correspondence*, i, pp. 147–8, 169, 249; Cruise O'Brien, *The*

Great Melody, pp. 46–57, and L. M. Cullen, 'Burke's Irish Views and Writings', in Ian Crowe, ed., *Edmund Burke, His Life and Legacy*. For Burke's immediate attempt to exonerate the Whiteboys from charges of sedition and conspiracy, see 'An Unfinished Paper of Mr. Burke's, relative to the Disturbances in Ireland at the Beginning of the Reign of George the Third', in *Correspondence of the Right Honourable Edmund Burke*, ed. Charles William, Earl Fitzwilliam, and Lieutenant-General Sir Richard Bourke (London: Francis and John Rivington, 1844).

5. Cullen, 'Burke's Irish Views and Writings', pp. 67–8. The successful defence line-up for the next wave of Whiteboy trials in Fermoy, February 1767, gives some idea of the results of Burke's groundwork, as it includes some of the most distinguished names in eighteenth-century Irish public life: John Fitzgibbon (the future Earl of Clare), Sir Lucius O'Brien, Barry Yelverton and John Scott.
6. *Public Advertiser*, 21 September 1769, cited in Lock, *Edmund Burke*, p. 272. See also Nicholas Robinson, *Edmund Burke: A Life in Caricature*, pp. 11–12.
7. Henry Giles, 'Ireland and the Irish in 1848', in *Lectures and Essays on Irish and Other Subjects* (New York: D. & J. Sadlier & Co., 1869), p. 50.
8. *The True Friends of Liberty: To the Whiteboys of the South, the Oakboys of the North, and the Liberty Boys of Dublin* (Dublin: John Exshaw, 1763), p. 6. It is worth noting that the London *Public Advertiser* also saw fit to mock Burke with the tag of '*Liberty Boy*'. Robinson, *Edmund Burke: A Life in Caricature*, p. 12.
9. Stephen K. White, *Edmund Burke: Modernity, Politics, and Aesthetics* (London: Sage, 1994), pp. 22, 29.
10. S. J. Connolly, 'Violence and Order in the Eighteenth Century', in Patrick O'Flanagan, Paul Ferguson, and Kevin Whelan, eds., *Rural Ireland: 1600–1900: Modernization and Change* (Cork: Cork University Press, 1987).
11. Edmund Burke to Rev. Dr Thomas Hussey, post 9 December 1796, *Correspondence*, ix, p. 161.
12. Edmund Burke, 'Fourth Letter on a Regicide Peace' [1796], *Works*, v, p. 415.
13. 'A Letter from the Right Honourable Edmund Burke to a Noble Lord' [1796], *Works*, v, p. 111. The mixture of fascination and horror in Burke's response to the revolution is evident in his statement that 'All circumstances taken together, the French revolution is the most astonishing thing that has hitherto happened in the world.' *Reflections*, p. 92.
14. Edmund Burke, 'Report, made on … the Lords' Journals, in relation to their Proceeding on the Trial of Warren Hastings' [1794], *Works*, vi, pp. 465–6.
15. White, *Edmund Burke*, 34.
16. Burke comments on the recalcitrance of the deeply embedded culture of India: 'We are not here to commend or blame the institutions or prejudices of a whole race of people, radicated in them by a long succession of ages, on which no reason or argument, on which no vicissitudes of things, no mixtures of men, or foreign conquest, have been able to make the smallest impression.' 'Impeachment: Fifth Day', vii, 190.
17. Edmund Burke, 'An Abridgement of English History', *Works*, vi, p. 280. See also his remarks, cited above, on relationships between nations: 'Men are not

tied to one another by papers and seals. They are led to associate by resemblances, by conformities, by sympathies... Nothing is so strong a tie of amity between nation and nation as correspondence in laws, customs, manners, and habits of life. They have more than the force of treaties in themselves. They are obligations written in the heart.' 'First Letter on a Regicide Peace' [1796], *Works*, v, pp. 213–14.

18. Edmund Burke, 'Speech on Conciliation with America' [1775], *Works*, i, p. 508 (subsequent references will take the form of 'Conciliation', followed by volume and page number, in parentheses in the text).

19. As Jeremy Black comments: 'Burke's use of historical example can be challenged, particularly in light of his failure to accept that the invasion, rebellion and usurpation of 1688–89 marked a major discontinuity in English history and was only enforced in Ireland and Scotland at the point of a sword.' Jeremy Black, 'Edmund Burke: History, Politics and Polemic', *History Today*, 37 (December 1987), 46. As is clear from n. 24 below, Burke himself was not unaware of the discontinuities masked by the 'organic' growth of the British constitution.

20. Edmund Burke, 'Speech on Conciliation with the Colonies' [1775], *Works*, i, p. 484.

21. Furniss, *Edmund Burke's Aesthetic Ideology*, p. 189.

22. Frances Ferguson, 'Legislating the Sublime', in Ralph Cohen, ed., *Studies in Eighteenth-Century British Art and Aesthetics* (Berkeley: University of California Press, 1995), p. 129.

23. 'With regard to that species of eternity which they attribute to the English law, to say nothing of the manifest contradictions in which those involve themselves who praise it for the frequent improvements it has received, and at the same time value it for having remained without any change in all the revolutions of government, it is obvious, on the very first view of the Saxon laws, that we have entirely altered the whole frame of our jurisprudence since the Conquest.' Edmund Burke, 'An Abridgement of English History', vi, p. 415.

24. Ibid., p. 422. There is a certain irony in Thomas Paine's charge that Burke, in looking to William the Conqueror, was basing the lineage of the constitution on a usurper and false foundations, for it is Burke in this instance who is prepared to allow that a revolution may confer a legitimate claim to government, whereas Paine, the great defender of revolution, implies that it can only render all subsequent regimes illegitimate. For the presentation of this argument, see Steven Blakemore, *Burke and the Fall of Language: The French Revolution as Linguistic Event* (Hanover, NH and London: University Press of New England, 1988), ch. 2.

25. Edmund Burke, 'Substance of the Speech in the Debate on the Army Estimates' [1790], *Works*, iii, p. 279.

26. Suleri, *The Rhetoric of English India*, p. 36.

27. Edmund Burke, 'Remarks on the Policy of the Allies' [1793], *Works*, iii, p. 455.

28. White, *Edmund Burke*, p. 73; Peter J. Stanlis, *Edmund Burke: The Enlightenment and Revolution* (New Brunswick, NJ: Transaction, 1991), pp. 235, 244.

29. Cruise O'Brien, *The Great Melody*, pp. 234–40. For Petty's influence on political economy, and Ireland's key role in his thought, see Mary Poovey, *A History of the Modern Fact: Problems of Knowledge* (Chicago: University of Chicago Press, 1998).
30. Charles O'Hara to Edmund Burke, 10 August 1762, *Correspondence*, i, pp. 144–6.
31. See Kevin Whelan, 'The Modern Landscape: From Plantation to Present', in F. H. A. Aalen, Kevin Whelan, and Matthew Stout, *Atlas of the Irish Rural Landscape* (Cork: Cork University Press, 1997), pp. 79ff.
32. Edmund Burke to Charles O' Hara, *ante* 23 August 1762. *Correspondence*, i, pp. 147–8. For Burke's views on Cortez, Pizarro and the brutalities of Spanish colonization, see Chapter 7 below, p. 202.
33. James N. Healy, *The Castles of County Cork* (Cork: Mercier Press, 1988), pp. 427–8.
34. O'Brien, *Edmund Burke as an Irishman*, pp. 12–13.
35. Edmund Burke, 'Letter to Richard Burke', *Works*, vi, p. 68 (subsequent references will take the form of 'Richard Burke', followed by volume and page number, in parentheses in the text).
36. Ferguson, 'Legislating the Sublime', p. 135.
37. Burke, *Correspondence between 1744 and 1797*, pp. 44–5.
38. Burke, 'A Letter to William Smith, Esq' [1795], *Works*, vi, pp. 54–5. See also his warning in 1792 to his son Richard, then acting as Secretary to the Catholic Committee, that the Protestant enemies of the Catholic cause 'will fall upon them in that Situation, and show them no Mercy. They are to look for the renovation of forged conspiracies, judicial murders, and all all [*sic*] the Horrors of the period from 1761 to 1766.' Edmund Burke to Richard Burke, 1 October 1792, in *Correspondence*, vii, p. 224.
39. Edmund Burke to Richard Burke, *post* 21 November 1792, *Correspondence*, vii, p. 301.
40. Edmund Burke to Richard Burke, 2 November 1792, *Correspondence*, vii, p. 283.
41. Edmund Burke to Rev. Thomas Hussey, *post* 9 December 1796, *Correspondence*, ix, p. 62.
42. Edmund Burke to Rev. Thomas Hussey, 18 January 1796, in *Correspondence*, viii, p. 378.
43. Cited in Bartlett, *The Fall and Rise of the Irish Nation*, pp. 244, 227.
44. For an insightful discussion of Burke's fears that the past might open rather than heal wounds, see Bruce James Smith, *Politics and Remembrance: Republican Themes in Machiavelli, Burke and Tocqueville* (Princeton: Princeton University Press, 1985), ch. 3.

6 BURKE AND COLONIALISM: THE ENLIGHTENMENT AND CULTURAL DIVERSITY

1. Edmund Husserl, *The Crisis in the European Sciences and Transcendental Philosophy*, trans. David Carr (Evanston, IL: Northwestern University Press, 1970),

pp. 281–5, cited in Dipesh Chakrabarty, 'Postcoloniality and the Artifice of History: Who Speaks for "Indian" Pasts?', *Representations*, 37 (Winter 1992).
2. For contemporary critiques of the Enlightenment, see James Schmidt, ed., *What is Enlightenment?: Eighteenth-Century Answers and Twentieth-Century Questions* (Berkeley: University of California Press, 1996).
3. Paul Gilroy, 'One Nation Under a Groove', in *Small Acts: Thoughts on the Politics of Black Cultures* (London: Serpent's Tail, 1993), p. 44. Gilroy's comment is made in the context of a discussion of C. L. R. James's classic study of the slave rebellion in Haiti, *The Black Jacobins* [1938] (London: Alison and Busby, 1980).
4. See Robin Blackburn, *The Overthrow of Colonial Slavery, 1776–1848* (London: Verso, 1988), pp. 51–60.
5. For Burke's views on slavery, see Francis Canavan, SJ, 'Burke as Reformer', in Peter Stanlis, ed., *The Relevance of Edmund Burke* (New York: P. J. Kennedy and Sons, 1964), pp. 95ff.; Blackburn, *The Overthrow of Colonial Slavery*, pp. 147–56.
6. See Markman Ellis, *The Politics of Sensibility: Race, Gender and the Sentimental Novel* (Cambridge: Cambridge University Press, 1996), ch. 2.
7. See Deane, *Strange Country*, ch. 1, and C. P. Courteney, *Montesquieu and Burke* (Oxford: Basil Blackwell, 1963).
8. Frederick G. Whelan, *Edmund Burke and India: Political Morality and Empire* (Pittsburgh: University of Pittsburgh Press, 1996), p. 5.
9. For Elster, tradition is simply 'mindlessly repeating or imitating today what one's ancestors did yesteryear': *The Cement of Social Society: A Study of Social Order* (Cambridge: Cambridge University Press, 1989), p. 104, cited in Whelan, *Edmund Burke and India*, p. 339.
10. For Burke's praise of William Robertson's debunking of a mythic golden age in his *History of America* (1777), see Chapter 7 below, p. 205.
11. David Hume, 'Of the Original Contract', in *Essays: Moral, Political and Literary* (Indianapolis: Liberty Fund, 1985).
12. See Winch, *Riches and Poverty*, parts I and II.
13. See below, Chapter 8.
14. Adam Smith, *Lectures on Jurisprudence* [1766], ed. R. L. Meek, D. D. Raphael, and L. G. Stein (Oxford: Clarendon Press, 1978), pp. 540–1.
15. For a comprehensive critical discussion of this aspect of the Scottish Enlightenment, see J. G. A. Pocock, *Barbarism and Religion: Narratives of Civil Government* (Cambridge University Press, 1999), ii, sections iii to vi.
16. Cited in MacIntyre, *Whose Justice?, Which Rationality?*, p. 252.
17. Letter from James Macdonald to Herder, November 1776, reprinted in Alexander Gillies, *Herder und Ossian* (Berlin: Junker und Dünnhaupt, 1933), p. 174. For other examples of the regular conferring of 'Irishness' on the more rebarbative aspects of the Highlands to Irish society, see Robert Clyde, *From Rebel to Hero: The Image of the Highlander, 1745–1830* (East Linton: Tuckwell Press, 1995), pp. 5, 7.
18. There was nothing intrinsically reactionary in such invocations of 'the ancient constitution': as noted above (p. 271, n. 47) the recourse to the liberties of the 'free-born Englishman', as established in Magna Carta and other precedents,

became standard rhetoric of the English radical politics in the 1790s. See Vernon, *Re-Reading the Constitution*, chs. 1, 2; and James Epstein, *Radical Expression: Political Language, Ritual and Symbol in England, 1790–1850* (New York: Oxford University Press, 1994).
19. Edmund Burke, 'Letter to the Sheriffs of Bristol' [1777], *Works*, ii, p. 36.
20. See Whelan, *Edmund Burke and India*, p. 340, n. 16; Viswanathan, *Masks of Conquest*, pp. 28–30, 121ff.; Suleri, *The Rhetoric of English India*, pp. 51–2, 66ff.
21. Burke, here, is clearly overlooking those sympathetic strands in 'Patriot' Protestant opinion, represented by Swift, Thomas Sheridan, and others early in the century, and carried forward to elements in the Volunteer and Patriot movement, and the translations of Charlotte Brooke and the cultural antiquarianism of the Royal Irish Academy at the end of the century, which were well disposed, to different degrees, to the Catholic cause and the plight of the native population. He was more concerned with the hegemonic ruling interest which exercised its autocratic colonial power once more in the period leading up to the 1798 rebellion.
22. See Matthew Arnold, *On the Study of Celtic Literature and Other Essays* (London: J. M. Dent and Son, n.d.). For a recent comprehensive appraisal, see Robert Young, *Colonial Desire: Hybridity in Theory, Culture and Race* (London: Routledge, 1995).
23. For Burke's influence on Arnold, see Seamus Deane, 'Arnold, Burke and the Celts', in *Celtic Revivals: Essays in Modern Irish Literature* (London: Faber and Faber, 1985).
24. Aubrey de Vere, *English Misrule and Irish Misdeeds* (London: Murray, 1848), p. 14; Isaac Butt, 'A Voice for Ireland, the Famine in the Land' [1847], in Seamus Deane, ed., *The Field Day Anthology of Irish Writing*, ii (Derry/London: Field Day/Faber and Faber, 1991), p. 165; John Mitchel, *Last Conquest of Ireland, Perhaps* [1861] (London: Burns Oates, n.d.), p. 94.
25. Alfred Cobban identifies at least five instances where Burke supported the necessity of major social upheavals or 'rebellions against authority': 'the Glorious Revolution of 1688, the American War of Independence, the struggle of the Corsicans for freedom, the attempt of the Poles to preserve their national independence, and the various revolts against the minions of Warren Hastings in India' (Alfred Cobban, *Edmund Burke and the Revolt against the Eighteenth Century* (London: George Allen and Unwin, 1960), p. 100). Cobban does not include Ireland in his list though, on Burke's own logic, it presented a very strong case for 'rebellion against authority'. See also above, Chapter 5, p. 164.
26. For the contrast between 'abstract rights' based concepts of freedom, and more culturally grounded notions of autonomy in dialogue with custom and tradition, see Manuela Carneiro da Cunha, 'Custom Is Not a Thing, It Is a Path: Reflections on the Brazilian Indian Case', in Abdullahi Ahmed An-Na'im, ed., *Human Rights in Cross-Cultural Perspectives: A Quest for Consensus* (Philadelphia: University of Pennsylvania Press, 1991).
27. Edmund Burke, 'Thoughts on French Affairs' [1791], *Works*, iii, p. 375. See Whelan, *Edmund Burke and India*, pp. 57ff. for an extended disscussion of the implication of this and related passages.

28. Whelan, *Edmund Burke and India*, p. 55; Cobban, *Edmund Burke and the Revolt against the Eighteenth Century*, pp. 109–11.
29. Burke, of course, was far from being alone in such an undertaking: Diderot, Voltaire, Raynal, and later Madame de Staël in France, and Herder in Germany, also broached these issues. See Martin Thom, *Republics, Nations and Tribes* (London: Verso, 1995), chs. 5, 7, 8; Anthony Pagden, 'The Effacement of Difference: Colonialism and the Origins of Nationalism in Diderot and Herder', in Gyan Prakash, *After Colonialism: Imperial Histories and Postcolonial Displacements* (Princeton: Princeton University Press, 1995).
30. James Tully, *Strange Multiplicity: Constitutionalism in an Age of Diversity* (Cambridge: Cambridge University Press, 1995); Will Kymlicka, *Politics in the Vernacular* (Oxford: Oxford University Press, 2001); Frank Ankersmidt, *Aesthetic Politics: Political Philosophy Beyond Fact and Value* (Stanford: Stanford University Press, 1996); Bruce Robbins, *Feeling Global: Internationalism in Distress* (New York: New York University, 1998); Timothy Brennan, 'Cosmopolitanism and Internationalism', *New Left Review*, 7 (January/February, 2001).
31. Iris Marion Young, 'Polity and Group Difference: A Critique of the Ideal of Universal Citizenship', in Cass R. Sunstein, ed., *Feminism and Political Theory* (Chicago: University of Chicago Press, 1990), pp. 124–5.
32. Mehta, *Liberalism and Empire*, pp. 42, 43.
33. See above, Chapter 4.
34. James Clifford, 'Of Other Peoples: Beyond the "Salvage" Paradigm', in Hal Foster, ed., *Discussions of Contemporary Culture. Number One* (Seattle: Bay Press, 1987).
35. Tully, *Strange Multiplicity*, p. 83.
36. See Hirschman, *The Rhetoric of Reaction*, as summarized in James Schmidt, 'Which Enlightenment Project?', paper presented to the Tenth International Congress on the Enlightenment, Dublin, 1999, p. 12.

7 'SUBTILIZED INTO SAVAGES': BURKE, PROGRESS, AND PRIMITIVISM

1. See Zygmunt Bauman, *Modernity and the Holocaust* (Cambridge: Polity Press, 1994).
2. Walter Benjamin, 'Theses on the Philosophy of History', in *Illuminations*, trans. Harry Zohn (London: Fontana, 1979), p. 258.
3. Francis Parkman, *France and England in North America*, i (New York: Library of America, 1983), p. 432.
4. Cited in Gordon M. Sayre, *Les sauvages américains: Representations of Native Americans in French and English Colonial Literature* (Chapel Hill: University of North Carolina Press, 1997), p. 253. Sayre also cites John Bartram's verdict from 1751: 'They are a subtile, prudent and judicious people in their councils, indefatigable, crafty, and revengeful in their wars.'
5. See Bruce Johansen, *Forgotten Founders: Benjamin Franklin, The Iroquois and the Rationale for American Revolution* (Ipswich, MA: Gambit, 1982).

Notes to pp. 186–9

6. For the response to the McCrea murder in contemporary diaries and newspapers, see Richard M. Ketchum, *Saratoga: Turning Point of America's Revolutionary War* (New York: Henry Holt, 1997), pp. 276–7. See also H. Nickerton, *Turning Point of the Revolution; or, Burgoyne in America* (Boston: Houghton Mifflin, 1928), pp. 470–2.
7. Among other works, the McCrea incident inspired Michel René Hilliard-d'Auberteuil's pioneering novel, *Miss McCrea* (1784), Philip Freneau's poem 'America Independent' (1786), a 1786 poem in Rev. Wheeler Case's *Revolutionary Memorials* (1852), and Joel Barlow's epic poem, the *Columbiad* (1807). For a list of other publications, see the excellent account of the controversy surrounding the incident in James Austin Holden, 'Influence of the Death of Jane McCrea on Burgoyne's Campaign', *New York State Historical Association Proceedings*, xii (1913).
8. Edmund Burke, 'Speech on the Use of Indians', *Writings and Speeches*, iii, eds., Warren Elofsen and John Woods (Oxford: Clarendon Press, 1996), p. 355 (subsequent references will take the form of 'Indians', followed by volume and page number, in parentheses in the text).
9. Linda Colley, 'A Magazine of Wisdom', *London Review of Books*, 19, 17, 4 September 1997, p. 5. The quotations cited by Colley are from Burke's speech.
10. *The Public Advertiser*, 7 February 1778, cited in *Speeches and Writings*, iii, p. 355. The account in the newspaper continued: '[Burke's] metaphors were Bold, his Expressions nervous... his Stile in general pathetic, eloquent, and sublime. But his Colourings, we hope, for the Honour of Human Nature, were too High, and the Act of an undisciplined Individual [Burgoyne?] perhaps exaggerated and... attributed to a whole people.'
11. Edmund Burke to Mary Palmer, 19 January 1786, *Correspondence*, v, ed. Holden Furber, with P. J. Marshall (Cambridge: Cambridge University Press, 1965), p. 255.
12. As cited in Horace Walpole's 'Last Journals', in *Writings and Speeches*, iii, p. 361. See also Ketchum, *Saratoga*, for the impact of Burke's speech on the American Campaign, pp. 145–6.
13. Robert Bisset, in one of the earliest biographies of Burke, gives an extended account of the speech on the use of Indians, but with prurient editorial tact, glosses over Burke's description of the murder of Jane McCrea: 'after *a particular detail* [Burke's speech] rose to a general survey of savage life'. Bisset, *The Life of Edmund Burke*, p. 6: my italics.
14. See also the account in the *Annual Register* of 1777, almost certainly written by Burke, which admonishes St Leger for the 'outrages of the savages' employed by him, in terms similar to the earlier speech: 'The friends of the royal cause, as well as its enemies, were equally victims to their indiscriminate rage. Among other instances of this nature, the murder of Miss McCrea, which happened some small time after, struck every breast with horror. Every circumstance of this horrid transaction served to render it more calamitous and affecting. The young lady is represented to have been in all the innocence of youth, and bloom of beauty. Her father was said to be deeply interested in the Royal cause;

and to wind up the catastrophe of this odious tragedy, she was to have been married to a British officer on the very day that she was massacred.' *Annual Register*, 1777 (London: Robert Dodsley, 1778), p. 156

15. 'Probably no event either in ancient or modern warfare', wrote the nineteenth-century historian William L. Stone, with the hyberbole characteristic of the story, 'has received so many versions as the killing of Miss McCrea, during the Revolutionary War... The slaying of Miss McCrea was, to the people of New York, what the battle of Lexington was to the New England Colonies.' *The Campaign of Lieut. Gen. John Burgoyne and the Expedition of Lieut. Col. Barry St Leger* (Albany, NY: Joel Munsell, 1877), pp. 302–3. For the best recent account, see June Namias, *White Captives: Gender and Ethnicity on the American Frontier* (Chapel Hill: University of North Carolina Press, 1993), and the extensive visual iconography relating to the incident is discussed in Samuel Y. Edgerton, Jr, 'The Murder of Jane McCrea: The Tragedy of an American *Tableau d'Histoire*', *Art Bulletin*, December (1965), p. 47.

16. Accounts differ as to the manner of her death. Most attribute her death to a blow from a tomahawk, but other versions, such as Stone's (*The Campaign of Lieut. Gen. John Burgoyne*, pp. 308ff.) claim she was shot accidentally by pursuing American soldiers before being scalped.

17. Edgerton, 'The Murder of Jane McCrea', p. 481.

18. Cited in *The Pictorial History of the Revolution* (New York: Robert Sears, 1847), p. 252.

19. According to James Wilkinson, who may have seen her, she was a 'country girl of honest family in circumstances of mediocrity, without either beauty or accomplishments'. Ketchum, *Saratoga*, p. 277.

20. Mrs Mercy Warren, *History of the Rise, Progress and Termination of the American Revolution* (Boston, 1805), ii, p. 27, cited in Edgerton, 'Murder of Jane McCrea', p. 484.

21. Michelle Burnham, *Captivity and Sentiment: Cultural Exchange in American Literature, 1682–1861* (Hanover, NH: University Press of New England, 1997), pp. 73–4.

22. Cited in ibid., p. 75.

23. Michel René Hilliard d'Aubertuil, *Miss McCrea: A Novel of the American Revolution* [1784], trans. Eric LaGuardia with introduction by Lewis Leary (Gainesville, FL: Scholars' Facsimiles & Imprints, 1958), p. 58 (subsequent references will take the form of 'Miss McCrea', followed by page number, in parenthesis in the text). Though written in French, '*Miss McCrea*', according to Leary, 'is the first book-length prose narrative to deal wholly with a national American incident and with America as the entire scene of the action' (p. 5).

24. Barlow's description may have been based on a drawing that inspired Vanderlyn. Barlow had asked the painter and inventor, Robert Fulton, to execute a painting on the theme, and Fulton's sketches may have inspired Barlow's own account in 'The Columbiad'. When Fulton proved unable to complete the

work, Barlow then turned to Vanderlyn, perhaps supplying him with Fulton's drawings. See Edgerton, 'The Murder of Jane McCrea', pp. 484–5.
25. Ibid., p. 485. The sexual subtext is clear from an earlier description of Jane McCrea's ministering to the wounds of her fiancé, David Jones (called 'Belton' in the novel), in Hilliard d'Auberteuil's *Miss McCrea:* 'In her eagerness she did not wait for the return of her servant to fetch the necessary bandages, but tore in pieces the kerchief that covered her fair bosom, which had been heaving violently for some moments. Belton opened his eyes and saw her in this charming disarray. Her eyes met his, she became disconcerted, her hand trembled, she could not finish. He fell at her feet; respect, gratitude, and love overwhelmed all his senses. Jane raised him up... supporting this dangerous enemy's head on her breast in order to bandage his wound' (pp. 26–7).
26. As Namias has suggested, Jane McCrea's fatal 'error' in the eyes of her American contemporaries may have been that she was a disobedient daughter. *White Captives*, p. 121.
27. Jay Fliegalman, *Prodigals and Pilgrims: The American Revolution against Patriarchal Authority, 1750–1800* (Cambridge: Cambridge University Press, 1982), p. 141.
28. Thomas Paine, *Common Sense: Political Writings*, ed. Bruce Kuklick (Cambridge: Cambridge University Press, 1989), p. 29, cited in Burnham, *Captivity and Sentiment*, p. 71.
29. See Barbara Graymont, *The Iroquois in the American Revolution* (Syracuse: Syracuse University Press, 1972), p. 151; Namias, *White Captives*, p. 119.
30. Namias, *White Captives*, p. 119.
31. See Burnham, *Captivity and Sentiment*, pp. 51ff.
32. See Bruce James Smith, *Politics and Remembrance*.
33. See Annette Kolodny, *The Lay of the Land: Metaphor as Experience and History in American Life and Letters* (Chapel Hill: University of North Carolina Press, 1975).
34. Cited in William Musgrave, 'That Monstrous Fiction: Radical Agency and Aesthetic Ideology in Burke', *Studies in Romanticism*, 37 (1998), p. 17.
35. Ronald Paulson, *Representations of Revolution* (New Haven, CT: Yale University Press, 1983), p. 61, and the related discussion of this metaphor in Musgrave, 'That Monstrous Fiction', pp. 14–15.
36. Edmund Burke, 'A Letter to a Member of the National Assembly' [1791], in *Works*, ii, p. 540 (subsequent references will take the form of 'Assembly', followed by volume and page number, in parentheses in the text).
37. See also Adam Phillips, 'Introduction' to Edmund Burke, *A Philosophical Enquiry into the Origin of our Ideas of the Sublime and Beautiful* (Oxford: Oxford University Press, 1990), pp. xi, 100.
38. Frances Ferguson, 'The Sublime of Edmund Burke, pp. 50–2.
39. Cotton Mather, '*A Notable Exploit*; *Wherein,* Dux Faemina Facti from *Magnalia Christi Americana*', in *Woman's Indian Captivity Narratives*, ed. Kathryn Zabelle Derounian-Stodola (New York: Penguin, 1998), p. 60.

40. Burnham, *Captivity and Sentiment*, p. 65.
41. Greg Sieminski, 'The Puritan Captivity Narrative and the Politics of the American Revolution', *American Quarterly*, 42 (1990), cited in Burnham, *Captivity and Sentiment*, pp. 65–7.
42. For an extended discussion of this trope, see Burnham 'Republican Motherhood and Political Representation in Postrevolutionary America', in *Captivity and Sentiment*, ch. 3.
43. Edmund and William Burke, *An Account of the European Settlements in America* (London: R. & J. Dodsley, 1757) (subsequent references will take the form of 'Account', followed by volume and page number). Unfortunately, this important text is omitted from vol. i of the new edition of Burke's speeches and writings, perhaps on account of its joint authorship with William, and has only begun to receive critical commentary in recent years. See Lock, *Edmund Burke*, ch. 5, and Fuchs, *Edmund Burke, Ireland and the Fashioning of Self*, ch. 4, and J. C. D. Clark's valuable critical edition of the *Reflections*, p. 227 (Edmund Burke, *Reflections on the Revolution in France*, ed. J. C. D. Clark (Stanford: Stanford University Press, 2000). In what follows, I ascribe to Edmund Burke those passages which echo distinctive passages in his other works – bearing in mind that this is clearly a matter of interpretation rather than an ascription of incontrovertible authorship.
44. As the editors of Burke's speech on the 'Use of Indians' point out, Burke's preparations for his speech indicate that 'he appears to have taken some trouble to study the history of Indians. The drafts refer to Cadawaller Colden (1688–1776), Pierre-Francois-Xavier de Charlevoix (1682–1761), Louis Hennepin (1640–c. 1700), Joseph Francis Lafitau (1681–1746), and Louis-Armand de Lom d'Arce (1666–c. 1713)' (*Writings and Speeches*, iii, 355, n. 1). As the *Account* is based on extensive borrowing from these authors, Burke's reading for his 'Use of Indian's' speech undoubtedly drew on this earlier research.
45. Sayre, *Les sauvages américains*, p. 263.
46. Burke is here following the ethnographic literature. According to the writings of Lafitau and other French observers, 'it was the women who determined the fate of prisoners, as it was generally men who were lost in war and whose labour power had to be replaced; in most accounts it was also women who pressed for wars in order that they might have these prisoners'. Sayre, *Les sauvages américains*, p. 295.
47. The *Account* notes how this extends to their hospitality and compassion: 'To those of their own nation they are likewise very humane and beneficent. Has any one of them succeeded ill in hunting? has his harvest failed? or is his house burned? He has no other effect of his misfortune than that it gives him an opportunity to experience the benevolence and regard of his fellow citizens, who for that purpose have almost all things in common.' *Account*, i, 165.
48. For Burke's relations to the Scottish Enlightenment and its views on progress, see James Coniff, *The Useful Cobbler: Edmund Burke and Political Economy* (Albany: State University of New York Press, 1994).

49. [Edmund Burke], Review of *William Robertson, History of America, The Annual Register* (London: R. Dodsley, 1778), p. 218. Note also Burke's excoriation of Cortez and Pizarro in a related Irish colonial context (Chapter 6 above, p. 158).
50. For extended discussions of the Scottish Enlightenment's stadial theories of development, see J. G. A. Pocock, *Barbarism and Religion: Narratives of Civil Government*; Ronald Meek, *Social Science and the Ignoble Savage* (Cambridge: Cambridge University Press, 1976).
51. [Edmund Burke], 'Characters', *The Annual Register, 1761* (London: Robert Dodsley, 1762), p. 1.
52. As J. G. A. Pocock observes in relation to this 'very odd passage', Burke may mean here 'that this regression to the shepherd stage is less the consequence of the terrain than of that of the abdication of civil government that might otherwise promote agriculture'. J. G. A. Pocock, 'Josiah Tucker on Burke, Locke and Price: A Study in the Varieties of Eighteenth-Century Conservatism', in *Virtue, Commerce and History* (Cambridge: Cambridge University Press, 1988), p. 163.
53. As noted above (p. 175), this echoes similar sentiments which he expressed in relation to great Asian civilizations: the people of India 'were for ages civilized and cultivated; cultivated by all the arts of polished life, whilst we were yet in the woods' ('East India', ii, 182).
54. The passage is from Tacitus, *Agricola*, 38, trans. J. Brian Benestad, as cited by Pagano.
55. Hence, for example, the argument, advanced in the *Enquiry*, that custom mitigates the impact of terror, recurs in the *Account*. The Indians were at first awe-struck at Columbus's forces, but he 'knowing that those things which appear most terrible at first, become every day less affecting by use, and that they even grow contemptible, when their real power is well known, determined to have cordial relations with them'. *Account*, i, 25.
56. Hugh Honour, *The New Golden Land* (New York: Pantheon, 1976), p. 125.
57. Review, *The History of America*, by William Robertson, pp. 214–15.
58. Steven Blakemore, *Intertextual War: Edmund Burke and the French Revolution in the Writings of Mary Wollstonecraft, Thomas Paine and James Mackintosh* (Madison, WI: Fairleigh Dickenson Press, 1997), p. 46.
59. Mary Wollstonecraft, 'A Vindication of the Rights of Woman' [1792] in *The Works of Mary Wollstonecraft*, ed. Janet Todd and Marilyn Butler (New York: New York University Press, 1989), v, p. 103.
60. Edmund Burke, 'Letter to a Noble Lord' [1795], *Works*, v, pp. 120–1. For a valuable discussion of both passages in relation to Burke's demonizing of 'female furies', see Linda M. G. Zerilli, *Signifying Woman: Culture and Chaos in Rousseau, Burke, and Mill* (Ithaca: Cornell University Press, 1994), ch. 3. The translation of Virgil is from Zerilli, p. 92.
61. See Chapter 5 above, pp. 161–2.
62. Edmund Burke, 'Address to the Colonists' [1777], *Writings and Speeches*, iii, p. 282 (my italics).

63. Ibid., p. 362.
64. Cited in Ketchum, *Saratoga*, p. 99.

8 'THE RETURN OF THE NATIVE': THE UNITED IRISHMEN, CULTURE, AND COLONIALISM

1. Cited in Thomas Moore, *The Life and Death of Lord Edward Fitzgerald* [1831], 2 vols. (London: Longman, 1831), i, p. 148 (subsequent reference will take the form of *Lord Edward Fitzgerald*, followed by page number, in parentheses in the text). For a vivid recent account of Lord Edward's exploits in America, see Stella Tillyard, *Citizen Lord: Edward Fitzgerald, 1763–1798* (London: Chatto and Windus, 1998).
2. See Hamilton Moore's account of Fitzgerald's journey, in a letter to the Duke of Richmond, in Moore, *Lord Edward Fitzgerald*, pp. 136–8.
3. See Robert L. Emerson, 'American Indians, Frenchmen, and Scots Philosophers', in Runte, ed., *Studies in Eighteenth-Century Culture*; David Noel Doyle, *Ireland, Irishmen and Revolutionary America, 1760–1820* (Cork: Mercier Press, 1981).
4. Cadwallader Colden, *The History of the Five Indian Nations of Canada, which are Dependent on the Province of New York* [1727] (New York: Atherton Book Company, 1902), pp. xxii, x–xi. According to Robert Waite, Colden was 'the best informed man in the New World on the affairs of the British American colonies.' 'Introduction', p. 36.
5. For the classic discussion of this theme – the shadow of tragedy even in paradise – see Erwin Panofsky, '*Et in Arcadia Ego*: Poussin and the Elegiac Tradition', in *Meaning in the Visual Arts* (New York: Doubleday Anchor Books, 1955).
6. See Thom, *Republic, Nations and Tribes*, p. 133, who cites Fenelon and Chateaubriand in this repect.
7. Zia Sardar, Ashis Nandy, and Merryl Wyn Davies, *Barbaric Others: A Manifesto on Western Racism* (London: Pluto Press, 1993), p. 54.
8. Thomas Hobbes, *Leviathan*, ed. J. G. A. Gaskin, i, 13, 9 (Oxford: Oxford University Press, 1998), p. 84.
9. John Locke, *Two Treatises on Government* [1690], ed. Peter Laslett, ii, v, 49 (New York: Mentor, 1965), p. 343.
10. William Robertson, *History of America*, iv, p. 2, in *The Life and Writings of William Robertson* (London: William Ball, 1841), p. 806.
11. Cited in Meek, *Social Science and the Ignoble Savage*, p. 103.
12. Robertson, *History of America*, iv, 8, p. 811.
13. That the threat presented by Ireland lurked constantly behind the fear of the Highlands is evident throughout the early modern period. As early as William Camden's *Britannia* (1586), Scotland is described as being composed of two cultures: 'With respect to the manners and ways of living, it is divided into the *High-land-men* and the *Low-land-men*. These are the more civilized, and use the language and habit of the English; the other more rude and barbarous, and

use that of the Irish.' Cited in Robert Crawford, *Devolving English Literature* (Oxford: Clarendon Press, 1992), p. 16.
14. Roy Harvey Pearce, *Savagism and Civilization: A Study of the Indian and the American Mind* (Berkeley: University of California Press, 1988), p. 82.
15. See Stuart Piggott, *Ancient Britons and the Antiquarian Imagination* (London: Thames and Husdon, 1989), pp. 75 ff.
16. Peter Womack, *Improvement and Romance: Constructing the Myth of the Scottish Highlands* (London: Macmillan, 1989), p. 23.
17. Cited in Marvin B. Becker. *The Emergence of Civil Society in the Eighteenth Century* (Bloomington: Indiana University Press, 1994), p. 82.
18. Adam Ferguson, *An Essay on the History of Civil Society* [1767], ed. Duncan Forbes (Edinburgh: Edinburgh University Press, 1966), pp. 76, 79.
19. Howard Gaskill, 'Introduction', *Ossian Revisited* (Edinburgh: Edinburgh University Press, 1991), pp. 6–16.
20. James Macpherson, 'A Dissertation Concerning the Poems of Ossian' [1765], in *The Poems of Ossian*, 2 vols., 1773 edition (Dublin: J. Moore, 1790), ii, p. 192.
21. Cited in Fiona Stafford, *The Sublime Savage: James Macpherson and the Poems of Ossian* (Edinburgh: Edinburgh University Press, 1988), pp. 83, 85.
22. Macpherson, 'A Dissertation', *The Poems of Ossian*, ii, pp. 199, 198, 192 (subsequent references will take the form of 'Dissertation', followed by volume number and page number, in parentheses in the text).
23. Ibid., p. 192. (My italics.)
24. Johannes Fabian, *Time and the Other: How Anthropology Makes its Object* (New York: Columbia University Press, 1983).
25. Hugh Blair, 'A Critical Dissertation on the Poems of Ossian' [1763], in *The Poems of Ossian*, ii, 246 .
26. Smith, *Lectures on Jurisprudence*, pp. 540–1.
27. As Thomas A. Horne points out, Hume occupies a pivotal position in Western political thought in rejecting 'medieval' natural law traditions of obligations towards the poor, even questioning the role of discretionary charity as an inducement to 'idleness and debauchery'. Horne, *Property Rights and Poverty*, p. 93.
28. Adam Smith, 'Digression Concerning the Corn Trade and Corn Laws', *The Wealth of Nations* [1776], ii, 4, v (London: Everyman's Library, 1991), p. 26.
29. James Hope, 'Jefferson's Daughter', in *Literary Remains of the United Irishmen of 1798* [1846], ed. R. R. Madden (Dublin: James Duffy, 1887), p. 102.
30. *The Autobiography of Archibald Hamilton Rowan*, ed. William H. Drummond [1840] (Shannon: Irish University Press, 1972), p. 291.
31. Paine, *The Rights of Man*, p. 87.
32. See, for example, R. B. McDowell, *Ireland in the Age of Imperialism and Revolution, 1760–1801* (Oxford : Clarendon Press, 1979), pp. 371; R. F. Foster, *Modern Ireland, 1600–1972* (London: Penguin, 1988), pp. 269–70.
33. *The Lives and Trials of Archibald Hamilton Rowan, and Others*, ed. Thomas MacNevin (Dublin: James Duffy, 1846), 91–2.

34. [Rev. James Porter, Thomas Russell, and William Sampson], *Review of the Lion of Old England, or, The Democracy Confounded,* 2nd edition (Belfast, 1794), p. 37 (subsequent references will take the form of *Review of the Lion,* followed by page number, in parentheses in the text).
35. See Burke's reference to the constitution as an edifice that has 'suffered waste and dilapidation', presumably in the seventeenth century, but which still possesses 'the walls, and in all the foundations of a noble and venerable castle' (*Reflections,* 121). This stands in stark contrast to his Gothic depiction of the ghostly ruins left behind in Ireland after Cromwell (see above, Chapter 5).
36. Helen Carr, *The American Primitive: Politics, Gender and the Representation of Native American Literary Traditions, 1789–1936* (Cork: Cork University Press, 1996), p. 35.
37. Thomas Russell, *A Letter to the People of Ireland on the Present Situation of the Country* (Belfast: Northern Star Office, 1796), p. 22.
38. Walter J. Walsh, 'Religion, Ethnicity, and History: Clues to the Cultural Construction of Law', in Ronald H. Bayor and Timothy J. Meagher, eds., *The New York Irish* (Baltimore: Johns Hopkins Unversity Press, 1996), p. 55.
39. William Sampson, 'Speech in Defence of the Journeymen Cordwainers of the City of New York; who were Prosecuted for a Combination to Obtain an Advance in Wages in the Spring of 1811', in *Beauties of the Shamrock, containing Biography, Eloquence, Essays, and Poetry* (Philadelphia: William D. Conway, 1812), pp. 123–4 (subsequent references will take the form of 'Speech in Defence', followed by page number, in parentheses in the text).
40. As we have noted in Chapter 5, Burke himself applied this logic to a defence of Asian civilization, and particularly the longevity of Indian society and culture in relation to its British counterparts.

CONCLUSION: TOWARDS A POST-COLONIAL ENLIGHTENMENT

1. Cited in Mary McNeill, *The Life and Times of Mary Ann McCracken, 1770–1866* (Dublin: Allen Figgis, 1960), p. 83.
2. Cited in Charlotte Milligan Fox, *Annals of the Irish Harpers* (London: Smith Elder, 1911), p. 98.
3. C. R. Fay, *Adam Smith and the Scotland of his Day* (Cambridge: Cambridge University Press, 1956), p. 10.
4. Gerhard Oestreich, *Neostoicism and the Early Modern State,* trans. David McLintock (Cambridge: Cambridge University Press, 1982).
5. Adam Smith, *Lectures on Rhetoric and Belles Lettres,* ed. J. C. Bryce (Oxford: Clarendon Press, 1983), pp. 136–7.
6. 'The Declaration of Independence', in *Thomas Jefferson: Writings* (New York: Library of America, 1984), p. 21. The reference is to the deployment of native Americans as agents of terror against the rebels, as discussed in Chapter 7.
7. See Thom, *Republics, Nations and Tribes,* p. 191.
8. For an outstanding critical exposition of Burke's understanding of place and belonging, see Mehta, *Liberalism and Empire,* ch. 4. As with his determination

to retain an ethical sense of communal obligation in a market economy (see above, Chapter 4), the difficulty for Burke was reconciling this sense of place with the age of 'improvement', enclosures, and agrarian capitalism. My argument in this study is that it is through the aesthetic agency of the sublime – at once a force of modernization, critique, and difference, and yet also a source of solidarity and sympathy – that Burke sought to bring these opposites together.

9. Walter Benjamin, 'Theses on the Philosophy of History', in *Illuminations*, p. 259.
10. Trumpener, *Bardic Nationalism*.
11. Theobald Wolfe Tone, *Journal*, 13 July 1792, in *Life of Theobald Wolfe Tone*, ed. Thomas Bartlett (Dublin: The Lilliput Press, 1998), p. 132.
12. Donal O'Sullivan, *Carolan: The Life, Times and Music of an Irish Harper*, 2 vols. (London: Routledge and Kegan Paul, 1958), ii, p. 130.
13. I deal with the intersections between 'Bardic' nationalism and radical republicanism at greater length in 'From Ossian to O'Carolan: The Bard as Separatist Symbol', in Fiona Stafford and Howard Gaskill, eds., *From Gaelic to Romantic: Ossianic Translations* (Amsterdam: Rodopi, 1998), and 'Republicanism and Radical Memory: The O'Conors, O'Carolan and the United Irishmen', in Jim Smyth, ed., *Revolution, Counter-Revolution and Union* (Cambridge University Press, 2000).
14. Matthew Arnold, *On the Study of Celtic Literature* [1867] (London: J. M. Dent, n.d.), p. 85.
15. John Stuart Mill, *Considerations of Representative Government* [1861], cited in 'Introduction' to Will Kymlicka, ed., *The Rights of Minority Cultures* (Oxford: Oxford University Press, 1996), p. 5.
16. Edmund Burke, 'Evidence on Begums at Oudh [1788]', *Writings and Speeches of Edmund Burke*, vol. vi, ed. P. J. Marshall (Oxford: Clarendon Press), p. 478.
17. Orlando Patterson, *Slavery and Social Death* (Cambridge, MA: Harvard University Press, 1982).
18. See Chapter 3 above, pp. 113–14. It is striking how William Cobbett drew on a similar *topos* of parent and child to depict the heartless morality of political economy in the face of destitution and famine. The state falls short of even animal standards, on Cobbett's reckoning, for even a hen, when it is almost a skeleton, will still feed her chicks first: 'And who has ever seen a labouring man, or his wife, not ready to endure, and frequently enduring, the torments of hunger, rather than suffer their children to want.' Molly Townsend, *Not by Bullets or Bayonets: Cobbett's Writings on the Irish Question, 1795–1835* (London: Sheed and Ward, 1983), p. 105.
19. Journal, 1, 2, 3 March 1797, *Life of Theobald Wolfe Tone*, p. 734.

Index

absorption 43–4, 54 (*see also* Fried, Michael)
Achilles 41, 210
Adorno, Theodor 63, 64, 68, 180, 252
Aeniad 206
Aeschylus 249
aesthetics
   aesthetic distance 25, 35, 46–7, 101, 111, 120, 253
   of the actual 6, 25, 110
   disinterestedness 43, 46–8
   of engagement 104, 110
   of extreme situations 79
   and revolution 156
   romanticism 112, 263
   of shock 106–7, 263
Affecting Distresses of Frederick Mannheim's Family 191
Agricola (Tacitus) 283
Ajax 58
Alexander the Great 112
Alfred, King 139, 271
allegory
   audience participation in 56
   debased forms of 57
   Diderot and 72, 251
   and emotion 105
   and the image 56
   national allegory 59, 78
   as 'other speech' 77
   as 'semantic wound' 77
   in Sheridan 66–8
   in Swift 64–8
   and theatricality 53
   (*see also* Barry)
America
   'America Independent' (Philip Freneau) 279
   and captivity narratives 185, 194
   as daughter figure 193, 197
   discovery of New World 212
   exclusions of Declaration of Independence 209, 230
   and republican mother figure 197
Americans, Native
   attempts to explain origins of 212
   as banditti 187
   cannibalism 200
   captivity narratives 186, 194
   and classical republicanism 205, 209–10, 214
   co-existence of sociability and violence 205
   communalism of 201, 282
   in Declaration of Independence
   denial of their cultural specificity 214, 226
   as doomed race 214
   Edmund Burke on 183–207 (*see also* under Burke, Edmund)
   exemplars of natural rights 210
   Inca civilization 202
   compared to Jacobins 183, 185, 194
   myth of individualism 214
   relationship to British and French settlers 184
   and Spanish colonization 184
   compared to Sparta 214
   torture and 200
   United Irishmen and 208, 221–9
American Revolution 11, 186
   Battle of Saratoga 186, 193–4
   General Burgoyne's use of Indians 188, 190
   Murder of Jane McCrea (*see* Jane McCrea)
Amnesty International 139
Ancient Constitution (*see under* 'Britain')
Ankersmidt, Frank 177–8
An-Na'im, Abdullahi Ahmed 277
Antoinette, Marie 114, 185, 191
Aongus, King of Munster 40
Apollo, Belvedere 205
Arensberg, Mary 264
Aristotle 138
Aristopateira 59
Armagh 14
Arnold, Matthew 174, 287
Ashfield, Andrew 240, 264

Index

Bacon, Francis 41, 98
Bagehot, Walter 170
Baillie, John 111
Barlow, Joel 191, 279, 280
Baroque, culture 234
Barrell, John 58, 59, 252, 255
Barry, James 10, 40, 240
  ancient Ireland and virtue 69–70, 255
  rejection of absorption in painting 55
  views on allegory 53, 57
  as 'bigoted Romanist' 78
  resemblances to Caravaggio 50
  concern about Catholic cause 73–5
  Catholics and civic culture 253
  cross-cultural contact 254
  and Druidic culture 254
  on Egyptian art 57
  eroticism of allegorical body 58
  female virtú 58
  friendship with Burke 254
  role of embodied spectator 45, 46–7, 52–5
  knowledge of Irish history 254
  influence of 'Philoctetes' print in Ireland 250
  on 'the intelligent eye' 57
  letter to Lord Shannon 73
  painting, a suitable medium for representing pain 45, 53
  painting, as 'virtú' 57
  Protestant origin of Divine right of kings 74–5
  against puritan reserve 54
  and republicanism 254, 255
  seeks to prevent divergence between word and image 52–3, 56
  on the sphinx 58
  use of theatricality in painting 45, 52–5
  use of flatness in paintings 46–50
  and Daniel Webb 74, 255
Barry, James, *Works*
  'Baptism of the King of Munster by St Patrick' 69–70, 255
  'Birth of Pandora' 58
  'Birth of Venus' 254
  Commonplace Book 254
  'Crowning the Victors at Olympia' 73
  'Distribution of the Premiums' 73
  'Elysium and Tartarus and the State of Final Retribution' 50
  'Fall of Satan' 49
  'Fragment on the Story and Painting of Pandora' 252
  An Inquiry into the Real and Imaginary Obstructions to the Acquisition of the Arts in England 72, 251
  Lectures on Painting Delivered at the Royal Academy 252
  'Philoctetes on the Isle of Lemnos' 40–1
  'Philoctetes on the Isle of Lemnos' (sketch) 250
  'Philoctetes on the Isle of Lemnos' (1777) 61, 73, 75
  'Philoctetes on the Isle of Lemnos' (c. 1792) 75
  'Progress of Human Culture' 72, 251
  'Satan and his Legions hurling Defiance Towards the Vault of Heaven' 49
  'Self-Portrait' 44–6, 48
  'Fragment on the Story and Painting of Pandora' 252
Barry, Norman 134, 137
Bartlett, Thomas 8, 73, 250, 275, 287
Bartram, John 204–7, 278
Bate, Walter Jackson 266
Bauman, Zymunt 184
Bayor, Ronald H. 286
beautiful, the
  ameliorating power 30, 120, 154, 160
  and custom 154
  in distress 196
  'fatal beauty' 196–7, 206
  mixed with the sublime 162, 164, 196, 271
  as restorative 155
  in *Review of the Lion of Old England* 223
  as social bond 107, 195
  as stability 150
  and sympathy 108
Becker, Marvin 259, 285
Belcham, John 244
Belfast Harp Festival (1792) 230, 232
Benjamin, Andrew 239
Benjamin, Walter 183–4, 229, 233
Berkeley, George 132
Bisset, Robert 267, 279
Black, Jeremy 274
Blackburn, Robin 276
Black Dog Riots 248
Blackstone, Sir William 227
Blair, Hugh 215, 217
Blake, William 40, 50
Blakemore, Steven 205, 274
Blummer, Hugo 251
body, wounded 10, 39, 40–5, 53, 59, 71, 73 (*see also* Pain)
Bolingbroke, Lord 130, 202
Bolla, Peter de 240, 264
Boston Massacre (1770) 197
Boswell, James 95
Boucher, François 40
Boulton, James T. 38, 41, 240, 246

Bourke, Sir Richard 273
Boylan, Thomas, A. 266
Boyle, Roger 74, 158, 159
Brady, Ciaran 255
Brady, John 244, 249
Brant, Joseph (Thayendenega) 183
Brennan, Mrs John 37
Brennan, Timothy 177
Breton culture 234
Bridge, John 245
Britannia (William Camden) 284
Britishness 84, 87
  ancient Britons 175, 227
  ancient constitution 14, 152, 223
  and impartial spectator 98
  and Scotland 92, 96
  United Irishmen's break from 221–3
Bromwich, David 5, 241, 244, 262
Brooke, Charlotte 277
Bruhm, Steven 13, 112, 117
Bryce, J. C. 259
Bryson, Gladys 261
Bunting, Edward 230, 234
Burgh, Thomas 71
Burgoyne, General John 188, 193, 207, 279
Burke, Edmund
  criticisms of abstraction 166
  aesthetics and politics 16, 149, 156 (*see also* sublime, beautiful)
  on aesthetic distance 101
  on agrarian improvement 159
  on American Indians 183, 185, 186, 188, 200, 201, 202, 203, 205, 260
  on American Revolution 11, 277
  contests myth of Anglo-Saxon liberty 156, 169, 274
  'anguish of spectatorship' 25, 94, 104
  at Ballitore 132, 154
  baroque theory of passions 105, 262
  in Barry's 'Distribution of the Premiums' 73
  relationship to Barry 254
  on the beautiful 7, 15, 120
  and cannibalism 38, 197, 199–200, 280
  castigates General Burgoyne 188
  as secret Catholic 32
  on charity 131, 133, 134–8, 140
  'clairvoyance' of 2, 241
  and colonialism 3, 8–9, 17, 99
  condition of Catholics 9, 69–71, 78, 99, 124, 129–32, 150, 159, 161, 225, 260
  on confiscation of Church property 138, 159
  confiscations of Irish land 161
  and Cobbett 272
  on mitigating effects of conquest 153, 155
  Cork upbringing 8, 10, 22, 23, 24, 34, 88, 130, 131, 246
  trope of convulsions/paroxysms 147, 153, 156, 163, 272
  metaphors of costume and drapery 195
  on Corsica 277
  on Cromwell 156–61
  on need for common culture 31, 132, 140
  on cultural longevity 175
  and cross-cultural solidarity 113, 116, 117–18, 174, 178, 235–7
  cultural diversity 171, 173, 175, 236
  not a cultural relativist 175–6, 237
  on violation of cultural taboos 115–19, 236
  on culture and commerce 271
  and custom 151, 153–4, 160, 161–5, 171, 201, 236, 277, 283
  respect for the dead 36–8
  on decay and ruin 203
  aligns himself with Defenders 15, 162–4
  distinguishes delight from pleasure 258
  departs from *laissez-faire* doctrine 134, 140
  disapproves of 'wild style' 104
  divided political loyalties 15, 23
  Dublin upbringing 2–3
  and the Enlightenment 113, 172, 176–7
  on executions 5, 24, 25, 30, 31–3, 35, 36–8, 110
  on exemplarity 99, 152
  exemplifies sublimity 87
  on famine 6, 8, 121, 122, 131, 134–5, 137, 138, 142, 266
  possible experience of famine 131
  breach with Charles Fox 104
  anti-foundationalism 5, 28, 152, 169, 240
  on free trade 125
  on friendship 2, 102–3, 111
  and gender transgressions 71
  on Germany 119
  Glorious Revolution 277
  contrasts Glorious and French Revolutions 29, 152–5, 169
  contrasts Glorious Revolution in England and Ireland 152–3, 274
  sees good coming out of evil 204
  and the Gothic 4, 10, 14, 161, 206, 244, 286
  breach with Hamilton 103
  Hobbesian aspects of thought 186
  and homosexuals 31, 247
  on 'horrors of Munster circuit' 158
  on humiliation 115–19, 236
  view of innocence 195
  and irony 85
  on Jacobitism 34
  justice and mercy in 84, 127, 133, 244, 249
  questions impartial standards 106, 177, 178–9

Index

on India 7, 13, 99, 107, 175
on Irish history 10, 159
on interrelatedness of mind and body 116, 235
sees Ireland as 'colonial garrison' 8–9, 173
relates Ireland to India 99, 263
and Irish language 267
Irishness of 69, 87–8, 148, 261
and Kant 264
linguistic excess of 262
on local and cultural particularism 3, 14, 96, 107, 168, 240, 265
and Longinus 106, 264
on love and violence 162–4
on Jane McCrea 186, 189
on madness and frenzy 162–4
critical of moderation 100
and modernity 166
relationship with mother 245
on Muslim customs 236
and Nagle family 88, 124, 158
on Norman conquest 169
favours obscurity 4, 26, 88, 105
oppression cause of insurrection 160, 161–2, 163
disputes Oriental despotism 175
and Patriot movement in Ireland 277
on perfect and imperfect obligation 134–7
on physical pain 113, 116, 117, 235–7
on mental pain 113, 115–19
on imaginative sharing of pain 110, 115–19, 237
patriarchy and property 71
philosophy as national narrative in 86
'politics of periphrasis' 23, 245
on condition of Irish poor 129–31, 132
protests against punishment of Hyland 99–101
on Poland 176, 277
against primitivism 175–6, 222, 271
on progress 11
on property 71, 127, 131
on Protestant Ascendancy 15, 132, 161–5, 169, 263
on providentialism 269
rejects racial prejudice 209
and Pufendorf 134–7, 270, 271
first mention of in public life 87
radicalism of 14, 15, 244
aversion to republicanism 5, 169, 260
response to *Theory of Moral Sentiments* 261
on resistance 14, 15, 162–4
on revolution 7, 15, 151, 168, 176, 277
as counter-revolutionary 168
satirized in *Review of the Lion of Old England* 223
on William Robertson 205, 276
on regression to savagery 203
and Scottish Enlightenment 282
Secretary to Irish Chief Secretary 87
on self-preservation 34, 35, 106, 108–11, 118, 235–7
rejects sensationalism 101
silence as complicity 100, 104, 162–4
on the state 141
on state intervention 125–6, 138, 141–2, 184
reservations about stoicism 71, 84, 98, 103, 261
related to Nicholas Sheehy 37, 245
on sexual violence 114, 186, 195–7
opposition to slavery 167
on social contract 169
on Spanish colonization 202, 203
critique of spectacle 25, 246
surrealist notion of the sublime 2
and sympathetic contagion 105–7, 115, 119, 262, 266
on sympathetic revenge 120
and sympathetic sublime 35, 105–7, 115, 166, 235
theory of sympathy 4, 11, 27, 105, 108, 109, 115, 117, 120, 263, 264
theory of sympathy contrasted with Adam Smith's 100, 112–13, 117, 120, 235, 264, 266
on tradition 12, 14, 151, 161–5, 168, 171, 275
on tragedy 25–7
on theatricality 26
and United Irishmen 138, 223, 225, 237
criticisms of universalism 134
on virtue in distress 114, 265
uses imagery of volcano 163
on women counterfeiting weakness 205
and Whiteboys 22, 87, 107, 148, 158, 162–4 (*see also* Whiteboys)
described as a 'Whiteboy' 148
recalls Whiteboy unrest in 1790s 163, 272–3
word and image in 4, 6, 26, 104
youthful anticipations of *Enquiry* 2–4, 7, 26, 149, 163, 241, 246
Young Ireland movement on 122, 272
Burke, Edmund, *Correspondence*
to Thomas Burgh 71
to Richard Burke 10, 14, 160, 163, 169, 275
to Sir Grey Cooper 32
to Rev. Robert Dodge 122, 272
to Adrien Jean-François Duport 122, 272
to Philip Francis 262
to John Hely Hutchinson 103–4
to Rev. Thomas Hussey 14, 100, 101, 150, 162, 164, 260
to Sir Hercules Langrishe 8–9, 11, 107, 124, 132, 138, 140, 150, 152, 155, 161, 173, 225, 263
to Charles O'Hara 1, 22, 23, 158, 245

Burke, Edmund, *Correspondence* (*cont.*)
  to John Monck Mason 103
  to Mary Palmer 279
  to John Ridge 21
  to Marquess of Rockingham 254
  to Edward Sexton Pery 78
  to Richard Shackleton 2–3, 34, 35, 102, 103–4, 249, 261
  to Adam Smith 261
  to William Smith 163, 272
  to William Windham 137, 271
  To Lord Fitzwilliam 99
Burke, Edmund, *Works Cited*
  'An Abridgement of English History' 151, 155, 156, 274
  (with William Burke) *An Account of European Settlements in America* 201, 204, 268, 283
  'Address to the Colonists' 206
  'An Appeal from the Old to the New Whigs' 28, 137, 167, 262
  'Characters' 203
  'An Epistle to Dr Nugent' 98
  'Evidence on Begums at Oudh' 236
  'First Day of Reply' May 28, 1794
  'First Letter on a Regicide Peace' 38
  'Fourth Letter on a Regicide Peace' 151, 275
  'Impeachment of Warren Hastings: Speech on the Sixth Charge' 119
  'A Letter to a Member of the National Assembly' 195, 199–200
  'Letter to a Noble Lord' 151, 206
  'Letters with Reflections on the Executions of the Rioters in 1780' 33, 34, 36–8
  'A Letter to the Sheriffs of Bristol' 172
  'A Letter to Thomas Burke, Esq' [1780]
  'Notes for "Speech on the Use of Indians"' 183, 188, 189, 203, 207
  'Opening Speech on Impeachment of Warren Hastings' 183
  A Philosophical Enquiry into the Origin of our Ideas of the Sublime and Beautiful 2, 4, 6, 10, 21, 23, 25, 27, 28, 29, 35, 38, 101, 103–4, 105, 106, 107, 108, 109, 110, 111, 112, 115, 117, 118, 119, 120, 147, 149, 153, 154, 155, 161–5, 196, 205, 225, 230, 233, 240, 244, 256, 286
  Reflections on the Revolution in France 9, 11, 12, 13, 17, 25–7, 29, 30, 104, 137, 138, 140, 141, 154, 156, 160, 176, 177, 179, 183, 194, 195, 200, 232, 233, 235, 249, 272, 273, 286
  The Reformer (1747–8) 26, 130, 131
  'Religion' 257
  'Remarks on the Policy of the Allies' 157
  'Report, made on . . . the Lords' Journals, in relation to their Proceeding on the Trial of Warren Hastings' 151

'Review of William Robertson, *History of America*' 202, 205
'Second Letter on a Regicide Peace' 245
'Several Scattered Hints concerning Philosophy and Learning' 247
'Speech on Conciliation with America' 152, 153, 176, 203
'Speech on . . . the Economical Reformation of the Civil and other Establishments' 138
'Speech at the Guildhall, in Bristol' 69–70
'Speech on the Impeachment of Warren Hastings', First Day 33, 119, 120
'Speech on the Impeachment of Warren Hastings', Third Day 151, 172, 175, 178
'Speech on the Impeachment of Warren Hastings', Fourth Day 175, 265
'Speech on the Impeachment of Warren Hastings', Fifth Day 8, 111–16, 119, 121, 154, 164, 165, 178, 237, 273
'Speech on the Impeachment of Warren Hastings', Seventh Day 116
'Speech on Mr Fox's East-India Bill' (1783) 9, 104, 118, 119, 172, 175, 203
'Speech on the Nabob of Arcot's Debts' 142
'Speech on the Punishment of the Pillory' 31
'Speech on the Use of Indians' 186, 188, 189
'Third Letter on a Regicide Peace' 11, 25, 126, 206
'Thoughts on French Affairs' 176
'Thoughts and Details on Scarcity' 126, 127, 134, 137, 141, 142
'Thoughts on the Present Discontents' 246
'Tracts Relative to the Laws against Popery in Ireland' [*c.* 1765] 10, 71, 118, 127, 128, 159–61
A Vindication of Natural Society 85, 202, 203
Burke, Richard (father) 246
  attorney for Sir James Cotter 24
  attorney for Joseph Nagle 24, 246
Burke, Richard (cousin) 245
Burke, Richard (son) 14, 160, 163, 238, 260, 275
Burke, Thomas 255
Burke, William 199–200, 265, 268, 282
Burke, The Rev. William P. 244
Burnham, Michelle 191, 197, 281
Burrowes, Peter 164, 260
Butler, Marilyn 283
Butler, Jospeh 88
Butt, Isaac 174
Buttimer, Cornelius G. 248
Buxton, James 148

Caesar, Julius 112, 216, 224
Caligula 112
Camden, William 284
Campanella, Thomas 117–18, 235

Campbell, Colin 257
Canavan, Francis, SJ 121, 270, 276
cannibalism
  Adorno and Horkheimer on 64
  and American Indians 200
  and defilement of female body 197
  Jacobins as 38, 197
  and the maternal 199–200
'Caoineadh Airt Uí Laoghaire' (Ní Chonail) 36
Caplan, Jay 55
Caravaggio 46–8, 50
Carleton, William 256
Carmichael, Gershom 135
Carr, Craig L. 270
Carr, David 276
Carr, Helen 226
Carteret, Lady 66
Carteret, Lord 66
Carthage 210
The Case of Ireland Stated (Molyneux) 65
Cassirer, Ernst 263
Catholics
  and American Revolution 73
  Catholic Committee 69, 72, 251
  docility of 72, 251
  emancipation 10, 32, 40, 75
  and Gordon Riots 31–3
  compared to injured body 59
  compared to shipwreck 147, 163, 272
  Penal Laws 9, 11, 22, 69–71, 133, 159
  silence as resentment 162–4
  strangers in their own land 78
  (*see also* Burke)
Celticism 13, 89
  as cultural imaginary 174
  feminization of the Celts 174
  myth of insular Celts 234
  Mathew Arnold and 174
  and Ossianic controversy 170
  as romantic consolation 174
  and sympathy 98
Chakrabarty, Dipesh 257, 275
Chardin, Jean Baptiste 36, 250
charity
  Charles Trevelyan on 134
  as discretionary 133
  as obligatory 134–8
  (*see also* Burke)
Charlemont, Lord 75
Charlevoix, Pierre-François-Xavier de 282
Chateaubriand, François René de 284
Chatham, Lord 73, 267
Clarendon, Edward Hyde, earl 10, 159
Clarendon, Lord 135
Clarissa (Samuel Richardson) 191

Clarke, Miss 234
Clifford, James 179
Clyde, Robert 276
Cobban, Alfred 260, 277, 278
Cobbett, William 139, 287
Cohen, Ralph 264, 274
Coke, Sir Richard 227
Colden, Cadwallader 210, 282, 284
collective violence
  as contagion 33, 35, 162–4
  Gordon riots 33
  (*see also* Whiteboys)
Colley, Linda 93, 137, 186, 202
Collins, Henry 266
'Columbiad' (Joel Barlow) 191, 279, 280
Columbus, Christopher 283
Common Sense (Tom Paine) 193
Coniff, James 282
Connolly, S. J. 8–10, 150, 248
Cooper, Sir Grey 32
Copeland, Thomas 240, 249
Copley, Stephen 248
Corlett, William 287
Cortez 158, 202, 222, 275, 283
Cosgrave, Brian 268
Cotter, Sir James 9, 23–4
Courbet, Gustave 47
Cox, Sir Richard 268
Crawford, Robert 92, 95, 259, 285
Croker, Thomas Crofton 36, 248
Cromwell, Oliver 5, 14, 286
  Burke on 156–61
Crow, Thomas 50, 250, 251
Crowe, Ian 245
crying 50–5
  as contagion 55
  masculinity and 51–3
  and propriety 50
  social nature of 60
  theatricality of 55
  (*see also* Philoctetes)
Cullen, L. M. 23, 31–2, 148, 245, 273
Culloden, Battle of (1746) 83, 89, 215, 231
culture 10
  based on sympathy 172
  common culture 31
  as source of conflict 172
Curran, John Philpot 75, 223
Curry, Dr John 9, 72, 163, 255, 272
Custom 30
  and beauty 154
  better than laws 151
  lethargic effects of 153–4
  offences against 154
  perpetuates conflict 161–5

Custom (*cont.*)
  relationship to rights 277
  as reconciling 153–4, 171, 283
  Scottish Enlightenment opposed to 208
  (*see also* Tradition)

Da Cunha, Manuela Carneiro 277
Damiens, Robert 25
danger
  immediate 2, 3, 35, 120
  safe distance from 29, 110, 147
Darwin, Erasmus 265
Davies, Sir John 195
Davies, Merryl Wyn 284
Davis, Herbert 253
Davis, Richard 272
Deane, Seamus 5, 11, 13, 276, 277
death
  defilement of corpses 37
  Irish respect for corpse 37
  wakes and keening 24, 36, 249
De Bruyn, Frans 25, 104, 126, 246
De Bry, Theodor 215
Defenders 13, 14, 15, 150, 162–4, 165, 226, 233, 243
De Lom, Louis Armand D'Arce 282
Delany, Dr Patrick 253
De La Potherie, Bacqueville 185
Deleuze, Gilles 106
Demosthenes 255
Dennis, Willam 248
Derounian-Stodola, Kathryn Zabelle 281
De Staël, Madame 278
Detroit 208
De Vere, Aubrey 174
Diogaras 59
Dickson, David 256, 268
Diderot, Denis 4, 72, 251, 278
  on absorption 43–4, 46–8, 54
  on allegory 72, 251
  opticality of painting 43
Discourses on Art (Reynolds) 58
Dobree Commissar 121
Dodge, Rev. Robert 266
Domat, Jean 270
Donnelly, James 249
Donoghue, Denis 253
Doyle, David Noel 284
Drennan, Willim 230, 234
Drouais, Jean Germain 40, 50, 251
Druids 224
Drummond, Willam 285
Duport, Adrien-Jean-François 266
Dustan, Hannah 191, 196
Dwyer, John 95, 259

Eagleton, Terry 240
Edgerton, Jr, Samuel Y. 280, 281
Edgeworth, Maria 84
Edgeworth, Richard Lovell 105, 256
Edward, King 224
Edwards, R. Dudley 268
Egmont, Earl of 268
Eisenstein, Sergei 106
Elliot, Gilbert 258
Ellis, Markman 276
Elster, Jon 169, 276
Emerson, Robert L. 284
England
  Chartism 139
  contrast with Irish famine conditions 127–8, 141–2
  destruction of bardic order 225
  'Freeborn Englishman' 16, 92, 139, 223, 276
  Glorious Revolution 29, 152–3, 155
  popular constitutonalism 139, 276
  scarcity in the 1790s 125–8
  Speenhamland system of poor relief 126
  suppression of monasteries 139
Enlightenment, the
  alternative Enlightenments 166, 236
  Burke and 4, 11, 113
  counter-Enlightenment 11
  and cultural diversity 12, 209, 278
  and cultural specificity 217, 225, 232
  as European 166, 167–8
  exclusions of 17, 174, 209
  Hirschman on 11, 180
  and natural liberty 209, 210
  and pain (*see* pain)
  and sympathy 70, 112, 113
  and universalism 16, 213
  vision and 13
  (*see also* Scottish Enlightenment)
Epstein, James 271, 277
Essay on the History of Civil Society (Adam Ferguson) 215
Euripides 249
Everett, Nigel 123, 128, 268
executions
  contrast with fictive tragedy 25, 110
  Foucault on 34
  judicial 24
  as shows of force 30, 32
  and sympathetic contagion 35, 36
  theatricality of 31, 34
  in Whiteboy and Gordon riots 31–3
  (*see also* Burke)
exemplarity 5, 10, 26, 152
  events 99, 260
  and executions 27, 30, 31–3

Index

Fabian, Johannes 216
Fabricant, Carole 64, 254
famine
  in *Enquiry* 6, 8
  in India 121, 142, 266
  and moral economy 174
  result of state intervention (Smith) 220
  right of necessity during 136
  1741 famine in Ireland 8, 131
Famine, Great (1845–51) 8, 12, 122–44
  absence of moral economy 140, 150, 158
  Achill during 122–3, 266
  contrast between Irish and English conditions 127–8, 132
  famine incompatible with civilization 128
  government's denial of famine 128, 135
  Lord John Russell on 158
  providentialism and 123, 131, 143
  Punch on 134
  Trevelyan on 134
Fant, Mr 162–4
Farrel, James 148
Fay, C. R. 237
Fénelon, Françis de 284
Ferguson, Adam 92, 215
Ferguson, Frances 1, 86, 155
Ferguson, Oliver W. 253
Ferguson, Sir Samuel 78
Fielding, Henry 33
'Fingal' (James Macpherson) 216
Fitzgerald, Lord Edward
  admitted to Iroquois 208
  in America 208
  contests primitivism 211
  idealization of Indians 208, 210–12
  sees Indians as contemporaries 221
  Moore compares to Jefferson 221
Fitzgibbon, John 273
Fitzwilliam, Earl 273
Fitzwilliam, Lord 99
Flanagan, Patrick 248
Flaxman, John 50
Fliegelman, Jay 193
Flood, Henry 255
Flood, Warden 255
Fludernik, Monika 265
Foley, Timothy P. 266
Forster, E. M. 259
Foster, R. F. 285
Foucault, Michel 14, 17, 34
foundationalism
  Burke against 5, 10, 152
  primitivism and 175–6, 222
Fox, Charles 241
Fox, Charlotte Milligan 286

France in England and North America (Francis Parkman) 184
Francklin, Thomas 250
Franklin, Benjamin 258
Fraser, General Simon 190
Freemans' Journal 21, 87, 244
French Revolution 166
  analogous to British colonialism 186
  and British radicalism 16
  Burke on 7, 11, 16, 122, 162, 166, 183–207, 243, 272
  and cannibalism 38, 197
  contrasted with Glorious Revolution 152–5
  defilement of the dead 38, 195–7
  and Gordon Riots 248
  and Ireland 162, 272
  Jacobinism 11, 16, 244–5
  march to Versailles 183, 200
  relation to India and Ireland 263
  and savagery 183–207
  and Scottish Enlightenment 16
  strong state during 138
  total revolution and 151
  (*see also* Burke)
Freneau, Philip 279
Fried, Michael 11, 43, 53
  on absorption 43–4, 54
  on Caravaggio 46–8
  contrasts absorption and theatricality 43
  on Courbet 46–7
  on Diderot 43–4
  on Greuze 54
Freud, Sigmund 259
Fuchs, Michel 7, 78, 241, 264, 268, 282
Fulton, Robert 280
Furber, Holden 279
Furniss, Tom 109, 154, 263, 264

Gaillie, Andrew 216
Gaskill, Howard 216, 287
Gaskin, J. G. A. 284
A General Collection of the Ancient Music of Ireland (Edward Bunting) 230
Georgia 222
Gide, André 40
Gilbert-Rolfe, Jeremy 239
Giles, Henry 148, 150
Gillies, Alexander 276
Gilroy, Paul 1, 166, 276
Glaucus 74, 250
Godwin, William 268
Golden Age, myth of 170, 205, 212, 215
Gordon Riots (1780) 31–3, 246, 248
Gorgon 206
Gothic 4, 10, 14, 161, 185, 240

Grattan, Henry 75
Grattan's Parliament 125
Gray, Peter 123
Graymont, Barbara 281
Greig, J. Y. T. 258
Greuze, Jean Baptiste 54, 72, 250, 251
Griswold, Charles L., Jr 259
Grotius, Hugo 135, 136, 212, 220, 270
Grousset, Paschal 39
Gutteridge, George H. 256

Haakonssen, Knud 270
Habberjam, Barbara 263
Haddon, Lieutenant James 207
Hamilton, William Gerard 37, 103, 148
Harding, John 66
Hardt, Michael 139
harp
   as emblem of United Irishmen 230
   vibrating strings, as metaphor for sympathy 230
Harp Festival, Belfast (1792) 230, 233
Harrison, Alan 252
Hass, Willy 266
Hastings, Warren 13, 24–8, 89, 204
   Burke's campaign against 113–20, 262
   Burke rejects his idea of Oriental despotism 175
   East India Company 184, 188
   excessses of colonization under 184, 204
   The History of the Trial of Warren Hastings (1796) 266
   interest in Indian culture 173
   responsible for torture 113
   ruin of India 121
Healy, James N. 275
Heaney, Seamus 40
Hegel, G. W. F. 40
Helen of Troy 196
Heller, Thomas C. 258
Hemskirk, Egbert van 46
Hennepin, Louis 282
Hennessy, John 246
Hennessys 22, 24, 148 (*see under* 'Burke')
Henry VIII 74
Hercules 40–1, 63–4, 210, 252
Herder, Johann Gottfried von 40, 105, 278
   on Celticism 171
   Essay on Language 59–63
   on Philoctetes 60
   on sympathetic contagion 105
Hill, David 208
Hilliard d'Auberteuil, Michael René 191, 279, 281
Himmelfarb, Gertrude 123–4, 128, 268

Hirschman, Albert 11, 180
Hispaniola 203
History of America (William Robertson) 202, 205, 213, 276
History of the Five Indian Nations (Cadwallader Colden) 210
History of Ireland (Geoffry Keating) 69
Hobbes, Thomas 88, 135, 213
Hogan, William 245
Holden, James Austin 279
Holocaust, the 1–2, 184, 239
Homer 210, 212
Honour, Hugh 283
Hope, James 222
Horkheimer, Max 63, 64, 180, 252
Horne, Thomas 270, 271, 285
Hume, David 10, 84, 85, 87, 92, 215, 257, 258, 263
   and Burke 257
   critique of social contract 170
   personal and political identity 91
   philosophy as national allegory in 86
   on the poor 219, 285
   reason and the passions 167
   on responses to pain 102
   and Scotland 91–2, 259
   and Scottish Enlightenment 91
   on the self 90–2
   on sympathy 87
   sympathy directed towards pleasure 87, 218
   critique of vernacular culture 215
   vibrating strings as metaphor for sympathy 230
   Whig principles and Tory affections 91
humiliation 115–19, 236
Humphry Clinker (Tobias Smollet) 95
Hunt, Lynn 244
Husserl, Edmund 166
Hussey, Rev. Thomas 14, 100, 101, 162, 164, 244, 260
Hutcheson, Francis 135, 240, 271
Hyland, James 99–101 (*see under* Burke)

Iconologia (Cesare Ripa) 57
imitation 108, 109, 111
Incas 202
India 9, 13, 15
   as civilization 166, 283
   colonial humiliation in 91–2, 115
   colonialism in 13, 14, 98, 121, 204
   and cross-cultural sympathy 172
   dowagers of Oudh 195
   effects on England 119
   famine in 121, 142, 269
   and Ireland 99, 156, 173, 264

murder of Nundcomer 5, 242
obduracy of Indian culture 151, 172, 175, 176, 273
torture in 104, 113, 114, 237
suttee in 265
(*see also* Hastings, Warren)
Ingoldsby, Hugh Massy 33
Innismurray 157–9
Inquiry into the Beauties of Painting (Webb) 74, 75
Institutes Political and Military . . . by the Great Timour 175
Iphigenia 74
Ireland
  Act of Union 174
  colonial status of 8–9, 242
  and India 99, 156, 173, 264
  Irish culture 4, 13, 133, 242
  Irish Gothic 4, 161, 242
  landlordism in 123–4, 133
  national character 261
  and 'national tale of terror' 14
  poverty in 66–8, 130–1, 132
  and Scottish Highlands 284
  and Williamite settlement 152–3
  as wounded body 39, 69–70
Iroquois 185, 200, 208, 227
  Britain's allies
  and idea of confederacy 185

Jacobitism 68
  Adam Smith on 170
  and Burke 24–5
  in Dublin 34, 248
  and the Pretender 22, 34, 245
  and Scotland 92
James, C. L. R. 276
James II, King 29, 152
Jameson, Fredric 86
Jebb, R. C. 78, 250
Jefferson, Thomas 16, 221, 286
'Jefferson's Daughter' (James Hope) 222
Jesenska, Milena 117
Johnson, Dr Samuel 73, 170, 216
Johnson, Sir Willam 210
Jones, Sir William 173
justice
  impartial spectator and 177–8
  and suffering 64

Kafka, Franz 117
Kames, Lord 214
Kant, Immanuel 264
Keating, Geoffry 69, 217, 254
Keats, John 263

Kelly, James 255
Kentucky 222
Keogh, Daire 256
Ketchum, Richard M. 279, 280, 284
Kilfeather, Siobhan 78
Kilkenny 37
Kilmallock 162–4
Kinealy, Christine 267
Knight, Richard Payne 45, 78, 87, 251, 257
Knights of St John of Jerusalem 159
Kolodny, Annette 281
Kramnick, Isaac 130
Kronick, Joseph 264
Kublick, Bruce 281
Kymlicka, Will 177, 287

La Capra, Dominic 257
Lafitau, Joseph Francis 209, 282
Langrishe, Sir Hercules 107, 124, 132, 150, 263
Laocoon (Lessing) 40, 50–4, 256
  dramatic and visual representation in 51, 54
  on masculinity and effeminacy 52
  on Philoctetes 52
  spatial and temporal form in 51
  on Winckelmann 51
Laslett, Peter 284
Lawson, John 240
Leary, Lewis 280
Lemnos 22
Lessing, Gotthold Ephraim 50, 256 (*see also* Laocoon)
Letters to the Men of Ireland (Joseph Pollock) 77
Linebaugh, Peter 247, 249
Livesy, Jim 166, 247
Lock, F. P. 184, 240, 250, 268, 282
Locke, John 98, 135, 170, 178, 213
London Corresponding Society 271
Longinus 5, 240
Longley, Neil 256
Louis XVI 25
Lovat, Lord 25, 246
Love, Walter D. 267
Lubbock, Sir John 262
Lucretius 147
Luhmann, Nicklas 258
Lyotard, Jean-François 1–2, 166

Macaulay, Lord 98, 173
McCalman, Iain 14, 248
McCrea, Jane
  Burke's speech on 5, 186
  descriptions of 190, 279, 280
  eroticism of 191, 195, 281
  fatal beauty of 196–7

McCrea, Jane (*cont.*)
  influence on Battle of Saratoga 185, 193–4, 280
  and Marie Antoinette 194
  Miss McCrea (Hilliard d'Auberteuil) 191, 279, 280, 281
  murder of 189, 279, 280
  transformation into rebel daughter figure 197
  Vanderlyn's painting of 186, 191, 193
  (*see also* Burke)
Macdonald, James 171
McDonnough, Terence 133
McDowell, R. B. 244, 256, 257, 260, 285
McGuinness, Philip 255
Machiavelli, Nicolò 88, 104
McIntire, Dr 267
MacIntyre, Alasdair 63, 177
McLoughlin, Thomas 242, 246
McMinn, Joseph 254
McNeal, Mrs 190
McNeill, Mary 238, 286
MacNevin, Thomas 285
Macpherson, James 14, 97, 216
  castigates Irish historians 217
  and Celticism 170
  Dr Johnson's challenge to 216
  denigration of oral tradition 216
  'improving' on tradition 216
  repudiates the local 97, 217
  (*see also* Ossian)
McTier, Martha 230, 234
Madden, R. R. 8, 21, 234, 243, 244–5, 285
Mahoney, Thomas H. D. 286
Mandeville, Bernard 88
Mansfield, Lord 32
Martyrs, Catholic 265
Marx, Karl 85, 257
Mather, Cotton 281
Mead, George Herbert 261
Meagher, Timothy J. 286
Meek, Ronald 213, 276, 283
Mehta, Uday Singh 83, 244, 257
Meisel, Perry 259
Melville, Stephen 250
Memoirs of Captain Rock (Moore) 21, 39
Methodism 247
Mill, James 173
Mill, John Stuart 234
Millar, John 89, 167, 203
Miller, George 240
Minerva 58
Mist's Weekly Journal 253
Mitchel, John 123, 174
modernity
  and barbarism 183

casualties of 62–3, 184
and the 'salvage paradigm' 179
spatialization of time 212
and the sublime 287
Molyneux, William 65, 68
Monaghan, Fr 122–3
Monanimy Castle 159
Monks of the Screw 75
Montag, Warren 254
Montage 106
Montesquieu, Baron de 168, 177, 213
Moore, Hamilton 284
Moore, Thomas 21, 39, 221, 284
  Life of Lord Edward Fitzgerald 208, 210–12, 221
  Memoirs of Captain Rock 21, 39
moral economy
  contested in Ireland 10, 140, 150, 158
  and executions 33
Moral Sense School of Philosophy 88
Morash, Chris 268
Morris, David, B. 1, 240
Morrow, Glenn R. 84
Mossner, Ernest C. 260
'Mourn – and then Onward' (W. B. Yeats) 234
Mullan, John 91, 99, 102, 258, 262
multiculturalism 179
Murray, Robert H. 261
Musgrave, William 281
Muskerry, Major 249

Nagle family 22, 23, 160, 245
Nagle, Garret 23–4, 148, 245
Nagle, James 148
Nagle, Joseph 24
Nagle, Nano 24
Nagle, Patrick 148
  and Whiteboy unrest 22, 23, 148
Nairn, Tom 89
Namias, June 202, 280–1
Nandy, Ashis 284
Nation, The 124, 143, 144, 267–72
National Volunteers 75
Nazism 184
Negri, Antonio 139
Newman, Barnett 1
Ní Chonaill, Eibhlín 36
Nickerson, H. 279
Nicomachean Ethics (Aristotle) 279
Nietzsche, Friedrich 11, 17
Non-Governmental Organizations (NGOs) 139
Norris, Christopher 239
North Briton 91
North, Lord 32, 242

Index

O'Brien, Conor Cruise 69, 123, 157, 163, 241, 248, 254, 272
O'Brien, James Bronterre 139
O'Brien, Sir Lucius 273
O'Brien, Patricia 244
O'Brien, William 85, 99, 159
Ó'Buachalla, Breandán 242
Ó'Buachalla, Liam 245
O'Carolan, Turlough 233, 234, 287
O'Ciardha, Eamonn 243
O'Connell, Basil 245, 246
O'Connell, Daniel 144
O'Connell, Philip 244
O'Connor, Arthur 14, 166, 247
O'Connor, Dermot 254
O'Conor, Charles 69, 72, 163, 254, 272
O'Conor, Denis 255
O'Conor, Matthew 162, 272
O'Dea, Michael 242
O'Donnell, Katherine 247
O'Flaherty, Roderic 217
O'Halloran (Burke's schoolnaster) 159
O'Hara, Charles 1, 22, 23, 157, 245
O'Leary, Rev. Arthur 76
O'Neill, Kevin 141
O'Neill, Thomas P. 128, 268
O'Rourke, Rev. J. 266
O'Sullivan, Donal 287
Oesterich, Gerhard 231
Ogilvie Mr 208
Oliver, Barbara C. 262
Onondaga 183, 185
Order of the Knights of St Patrick 75
Orr, William 36
Ossian 13, 170, 231, 287
  absence of clans in 217
  authenticity of 216
  and Celticism 174, 216
  Irish claims contested 171
  universalism of 217
  (*see also* Macpherson)
Oxfam 139

Pagano, Frank N. 256, 283
Pagden, Anthony 278
pain 10, 11, 27, 39, 45
  American Indians 200, 210
  composure under 51, 54
  connoisseurs of 102
  and diseased limb 69–70, 72
  and the Enlightenment 39, 40–5, 218
  and humiliation 111–19
  and justice 64
  Laocoon and 50–4
  and the lash 100, 101
  leading to convulsions 147
  physical and mental 41, 86, 116, 117, 119, 265
  privacy of 41, 43–4
  on the rack 65, 67, 83, 253
  sexual violence 114
  social nature of 41, 43, 60
  and solidarity 115–19, 235–7
  and the sublime 110
  torture in India 113
  turns us in on ourselves 220, 234
  Webb, Daniel on 74, 75
Paine, Thomas 13, 100, 104, 166, 193, 222, 237, 266, 274
Pandora 58
Panofsky, Erwin 284
Panther (Wyondat) 190
Parkman, Francis 184
Parrhasius 74, 250
'The Parting of Friends' (O'Carolan) 234
Pascal, Blaise 116
Patriot movement, in Ireland 75–7, 111, 277
Patterson, Orlando 287
Paulson, Ronald 1, 7, 195
Petro, Patrice 263
Petty, Sir William 157
Phillips, Adam 196
Phillips, Charles 256
Philoctetes 10, 40, 234
  Adam Smith on 99
  as allegory of Ireland 40, 59, 67
  and Aongus, King of Munster 69
  contrasted with Laocoon 52
  Drouais's painting of 250
  healing as solidarity 63, 256
  Herder on 60
  isolation of 41, 44–6, 48
  and losers of history 63
  and Pandora 59
  and Prometheus 40, 249
  previous treatments of 40
  and Rousseau 60
  Sheridan's translation of 66–8
  story of 40–1
  tears and crying 50–5, 60
  (*see also* Barry, James)
Phoenicia 210, 212
The Pictorial History of the Revolution 281
picturesque, the 15, 223
Piggott, Stuart 285
Pine-Coffin, Commissary General 132, 141
Pizarro 158, 202, 275, 283
Pocock, J. G. A. 138, 140, 271, 272, 276, 283
Pollock, Joseph 75–7
Poovey, Mary 275
Port au Prince 166

Porter, Rev. James 223
Power, Thomas 244
Prakesh, Gyan 278
Pressly, William 46, 69, 75, 251, 254, 255
Price, Dr Richard 152, 157, 183
Priestley, Joseph 152
primitivism
  Adorno and Horkheimer on 252
  and native Americans 183–4
  Anglo-Saxonism and 169
  Burke's distrust of 177, 205, 213, 225, 271
  and Celticism 171
  and modernity 185
  and myth of Golden Age 170, 205
  progress and 179, 183–4, 201
  and radical antiquarianism 271
  and republicanism 205, 209–10, 214
  and salvage paradigm 179
  and state of nature 136, 213, 225
progress
  Adorno and Horkheimer on 63
  Burke on 11, 107
  commercial progress 128
  cultural diversity 209
  cultural superiority 168
  exclusions from 174
  linear and cyclical theories of history 212
  and primitivism 179, 183–4, 201
  and the Scottish Enlightenment 89, 211, 213
  stadial theories of development 211, 213
Prometheus 40, 249
Prud'hon, Pierre-Paul 40
psychic economy 92, 167, 259
Public Advertiser, The 148, 273, 279
Pufendorf, Samuel

Quilligan, Maureen 56

radical antiquarianism 271
Radner, John B. 89
Raphael, D. D. 101, 276
Raynal, Abbé de 278
Raynor, David 258
reason
  instrumental 62–4, 252
  and narrative 85–8, 118
  as national narrative 85–8
  prerogative of Western culture 257, 275
  subject to the passions 85
  universal reason 166
republicanism
  Adam Smith and 244
  and native Americans 205, 209–10
  British radicalism and 244
  in Ireland 13–14

privileging antiquity over tradition 222
overrides cultural specificity 222
engages with vernacular traditions 233
(*see also* French Revolution; United Irishmen; Paine)
Revere, Paul 197
Review of the Lion of Old England (Porter, Russell, Sampson) 223
Revolutionary Memorials (Wheeler-Case) 279
Reynolds, Sir Joshua 50, 58, 254
Richardson, Samuel 191, 196
Richmond, Duke of 284
Richter, Simon 60
right(s)
  abstract conceptions of 12, 13, 65, 118
  cultural 116, 168, 177–8, 277
  of man 167, 168
  natural 135, 178, 210, 212
  of necessity 12, 135, 179
  to property 135
  to 'roar on the rack' (Swift) 65
Ripa, Cesare 57
Robbins, Bruce 177
Robertson, William 89, 202, 203, 205, 213, 214, 276
Robinson, Nicholas 87, 257, 273
Roche, Mark 249
Romanticism 113, 209, 210–12 (*see also* Celticism; primitivism)
Romney, George 50
Ross, Ian Simpson 260
Rousseau, Jean-Jacques 25, 60, 130, 238, 286
Routh, Sir Randolph 122–3, 266
Rowan, Archibald Hamilton 222, 223
Rowlandson, Mary 197
Royal Irish Academy 277
Rule, John G. 247
Runte, Roseann 253, 258, 284
Russell, Lord John 143, 268, 272
Russell, Thomas 13, 222, 223, 226, 243
  on American Indians 226
  on savagery of British constitution 226
  on the sublime and beautiful 13
  on slavery 226
Ryan, Charles 255

Sacheverall, Henry 27, 247
Sadlier, Mrs 244–5
salvage paradigm 179
Sampson, William
  criticizes ancient constitution 227
  on freedom of religious worship 226
  Review of the Lion of Old England 223
  ridicules imputation of barbarism against the Irish 227

on the Irish language 227
longevity and civility 227
claims of the Iroquois to civility 227
defends 'primitive' cultures 228, 229
on Scottish law 228
on the Brehon law 228
Sardar, Zia 284
savagery
   and American Indians 11, 183
   and British colonial policy 206
   and Christian history 210
   Lord Edward Fitzgerald on 208
   and Jewish history 210, 212
   noble savage 209
   scalping 205
   and sociability 201, 212, 214
   Western culture and 210
Savile, Sir George 32
Sayre, Gordon M. 200, 282
Scarry, Elaine 39, 50
Schmidt, James 276
Scotland
   Act of Union 86, 87, 89, 92, 98, 259, 269
   as insular Celts 234
   cultural improvement in 95
   Highlands 171, 215, 217, 218, 284
   post-Culloden culture 84
   and primitivism 171
Scott, James C. 243
Scott, John 273
Scott, Sir Walter 84, 233
Scottish Enlightenment 178
   and Act of Union 86, 87, 89, 92
   and Britishness 96
   Burke's relationship to 282
   opposes clan society 208
   and colonialism 167
   and cultural improvement 95
   and doomed cultures 214
   role of feeling in 167
   and Gaelic culture 208
   severance of local attachments 97
   attraction to London 95–6
   and loss of cultural esteem 92
   on primitivism 201, 214
   and progress 89, 92, 203, 211, 213, 214
   on savagery and barbarism 170, 215
   on sociability 214
   counters superstition 170
   and sympathy 84–98, 107
   opposes vernacular culture 215
Scythians 212
Sebright, Sir John 267
Segal, Charles 62, 66, 249, 252
Seidler, Michael J. 270

Seneca 261
Senior, Nassau 128
sensibility 88
   and sympathy 89, 167
   cult of sensibility 167
sentimentalism
   Burke's criticisms of 71, 101, 261
   and charity 102
   in novels 191
   sensationalism 101, 261
Shackleton, Richard 2–3, 31–2, 34, 102, 105, 240, 256, 261
Shaftesbury, Lord 88
Shakespeare, William 98
shame 115–19, 236
Shannon, Lord 73
Shapiro, Michael, J. 86
Sheehy, Catherine 37
Sheehy, Edmund 37, 148
Sheehy, Fr Nicholas 5, 9, 21–4, 36, 39, 148, 242, 245, 249
   grave of 21, 248
   revenge for death of 36
Shelburne, Lord 157
Sher, Richard B. 259
Sheridan, Richard Brinsley 167, 243
Sheridan, Dr Thomas 10, 40
   The Art of Punning 253
   and Cavan residence 254
   translation of *Philoctetes* 66–8
   The Intelligencer 67–8
   concern for Irish poor 68, 277
   Jacobite associations 66, 68
   (*see also* Swift; Philoctetes)
Sicily 201
Sieminski, Greg 197
Simms, J. G. 252
Simpson, Kenneth 92, 258, 259
Slator Eamonn 133
slavery
   abolition of 167
   Burke on
   Haiti 167–8
   and Jefferson 16, 222
   Philoctetes and 59
   Swift on 253
Smith, Adam 10, 11, 13, 83, 84, 89, 92, 203, 235, 260, 266
   and Act of Union 98
   agreeableness of expressing sympathy 94
   Burke's response to *Theory of Moral Sentiments* 261
   contrast with Burke 100, 106–7, 112–13, 117, 120, 266, 267
   criticisms of clan society 218, 220

Smith, Adam (*cont.*)
  and colonialism 88, 92
  compassion not part of justice 135, 219
  on economic rationality 97
  and Englishness 95–6
  famine a result of state intervention 220
  Gaelic prose, on absence of 231
  Gaelic, incompatible with commerce 231
  and 'impartial spectator' 96–8, 260
  individualist theory of sympathy 112–13, 116
  influence on government policy during Great Famine 122, 272
  influence on education in India 98
  and 'invisible hand' 269
  on Jacobite invasion 170, 218
  rejects local attachments 96, 97
  decries lack of martial spirit in commercial age 218
  and mass society 96
  opposed to self-indulgence 94
  opposition to slavery 167
  pain shuts out fellow feeling 219, 220
  on physical suffering 83, 93
  on Philoctetes 83
  philosophy as national narrative in 86
  on propriety 219
  and Scottish Highlands 231
  on sovereignty and exchange 86
  on spectatorial aloofness 99, 101
  stoicism in 83, 84, 94–8
  on comfort of strangers 96–7
  sympathy absent in primitive societies 220, 221
  sympathy as aestheticized 101
  sympathy and generalized other 102, 107
  sympathy as two-way transaction 94
  sympathy as willed uninvolvement 102
  and talking cure 96
  two-tiered nature of sympathy 102
  (*see also* sympathy)
Smith, Bruce James 275, 281
Smith, Robert A. 244, 260
Smith, William 163, 272
Smollett, Tobias 95
Smyth, James 287
social death 236
Solemn League and Covenant 156
Somerset, H. M. V. 247, 248
Sophocles (*see also* Philoctetes) 10, 40, 41–3, 44, 51, 249
Sosna, Morton 258
Spufford, Francis 1
Stafford, Fiona 285, 287
Stage-Irishman 77
St Andrew 74

Stack, Richard 6, 111, 118, 240
Stanlis, Peter J. 157, 269, 274, 276
state of nature (*see* primitivism)
Steen, Jan 3, 46
Stein, L. G. 276
St Leger, Colonel Barry 189, 279
Stern, James 266
Stern, Laura 266
St Patrick 69
stoicism
  and native Americans 210–12
  and ancient Ireland 40
  Barry's reservations about 74, 261
  Burke's reservations about 71
  as complicity with oppression 79
  neo-stoical conception of citizen 11, 231, 235
  and self-control 120
  and sympathy 94–8
  undramatical 54
  and visual representation 54
  (*see also* Smith; Burke; sympathy)
Stone, William L. 280
Strachey, Lytton 259
Strahan, William 260
Suarez, Francisco 123
sublime, the
  alarms into reflection 104
  arctic 1
  and the beautiful 107, 120, 160, 162, 164, 196
  and Burke's early experiences 2, 34
  and colonialism 4, 13, 23
  and contingency 3
  and custom 161–5
  'egotistical sublime' (Keats) 263
  as empowerment 28, 107, 112, 265
  and fear 7
  and French Revolution 1, 7
  Gothic 240
  and heroism 111, 264
  and the Holocaust 1, 239
  and imperialism 111, 264
  Indian sublime 1, 7
  and individualism 263, 264
  inexpressible 1, 5, 23, 84, 105
  and Ireland 2, 8, 87
  Irish sublime 240
  and language 4, 104, 105, 109
  Longinus 240, 265
  and masculinity 161–3
  and modernity 287
  as montage 106
  nuclear 1
  and obscurity 6, 29, 105, 109
  and pain 1, 2, 10

perpetual sublime 161–2, 206
and politics 7, 15
reflexivity of 105
resides in details 6
as restorative 30
as resistance 3, 28, 111
in *Review of the Lion of Old England* 224
and self-preservation 34, 256
as social 15, 34, 109, 110, 112, 241, 264
as shock 5, 105–7, 110, 263
slave sublime 1
surrealism 2
and sympathy 4, 105–7, 109, 115, 264
and sympathetic contagion 105–7, 115, 176
sympathetic sublime 13, 89, 105–7, 109, 115, 120, 175, 176, 235, 237, 264
terror 31, 108
as transport 106
and vision 4, 6, 104, 105, 109
(*see also* Burke; pain; sympathy)
Suleri, Sara 1, 6, 104, 106, 266, 277
superstition 170
Suttee 265
Swift, Jonathan 10, 11, 40, 64–8, 83
and allegory 65–6
The Art of Punning 253
Drapier's Letters 65–6
The Intelligencer 67–8
and the Irish people 68, 254
A Modest Proposal 64
rejection of abstract rights 65
right to 'roar on the rack' 65
as Patriot 277
sympathy
aestheticized forms of 101
and the beautiful 108
consolidating Act of Union (1800) 84
and Celticism 89
communalist theories of 112
and compassion 101
sympathetic contagion 35, 105–7, 115, 119, 162–4, 262, 266
cross-cultural solidarity and 13, 93, 97, 172, 235–7
as cultural form 172, 236–7
as emulation 10
and exchange 86
at executions 31, 36
as fellow-feeling 86, 89, 93, 112, 116
in Hume 10, 90
individualist theories of 112
as Irish and Scottish contribution to philosophy 89
oriented towards pleasure, not pain 87, 218

takes over from description 105
and language 27, 85
morality grounded in 12, 93
painting and 53, 55
and personal identity 90
absent in primitive societies 220, 221
and propriety 95–8
requires affluence 220
solidarity of the oppressed 220
sympathetic revenge 107
sentimentalism and 101
as social bond 264, 274
and spectatorship 101
and comfort of strangers 92
and the sublime 4, 105–7, 109, 115, 235–7, 264
(*see also* sympathetic sublime)
and suffering 11, 102
two-way transaction 94
vibrating strings and 230
and voyeurism 109

Tacitus 115–19, 216
Tamerlane 169
Taylor, William 268
Teichgraber, Richard F. 97
Temple, Lord 4, 75, 159
theatricality
contrasted with absorption 43
use of in painting 45, 52–5
Thom, Martin 278, 284, 286
Thompson, E. P. 2, 26, 125–8, 139, 150, 247
Tillyard, Stella 284
Timbs, John 241
Todd, Janet 244, 283
Toland, John 254
Tomlinson, Hugh 263
Tone, Matilda 234
Tone, Theobald Wolfe 14, 162–4, 233, 234, 237
Townsend, Molly 287
tragedy 83
Trant, Dominick 147
Trevelyan, Sir Charles 121, 123, 124, 132, 134, 135, 143
Trinity College, Dublin 2, 26, 122, 246, 248
Tristram Shandy (Sterne) 27
Troy 41–3
Trumpener, Katie 233
Tully, James 177, 179, 270

Usher, James 240

Vallancey, Charles 267
Vanderlyn, John 186, 195, 205, 280–1
Vernon, James 166, 180
Virgil 51, 206, 211

Viswanathan, Gauri 98, 166
Voltaire 278

Waite, Robert 284
'Wake of William Orr' (Drennan) 36
Walcott, Derek 40
Wales 234
Walpole, Horace 279
Walsh, T. J. 246
Walsh, Walter J. 227
Ward, Catherine Coogan 255
Ward, Robert F. 255
Wark, Robert R. 46–50, 251, 252
Warren, Mrs Mercy 190
Webb, Daniel 74, 75, 255
Weinsheimer, Joel C. 91, 263
Weiskel, Thomas 264
Wellbery, David 251, 258
West, Benjamin 50, 205
Wheeler-Case, Rev. 279
Whelan, Frederick 168, 265, 276, 277
Whelan, Kevin 243, 244, 256, 275
White, John 215
White, Stephen K. 149, 151, 157
Whiteboys 22, 87, 107, 148, 158, 162–4
   Burke receives first communication of 148
   Burke described as 148
   Burke family connections with 22, 23–4, 148, 160, 245
   Burke visits Ireland to organize defence of 22, 23, 148, 160, 245
Wilkes, David 215
Wilkes, John 91, 92, 246

Wilkins, Burleigh T. 108, 267
Wilkinson, James 280
William (of Orange), King 14
William the Conquerer 274
Williams, Raymond 16
Williams, T. Desmond 268
Wilson, Edmund 249
Wilson, Rob 1
Wilton, Andrew 261
Winch, Donald 244
Winckelmann, J. J. 50
Windham, William 271
Winslow, Cal 247
Wittkower, Rudolf 44–6, 48
Wollstonecraft, Mary 15, 263
Womack, Peter 215
Wood, Charles 135
Woods, John A. 242, 248, 260, 279
Woodham-Smith, Cecil 270
Woolooch, Isser 243
Wordsworth, William 40
Woolley, James 253, 254

Xenos, Nicholas 87, 257

Yeats, W. B. 234
Yelverton, Barry 75, 256, 273
York, Neil Longley
Young, Arthur 252
Young, Iris Marion 177
Young, Robert 277

Zerilli, Linda M. G. 283